08

Enhancing Learning Through Human Computer Interaction

Elspeth McKay
RMIT, Australia

IDEA GROUP REFERENCE
Hershey · London · Melbourne · Singapore

Acquisitions Editor:	Kristin Klinger
Development Editor:	Kristin Roth
Senior Managing Editor:	Jennifer Neidig
Managing Editor:	Sara Reed
Assistant Managing Editor:	Sharon Berger
Copy Editor:	Julie LeBlanc
Typesetter:	Sara Reed
Cover Design:	Lisa Tosheff
Printed at:	Yurchak Printing Inc.

Published in the United States of America by
Idea Group Reference (an imprint of Idea Group Inc.)
701 E. Chocolate Avenue, Suite 200
Hershey PA 17033
Tel: 717-533-8845
Fax: 717-533-8661
E-mail: cust@idea-group.com
Web site: http://www.idea-group-ref.com

and in the United Kingdom by
Idea Group Reference (an imprint of Idea Group Inc.)
3 Henrietta Street
Covent Garden
London WC2E 8LU
Tel: 44 20 7240 0856
Fax: 44 20 7379 0609
Web site: http://www.eurospanonline.com

Library of Congress Cataloging-in-Publication Data

Enhancing learning through human computer interaction / Elspeth McKay, editor.

    p. cm.

  Summary: "This book is a manual for the novice-Human Computer Interaction (HCI) designer. It compares and contrasts online business training programs with e-Learning in the higher education sector and provides a range of positive outcomes for linking information management techniques, which exploit the educational benefits of Web-mediated learning in computer supported collaborative learning"--Provided by publisher.

  Includes bibliographical references and index.

  ISBN 1-59904-328-9 (hardcover) -- ISBN 1-59904-330-0 (ebook)

  1. Human-computer interaction. I. McKay, Elspeth.

  QA76.9.H85E535 2007

  004'.019--dc22

                            2006033668

British Cataloguing in Publication Data
A Cataloguing in Publication record for this book is available from the British Library.

All work contributed to this book set is new, previously-unpublished material. The views expressed in this book are those of the authors, but not necessarily of the publisher.

Table of Contents

Section I
Technology Management and Change

Section II
Collaborative Learning Through HCI

Section III
Teacher and Student Use of HCI

Section IV
HCI in Educational Practice

Detailed Table of Contents

Section I
Technology Management and Change

Chapter I

Our book opens with a chapter that presents an in-depth examination of the challenges facing Canadian universities in their quest to implement quality ICT to enhance student learning. Case studies are used to draw out cultural aspects that are certainly relevant to other communities of learning. The issues are well organized and provide an excellent testimony of professional practice that serves as a well-researched literature resource for postgraduate students.

Chapter II

Here is a well-written chapter that is easy to understand. Although it deals with advanced technological techniques, the writing style is accessible to a broad audience. The authors present an historical overview and their motivation for this innovative classroom interface. They uncover many practical HCI issues that arise when interacting with ICT in the classroom.

Chapter III

This chapter describes a trial project that involves seven major Australian universities. As such, it adds a meaningful contribution to the emerging debate on tutoring online and student retention rates for distance education learners.

Chapter IV

Understanding how students organize themselves in an online educational context is a fascinating topic for all practitioners wishing to implement learning environments that involve the newer ICT tools available today. These authors utilize a Tablet PCs blog-forum as their effective HCI interface that provides an enlightened account of second year undergraduate students' knowledge construction.

Section II
Collaborative Learning Through HCI

Chapter V

In these days where we continually need to do more for less, this chapter conveys useful information on various ways of conducting online discussion with actual examples on questions and assessment. It makes practical suggestions on large-class management in a blended learning environment that involves partial online and partial face-to-face instructional strategies.

Chapter VI

This chapter presents a comprehensive summary of a relatively new type of workplace. It clearly points to the requirement for further work in the area of virtual workspace. The author points out that creating effective HCI in such virtual work environments raises particular technological issues for collaborative and informal learning.

Section III
Teacher and Student Use of HCI

Chapter VII

This is a multi-disciplinary approach toward successful implementation of effective HCI to enhance learning in a university environment. Issues, problems, and trends in the area of electronic personae design are uncovered in this chapter. It emphasizes a student-centered approach to educational information systems design, showing how to match a student's learning profile and his or her needs with an appropriate learning environment. A blended bibliography can be utilized as a student reference resource.

Academic culture of adult distance learners is described in this chapter as individuals who need a great deal of learning support from tutors, as well as from their peer group. Set in the Open University Malaysia, it provides an informative and enjoyable read about learners' experiences in distance learning programs.

The strength of this chapter lies in its ability to show how a sound pedagogy can be translated into effective HCI principles in a practical application through an interesting and innovative platform. The theory and principles that support the framework are many and detailed. A meaningful set of tables is used to summarize the learning program.

Here is a rendition of another rapidly growing area of research with its logical extension to learning technologies that sets this chapter comfortably within the bounds of our book. A natural spin-off from this work is to initiate a new style of educational research that diverges away from a more classical approach to HCI research.

There are some wonderful insights into online learning environments that are brought forward by the authors of this chapter. HCI's role is described in this educational technology scenario in an interesting manner for readers to enjoy.

The impressive authorship of this chapter gives rise to a clear, coherent, and very well researched topic. Perhaps the most pleasing contribution of this work is the tremendous practical value for educators interested in ICT. Moreover, the points of interest lie in the effectiveness of the HCI components and how this interaction has improved the students' learning.

Section IV
HCI in Educational Practice

Chapter XIII

The clarity of language in this chapter is easy to follow. The authors have given us a generous account of their professional practice. It is clear that the authors have been aware of the changes taking place around them, not only in technological and pedagogical terms, but also in the diversifying student background.

Chapter XIV

Now to the chapter that ends our book—last, but not at all the least, in terms of informative dissemination. Readers will be fascinated by this author's point of view, as she unravels her intuitive technological strategies as they apply to architectural course design. Her use of a transformer toy metaphor, together with her connection with systems thinking, can only be seen as inspirational. This is a practice-based pedagogical exercise that is truly interesting, offering nothing but exciting learning outcomes.

Foreword

Education is the most powerful weapon that you can use to change the world. – Nelson Mandela

As teachers and professors we change the world by guiding our students to understand issues from different perspectives. As we interact with students and they interact with each other, everyone continually enhances each other's learning.

To teach and learn successfully we need well-designed tools. The availability of information and communication technologies (ICTs) is not enough, ICTs must be useful, usable, understandable, satisfying to use, and universally available. In other words, ICTs must be designed using the principles of human computer interaction (HCI). Unlike most other books about the role of ICTs in education, this book embraces HCI and goes one step further to advocate *Enhancing Learning Through Human Computer Interaction*. Why, you might ask, is this important? It is important because it is hard to integrate theories and practices across disciplines.

We are fortunate to live in an information-rich world, but it is also a burden because information must be managed. One strategy for doing this is to compartmentalize knowledge. This encourages specialization, but it also limits creativity. Indeed, it is often at the boundaries of disciplines that new ideas arise as in bio-informatics and nano-technology. Research in these areas brings together skills and knowledge from two or more disciplines to solve important interdisciplinary problems. *Enhancing Learning Through Human Computer Interaction* strives to attain this goal; it brings together learning theory and practice with knowledge and skills from HCI to create and enhance ICTs for learning. It is thrilling to see this approach because all too often pioneering work in education and in HCI fails to influence each other. By taking this interdisciplinary approach, the authors of *Enhancing Learning Through Human Computer Interaction* provide readers with more than the sum of the individual parts. Elspeth McKay, the editor is also to be complimented for bringing together an impressive group of international authors and for shaping the book so that it is intellectually insightful as well as practically useful.

Enhancing Learning Through Human Computer Interaction speaks to everyone involved in teaching because it is a book of ideas brought to life with meaningful examples. While each chapter may not speak directly to every reader, readers will gain insights that they can adapt and apply to their own situations. The 14 chapters are organized into four themes: *Technology Management and Change, Collaborative Learning Through HCI, Teacher and Student Use of HCI,* and *HCI in Education Practice.* A useful preface guides readers through the book and provides valuable contextual information to help readers. Some readers may opt to read the book straight through, but a more likely approach will be to focus on specific chapters.

A strength of *Enhancing Learning Through Human Computer Interaction* is that it addresses important themes from different perspectives. Several authors point out that ICT developers and users need to take account of different learning styles by ensuring that human computer interfaces, pedagogic structure, and appropriate terminology are used to meet the needs of different learners. Some chapters include case studies that ground educational theory and demonstrate how it can be put into practice. In this way, useful models are provided for others to emulate and adapt. Many authors discuss the importance of "learning by doing and experiencing," reminding us of the Chinese proverb: *I hear, and I forget. I see and I remember. I do and I understand.* Those interested in the application of state-of-the-art technologies will enjoy discussions about how visualizations, online communities, and mobile technologies facilitate learning. The international authorship provides perspectives from different countries and cultures reminding us that education and learning are becoming increasingly global and that judicious use of ICTs can help to reduce the digital divide.

Personally, what I like best about *Enhancing Learning Through Human Computer Interaction* is that it strongly embraces the philosophy that learning is social and collaborative. Not only do we learn by doing, we learn even more by doing it with and for others. In addition to presenting issues that are important, this book also addresses how ICTs can be designed and used taking account of usability and sociability. The authors recognize the advantages and challenges of using ICTs to transform education by supporting social interaction within classrooms, neighborhoods, and with others across the world.

For these reasons *Enhancing Learning Through Human Computer Interaction* is a "must read book" for anyone who wants to improve the world through education.

Jenny Preece
Dean and Professor
University of Maryland, USA

Jenny Preece is a professor and dean of the College of Information Studies at the University of Maryland (USA). Prior to joining the University of Maryland in 2005, Preece was a professor and department chair of information systems at the University of Maryland, Baltimore Count (UMBC). Before coming to the U.S. in 1996, Preece was a research professor at South Bank University, London, for two years, where she created and directed an interdisciplinary center for people and systems interaction. In the mid-1980s, Preece joined the Open University (OU) where she was an associate professor. At the Open University she worked on a variety of projects in computer-based education, human computer interaction, and computer education. With a team of academics from the UK and Holland, Preece assisted in developing the first master's distance learning course on human computer interaction, which was regularly studied by around 1,000 students. This experience provided the foundation for authoring one of the first major texts in HCI—human computer interaction (Preece, Rogers, Sharp, Benyon, Holland, & Carey, 1994)—and initiated the successful authoring partnership between Helen, Yvonne, and Jenny. Preece's teaching and research interests include online communities of interest, communities of practice, social computing, and human computer interaction. She was one of the first researchers to point out the importance of online communities for providing social and emotional support to their members as well as for obtaining and exchanging information, particularly in patient support communities. She has also researched the differences in participants' behavior in different types of online communities including the reasons why people do or not participate. Preece has written extensively on these topics. Her work includes a book titled Online Communities: Designing Usability, Supporting Sociability *(Preece, 2000).*

Preface

OVERVIEW

Information communications technology (ICT) has been found to be one of the most potent tools for promoting equity and access to education, and a great resource in bridging the gap of the digital divide. ICT affects almost all of our everyday activities, be it business, defense, or space exploration. Being informed of the latest information has become essential for survival. Educational enterprises also benefit from the advantages and technological learning tools offered by ICT. ICT is indispensable for creating effective distance education learning environments. Consequently, the developments in *human computer interaction* (HCI) now assume greater significance, with our increasing reliance on the plethora of smart electronic devices that enable seamless access to our computer files from almost anywhere, anytime. Since the advent of the Internet, geographical boundaries no longer present barriers to communication. The global nature of this book's authorship provides a testimony of the trends in HCI toward collaborative international partnerships in a social context of shared knowledge. Today, there is more awareness for effective HCI through the increased laptop usage that is emerging as a commonplace information management tool. Moreover, laptop computers are already being adopted for basic operations in and around the home for e-mail, scanning interesting materials for school homework projects, and controlling household appliances.

INTEGRATING INTERACTIVITY INTO LEARNING

Within the education sector, ICTs are widely believed to offer new options, based on a paradigmatic approach, to individualize the instructional requirements of diverse cohorts of students. More specifically, multimedia and Web-based courseware development is seen to accentuate a presumed requirement for highly graphical *(or visual)* instructional resources. While most electronic courseware may appear to allow a learner to proceed at their own pace, the assumption is commonly made by the designers of such courseware, that to facilitate learning all learners are capable of assimilating graphical instructional material with their current experiential knowledge. Often, there is little or no consideration for differences in cognitive styles (McKay, 2000).

There is a consequential need to accommodate co-existing instructional paradigms in any computerized learning/courseware authoring process. This inevitably requires the dynamic evaluation of task knowledge level requirements (Dick, Carey, & O'Carey, 2004) to respond to individual cognitive styles and to deduce the student's knowledge acquisition requirements. Now with the reality of the *Semantic Web* (Berners-Lee, Hendler, & Lassila, 2001; Emonds-Banfield, 2006), meta-knowledge acquisition strategies are thus even more essential to provide the mechanism for dynamic knowledge analysis and for seemingly free flowing knowledge-mediated instructional processes.

DEFINING EFFECTIVE HCI

Although agreement on what constitutes HCI has not been reached (Hewett, Baecker, Card, Carey, Gasen, Mantei, Perlman, Strong, & Verplank, 2004), practicing professionals from the Association for Computing Machinery offer this working definition of HCI:

Human computer interaction is a discipline concerned with the design, evaluation, and implementation of inter-active computing systems for human use and with the study of major phenomena surrounding them.

Yet another focus that takes a view that reflects a human-dimensional quality for HCI:

"...HCI is about designing computer systems that support people so that they can carry out their activities productively and safely." (Preece, Rogers, Sharp, Benyon, Holland, & Carey, 1994)

These two views have much in common despite the mechanistic orientation of the first, where there is an emphasis on the technology per se, while the latter reflects a sense of social connectedness, showing a priority for the *human-dimension* of computer interaction.

How then can we define *effective HCI*? As before, one view will concentrate on the machine-fit and adaptation of the ICTs, while the other will emanate from an inherent drive for social organization and the comfortable working environmental effects of the ICTs (Hewett et al., 2004). Given that the general audience of this edited book will largely be novice-educational courseware designers, and in the interest of preserving space and leaving room for the insightful contributions from our authorship, we support the *human-dimension when we promote this meaning:*

Effective HCI means having a trusted, interactive and communicative computing environment that lets users decide whether to trust it for a particular purpose, or not; furthermore, effective educational HCI is about knowing how to develop a learning design that provides access to an educational information system that is easy to use, offering a safe environment for knowledge and cognitive skill development that supports the joy for life-long learning.

CURRENT PRACTICE

Due to the multi-disciplinary orientation of HCI, and indeed the authorship of this edited book, each chapter may be read in isolation from the complete work; it may appear that various concepts are covered a number of times, in separate ways. This is the intention in offering a reading framework that is appropriate to the multiple viewpoints that surround ICT in the practice of education. Naturally, the authorship hopes that the overall perspective on what constitutes *effective HCI* for enhanced learning will generate considerable interest in the relationships between *cognitive psychology, educational technology research, instructional science, and life-long learning,* which have not previously been elaborated in a unifying context.

The overall intention of this book is therefore to bring forward current practice in the form of a useful handbook on HCI for novice courseware designers and those interested in designing learning resources within the education and training sectors. As mentioned earlier, observing the increased acceptance and importance of ICT in the general community and perhaps more specifically outside the education arena, the authors go beyond a purely mechanistic vein that leaves aside the semiotic context or *human-dimension* so necessary for the success of an *effective HCI* learning environment. Consequently, the chapters in this book are devised to generate interest in e-learning best practice in corporate performance that is applicable to the education sector. So doing, it brings forward traditional instructional design expressed as *effective HCI* frameworks that have succeeded in business, in a language that is familiar for teaching and learning institutions in schools and institutions of higher education.

AUDIENCE

This book will be of interest to industry training developers, corporate trainers, courseware designers, government sector specialists, infrastructure policy makers, educational technology practitioners (schoolteachers, higher education), postgraduate students, and anyone with a keen eye for spotting the applicability of the chapter material for their own learning environment.

SCHOLARLY VALUE AND CONTRIBUTION

The chapters in this book will directly compare and contrast e-learning in a variety of higher education, corporate and elementary/secondary school settings. As such, it provides a range of positive outcomes for linking information management techniques that exploit the educational benefits of Web-based learning in computer supported collaborative learning environments. Through the global nature of the authorship, their diverse cultural factors impact on the educational aspects of HCI to reveal practical approaches for increasing the *human-dimension* of HCI through enlightened case studies that effectively utilize ICT tools. Commendable books on HCI that are currently available (de Souza & Preece, 2004; Preece, 2000; Preece, Rogers, & Sharp, 2002) are mostly for use in both corporate and educational sectors. These texts offer excellent online resources as teaching tools, for both the facilitators as well as students. Other experts provide some hints of HCI guidelines (Shneiderman & Plaisant, 2005; UsabilityNet, 2006); however, there is a distinct lack of other monographs that address the issues that surround the *human-dimension* of HCI in an educational setting.

At the time of preparing for this book, the educationalists in need of practical solutions to solving their courseware design problems would find it difficult to gain access to the professional practice of educational ICT tool development. Often, the books that are available represent a generalist's view of HCI. As such, they do not cover the pedagogical content that educational technologists/corporate trainer development specialists require. While others provide excellent historical accounts of HCI, it is possible to read valuable material on cognitive perspectives (Carroll, 2003), but they do not address strategies that can be easily translated as pedagogy models.

CONTRIBUTIONS

This book is organized into 14 chapters, which fall into four main themes that offer practical examples of: *Technology Management and Change, Collaborative Learning Through HCI, Teacher and Student Use of HCI,* and *HCI in Educational Practice.*

Section I. Technology Management and Change

There can be no doubt that we are witnessing a critical shift in the ways people view teaching and learning. Most noticeable is the tendency to move away from a traditional classroom approach where the teachers' reliance on educational technology for their presentation of learning resources is minimal to one where ICT tools are maximized. None of these techno-driven classrooms would operate without the strategic decisions that would need to be made for the organizational change management necessary to support the increased focus on HCI. These first four chapters deal with classroom management techniques, which reveal the importance of the global online learning environment.

Chapter I: Visualizing ICT Change in the Academy: This opening chapter serves as an excellent example to introduce the issues that exist in universities for learners and the ways in which universities might respond to the needs of learners in the 21st century. Set in Canada, it presents a well-researched study of the literature that validates the context for the policies necessary for change management, with higher education. An argument is made that the strategic adaptation of the academy's structures, cultures, economies, and pedagogical praxes to the knowledge economy can help build a future where academy-based distributed learning networks will transmit ICT-mediated learning opportunities around the world, thus providing flexible access for a wide range of learners to fully participate in the global learning society. The author posits attunements to policies and practices to support institution-wide involvement in ICT initiatives.

Chapter II: HumanComputer Interaction for Computer-Based Classroom Teaching: Based in Germany, the authors of this chapter have captured the spirit of excellence in bringing ICT into the classroom. Their approach combines the traditional techniques of talk-n-chalk with technological aids that provide effective collaborative knowledge development through their expertise and management of the ICT tools they employ to support their instructional strategies. It investigates different input devices on their usage and interactivity for classroom teaching and argues that pen-based computing is the mode of choice for lecturing in modern lecture halls. It also discusses the software design of the interface where digital ink, as a first class data type, is used to communicate visual contents and interaction with the ICT.

Chapter III: Project Student Rescue: Online Learning Facilitation in Higher Education to Improve Retention Rates for Distance Learners: This chapter, set in Australia, provides a collective view of distance education in a consortium of seven universities. It raises awareness for effective online tutoring support facility to increase retention rates of online learning programs. Distance learning students often still need and require the support of a learning facilitator within the online learning environment. Preliminary studies at Open Universities Australia have shown that additional learning facilitation by online tutors have increased student motivation and student retention rates in certain critical first year subjects. This chapter describes an ongoing project that is currently being conducted at the Open Universities that investigates the impact of additional online tutorial support to increase student retention whereby the computer and Web-based environment is utilized to facilitate the student-tutor *(learning facilitator)* interaction.

Chapter IV: Enhancing Learning Through Mobile Computing: Once again from Australia, this chapter explores teaching and learning alternatives that shift the discussion away from the pedagogy of traditional classrooms to effective ways in which to engage students in their learning through flexible educational strategies. The chapter presents the students' view of their experiential learning, providing a refreshing and energetic account of the new-age technologies. The authors examine technology management and change from a student's perspective. They have given Tablet PCs to multimedia students to enable mobility and flexibility and to investigate what this increased HCI means for students who are learning design. They employ the principles of ethnographic action research as the methodology for their study and report their findings from surveys conducted and focus group meetings. This chapter explores how HCI has become mobile through the use of wireless networks, blogs, and customized agent software.

Section II. Collaborative Learning Through HCI

Innovations in online training and skill acquisition processes are being driven by demands on the human workforce to maintain their competency and knowledge in a period of rapid technological change and international competitiveness (Rosenberg, 2001). The potential for Web-based learning programs to offer a medium of collaboration, where conversation, discussion, and exchange of ideas that enables learners to work and learn together has naturally excited considerable interest. Asynchronous learning networks (ALNs) is a term used to describe a style of learning that involves an instructor who leads a class in separate transactions amongst individual learners through some form of communication media. ALNs are the subject of intensive research into context-mediated knowledge exchange. However, productive access to distributed knowledge sources requires new advances in the learning sciences (Shank, 2001), and the complexity issues in sharing experiential knowledge using ALNs and Web-based ICT educational tools commands urgent investigation. The next two chapters take up this challenge, providing interesting accounts of how the authors went about increasing their students' knowledge development.

Chapter V: Online Discourse: Encouraging Active Student Participation in Large Classes: Facilitating the learning environments for large classes can present many headaches for both teachers and learners alike. This chapter provides an account of an Australian study that investigated the effects of dealing with smaller groups from a large student cohort. The chapter demonstrates how asynchronous discourse within small groups can enhance the learning opportunity for students in large classes. It shows how ICTs encourage students to share their conceptual knowledge, and through this, to develop critical analytical and reflective skills. The HCI creates a learning environment that is flexible; it enables students to consider and respond to different views over time, and leads to closer relationships if designed to enable small group discourse. The research recommends that the best HCI will occur where ICTs are utilized effectively to augment rather than replace the face-to-face learning environment.

Chapter VI: Facilitating Social Learning in Virtual Communities of Practice: Italy is home base for the next author, yet the collaborative learning strategies described here extend the classroom much further through the virtual space provided by the powerful ICT tools and the Internet. The discussion provides a voice from both sides of the machine/human-dimensional environment of HCI. On one hand the author concurs that the machine-dimension of virtual collaborative learning spaces must deal with the complexity of the software issues to enable the virtual space to succeed, while also saying that the virtual community of practice does require a human intervention to succeed.

The chapter introduces communities of practice as a means to explore HCI in online collaborative environments. Through a wide review of the literature on communities of practice and their virtual counterparts, it argues that the focus for successful interaction design in these communities lies on those sociability and usability aspects that allow greater participation in social learning. It also argues that the facilitator assumes a fundamental role in guiding a virtual community of practice to accomplish work-related informal learning activities in a climate of trust and collaboration. The author hopes that understanding the special opportunities provided by virtual communities of practice will advocate for their widespread and routine use.

Section III. Teacher and Student Use of HCI

Until now much of the discourse surrounding online learning relates to the fall out of techno-catch-up experienced by the education sector while it struggles with the transition from being a print-based learning environment to one that supports online courseware delivery (Anderson & Elloumi, 2004). Trial-and-error has been the order of the day for many of the Web-based educational programs that involve distance education, digital library services, e-commerce, and learning systems' management. The popularity of HCI for teaching and learning within the literature is limited to collections of disparate activities, where the boundaries between teacher and students are well defined. However the six chapters in this next section integrate the facilitation of learning, with a seamless approach toward HCI and the classroom experience.

Chapter VII: Design-Personae: Matching Students' Learning Profiles in Web-Based Education: This chapter from Australia uses a theoretical case study example to explain to novice-courseware designers how to employ HCI in flexible student-centered learning programs. The authors propose a *Student Empowerment Model* to articulate an individual student's wants, desires, and expectations. Ever since the enthralling book *Rethinking university teaching: A framework for the effective use of educational technology* (Laurillard, 1993), the literature has burst forth with a plethora of new and exciting ways for teacher and student use of ICT to enhance learning. This chapter mirrors the enormous spread of professional practice involved in bringing about effective HCI for Web-based education.

Chapter VIII: Enlivening the Promise of Education: Building Collaborative Learning Communities Through Online Discussion: This chapter is set in the Malaysia, providing the reader with literature that supports the context upon which the analysis takes place. The importance of acknowledging the social environment is gaining momentum (Wallace, 1999). However, we still have much to understand about the effects of the human-dimension on online behavior (Preece, 2000). This interesting chapter explains a student-centered virtual discussion forum that cultivates social interdependence. An important dimension in education is interaction, that is, in the coming together of a number of people to discuss, debate, and deliberate about issues of common concern. In distance education, such social environments are as much present in online learning contexts as they are in face-to-face learning contexts such as tutorials. This chapter expands the notion of teacher and student use of HCI to focus on integrating HCI in the curriculum through the use of online discussion forums at Open University Malaysia to build collaborative online communities using common principles of teaching and learning.

Chapter IX: APEC Cyber Academy: Integration of Pedagogical and HCI Principles in an International Networked Learning Environment: Taiwan and the U.S. stand to provide an excellent international context for linking pedagogy to HCI in a practical environment. One of the many strengths of this chapter is the tying of the Asia Pacific Economic Cooperation (APEC) Cyber Academy framework to pedagogical principles. The authors' expertise and knowledge of instructional design are evident in their choice of their Cyber Camp learning modules that offer effective HCI. The APEC Cyber Academy provides learning opportunities through collaboration and HCI in an international networked learning environment. The HCI tools are employed to support the pedagogical principles that are steeped in constructivism and self-regulated learning. These tools, including video chat room, forum, intelligent agent, peer evaluation assistant, learner profile, and interpersonal communication system, have fostered a conducive learning environment and attracted more than 10,000 K-12 participants from 22 countries to engage in online learning activities.

Chapter X: Tangible User Interfaces as Mediating Tools within Adaptive Educational Environments: This Australian-based chapter draws on work from the UK to deal with mechanisms that integrate adaptive experiential awareness of effective HCI in classrooms. The author describes a learning ecology that involves interesting multi-relationships between students/teachers, cognitive diversity, and pedagogical choice. The chapter proposes tangible user interfaces as an effective HCI that can scaffold rich classroom experiences if they are coupled and generated within multi-pedagogical frameworks that adopt concepts such as multimodality, multi-sensoriality, and multi-literacies. It provides an overview of some necessary conditions for these tools to be effective, arguing that tangible user interfaces and multi-pedagogies are efficient when they are conceptualized as part of adaptive educational environments—teaching and learning ecologies where learners and teachers are seen as co-creators of content and of new ways of interacting with such content.

Chapter XI: Building the Virtual into Teacher Education: This Australian-based chapter describes the online environment and the evolving context to provide novice-teachers with some wonderful insight into the evolution of a virtual learning environment. The authors provide a detailed motivation for their approach, which is also backed by their referenced literature. Traditional teacher and student design and use of HCI are contested, as two teacher educators *(with the assistance of Web designers)* worked to unsettle known practices of schooling. The authors advocate new learning pedagogies and share how a virtual primary school alongside face-to-face teaching is helping pre-service teachers to manage purposeful change. The environment has been built with attention to being dynamic and unpredictable. Novice teachers have a placement in this virtual school.

Chapter XII: Integrating Human Computer Interaction in Veterinary Medicine Curricula: This Canadian chapter moves the discussion on effective HCI to a position that reflects the serious nature of global issues that impose on us all. The authorship is an impressive collection of 11 professional practitioners expressing the desire to differentiate between what they teach and the manner in which this teaching is carried out. The chapter discusses contemporary global challenges facing veterinary educators and summarizes some of the economic, social, political, and technological pressures underlying curricular and pedagogical change initiatives. Integrating HCI into veterinary medicine curricula, as a strategy for implementing pedagogical transformation, is reviewed. Computer-assisted learning (CAL) projects recently developed at a veterinary college are described. Results of studies evaluating the effectiveness of CAL approaches to HCI integration within the veterinary medicine curricula are reported, and future research directions are proposed.

Section IV. HCI in Educational Practice

This fourth and final group of two chapters is about the practicalities of existing educational program delivery. The first falls with the professional practice of *educational and training design—support systems and models* to present a clearly explained and interesting chapter of an obviously well designed postgraduate course. It provides an excellent case study that outlines the issues and problems encountered in running the course, offering solutions to the dilemmas that face many distance education learning environments. The second chapter deals with *simulation and managerial gaming issues.* While this chapter may have been placed last in the book by some Freudian quirk, it is by no means without substance; it offers a rare and insightful approach toward holistic instructional strategies that employ *effective HCI* to address the complexity of the real world problems architectural students will need to face as professionals.

Chapter XIII: Problem-Based Learning at a Distance: Course Design and HCI in an Environmental Management Master's Program: The use of HCI in an environmental management master's program. Ralph Horne and Jon Kellett present their experiences of incrementally developing a master's course from face-to-face mode to HCI. Using a case study approach they show how the design process works in practice. Drawing on theory from the established literature and using their own experience and external examiners' comments as a guide, the authors take the reader through the educational design process, which culminates in an attractive and valuable virtual learning product. Their chapter demonstrates the complex range of issues that influence the design of successful HCI.

Chapter XIV: An Integrative Approach to Teaching 3D Modelling in Architecture: The argument presented here is that computer courses in architecture must reach beyond the comfortable cushion of conventional teaching practices and provide students with a way to come to grips with the complexity present in real world problems. It provides as evidence a digital graphic literacy course for architecture students using transformer robot toys as a metaphor for introducing the concept of adaptive kinetic architecture, a form of complex dynamic systems. The transformer robot toy is the manipulative device with which students develop 3D digital modeling and rendering skills and make a tangible connection to dynamic architectural systems. The course approach is described, and observations about the students' work are offered. Further investigation is proposed to ascertain the most appropriate delivery for reciprocal and complementary knowledge.

CONCLUSION

The collective contributions from authors based in many different countries identify the complexity of the visual learning environment and outline prospects for customizing Web-mediated learning. Progress is thus possible in linking research outcomes to actual learning contexts. The prospect of customized learning shells, tailored dynamically to the requirements of individual students, has stimulated contemporary research into knowledge mediation, and the associated meta-knowledge acquisition strategies, of actual learning contexts within asynchronous learning frameworks (Fredericksen, Pickett, Shea, Peiz, & Swan, 2000).

Within the context of online asynchronous learning platforms, there is a noticeable shift from traditional teaching methods, which act as the sole content provider, toward a multiple mentor-guiding approach. This approach supports learners through the process of knowledge acquisition, largely directed by the learners themselves, reflecting the lack of understanding of the effect of Web-based learning on the population at large. Web-based pedagogy is complex, and instructional courseware designers need to ensure that careful attention is paid to implement sound and well-founded instructional design principles (Merrill, 2002).

While multi-sensory instruction is known to improve a student's capacity to learn effectively, the overarching role of knowledge-mediated HCI has been poorly understood in the design of instructional strategies that integrate contextual components in asynchronous learning frameworks. The limitations of contemporary approaches to instructional design appear to lie in the failure to recognize and accommodate learning process dynamics, specifically the interactive effects between cognitive style and instructional format, and the need to adapt the instructional format dynamically. It may be concluded that the mechanism to achieve such dynamics lies in the concurrent acquisition of knowledge about the learner's cognitive performance within a contextual framework defined by a knowledge level analysis of task difficulty.

REFERENCES

Anderson, T., & Elloumi, F. (Eds.). (2004). *Theory and practice of online learning*. Athabasca University. Retrieved May 11, 2006, from http://cde.athabascau.ca/online_book/copyright.html

Baggett, P., & Ehrenfeucht, A. (1985). *Conceptualizing in assembly tasks* (Tech. Rep. No. 139). Boulder Inst. of Cognitive Science.

Berners-Lee, T., Hendler, J., & Lassila, O. (2001). The semantic Web: A new form of Web content that is meaningful to computers will unleash a revolution of new possibilities. *Scientific American, 284*(5), 28-37.

Bruder, I. (1991). Guide to multimedia: How it changes the way we teach & learn. *Electronic Learning,* (September), 22-26.

Carroll, J. M. (Ed.). (2003). *HCI models, theories: Toward a multidisciplinary science*. San Francisco: Elsevier Science.

de Souza, C. S., & Preece, J. (2004). A framework for analyzing and understanding online communities. *Journal, Interacting with Computers, 6*, 579-610. Retrieved March 4, 2006, from http://www.ifsm.umbc.edu/preece/Papers/Framework_desouza_preece2003.pdf

Dick, W. O., Carey, L., & O'Carey, J. (2004). *The systematic design of instruction* (6th ed.). Allyn & Bacon.

Dowding, T. J. (1993). The application of a spiral curriculum model to technical training curricula. *Educational Technology,* (July), 18-28.

Emonds-Banfield, P. (2006, February 1). Building the Semantic Web. *Orange Journal*. Retrieved May 13, 2006, from http://orange.eserver.org/issues/3-2/emonds-banfield.html

Fredericksen, E., Pickett, A., Shea, P., Peiz, W., & Swan, K. (2000). Student satisfaction and perceived learning with online courses: Principles and examples from the suny learning network. In J. Bourne (Ed.), *On-line education: Learning effectiveness and faculty satisfaction, Proceedings of the 1999 Sloan Summer Workshop on Asynchronous Learning Networks* (p. 288). Nashville: ALN Centre, Vanderbilt University.

Gillis, P. D. (1993). ICACT: An instruction and control architecture for classroom training. *Educational Technology,* (June), 41-45.

Hewett, T. T., Baecker, R., Card, S., Carey, L., Gasen, J., Mantei, M., Perlman, G., Strong, G., & Verplank, W. (2004). *Acm sigchi curricula for human-computer interaction*. Association for Computing Machinery, Inc. Retrieved May 13, 2006, from http://www.sigchi.org/cdg/cdg2.html

Laurillard, D. (1993). *Rethinking university teaching: A framework for the effective use of educational technology*. UK: Routledge.

McKay, E. (2000). *Instructional strategies integrating the cognitive style construct: A meta-knowledge processing model (contextual components that facilitate spatial/logical task performance).* Published doctoral dissertation (Computer Science and Information Systems). Total fulfillment, Deakin Univ., Australia.

Merrill, M. D. (2002). First principles of instruction. *ETR&D, 50*(3), 43-59. Retrieved January 11, 2006, from http://www.indiana.edu/~tedfrick/aect2002/firstprinciplesbymerrill.pdf

Preece, J. (2000). *Online communities: Designing usability, supporting sociability.* New York: John Wiley & Sons: UK.

Preece, J., Rogers, Y., & Sharp, H. (2002). *Interaction design: Beyond human-computer interaction* (1st ed.). Harlow, UK: Addison-Wesley.

Preece, J., Rogers, Y., Sharp, H., Benyon, D., Holland, S., & Carey, T. (1994). *Human-computer interaction.* Harlow, UK: Addison-Wesley.

Rosenberg, M. J. (2001). *E-learning: Strategies for delivering knowledge in the digital age.* New York: Mc-Graw-Hill.

Shank, R. C. (2001). Revolutionizing the traditional classroom course. *Log on Education Column: in Communications of the ACM, 44*(12). Retrieved from http://www.acm.org/cacm/1201/1201toc.html

Shneiderman, S., & Plaisant, C. (2005). *Designing the user interface: Strategies for effective human-computer interaction* (4th ed.). Reading, MA: Addison-Wesley.

Wallace, P. (1999). *The psychology of the Internet.* UK: Cambridge University Press.

Acknowledgments

I would like to thank everyone who contributed to making this book possible. The enthusiasm from the reviewers is acknowledged. I extend my gratitude and appreciation to this seemingly tireless group of academics. The review results were sent to each primary chapter author as constructive recommendations to improve their work. This type of supportive collegial environment continues my goal to promote the best quality research and project findings into the future. To the countless number of proofreaders, your scholarly efforts are appreciated by experienced academics as well as those new to this type of dissemination. To those authors of the chapters not selected for publication, please know that your efforts are acknowledged with thankfulness; selection decisions were most difficult, with topic coverage dictating final acceptance.

I would also like to express gratitude to RMIT University, which provided me with time away from School duties to complete the book. To the staff at Idea Group Inc., thank you for the continued professional advice that was always forthcoming and timely throughout the yearlong preparation process. A special word of appreciation is to be sent to Ramesh C. Sharma, Regional Director, Indira Gandhi National Open University, Haryana, India, for his encouragement with the early concept to bring forward this manuscript.

The following reviewer listing reflects the global interest in effective HCI for education and training:

Alain G. N. Anyounza, *Cougaar Software Inc., U.S.*
Adam Parker, *RMIT Univ., Australia*
Alexandra Uitdenborerd, *RMIT Univ., Australia*
Any Avny, Consultant, *Italy*
Ben Daniel, *Univ. of the West Indies, Trinidad & Tobago*
Brian Garner, *Deakin Univ., Australia*
Candace Chou,   *Univ. of St. Thomas, U.S.*
Carmina Sanchez, *Hampton University, Virgina, U.S.*
Carole Bagley, *Univ. of St. Thomas, U.S.*
Daniel Peraya, *Univ. of Geneva, Switzerland*
Daria Loi, *RMIT Univ., Australia*
Dina Lewis, *Univ. of Hull, UK*
Elizabeth Berry, *Univ. of Leeds, UK*
Gale Parchoma, *Univ. of Saskatchewan, Canada*
Gloria Latham, *RMIT Univ., Australia*
Ian Cole, *Univ. of York, UK*
John Izard, *Human Performance Measurement Consultant, Australia*
Julie Faulkner, *RMIT Univ., Australia*
Keven Asquith, *Project Management Consultant, Melbourne, Australia*
L. Odette Dewhurst, *Univ. of Leeds, UK*
Margaret Hamilton, *RMIT Univ., Australia*
Marsha Berry, *RMIT Univ., Australia*
Maureen Farrell, *RMIT Univ., Australia*
Mitch Parsell, *Macquarie University, Australia*
Permanand Mohan, *Univ. of the West Indies, Trinidad and Tobago*

Phillipe Dessus, *Univ. of Grenoble, France*
Ralph Horne, *RMIT Univ., Australia*
Rosanna Tarsiero, *Gionnethics, Italy*
S. E. Bacon, *Leeds Teaching Hospital, UK*
Sandra Jones, *RMIT Univ., Australia*
Syamal Kumar Sen, *Florida Institute of Technology, U.S.*
Wolfgang Hürst, *Albert-Ludwigs-Universität Freiburg, Germany*

Elspeth McKay, PhD
RMIT, Australia

About the Editor

Elspeth McKay has a mix of experience that involves two decades as a business sector information systems trainer, lecturer in business computing, and an active researcher into online learning and courseware development. Her research has involved the design and development of interactive e-learning systems, which enhance opportunities for the special requirements of vocational rehabilitation for disabled members of the community. Her work on cognitive performance measurement for assessing readiness for returning to study/retraining breaks new ground, bringing the richness of ICT to enhance the human-dimensions of HCI in an educational/corporate training context.

Section I
Technology
Management and Change

Chapter I
Visualizing ICT Change in the Academy

Gale Parchoma
University of Saskatchewan, Canada

ABSTRACT

This chapter introduces complexity theory as a theoretical framework for analyzing the influences of information and computer technologies (ICTs) on the structures, cultures, economies (reward systems), and pedagogical praxes within the Academy. An argument is made that the strategic adaptation of the academy's structures, cultures, economies, and pedagogical praxes to the knowledge economy can help build a future where Academy-based distributed learning networks will transmit ICT-mediated learning opportunities around the world, thus providing flexible access for a wide range of learners to fully participate in the global learning society. The author posits attunements to policies and practices to support institution-wide involvement in ICT initiatives.

OVERVIEW

This chapter addresses the technology management and change theme through the application of complexity theory to information and communications technologies (ICT) change initiatives directed toward enhancing learners' access to higher education, opportunities to succeed, and experiences with human computer interaction (HCI). Academic organizational structures, cultures, economies, and pedagogies are analyzed for their alignment with successful integration of human computer interaction into learning experiences as a core activity within higher education. A variety of challenges to achieving institution-wide involvement in HCI are addressed. A series of adjustments to policy and practice is posited.

INTRODUCTION

The contemporary global learning society's demands upon individuals for life-long learning are now transforming and will continue to transform the traditional Academy. The adoption of information and computer technologies (ICT) to provide flexible access to distributed learning opportunities for working adults underpins this transformation. The external economic forces of the new economy and its information technology paradigm may be the most powerful influence for this change. Simultaneously, the social forces of postmodernism, the interpretive turn, identity politics, and globalization are affecting change in the organizational culture of higher education and increasing demands for collaborative and distributed learning opportunities. At this juncture, traditional research universities may need to re-examine their policies and practices to effectively adapt to a complex, ambiguous, and dynamic, and technologically driven external environment. University leadership may need to strategically respond to these external pressing demands for change.

Internal organizational structures, cultures, economies (reward systems), and pedagogical praxes may need to be attuned to changing academic times. At the heart of this need for adjustment of university policies, procedures, and customs is the groundswell of demands for lifelong, personalized, customized, and distributed learning opportunities (Daniel & Mohan, 2004; McCalla, 2004; Tjeldvoll, 1998). Strategic responses to these demands are required to ensure that ICT-mediated solutions provide flexible access to high quality higher education and forestall the potential of models rapidly being developed by new for-profit higher education competitors (DiPaolo, 2003) from becoming disruptive technologies and eclipsing the role of traditional universities in the higher education sector (Archer, Garrison, & Anderson, 1999; Christensen, 1997). The Academy needs to embrace ICT solutions and their associated service orientation to ensure its ongoing position as the best option for higher education.

In order to achieve this transformation, leaders in traditional research universities may need to increase their capacity to effectively manage complexity. Control and direction need to be abandoned in favor of influence. Contextualized solutions to complex problems need to be determined via inclusionary, polycultural approaches to change (Sackney & Mitchell, 2002; Suter, 2001). Faculty members need to be engaged and willing to take innovative risks (Bates, 2000; Brown & Jackson, 2001; Olcott & Schmidt, 2000). Cost-effective, scalable innovations need to be researched and developed (Daniel & Mohan, 2004). To make this transformation possible, individual institutions need to more thoroughly understand their current situations and collegially create effective visions for the future—a future where Academy-based distributed learning networks will transmit ICT-mediated learning opportunities around the world, thus providing flexible access for a wide range of learners to fully participate in the global learning society.

THEORETICAL FRAMEWORK

Structural, cultural, economic, and pedagogical value positions within the Academy may not be closely allied to the potential for successfully increasing access to higher education via ICT-mediated learning opportunities (Brown & Jackson, 2001; Graves, 2001; Hanna, 2000a). Dealing with the complexity of issues in this range of value positions "does not mean controlling or eliminating them. It means tapping the power of complexity by accepting it, understanding its principles, and working with it as academic institutions work with faculty to transform teaching and learning" (Suter, 2001, p. 25).

Suter (2001) applies complexity theory in her development of five principles for transforming the Academy into a postmodern, technologically advanced organization. She argues, "When the speed of change (in demographics, demand, workforce, technology, economics) leads us to the edge of chaos, the command-and-control model" of organizational structures and functions "is not only counterproductive, it is simply not possible" (p. 25). Suter's first principle advises academic leaders to "give up control and aim for influence" through systematic sharing of "information," "authority, responsibility, and the power to oppose" (p. 26). She argues that accelerating change requires institution-wide involvement and distributed leadership.

Secondly, adopting a stance of studying the Academy as if it were an artwork, is posited as an avenue to the creation of an "institutional vision" for a future where shared "goals worth working toward" can be achieved through "tracking important patterns" (pp. 28-29). Using an analogy to nature, Suter prescribes a reduce and reuse approach to creating streamlined, useful structures that fulfill multiple purposes, as well an over-arching common structure for institutional coherence. Paradoxically, she suggests investing in "polyculture and prototyping," experimenting with diverse approaches, and accepting that "failure is necessary to create the conditions for successful change" (p. 31).

Finally, Suter promotes tapping "the power of limits," through setting and communicating clear "boundary conditions" (p. 32). Boundary conditions are defined as limits within which the organization must manage its resources. An example of "the power of limits" is the extended use of research funding through application of findings to teaching and learning settings. Using Suter's (2001) managing complexity framework, an examination of five aspects of each of structural, cultural, economic, and pedagogical value positions follows.

Organizational Structure

Five aspects of organizational structure, which have an impact on the successful adoption of ICT-mediated learning, include: tensions between hierarchical and decentralized organizational forms; bureaucratic and autonomous functions; individual and distributed leadership models; the relative comfort of gradual change and need

for more rapid change; pressures for sustaining independent faculty roles; and pressures to include emergent professions in collaborative, interdependent activities. Strategically mediating these tensions contributes to the "health" of the Academy:

'Healthy' institutions are 'fit for purpose'; in other words, they are organized to ensure their goals and purposes are achieved in the most effective and efficient manner. The current structure and organization of most universities and colleges is largely historical and ... unsuited to new forms of technological delivery. (Bates, 2000, p. 36)

Despite this criticism, Bates (2000) acknowledges an important way in which traditional universities are well prepared to become highly functional, postmodern organizations. He notes a form and function paradox, which serves two basic needs of a postmodern organization: the need for a clear vision of organizational goals and purposes, and the need for flexibility and adaptability to effectively and efficiently meet those goals and purposes. "Despite its hierarchical organizational structure, a [traditional research] university is in practice an extremely decentralized organization" (p. 41). The existing hierarchical form provides opportunities for "strong leadership, characterized by clear but broad vision and objectives," and an "integrating, coordinating and facilitating role" for senior management (p. 40). The functionally distributed decision-making ability allows a "large and creative 'core' of staff—faculty—who are able and willing to operate relatively autonomously, are concerned with the creation and transmission of knowledge, and have the power to develop and implement new ways of doing things" (p. 41), thus allowing the organization to be flexible and adaptable. This paradox of form and function has the potential to balance tension between centralized and decentralized control. It allows leaders to, at once, "give up control while ensuring that there are commonly shared principles for decision making aligned with the institution's goals" (Suter, 2001, p. 27). In theory, strategic planning and faculty autonomy can co-exist within the distributed leadership environment of the Academy.

However, faculty autonomy is a factor that affects the pace of organizational change. Few organizations allow the scope of latitude afforded to university and college faculty (Cahn, 1986). "The tradition-bound nature of the Academy has accommodated this latitude, and the slow pace of change in almost every aspect of campus life has made it a tolerable part of the academic landscape" (Hagner & Schneebeck, 2001, p. 2). Conversely, rapid technological development and change, especially rapidly accelerating "dependence on information technology," "networking" (Bates, 2000, p. 40), and "prototyping" (Suter, 2001, p. 31) are hallmarks of postmodern organizations. The mismatch of the respective paces of traditional academic culture and postmodern organizational culture is a potentially powerful source of resistance to change (Hagner & Schneebeck, 2001; Hanna, 2000a). If the Academy is going to become flexible, adaptable organization, capable of providing learners with the necessary experiences "to develop knowledge and skills appropriate for living and working in a rapidly changing, technology-based society" (Hanna, 2000a, p. 46), the challenge of accelerating the pace of change within the Academy must be met. Engaging faculty in the process of change through clear and open communication and decision-making channels may provide leaders with sufficient influence to do so (Suter, 2001).

A further structural concern, one that impacts faculty autonomy, is a shift from independence to interdependence in scholarly work. In particular, emergent professions are beginning to be involved in the scholarly work of teaching. Traditionally, "university and college staffs have been highly skilled and … well-trained for *research*" (Bates, 2000, p. 41). However, "*teaching* has not been not professionalized in the sense of being based on skills resulting from research into and analysis of teaching and learning processes" (p. 41). Rather, teaching has most often been an independent, role model-based *art* or *craft*, which in comparison to research has "not [been] well rewarded" (Boyer, 1990, p. xii). However, in the development and implementation of ICT-mediated learning opportunities, the professionalization of teaching through study of such areas of knowledge as, "psychology of learning, organizational management research, communications theories, [and] human-machine interaction" (Bates, 2000, p. 41) is critical.

Yet, acquiring and maintaining current, in-depth understanding of these disparate fields, in addition to a specialty area of knowledge, is not always possible. Therefore, many, if not most, faculty members need to work collaboratively with teams of specialists occupying emergent roles (Bates, 2000; Hanley, 2001; Hanna, 2000a; Hutchins, 2000; Luker, 2000). Teaching with technology requires a shift from perceiving teaching as fulfilling a traditional, independent role to "one where teaching and learning are the products of an integrated group of individuals" (Hanley, 2001, p. 59). Emerging roles within the realm of academic teaching and scholarship include instructional designers, educational technologists, Web programmers, multimedia experts, computer scientists, and system engineers. In order to support a team-based approach to instructional development, academic leaders need to promote a culture of collaboration and change tenure and promotion standards that sufficiently reward faculty for time spent on collaborative instructional development activities.

Figure 1 illustrates five continua of organizational structure within the Academy: hierarchical to decentralized organizational forms, bureaucratic to autonomous functions, individual to distributed leadership models, gradual to rapid responses to change, independent to interdependent roles. In addition, in Figure 1 current and required conditions for successful adoption of ICT-mediated learning are hypothesized through

Figure 1. Organizational cultures "in tune" with ICT initiatives

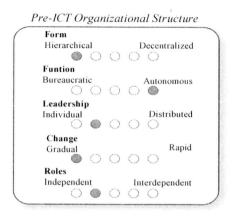 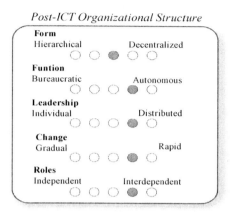

the use of a stereo analogy. The premise of this analogy is that just as tone, balance, bass, and treble need to be adjusted to suit an audio recording, organizational structures need to be "in tune" with ICT initiatives.

Organizational Culture

Shafritz and Ott (2001) define organizational culture as a collage of ephemeral phenomena, including "values, beliefs, assumptions, perceptions, behavioral norms, artifacts, and patterns of behavior," each of which contribute to "meaning, direction, and mobilization" (p. 361). Schein (1993) argues that a useful way to perceive organizational culture is "as the accumulated shared learning of a given group, covering behavioral, emotional, and cognitive elements or the group members' total psychological functioning" (p. 372). An organizational culture requires a "common language" and "a common system of communication" as the basis for "group learning"—the ability to acquire and dispel "shared basic assumptions" (p. 373).

When elements of an organizational culture "have become maladapted" to the external environment, "it is ultimately the function of leadership to recognize and do something about the situation" (Schein, 1993, p. 370). Trice and Beyer (1993) argue that *doing something about the*

situation, changing an organizational culture, "is a relatively drawn out and slow process," which "usually takes several years to accomplish" (p. 415). They recommend initiating change at "propitious moments, when some obvious problem, opportunity, or change in circumstances makes change desirable" (p. 417). The accumulative problems of decreasing public funding (Archer, Garrison, & Anderson, 1999; Bates, 2000; Hanna, 2000a; Mackay, 1996; Nesbit, 2004), opportunities to extend the Academy to better serve the needs of a global learning society (Alclay, 2003; Archer & Wright, 1999; Maduro, 1998; McLuhan, 1964; Norton, 2000; O'Driscoll, 2003), and changes in circumstances, such as the entrance of for-profit competition (Bates, 2000; Hanna, 2000a; Maduro, 1998), as well as the impacts of advanced information and learning technologies (Archer, Garrison, & Anderson, 1999; Bates, 2000; Hanna, 2000a; Nesbit, 2004) currently facing higher education, suggest that a *propitious moment* for cultural change is at hand:

The most important and immediate task for universities facing an uncertain future is to build a culture that is friendly to and supportive of innovation and change at all levels of the organization. (Hanna, 2000a, p. 348)

Again employing Suter's (2001) managing complexity approach, an examination of five elements of academic organizational culture that affect successful adoption of ICT-mediated learning follows. Beliefs about institutional operations are examined along an independence/interdependence continuum. Values are traced from the tradition of emphasis on open discourse to inclusion of teaching marketable skills. Assumptions about the appropriate role of continuing education units within the Academy scan a range from public service to entrepreneurial venture. Perceptions of technology—from skepticism to enthusiasm—are explored. Artifacts, from lecture notes, assignments, and exams to ICT-mediated learning opportunities, are described in terms of the cultural changes associated with their use. Each of these elements is examined for alignment with the external forces driving and restraining change.

"The curtailment of public funding has become a year-to-year fact of planning life on the campuses" (MacKay, 1996, p. 10). As public funding is withdrawn "and as the ability of the universities, for reasons of equity and practicality, to replace these funds with other sources of revenue, such as tuition, becomes more restricted or disappears, the universities again face the fundamental question of how to rebalance themselves" (p. 10). Increasingly, public pressure is mounting "to ensure that, where possible, the universities act in a cooperative and complementary fashion as they conduct their institutional missions" (p. 10). As a result, "memoranda of understanding" between/among universities are being developed. At a basic level, these memoranda may outline credit transfer policies and joint course development and delivery initiatives among universities. More recent types of memoranda, made possible by ICT-mediated learning, include franchise arrangements, which allow for use, revision, and reuse of electronic learning resources. This cooperative "reduce and reuse" (Suter, 2001, p. 28) approach to creating

and managing resources is a well-suited response to an environment of fiscal restraint.

Fiscal pressure is also fostering a need "to forge many linkages and partnerships with external associations" (Hanna, 2000a, p. 339). Traditional research universities are under significant pressure to abandon the posture of "quiet enclaves for the pursuit of truth far removed from the busy world of commerce and industry" and to assume close linkages "with national economic and scientific objectives" (Nesbit, 2004, p. 104). A pervasive debate within the Academy involves increasing tensions between the academic value attached to "the traditional academic mandate of [fostering] a 'lively exchange of ideas'" through open discourse and the economic value of "the teaching of [marketable] skills that can lead to required and satisfying careers" (Maduro, 1998, p. 42). Arguments against shifting the mandate further toward marketable skills include: such a change would amount to "prostitution of education"; and the Academy would end up "being in the pockets of industry" (p. 42). Given the "rapid growth in opportunities to profit from the production of knowledge," the risk of "conflicts of interest" merits recognition (Nesbit, 2004, p. 106). However, counter-arguments, such as "the 'job-readiness' gap is growing," and that "skill deficits" are contributing to Canadian "non-competitiveness," (Maduro, 1998, p. 40) are equally worthy of note. While the clash between "commercial and academic values" (Nesbit, 2004, p. 106) requires significant deliberation, resolution may be found. Acknowledging the "polyculture" of the Academy (Suter, 2001)—in particular, the role that continuing education (CE) units can play in skills training (Hanna, 2000a; Maduro, 1998)—may provide an acceptable balance, attuned to both academic values and knowledge economy pressures.

The appropriate role of CE units is another source of debate. Many North American CE units' mandates originally referenced "'the Wisconsin Idea': [that] the purpose of a university was not to educate a small, elite class, but rather to serve the educational needs of the community" (Archer & Wright, 1999, Three eras in university extension, para. 2). Subsequently, CE units have commonly been tasked with dual responsibilities of providing high quality educational services as a public service function and increasing accessibility to programming to non-traditional learners. Conversely, "especially in research universities, many faculty members question whether providing lifelong learning, especially for those in the workforce, is an appropriate mandate" (Bates, 2000, p. 15). As a result, "departments of continuing education (CE) usually have both fewer resources and a lower status than other university units" (Nesbit, 2004, p. 105). Long-term erosion of institutional support for public service programming through declining financial support from university administrations (Bates, 2000; Maduro, 1998) has created significant fiscal challenges for CE units. Increasingly, CE units are expected to operate on a cost-recovery basis (Nesbit, 2004). However, undertaking entrepreneurial ventures tends to garner criticism from students and faculty, resulting in further erosion of academic status across the Academy (Maduro, 1998; Nesbit, 2004). This stalemate has contributed to North American universities losing an estimated "70 billion dollars a year" to "corporate universities" and "training centers," where in-house programs address CE gaps (Maduro, 1998, pp. 43-44).

Given the significance of the need for lifelong learning, driven by the knowledge and skill demands of the economy combined with the public perception that publicly funded universities have a major obligation to share new knowledge via new information technologies and support for lifelong learning, reconsideration of institutional support for CE units, and their use of ICT is warranted (Hanna, 2000a). An institutional vision for a future where public learning needs are addressed through a reduction of the "rigidity of boundaries between [universities] and their external publics"

through "interaction made possible by increasingly powerful technologies" (p. 343) has the potential to revitalize the relationship between the Academy and society.

If ICT-mediated knowledge sharing is to become a basic tenet of the future Academy, the challenge of developing technically competent faculties must be addressed by university leaders. Rogers' (1995) theory of *diffusion of innovations* "has quite deservedly been recognized as the baseline work" (Hagner & Schneebeck, 2001, p. 1) on perceptions of technological innovations. Findings based upon "intensive interviews with 240 faculty at the University of Hartford" strongly suggest that faculty tend to "demonstrate predominant characteristics" of Rodgers' four technological adoption groupings (p. 2).

The "first wave" or early adopters are "professors who represent the vanguard of innovation in teaching and learning" with technology (Hagner & Schneebeck, 2001, p. 3). However, "their work tends to be idiosyncratic" and is not scalable for broader use (p. 3). Engaging early adopters in scalable solutions requires clearly articulated processes and procedures, which are evidently more effective and efficient than individual efforts.

The "second wave" or "risk adversives" are committed to quality teaching and learning opportunities, and they are attracted to the potential of "new technologies" for improving "what they do"; however, they often lack "technological expertise," and require "significant levels of instructional support" (Hagner & Schneebeck, 2001, pp. 2-3). Risk adversives are often afraid that "their current success in teaching will not translate into the new teaching environments" (p. 2). Some "are hesitant to become engaged in the process of self-examination" (p. 2). Technological and peer support are critical for this group.

The "third wave" or "reward seekers" tend to focus on use of technology "to advance their professional careers"; therefore, their motivation "is closely tied to the university's reward structure" (Hagner & Schneebeck, 2001, p. 4). "When they view adoption of new teaching and learning techniques as having a positive impact on tenure, promotion, and salary decisions, they will be more willing to transform" (p. 4).

The "fourth group" or "reluctants" are "those who are computer illiterate or firmly believe that traditional models of learning are superior" (Hagner & Schneebeck, 2001, p. 4). In some academic institutions, "there is a pervasive belief that faculty jobs are going to be replaced by the adoption of technology" (Olcott & Schmidt, 2000, p. 262). Fearful and "philosophically resistant faculty" increasingly risk being perceived as "anachronistic" and the professional consequences of that perception, including "an adverse impact on the evaluation of their teaching" (Hagner & Schneebeck, 2001, p. 5). One effective leadership method with this group is to communicate these risks through "faculty bodies, such as faculty senates" (Hagner & Schneebeck, 2001, p. 6).

Variant perceptions of technology—from the skepticism of reluctants to the enthusiasm of early adopters—warrant consideration in the design of engagement strategies. To circumvent cultural resistance to technological innovation, institutions need to determine their [particular] faculty mix and strategically plan appropriate support mechanisms and communication channels for each adoption group.

Organizational culture is often expressed through the use of artifacts for cultural activities. Whereas lecture notes, assignments, books, and exams are predominant artifacts in traditional educational settings, ICT-mediated learning artifacts include electronic learning resources and environments, and electronically mediated personal and professional experiences. The use of traditional educational artifacts emphasized concerted individual, isolated effort directed toward "abstract and relatively unconnected assessment processes such as … content examinations" (Hanna, 2000a, p. 345). ICT artifacts increasingly focus on "the ability to work in teams, to develop creative approaches to problem solving, and to learn continuously" (p. 344). Networked universities are becoming "more and more concerned with ensuring that students know how to learn and to apply what they learn to real situations" (p. 344). This activity-centered approach to demonstrating learning represents a cultural shift from valuing abstract knowledge to valuing applied knowledge and skills—the same skills that are "necessary to live and work in a rapidly changing economy" (p. 64).

Figure 2. Organizational cultures "in tune" with ICT initiatives

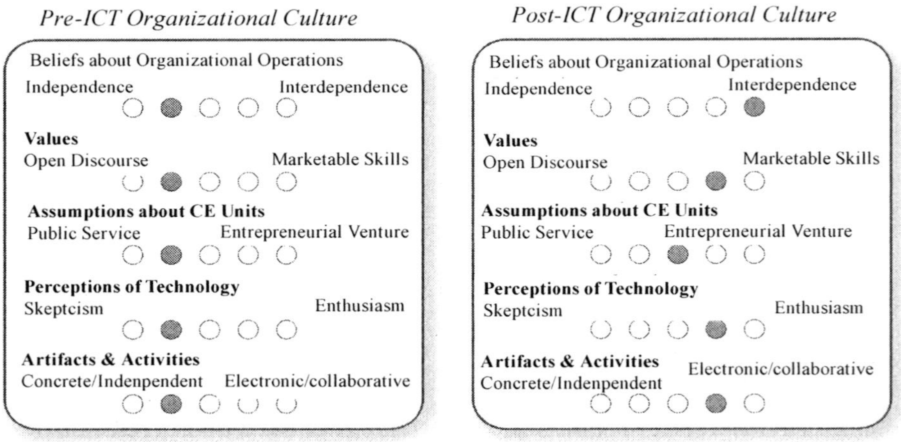

Figure 2 illustrates two hypotheses: one suggests a current state of academic culture, and one recommends cultural attunement for successful adoption of ICT-mediated learning opportunities.

Organizational Economies (Institutional Reward Systems)

Five aspects of organizational economies (institutional reward systems) that have an impact on the successful adoption of ICT-mediated learning opportunities include: tensions created by an emphasis on rewarding research activities more substantially than teaching activities; restricting the involvement of junior faculty in ICT development through out-date tenure and promotion criteria; emergent tensions between institutional rewards for commercialization of research discoveries and innovations and commercialization of ICT development activities; emergent issues about ICT intellectual property rights; and valuing work with graduate and traditional (full-time, on-campus) learners more than undergraduate and non-traditional (part-time, distance) learners.

Extending Suter's (2001) approach to managing complexity, an analysis of these five elements of institutional reward systems that affect successful adoption of ICT-mediated learning follows:

Today... there is a recognition that the faculty reward system does not match the full range of academic functions and that professors are often caught between completing obligations... According to the dominant view, to be a scholar is to be a researcher—and publication is the primary yardstick by which scholarly activity is measured... Given these tensions, what is the balance to be struck between research and teaching? (Boyer, 1990)

More than a decade after Boyer (1990) posed his question, the advent of ICT development as a teaching activity for faculty adds salience to it.

ICT design, development, and delivery involve significant time investments from faculty (Bates, 2000; Hanley, 2001). Conversely, the same time investment could be made in research activities. If the Academy is serious about technological innovation in teaching praxis and does not adjust this mismatch of rewards, it will be difficult to engage faculty in ICT development initiatives (Archer, Garrison, & Anderson, 1999; Olcott & Schmidt, 2000).

Junior faculty members—the group that initially may seem most likely to adopt innovations—are, in fact, systematically discouraged by existing reward systems:

Interestingly, senior tenured faculty can venture out and be innovative, while junior non-tenured faculty must adhere to traditional norms. Translated, this means strict adherence to promotion and tenure criteria. In sum, for many junior faculty members there are not only few incentives but, in fact, underlying disincentives operating in this subculture. (Olcott & Schmidt, 2000, p. 264)

If technological innovation is to take hold in the Academy, the criteria for tenure and promotion must become more inclusive in determining legitimate scholarly activities, and this change needs to be perceived as an immediate, rather than a future, concern:

The currency of the Knowledge Age is information. More precisely, it is the creation, analysis, preservation, and distribution of information in efficient, easily accessible venues that give users the immediate capacity to apply information and knowledge. (Olcott & Schmidt, 2000, p. 259)

In the new economy, the academic tradition of autonomous pursuit of knowledge, for its own sake, is coming under increasingly powerful political-economic pressures. Fiscal challenges, combined with expanded opportunities to commercialize discoveries and innovations, are driving academic leaders to reward faculty for commercialization of research (Boyer, 1990; Nesbit, 2004). To date, few examples of commercialization of ICT-mediated learning can be found, but that may change. Increasingly, faculties who are skilled and experienced in ICT development are being "courted by private-sector companies, publishing firms, and government to develop technology-based content and instructional packages" (Olcott & Schmidt, p. 266). A logical next step would be to reward faculty for commercialization of teaching activities in comparable terms to those that currently exist for commercialization of research activities.

One element of commercialization of electronic learning resources that deserves particular attention is the question of who owns the intellectual property (IP) rights to ICT products that have been funded by academic institutions, and developed by faculty members in collaboration with instructional designers, multimedia, and information technology specialists. This question is complex, and to date, unanswered. Given that "cases have held ... that a professor who creates his or her own lectures (assuming they meet the test of originality and fixation, that is, recorded in a fixed format, such as print) owns the copyright in his or her own works" (Tallman, 2000, p. 194), it seems arguable that similar criteria would be applied to ICT-mediated learning artifacts. However, given the "vast resources the university invests in the creation" of ICT-mediated learning, "it is understandable that a university will claim ... ownership" (p. 194).

A further complicating factor is the status of the collaborators in the IP picture. Whereas multimedia and information technology specialists routinely belong to professional associations whose contractual relationship with the university includes relinquishing IP ownership of "work-made-for-hire" (Tallman, 2000, p. 194), instructional designers often hold faculty positions. The latter consideration brings to the fore questions concerning the respective values of content and

design in ICT-mediated learning. As muddy as the IP waters appear to be, "there is a middle ground: copyright can be owned jointly" (p. 195). In sum, legal guidelines for sharing profits derived from the commercial exploitation of ICT-mediated learning artifacts may soon be a matter of significant contention between academic faculties and leaders. The manner in which this matter is managed could become a critical element in either driving or inhibiting faculty engagement in technological innovation.

A fifth consideration of existing reward systems are the variant returns on investment faculty receive for teaching and advising different types of students. The least profitable learners in the educational sector are individuals, who for geographic, economic, or academic reasons, cannot access a conventional university program. Typically, these non-traditional learners have registered in unclassified or non-degree programs offered via distance learning options. Distance education within traditional universities has typically been marginalized in continuing education and extension divisions, and is of little interest to the Academy at large (because neither status nor rewards were offered for this work); therefore, the tasks of teaching and advising non-traditional, part-time learners has often been contracted to sessional lecturers.

"In the environment of public universities in Canada, it is easy to identify [traditional, on-campus] undergraduates as being ... the university's [second] 'least profitable customers'" because they do not contribute to the most "lucrative part of the 'market' addressed by research universities" (Archer, Garrison, & Anderson, 1999, p. 18). As research is the currency of traditional universities—the predominant source of tenure and promotion for faculty—and as undergraduate students rarely contribute to this currency, emphasis on undergraduate teaching may be less valued.

Recently, for-profit corporate universities have entered the post-secondary educational *market*, and have with variant levels of success, established themselves as players in the graduate "sector" (Bates, 2000; DiPaolo, 2003). In response to this emerging competition, traditional universities, to variant degrees, have implemented changes to graduate studies admission and residency requirements, and as a result, have created a third class of academic clients: professional or executive graduate students. The Universities of Toronto, Saint Mary's, Western Ontario, McGill, Brock, and Concordia, for example, have launched Executive Master of Business Administration programs, all of which involve flexible access, such as weekend and evening classes, and many of which include part-time and e-learning options. While learners in programs such as these are involved in research, as part-time and/or remote program participants they are unlikely to contribute significantly to campus-based research programs. However, with annual tuition fees as high as $20,000 (McGill, 2006) and $16,500 (Brock, 2006) per year for e-learning options, tuition revenues can significantly contribute to funding on-campus research.

The fourth, and arguably still most-valued class of learners in traditional research universities, remains full-time, on-campus graduate students. These learners make significant contributions to the Academy through research and teaching assistant positions, thus freeing faculty to focus their time and energy on research and publication (Archer, Garrison, and Anderson, 1999; Olcott & Schmidt, 2000). As a result, the activities of full-time, on-campus graduate students currently are most closely aligned to existing faculty reward systems, thus providing the most return on investment for faculty time.

However, the influence of the New Economy, combined with rapidly increasing educational costs (Bates, 2000), and the available option of e-learning may make full-time, on-campus graduate study less attractive. Further, "the public, the legislature, and consumers care about quality," but they also increasingly focus attention on "cost-effectiveness" (Olcott & Schmidt, 2000,

p. 269). Scalable e-learning systems are gradually becoming more cost-effective than campus-based programs (Bates, 2000), and if one takes a broader view, productivity and wage losses due to long-term study-related career interruptions are arguably also measures of cost-effectiveness. The "new generation of students who are more demanding, selective, and vocal about their educational" and financial needs may less often choose the full-time, on-campus route through graduate studies (Olcott & Schmidt, 2000, p. 268). Therefore, traditional research universities may be well advised to consider re-evaluating existing reward systems to provide incentives for increased faculty involvement with a broader variety of learners.

Figure 3 illustrates two hypotheses: one suggests a current "economic" state of the Academy, and one recommends reward-system attunement for successful adoption of ICT-mediated learning opportunities.

Pedagogical Praxis

With the advent of ICT-mediated learning opportunities, "faculty must begin to *design* instruction and not just *deliver* instruction (Olcott & Schmidt, 2000, p. 274). The professionalization of teaching, as a critical component of successful adoption of ICT-mediated learning, requires that faculty re-evaluate their pedagogical practices. "Habit, tradition, and culture have so far kept [many] faculty from addressing pedagogical practice and technological innovation" (Olcott & Schmidt, 2000, p. 274). An increasingly common institutional approach to address pedagogical practices in the development of ICT-mediated learning is to involve instructional designers.

Instructional design—a combined art and science of teaching—is based upon principles of learning psychology, "cognitive science research and instructional models" (Olcott & Schmidt, 2000, p. 274). Research conducted through EDUCAUSE, a non-profit organization, whose

Figure 3. Organizational economy/reward systems "in tune" with ICT initiatives

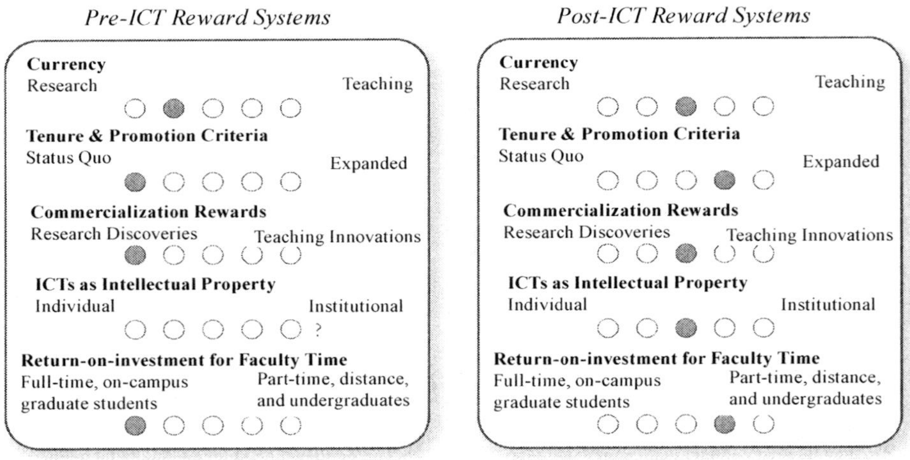

Pre-ICT Reward Systems

Currency
Research   Teaching

Tenure & Promotion Criteria
Status Quo   Expanded

Commercialization Rewards
Research Discoveries   Teaching Innovations

ICTs as Intellectual Property
Individual   Institutional
                                                    ?

Return-on-investment for Faculty Time
Full-time, on-campus   Part-time, distance,
graduate students   and undergraduates

Post-ICT Reward Systems

Currency
Research   Teaching

Tenure & Promotion Criteria
Status Quo   Expanded

Commercialization Rewards
Research Discoveries   Teaching Innovations

ICTs as Intellectual Property
Individual   Institutional

Return-on-investment for Faculty Time
Full-time, on-campus   Part-time, distance,
graduate students   and undergraduates

membership includes "more than 1,800 campuses, organizations, and corporations" (Barone & Hagner, 2001, p. viii), strongly suggests the involvement of instructional designers, or at a minimum, provision of instructional design resources for ICT development initiatives "serves to increase quality and reduce risk" (Hartman & Truman-Davis, 2001, p. 51). Increasing quality and reducing risk are two of the most important concerns in ICT initiatives. Thus, a series of pedagogical considerations is warranted.

Five pedagogical considerations that have an impact on the successful adoption of ICT-mediated learning include: the changing nature of student enrollment patterns; customization and personalization of learning environments and experiences; transitioning from content-focused to learner-centered and service-oriented instruction; transforming classroom-based and distance education models into distributed learning opportunities; and designing ICT-mediated learning for reuse. Thoughtful, strategic responses of these five pedagogical issues can contribute to successfully managing the complexities of ICT initiatives.

One of the major challenges that traditional research universities face in the digital era—perhaps the most salient one—is determining who their prospective learners are and who future learners

will be. Whereas geographical area, institutional reputation and mandate, as well as fee structures, may have been the criteria via which defined institutional "clientele" in the past, increasing job market demands, e-learning options, and lifelong learning needs are influencing the "student mix and competitive position" of universities (Hanna, 2000a, p. 337). Diversity in the range of job-related skills in demand and diversity in the range of learners *shopping* for courses and programs are contributing to demand for customized or personalized learning experiences:

Personalizing learning will require the development of new administrative and pedagogical processes, and learning technologies will play an important role in being able to accomplish this personalization effectively. (Hanna, 2000a, p. 337)

Personalizing learning also requires knowing who the learners will be and the range of individual needs that must be met. Failure to address the personalization issue has already caused a significant number of institutions to experience significant difficulty in implementing e-learning initiatives.

Rapidly increasing enrollments in higher education e-learning programs may not result in the equally high successful completion rates. Carr (2000, para. 13) reports a range of 20% to 50% attrition rates in distance education programs in American colleges. While these rates vary significantly among institutions, administrators generally concur that "course-completion rates are often 10 to 20 percentage points higher in traditional courses than in distance offerings" (para. 13). A metastudy of a broad range of correspondence-based distance education results, undertaken by the World Bank, reported "dropout rates ranging from 19% to 90% and an overall rate of 40%" (Potashnik & Capper, 1998, p. 43). Potashnik and Capper suggest that "while similar studies have yet to be conducted for technology-based distance learning, both intuition and the limited research already done suggest that the interactivity and novelty provided by most technology-based approaches may contribute to higher completion rates" (p. 43).

However, recent studies of attrition rates in online learning programs provide little supportive evidence that ICT-based approaches can ensure higher completion rates. Jameson (2002) argues, "It is common in Web-based instruction to have high attrition rates" (p. 2). Neil (2002) reports, "Enrollment and attrition rates are both statistically greater in the online format" (p. 66). Lorenzetti (2002) concurs that while it is relatively easy to attract learners to online distance education courses, dropout rates can "range as high as 50%" (p. 1). MacGregor (2001) argues that not all learners are willing to try online approaches to distance learning, and "those who do sign up drop out in higher numbers than in a traditional face-to-face course" (p. 143). "Retention has been indicated as one of the greatest weaknesses in online instruction" (O'Brien, 2002, para. 1). Given these preliminary findings, the success of electronically delivered distance education products and services may not be as secure as projected demand statistics predict. Whether or not e-learning will be successful is a question that the learners, not the technologists, will ultimately answer. In short, the predominant question about e-learning has been, "If we build it, will they come?" Currently, the question is, "How do we design it to ensure they stay?"

One strategy for increasing retention rates is to place stronger emphasis on the needs of learners during the development and delivery phases of e-learning projects. This strategy involves moving away from traditional domain-centered pedagogy and toward a learner-centered perspective. The shift from domain-centered to learner-centered design is being undertaken in order to increase the effectiveness and relevance of teaching practice.

To date, comparative research on the effectiveness of online learning has tended to focus on classroom-based learning. As a result of this context, many early versions of online instruction extended classroom-based pedagogical practice into online learning environments (Gifford & Enyedy, 1999). Traditional classroom-based pedagogical practice has been highly dependent upon "the transmission model of knowledge transfer...[in which] knowledge is an identifiable object that is possessed by a person, detached from any social context, that can be conveyed from the mind of the instructor to the mind of the student" (Gifford & Enyedy, 1999, p. 2). Given the epistemological perspective that knowledge-to-be-learned is an object that may be possessed and transferred, domain centered design (DCD) tends to focus on design and development activities that lead to well-organized and well-presented knowledge objects (Sims, 2001). Rather than taking into account the needs, wants, and desires of the learner, "the focus of pedagogy from this perspective is to make transmission more efficient" (Gifford & Enyedy, 1999, p. 2). As a result, learners who use online products and services created from a DCD perspective tend to struggle with difficulties similar to those that have long challenged traditional distance learners who have used print-based materials (Beffa-Negrini, Miller, & Cohen, 2002).

In contrast to DCD models of knowledge acquisition, learner-centered, activity-centered, situated, and participatory models of instructional design and development focus on demographic and cognitive profiles of learners, prior knowledge, perceptions, preferences, needs, goals, characteristics, and experiences of learners. While individual theorists draw distinctions among learner-centered, activity-centered, situated, and participatory models (Gifford & Enyedy, 1999; Reeves, 1999; Vinicini, 2001; Wilson, 1995), for the purposes of this chapter, the commonalities among these models will be considered and will be referred to as learner-centered design (LCD).

The underpinning tenet of each of these models is a shift of *focus* from what is known about and what is valued within a content domain (DCD) to what is known about and what is valued by learners (LCD). This shift is away from primary concern for what will be taught to a careful examination of learner characteristics and to ensuring that learners will perceive content as worth knowing (Sims, 2001). Subsequent development activities are focused on ensuring that essential content is contextualized in learner experiences and/or goals, so that learners will be motivated to value it.

A Boise State University (BSU) case study exemplifies the difference that may be made by a shift from DCD to LCD. In 1989 Boise State launched a distance learning online/off-Web, Masters' degree program in Instructional Performance and Technology (IPT). A variety of undergraduate degrees were accepted for entrance into the program; however, much of the curriculum assumed prior knowledge in the fields of psychology, educational psychology, and instructional design. Most students were full-time working professionals in fields other than education or instructional design. A common motivation for entering the program was to make a career change or to specialize in training within an existing profession. All students were required to make substantial commitments of weekly time and long-term planning. The program was, for

its time, rather expensive, and its service level to students did not match either its fee level or learner needs. Students were required to have access 15 hours per week to a computer system valued at approximately US$3,000 in order to interact with the *FirstReader* courseware system that delivered the program. Tuition fees per 3-credit course, by 1995, had reached US$999. Despite their considerable initial commitments, "between fall 1989 and fall 1996, 44% of the students had dropped out" (School's Founder, 2002, p. 4). In a series of exit interviews conducted by Chyung (2001), the most often cited reason for attrition was "discrepancies between… professional or personal interests and the curriculum or the course structure" (Cause analysis, para. 1). Course developers at Boise State took this feedback seriously. A series of changes were made to the *IPT* curriculum and course structure. By the end of the 2000 term:

BSU's department of Instructional Performance and Technology had decreased online attrition to 15% by focusing on its first-time Internet learners… The department also devised interventions to address students' unfamiliarity with the subject matter; varying interests, goals, and learning styles; and desires for personal contact and social interaction. (School's Founder, 2002, p. 4)

Aligning the *IPT* program more closely with learners' needs, wants, and goals, as well as providing additional student support mechanisms, resulted in significantly improved retention rates and student satisfaction ratings, which in turn, resulted in the continuance of the *IPT* program. A lesson learned in the *IPT* case is that for-profit e-learning ventures where discrepancies between fee and service levels persist, and where learner needs and aspirations are ignored, are unlikely to be sustainable over the long term.

Transforming classroom-based and distance education models into distributed learning opportunities has the potential to better serve traditional, on-campus learners and non-traditional, distance learners. Distributed learning adopts a learner-centered approach to pedagogy and "integrates a number of technologies to enable opportunities for activities and interaction in both asynchronous and real-time modes... This approach gives instructors the flexibility to meet the needs of diverse student populations, while providing both high quality and cost-effective learning" (Bates, 2000, p. 27). Distributed learning models provide faculty with more flexible working conditions, which in turn allow faculty the opportunity to more easily balance teaching and research responsibilities.

An element that distinguishes distributed learning from other modes of instruction is its use of ICT-mediated learning opportunities to facilitate peer-to-peer learning: "Students do not so much interact *with* the technology as *through* the technology with teachers and other learners" (Bates, 2000, p. 27). Interacting with peers via online communication promotes "collaborative learning," and builds teamwork capacities (p. 27). Interacting with teachers, and in some cases external experts in the field of study, extends learning for both traditional and non-traditional learners well beyond the campus of the university, potentially into previously inaccessible work- and research-related arenas. Thus, the benefits of distributed learning opportunities are well suited to the demands of the global learning society and strategically suited to university goals, such as the provision of high quality and cost-effective learning.

Finally, designing ICT-mediated learning opportunities for reuse is a topic of increasing interest. The escalating costs of designing and developing high quality ICT-mediated learning opportunities is driving this interest and creating a new area of educational research: reusable learning objects (RLOs). RLOs and RLO repositories are currently hot topics of debate across the educational sector (Wiley, 2002).

Even the definitions for these terms are controversial. The Institute of Electrical and Electronics Engineers' Learning Objects Metadata (LOM) Working Group (2002) defines learning objects as "any entity, digital or non-digital, that may be used for learning, education or training" (Institute of Electrical and Electronics Engineers, 2004, para. 1). This definition has been broadly applied in commercial venues, but has received significant criticism from the educational community because its breadth is perceived as meaningless. Wiley (2002) alternatively defines learning objects as "any digital resource that can be reused to support learning" (p. 6). Merrill (2001) offers a distinction between learning objects and knowledge objects: knowledge objects include "only the content to be learned but not an objective, presentation, or assessment; learning objects are distinct from knowledge objects in that they also include an objective, some instructional information, and assessment" (Wiley, 2002, p. 11).

Similar controversy surrounds the definition of learning objects repositories. Definitions range from an alternative term for a database to a specialized computer server that houses information in a structured environment, which is organized and accessed via metadata. "Metadata, literally 'data about data' is the descriptive information" about both knowledge and learning objects that allows them to be retrieved from an electronic repository via a search mechanism (Wiley, 2002, p. 8).

Definitional debates aside, reusable electronic learning objects and the repositories that house them promise sufficient cost-effectiveness to warrant attention (Barritt & Alderman, 2004; Daniel & Mohan, 2004). CANARIE, Canada's advanced Internet development organization, has contributed $10 million over the past five years to the research and development of reusable electronic learning objects and learning objects repositories (Wosk, 2003). This investment has been aimed at "attaining critical mass [of RLO users] to demonstrate value" and "addressing [the] major problem" of developing cost-effective approaches to managing ICT-mediated learning opportunities (p. 2).

Figure 4. Pedagogical praxis "in tune" with ICT initiatives

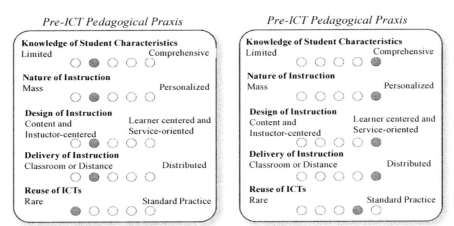

In more advanced e-learning environments, learning agents can broker relationships among learners, experts, and objects by matching learner profile information for the purposes of recommending specific resources and peer-to-peer, as well as expert-to-novice, support (McCalla, 2004; Mohan & Greer, 2003). In combination with learning objects and agents, user-tracing software can detect user-behavior, analyze behavior patterns, and assist the agents in making increasingly accurate recommendations (Zaiane, 2002). Thus, the system can *learn* to effectively link individuals to others who share their interests and who can provide peer or professional assistance. The system can also *learn* to recognize resources that match individuals' learning styles and learner goals, thus enabling individualization of user experiences (McCalla, 2004). While data-mining and expertise-location tools are still in the research and development phase, in combination with learning objects technologies, their development holds significant promise for future community-building functionalities within e-learning systems.

Finding or creating cost-effective avenues to create, customize, use, and reuse ICT-mediated learning artifacts, and to create the conditions for communities of users to support each other in their learning goals, are emerging fields of research and development, which will be of significant interest to university leaders, who face concerns about "how and where to invest scarce resources" (Suter, 2001, p. 29) in technological innovations for teaching and learning. As accumulating existing ICT resources reach a management and maintenance crisis-point, these issues will come to the fore of the list leadership challenges in higher education.

Figure 4 illustrates two hypotheses: one suggests a current state of the pedagogical praxis within the Academy, and one recommends pedagogical attunement for successful adoption of ICT-mediated learning.

CONCLUSION AND RECOMMENDATIONS

The global learning society, and its demands upon members of society to learn their living, are now and will continue to transform the Academy. At this juncture, traditional research universities may need to examine their e-learning policies and practices to effectively adapt to a complex, ambiguous, and dynamic external environment. University leadership needs to strategically respond to the pressing demands of external forces for change. By attuning internal organizational structures, cultures, economies (reward systems), and pedagogical praxes to changing academic times, the Academy can embrace ICT solutions and their associated service orientation to ensure its ongoing position as *the best option* for higher education.

ACKNOWLEDGMENTS

The graphics in this chapter were created by Carmen Perret-Smith at the University of Saskatchewan.

REFERENCES

Alcaly, R. E. (2003). *The new economy: What it is, how it happened, and why it is likely to last.* New York: Farrar, Stratus, & Giroux.

Archer, W., Garrison, D. R., & Anderson, T. D. (1999). Adopting disruptive technologies in traditional universities: Continuing education as an incubator for innovation. *Canadian Journal of University Continuing Education, 25*(1), 13-44.

Archer, W., & Wright, K. (1999). Back to the future: Adjusting university continuing education research to an emerging trend. *Canadian Journal of University Continuing Education, 25*(22), 61-84.

Barone, C. A., & Hagner, P. R. (2001). Preface. In C. Barone & P. Hagner (Vol. Eds.), *Educause leadership strategies: Vol.5. Technology-enhanced teaching and learning: Leading and supporting transformation on your campus* (pp. 35-54). San Francisco: Jossey Bass.

Barritt, C., & Alderman, F. L. (2004). *Creating a reusable learning objects strategy: Levering information and learning in a knowledge economy.* San Francisco: Pfeiffer.

Bates, A. W. (2000). *Managing technological change: Strategies for college and university leaders.* San Francisco: Jossey-Bass.

Beffa-Negrini, P. A., Miller, B., & Cohen, N. L. (2002). Factors related to success and satisfaction in online learning. *Academic Exchange Quarterly, 6*(3), 105-114.

Bok, D. (2003). *Universities in the marketplace: The commercialization of higher education.* Princeton, NJ: Princeton University Press.

Boyer, E. L. (1990). *Scholarship reconsidered: Priorities of the professoriate.* Princeton, NJ: The Carnegie Foundation for the Advancement of Teaching.

Brown, D. G., & Jackson, S. (2001). Creating a context for consensus. In C. Barone & P. Hagner (Vol. Eds.), *Educause leadership strategies: Vol.5. Technology-enhanced teaching and learning: Leading and supporting transformation on your campus* (pp. 35-54). San Francisco: Jossey Bass.

Cahn, S. M. (1986). *Saints and scamps: Ethics in Academia.* Lanham, MD: Rowman & Littlefield.

Carr, S. (2000). As distance education comes of age, the challenge is keeping the students [Electronic version]. *Chronicle of Higher Education.* Retrieved April 20, 2006, from http://chronicle.com/free/v46/i23/23a00101.htm

Christensen, C. M. (1997). *The innovator's dilemma: When new technologies cause great firms to fail.* Boston: Harvard Business School Press.

Chyung, Y. (2001). Improve the motivational appeal of online instruction for adult learners: What's in it for me? Retrieved April 20, 2006, from http://coen.boisestate.edu/ychyung/researchpaper.htm

Collins, M., & Berge, Z. (1996, June). *Facilitating interaction in computer mediated online courses.*

Paper presented at the FSU/AECT Distance Education Conference, Tallahassee, FL.

Daniel, B. K., & Mohan, P. (2004, July). *Re-engineering the public university with reusable learning objects approach.* Paper presented at the International Conference on Education and Information Systems: Technologies and Applications, Orlando, FL.

DiPaolo, A. (2003, December). *Choices and challenges: Lessons learned in the evolution of online education.* Paper presented at the Association of Pacific Rim Universities' 2003 Distance Learning and the Internet conference. Retrieved April 20, 2006, from http://www.cit.nus.edu.sg/dli2003/Presentation/Andy_DiPaolo.pdf

Fees. (2006). Retrieved April 20, 2006, from the Brock University Web site: http://www.bus.brocku.ca/mba/mba_fees.html

Gifford, B., & Enyedy, N. (1999, December). *Activity centered design: Towards a theoretical framework for CSCL.* Paper presented at the Third International Conference on Computer Support for Collaborative Learning, Stanford, CA. Retrieved April 20, 2006, from http://www.ee.upatras.gr/hci/courses/colaborative_technology/Gifford_Enyedy_CSCL_1999.pdf

Graves, W. H. (2001). Transforming traditional faculty roles. In C. Barone & P. Hagner (Vol. Eds.), *Educause leadership strategies: Vol.5. Technology-enhanced teaching and learning: Leading and supporting transformation on your campus* (pp. 35-43). San Francisco: Jossey Bass.

Hagner, P. R., & Schneebeck, C. A. (2001). Engaging the faculty. In C. Barone & P. Hagner (Vol. Eds.), *Educause leadership strategies: Vol.5. Technology-enhanced teaching and learning: Leading and supporting transformation on your campus* (pp. 1-12). San Francisco: Jossey Bass.

Hanley, G. L. (2001). Designing and delivering instructional technology: A team approach. In C.

Barone & P. Hagner (Vol. Eds.), *Educause leadership strategies: Vol.5. Technology-enhanced teaching and learning: Leading and supporting transformation on your campus* (pp. 57-64). San Francisco: Jossey Bass.

Hanna, D. E. (2000a). Emerging organizational models: The extended traditional university. In D. Hanna & Associates (Eds.), *Higher education in an era of digital competition: Choices and challenges* (pp. 93-116). Madison, WI: Atwood.

Hanna, D. E. (2000b). Emerging approaches to learning in collegiate classrooms. In D. Hanna & Associates (Eds.), *Higher education in an era of digital competition: Choices and challenges* (pp. 45-65). Madison, WI: Atwood.

Hartman, J. L., & Truman-Davis, B. (2001). The holy grail: Developing scalable and sustainable support solutions. In C. Barone & P. Hagner (Vol. Eds.), *Educause leadership strategies: Vol.5. Technology-enhanced teaching and learning: Leading and supporting transformation on your campus* (pp. 45-56). San Francisco: Jossey Bass.

Hutchins, R. (2000). Working with your neighbors. In M. Luker (Vol. Ed.), *Educause leadership strategies: Vol.1. Preparing your campus for a networked future* (pp. 59-70). San Francisco: Jossey Bass.

Institute of Electrical and Electronics Engineers. (2004). WG12: Learning object metadata. Retrieved April 20, 2006, from http://ltsc.ieee.org/wg12/index.html

Jameson, T. (2002). Theory-driven motivational study aims to assist retention. *Distance Education Report, 6*(22), 5-6.

Lincoln, Y. S. (2001, April). *The fourth generation view of evaluation: The future for evaluation in a new millennium.* Paper presented at the 2001 Arizona Evaluation Network's Spring Conference.

Lorenzetti, J. P. (2002). Before they drift away: Two experts pool retention insights. *Distance Education Report, 6*(8), 1-2.

Luker, M. A. (2000). What campus leaders can do today. In M. Luker (Vol. Ed.), *Educause leadership strategies: Vol. 1: Preparing your campus for a networked future* (pp. 93-100). San Francisco: Jossey-Bass.

MacGregor, C. J. (2001). A comparison of student perceptions in traditional and online classes. *Academic Exchange Quarterly, 5*(4), 143-146.

Mackay, H. H. (1996). The MacKay report on universities. Retrieved April 20, 2006, from http://www.sasked.gov.sk.ca/branches/university_services/mackay/mackaytc.html

Maduro, M. (1998). The issue of competitiveness and skills training in continuing education today. *Canadian Journal of University Continuing Education, 24*(2), 37-46.

McCalla, G. (2004). The ecological approach to the design of e-learning environments: Purpose-based capture and use of information about learners [Electronic version]. *Journal of Interactive Media in Education,* (7). Retrieved April 20, 2006, from www-jime.open.ac.uk/2004/7

McLuhan, M. (1964). *Understanding media: The extensions of man* (2nd ed.). Toronto: The New American Library of Canada.

Merrill, M. D. (2001). Knowledge objects and mental-models. Retrieved April 20, 2006, from http://cito.byuh.edu/merrill/text/papers/KOMM. PDF

Mohan, P., & Greer, J. (2003, August). *Using learning object technology to tackle the educational challenges of the Caribbean.* Paper presented at IEEE 1st International Workshop on Technology for Education in Developing Countries, Newark, NJ.

Nesbit, T. (2004). [Review of the book Universities in the marketplace: The commercialization of higher education]. *Canadian Journal of University Continuing Education, 30*(1), 104-106.

Norton, R. D. (2000). *Creating the new economy: The entrepreneur and the U.S. resurgence.* Northampton, MA: Edward Elgar.

O'Brien, B. (2002). Online student retention: Can it be done? *World Conference on Educational Multimedia, Hypermedia and Telecommunications 2002* (1), 1479-1483. [Online]. Retrieved January 4, 2005, from http://dl.aace.org/10372

O'Driscoll, T. (2003). Proposing an optimal learning architecture for the digital enterprise. *Educational Technology, 43*(1), 12-18.

Olcott, D., & Schmidt, K. (2000). Redefining faculty policies and practices for the knowledge age. In D. Hanna & Associates (Eds.), *Higher education in an era of digital competition* (pp. 258-286). Madison, WI: Atwood.

Palloff, R. M., & Pratt, K. (1999). *Building learning communities in cyberspace: Effective strategies for the online classroom* (1st ed.). San Francisco: Jossey-Bass.

Potashnik, M., & Capper, J. (1998). Distance education: Growth and diversity. *International Monetary Fund and the International Bank for Reconstruction and Development/The World Bank.* Retrieved April 20, 2006, from http://www.worldbank.org/fandd/english/0398/articles/0110398.htm

Reeves, W. (1999). *Learner-centered design: A cognitive view of managing complexity in product, information, and environmental design.* Thousand Oaks, CA: Sage.

Rogers, E. M. (1995). *Diffusion of innovations* (4th ed.). New York: The Free Press.

Ruttenbar, B. W., Spickler, G. C., & Lurie, S. (2000). *E-learning: The engine of the knowledge economy.* Retrieved April 20, 2006, from http://www.internettime.com/itimegroup/morgankeegan.pdf

Sackney, L., & Mitchell, C. (2002). Postmodern expressions of educational leadership. In K. Leithwood & P. Hallinger (Eds.), *Second international handbook of educational leadership and administration* (Vol. 2, pp. 881-913). Boston: Kluwer Academic Publishers.

Schein, E. H. (1993). Organizational culture and sense making. In J. M. Shafritz & J. S. Ott (Eds.), *Classics of organization theory* (5th ed.) (pp. 369-376). Belmont, CA: Wadsworth.

School's founder says dumping the traditional is secret to retention success online. (2002). *Recruitment and Retention in Higher Education, 16*(3), 4-5.

Shafritz, J. M., & Ott, J. S. (2001). Organizational culture and sense making. In J. M. Shafritz & J. S. Ott (Eds.), *Classics of organization theory* (5th ed.) (pp. 361-368). Belmont, CA: Wadsworth.

Sims, R. C. (2001). *From art to alchemy: Achieving success with online learning.* Retrieved April 20, 2006, from http://it.coe.uga.edu/itforum/paper55/paper55.htm

Suter, V. N. (2001). Managing complexity in a transforming environment. In C. Barone & P. Hagner (Vol. Eds.), *Educause leadership strategies: Vol.5. Technology-enhanced teaching and learning: Leading and supporting transformation on your campus* (pp. 25-34). San Francisco: Jossey Bass.

Tallman, J. (2000). Who owns knowledge in a networked world? In D. Hanna & Associates (Eds.), *Higher education in an era of digital competition: Choices and challenges* (pp. 185-218). Madison, WI: Atwood.

Tjeldvoll, A. (1998, Fall). The idea of the service university [Electronic version]. *International Higher Education.* Retrieved April 20, 2006, from http://www.bc.edu/bc_org/avp/soe/cihe/newsletter/News13/text4.html

Trice, H. M., & Beyer, M. (1993). Changing organizational cultures. In J. M. Shafritz & J. S. Ott (Eds.), *Classics of organization theory* (5th ed.) (pp. 361-368). Belmont, CA: Wadsworth.

Tuition fees and expenses. (2006). Retrieved April 20, 2006, from http://www.mcgill.ca/mba/financing/tuition/

Vinicini, P. (2001). The use of participatory design methods in a learner-centered design process. *ITFORUM 54.* Retrieved April 20, 2006, from http://it.coe.uga.edu/itforum/paper54/paper54.html

Wiley, D. A. (2002). Connecting learning objects to instuctional design theory: A definition, a metaphor, and a taxonomy. In D. Wiley (Ed.), *The instuctional use of learning objects.* Bloomington, ID: Agency for Instructional Technology and Association for Communications & Technology.

Wilson, B. G. (1995). Situated instructional design: Blurring the distinctions between theory and practice, design and implementation, curriculum and instruction. In M. Simonson (Ed.), *Proceedings of selected research and development presentations.* Washington DC: Association for Educational Communications and Technology [Electronic version]. Retrieved April 20, 2006, from http://carbon.cudenver.edu/~bwilson/sitid.html

Wosk, M. J. (2003, November). *CANARIE: Mini-summit on learning object repository implementation.* Canarie, Inc.: Vancouver.

Zaïane, O. R. (2002). *Building a recommender agent for e-learning systems.* Retrieved April 20, 2006, from http://www.cs.ualberta.ca/~zaiane/postscript/icce02.pdf

Chapter II
Human Computer Interaction for Computer–Based Classroom Teaching

Wolfgang Hürst
Albert-Ludwigs-Universität Freiburg, Germany

Khaireel A. Mohamed
Albert-Ludwigs-Universität Freiburg, Germany

ABSTRACT

This chapter focuses on HCI aspects to overcome problems arising from technologies and applications that may hinder the normal teaching process in ICT-ready classrooms. It investigates different input devices on their usage and interactivity for classroom teaching and argues that pen-based computing is the mode of choice for lecturing in modern lecture halls. It also discusses the software design of the interface where digital ink, as a "first class" data type is used to communicate visual contents and interact with the ICT.

INTRODUCTION

Utilizing *information and communication technology (ICT)* in modern classrooms for the purpose of teaching offers several advantages. These include (worldwide) access to digital materials during lectures, recording and archiving of both the presented materials as well as the whole live event, and transmitting the lecture (live or recorded) to remote locations—a concept of tele-teaching. Consequently, conventional equipment,

such as blackboards and chalk as well as overhead projectors and transparencies, have almost disappeared from the classrooms and lecture halls at many institutions and have been replaced with computers and data projectors. Integrating ICT in the classroom raises a myriad of technical questions related to the implementation of the respective devices and services. It is generally agreed, that details of the technical installation should be hidden from the presenters and teachers. Thus, in an ideal scenario, the teacher walks into the lecture room and, if anything, just has to press one button in order to switch on the whole equipment and having all the infrastructure readily available. In this chapter, we are concentrating on the user's perspective once all equipment is up and running and operated by the teacher during the lecture. In doing so, we focus on questions related to *human computer interaction (HCI)*: How can people access the functionality offered by the installed ICT? How do they interact with the available infrastructure? What are the best possible approaches for the interface design in order to support the teaching process? And so on.

Generally, the way in which people interact with any kind of ICT is influenced by two aspects. The first aspect is the input devices, that is, the hardware that specifies what information is exchanged between man and machine and how this exchange takes place. For example, by moving a mouse, a user sends "events" to a computer that encodes information such as relative coordinates representing mouse movements. The second aspect is the software design of the user interface and the way in which the technical signals exchanged by the hardware are interpreted. For example, incoming signals from mouse movements (representing relative coordinates) are generally mapped to absolute pointer movements on the screen and as such visualized to the user. Unfortunately, traditional HCI concepts, such as conventional "desktop" input devices (the keyboard and mouse) and their related classical interface designs are not well suited for the tasks appearing in a classroom, forcing teachers to modify and adapt their teaching styles to the used equipment.

Following the point of view described before, this chapter is organized into two parts. First, we address input devices, that is, hardware-related issues for operating and using ICT in classrooms. We describe current and future trends in the usage of different devices using examples and case studies from our past and ongoing research projects as well as our experiences in actual teaching scenarios. We identify a subtle, yet promising trend that can be observed developing in the educational world—more and more pen-based input devices are used in classrooms and lecture halls. Examples of such devices include interactive electronic whiteboards, graphics tablets, Tablet PCs, and personal digital assistants. The second part of this chapter is devoted to the software designs and interaction paradigms for interactive classroom teaching using ICT. We describe different aspects in relation to pen-based interaction with the installed ICT. "Digital ink" is described as a new, "first-class" data type serving both, an exchange of information between teacher and students, as well as a new metaphor for interacting with the installed ICT via newly introduced gesture commands. Generally, we concentrate on instructional talks and presentations, where a presenter (i.e., the teacher) faces an audience (i.e., the students) and presents some content in a typical classroom setting. More interactive classroom settings, such as seminars or other arrangements involving group work, are discussed in a concluding future trends section at the end of this chapter.

HARDWARE-RELATED ISSUES: INPUT DEVICES

Background: Ubiquitous Computing Environments

As mentioned in the introduction, ICT usage in classrooms offers great opportunities to support and improve teaching. However, traditional input and output devices often prove to be a hindrance for the direct interaction between teacher and students. They draw too much of the lecturer's attention to the operation of the respective hardware. Keyboard and mouse cannot be used to provide content to the students as naturally as chalk is used to write on blackboards. Monitors, even the small ones from laptop computers, can stand between the audience and the teacher building a virtual barrier, and so on.

In a perfect scenario, all ICT equipment should be seamlessly integrated into the environment, that is, the classroom, and not interfere with the activity of teaching but support the lecturer in the best possible way. Presenters must be able to naturally access and handle the additional functionality provided by the respective devices alongside in a way that enables them to fully concentrate on their teaching and the interaction with the audience. Hence, the appropriate usage of ICT in classrooms is an ideal example for a concept of computing introduced by Marc Weiser in 1991 as *ubiquitous computing* (Weiser, 1991). Generally, the term ubiquitous computing refers to "an environment in which a large number of computers, ranging from hundreds of palm-sized to a few wall-sized units will be seamlessly integrated into our immediate surroundings, connected by wireless networks" (MacIntyre & Feiner, 1996, p. 251). While originally being applied mainly in the academic world, we now have the technology available to make Weiser's vision of a ubiquitous computing environment a reality by building a classroom where all computing functionality is integrated into the environment. Many universities are already equipped with wireless networks. Large touch sensitive displays for integration into classrooms are available at prices affordable by most universities, and so forth.

However, to really create an "intelligent" classroom that does not constrain teachers but fully supports them, some open problems and challenges still remain, especially related to HCI. In the following, we give a historical overview about the usage of computers and different input devices in the classroom over the last couple of years. We discuss our experiences gained from utilizing such devices at our university and from observing other project- and user-groups. The aims of this overview are to highlight the advantages and disadvantages of the respective devices, identify interaction and usage styles, provide advice for the appropriate usage of the technology, and

pinpoint open problems for further HCI-related research. Pen-based interfaces are identified as a trend-setting and essential aspect for ICT-based classroom teaching. Afterward, two case studies of innovative usage of pen-based input-devices are presented, which give direction to the future usage of pen-based interaction in an interactive classroom.

Input Devices for Computer Usage in Classrooms: An Historical Overview

Traditional teaching: blackboards, overhead projectors, and freehand writings. Teaching a class involves a lot of interaction between teacher and students, through the *freehand writings* on blackboards or chalkboards. *Blackboards* have traditionally been by far the most widely used medium for lecture presentations in institutes of higher learning, and they are very effective. Not only do they allow instructors to communicate all or part of the course materials in natural handwriting, but they also take away the attention to details for their use. Freehand writings and annotations take an important role in classroom teaching, even if a lesson is delivered via previously prepared slides or transparencies that are presented to the students using an *overhead projector*. Essentially, as classes progress, teachers will write, highlight, underline, draw, and formulate on those slides to put forth their points to the students. By using "empty" slides, they can spontaneously write on them, what actually facilitates discussions amongst students, helps to illustrate complex mathematical proofs, and demonstrates diagrammatic facts more clearly. Studies show that the combination of handwritten annotations, the development of thoughts through freehand writings, and the verbal explanations of the lecturers, are indeed crucial in assisting students' understanding of the subjects (Mukhopadhyay & Smith, 1999; Zupancic & Horz, 2002).

Early computer usage: data projectors and presentation software. With the rising popularity of *presentation software tools*, such as Microsoft's PowerPoint, in the mid and late 1990s, a sizable number of teachers moved from using chalk and blackboards or overhead transparencies to using electronic slides and computers for classroom teaching. The increase of processing power and the decrease in hardware pricing led to the augmentation of lecture halls and classrooms with *data projectors* connected to background computer systems. By observing how teachers took to using these new tools, three different trends can be discovered:

1.   Due to the lack of a flexible and effective input device such as the pen and partly due to a less than perfect interface design, some lecturers adapted from their very lively teaching style, to a scenario where the materials presented to the students were prepared electronically in advance and shown in a pure "slide show" style presentation. Hence our observation that whenever computers are exploited in classrooms, the teaching styles of the instructors are often made to adapt to the currently available interfaces and not vice versa.

2.   Some teachers have tried to revert back to their old, traditional approach of slowly developing a topic by continuously adding and annotating their contents. This often results in their sitting down behind a computer screen and using traditional input devices, such as the keyboard and mouse, to add and modify the presented materials during the lecture. Where instead of writing in freehand and annotating on the slides, they type the text with the keyboard and make annotations by drawing straight lines and boxes with the mouse. So, again, the teachers go off their traditional way of teaching and adapting to a new and less appropriate style of interaction. In addition, sitting down and "hiding" behind a big computer monitor led to a loss of contact with the students.

3.   Chong and Sakauchi (2000) observed that when presentation slides are available (either as overhead projected slides or PowerPoint slides from a data projector), the use of the chalkboard is significantly reduced during the course of the lecture. However, when it comes to facilitating questions and answers, the chalkboard is conveniently used again to demonstrate facts, confirm equations, and diagrammatically illustrate flowcharts. But making a direct reference from the chalkboards to any of the slides can be a hassle, and sometimes the instructors resort to annotating on those slides in whatever little space is available, and may even compromise on legibility.

In all three scenarios, we can observe that forced by inappropriate user interfaces, teachers generally adapt their teaching style in a less preferable way to the available technology. As for the students, they normally appreciate the fact of having an electronic version of the presented material after the lecture. It enables them to pay more attention to the class, and it gives them the time to make more appropriate and "intelligent" annotations during the live event because they do not have to copy everything the presenter shows them. However, pure slide shows are generally considered too exhaustive. Students often complain that such presentations are too fast for their liking, while the required speed for handwriting naturally slows down the pace of the lecture to a speed that is generally considered more appropriate and pleasant.

Initial usage of pen-based devices: Graphics tablets and touch screens. Considering the negative observations described previously, it is no surprise that with the advent of devices for *pen-based computing*, presenters quickly started to experiment with them in their classrooms and lecture halls. People first started using *touch screens* (where users communicate with the computer by direct touching of the screen) and *digitizing* or *graphics tablets* (where a digital pen is moved over a separate surface in order to remotely control and operate the computer, similar to moving a mouse in order to operate the mouse pointer on the screen, cf. Figure 1). These input modalities improved the situation in so far as teachers are at least able to write natural freehand annotations. The devices, however, still lacked the usability and simplicity of markers or chalk. For example, in the case of graphics tablets, not every teacher feels comfortable with the remote control of a digital pen, but prefers to write directly onto the visualized electronic slide. Touch screens are hard to write on when the monitor is standing upright. Ideally, the screen should be mounted horizontally. However, touch screens do not only react to pen input but to any kind of physical contacts, thus making it impossible for teachers to rest their hand on the surface while writing. A detailed discussion about the initial usage of pen-based input devices in the classroom can be found in [*].

Advanced pen-based input devices: Interactive LCD panels and electronic whiteboards. The previously described input devices represented an improvement over traditional ways for human computer interaction such as keyboard and mouse. However, it was only after large, blackboard-like electronic whiteboards and LCD panels with in-tegrated tablet became available at a reasonable price when pen-based computing became a real alternative to chalk and blackboard usage.

Originally targeted toward special interest groups and professions (such as graphic designers), the first LCD displays with integrated tablet, in the following called *interactive LCD panels* (cf. Figure 2), became available for the average consumer by the end of the 1990s. These devices operate like regular graphics tablets described before with the main difference being that the tablet is transparent and mounted on top of an LCD panel. Hence, compared to common touch screens, the surface does not react to any kind of contact, but only to the input of a special pen, thus enabling presenters to naturally write on a horizontally mounted screen. Using the pen, people can directly interact with the applications (e.g., by making annotations on the presented slides, navigating through subsequent slides, etc.). Teachers generally see this as a big improvement compared to normal touch screens or graphics tablets. However, early versions often proved to be too small, had a resolution that was too low, and a limited processing power that resulted in a noticeable time delay during freehand writing. Nowadays, we observe significant advancements in display size, screen resolution, as well as processing power, paired with lower prices. Hence,

Figure 1. Examples of pen-based input via graphics tablets in different sizes

Figure 2. Examples of interactive LCD panels where the user can write directly on the computer screen using a special digital pen. While original versions were rather small (top right), newer versions (left and bottom right) are now available at reasonable sizes and prices.

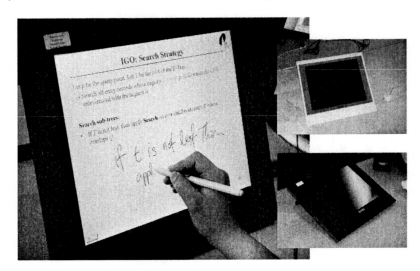

when mounted horizontally such devices provide the same ease of use as traditional overhead projectors while at the same time enabling users to access and use the full functionality offered by the underlying ICT installation.

An *electronic whiteboard* (cf. Figure 3) is the equivalent of a chalkboard, but on a large, wall-mounted, touch-sensitive digital screen that is connected to a data projector and a computer (see, for example, Smart Technologies Inc. [Online]). This computer can be controlled directly from the digital screen with a digital pen or by simply using a finger to touch it. Other known terminologies of the electronic whiteboards include the "eBoard," "digital whiteboard," "smart board," or "interactive whiteboard." They carry slightly different meanings to different people depending on their environment of application. However, these terms all describe in general, the group of technologies that are brought together to support classroom activities. Different versions exist that rely on front or rear projection. In the case of front projection, there are also whiteboard solutions that do not react to any kind of

contact, but (similar to interactive LCD panels) use a special pen for interaction. While such an approach is preferable for LCD panels or any kind of horizontally mounted input surface, it is less important for vertically wall-mounted boards since users generally do not rest their hand on the board during writing.

Similar to early interactive LCD panels, first versions of electronic whiteboards had limitations regarding size, resolution, and processing power and were often too expensive for large-scale usage. Again, the situation is improved significantly today, and we can observe how more and more classrooms are becoming equipped with such devices. In fact, there is a growing trend amongst learning institutions approving the integration of electronic whiteboards into their classrooms. There are also many reports in the emerging body of literature suggesting that vendors of education and teaching instructors alike find the electronic whiteboards relatively easy and compelling to use (BECTA, 2003; Glover & Miller, 2001). However, the authors also caution that becoming confident in their use often requires effort in commitment

Figure 3. Examples of electronic whiteboards which enable direct interaction and freehand writing to the users (top right). Earlier versions were rather small and often used front projection (top left) while newer versions increased in size and offer rear projection at reasonable prices (top middle and bottom).

in terms of both training and independent exploration.

The situation today. As described previously, we saw that pen-based input devices offer promising perspectives for usage in classroom teaching, but initial versions had limitations and disadvantages. Due to advancements in hardware (such as size, resolution, and processing power) and dropping prices we can now say that electronic whiteboards and interactive LCD panels have become a real alternative to traditional blackboards and overhead projectors, respectively. Both devices offer a similar ease of use as their traditional counterparts while at the same time opening various new opportunities by providing full access to the underlying computer systems and infrastructure. In addition, new developments such as *Tablet PCs* (cf. Figure 4) incorporate the pen-based input technology and are more and more used for giving presentations and classroom lectures as well. Tablet PCs are a special kind of computer in the size of a laptop

with a pen-operated graphics tablet integrated into the screen, similar to the interactive LCD panels described previously. Some Tablet PCs purely rely on pen-based user interaction, while others, called *convertibles* or *hybrids*, offer pen-based operation in addition to a regular keyboard and mouse or touch pad input.

Based on the feedback we received in various situations at our university, we argue that the equipment available today can finally be used to replace blackboards and overhead projectors through their electronic counterparts in a reasonable way. We observed that even people who are rather skeptical about using computers in classrooms and still stood with the old, traditional form of classroom teaching are more and more switching to computer supported presentations due to these new input devices. Overall, we can conclude that pen-based computing will be an important if not essential part of computer usage in future classrooms. It seems likely that in the near future, more and more classrooms will be equipped with pen-based input devices, in a similar way as not so long ago, blackboards and overhead projectors were complemented and slowly replaced with electronic data projectors.

In the following section, we describe two case studies of actual equipment used at our university for teaching. The purpose of this description is to describe the respective technology and how it is best used, to illustrate how people take advantage of it, and to identify open problems and future trends. We will see that with this technology we are able to build real ubiquitous computing environments as described before as the ultimate goal in the "Background" section.

Case Studies of Actual Equipment Used in a Ubiquitous Computing Environment

Electronic whiteboards as blackboard replacement. As mentioned before, today's electronic whiteboards are larger in size, offer a higher resolution, are technically more reliable, and are easier to handle. However, their absolute size still

remains an issue when compared to traditional blackboards. As a consequence, some people started placing two boards next to each other in order to increase their writing space by forming a large electronic whiteboard (Prante, Streitz, & Tandler, 2004). Examples of such "twofold" whiteboard installations at our university can be found in Figure 5. The boards shown at the top and bottom left of Figure 5 are integrated into the front wall of the lecture room thus hiding the required technology from the presenter and providing an environment, where the computing functionality can be directly accessed by the teacher through interacting with the electronic whiteboards, but the whole technology does not interfere with regular teaching. All technologies are hidden as much as possible in order to let the presenter concentrate on the talk without distraction from any of the hardware. In our installation, both boards can be connected to one computer. People are able to place one application window (e.g. from the used presentation software) over two boards thus creating one large "virtual" electronic whiteboard. Experience with users has shown that the border

Figure 4. Examples of Tablet PCs which enable pen-based input via a transparent graphics tablet mounted on top of the LCD screen. While some versions purely rely on pen-based input (top) others, called hybrids (bottom), feature a rotating display thus supporting both, traditional as well as pen-based interaction.

in the middle of these two boards is generally not considered critical since most presenters prefer to write on the board in columns anyway. While connecting several input and output devices to one computer was still considered critical a few years ago (MacIntyre & Feiner, 1996), today's windowing systems generally support this kind of functionality without any problems.

When observing how people are using such an installation, we realized different approaches. Some presenters like to have just one application window that extends over both whiteboards, either using it to present two slides next to each other or to start with two empty slides and an increased writing surface. Others prefer to have two separate applications running, for example, in order to show an overview slide of the lecture on the left board while presenting the current slide on the right side. Some teachers use one board for slides and the other one to show a different application, such as a player for video clips or animations. People can also connect their own laptop to one of the boards, which is used, for example, by some presenters to

show their slides from the laptop, while referring to the other board (and the connected computer in the classroom) when accessing and presenting information from the Internet. Using the two output devices for different applications is a common practice often chosen when using multiple monitors for desktop computing as, for example, Grudin's studies pointed out; there, participants used multiple monitors rather for partitioning than to increase space (Grudin, 2001).

Overall, we can observe that people take great advantage of the additional working space. No single trend in using this installation can be observed, but a variety of different usage scenarios exists. Hence, instead of having the teachers adapt to a certain interface or style of interaction, this setup enables them to choose among different approaches and to use the respective tools in the way they personally prefer.

Integrated interactive LCD panel as overhead projector replacement. In addition to the boards, we built a high desk or lectern with integrated computing facilities that can serve as a true re-

Figure 5. Putting two electronic whiteboards next to each other, in order to form a larger input and output area, resemble traditional blackboards

Figure 6. Lectern with integrated computing facilities and pen-based input device. The interactive LCD panel is integrated into the surface in order to support freehand writing on the presented slides and pen-based operation of the used applications.

placement of the traditional overhead projector (cf. Figure 6). As input device, a horizontally mounted LCD display with pen-based interaction functionality is integrated into the surface of the lectern. All other equipment needed for a talk is embedded into the lectern, but again hidden to the user as much as possible. This includes even audio recording facilities if the presenter wants to record the lecture with some lecture recording software (Müller & Ottmann, 2000) and preserve it for further, off-line usage. Hence, the normal user just has to connect the lectern to the power source and data projector and press a button to turn it on. Including all required equipment into the lectern provides several advantages, because it enables us to make the whole device mobile by putting it on wheels. Thus, it can be easily maintained and replaced by technical staff if necessary. In addition, it can be transferred to different rooms, which is important in case not all rooms can be provided with the full range of technical equipment. It also allows one to easily put it away and lock it, in case it is not possible to always lock the room.

Considering the usage by the presenters, most of them reported that handwriting and making annotations is much easier, since they can do this on a horizontally mounted surface placed in front of them. Some also expressed their appreciation that they can face their material and the audience at the same time and do not have to continuously turn their back to the students when presenting their material. Meanwhile, several of these lecterns were built and used in various lecture halls at our as well as other institutions.

Both the lectern as well as the large interactive whiteboard described before turned out to be reasonable replacements for traditional devices used in classrooms, that is, blackboards and overhead projectors. If integrated into the environment as shown, for example, in Figure 5 and 6, they do not interfere with the normal teaching process of the presenter while at the same time offering full access to the computing functionality offered by the underlying computing system and network infrastructure.

SOFTWARE-RELATED ISSUES: INTERACTION PARADIGM

Background: Digital Ink

In the previous section we argued that the pen is the natural choice for interaction with wall-mounted boards and interactive tablets. It enables users to interact directly with the respective tools instead of remotely as with a mouse pointer. Freehand writing proves to be more intuitive and flexible to enter content during a lecture than a keyboard. Hence, handwriting becomes a "first-class" data type, on an equal footing with text entered via keyboards. However, common interface designs and *graphical user interfaces (GUIs)* usually follow the desktop metaphor and are therefore optimized for input devices such as keyboard and mouse. For example, navigation through nested menus can easily be done with a mouse, but is hard to do with a pen. For pen-based interaction, earlier research on pie menus proved an advantage for users of digital screens, as people tend to better remember the cyclic position, and as such expedites the selection process (Callahan, Hopkins, Weiser, & Shneiderman, 1988). Hence, we see ourselves confronted with two different demands: on the one hand, the aim of using pen-based input devices in order to present information to the students, while on the other hand, the need to rely on traditional, mouse-based input in order to interact with the ICT and to operate the respective programs. To avoid the unfavorable switching between different devices, we propose a new interaction mode purely based on pen input and the notion of digital ink described in the following sections.

Digital Ink. Motivated by the treatment of handwriting as a "first-class" data type, we introduce the notion of *digital ink*, which is used not only to enter and represent contents, but also to operate the ICT via *gesture commands*. A gesture command is the resultant process of invoking gesture-like movements with the pen,

that resemble special shapes drawn in a certain distinctive way, recognized by the program as certain predefined instructions for it to carry out. The digital ink derives its name from the data class that represents any kind of information created when using a digital pen to draw strokes on a screen of a pen-based input device. While the strokes received on the pen-computer's surface get recorded as digital ink, its consequential markings are reflected noticeably onto the screen simultaneously. Any digital ink that was written is either kept in its raw form or goes through a process that translates it into recognizable texts or graphic objects. Often, in many pen-based applications, the ink goes further to be tried as a possible pen-gesture. In this case, when the ink is confirmed to be a gesture command, its visual trace on the screen is removed upon the execution of the respective gesture command.

Digital ink in its raw representation as processed by the respective hardware and software holds far greater amounts of information than are immediately apparent. These include, among others, the type of pen tip, the amount of pressure used to create a stroke, the height of the pen above the screen surface, opacity value, color, and timing data. As a result, the digital ink is acknowledged in serious enterprises such as one for secure handwritten signatures (Cyber SIGN, Inc., 2005; Gries, 2000; Hangai, Yamanaka, & Hamamoto, 2000), as well as in everyday norms of handwriting e-mail messages (Pen&Internet® LLC, 2005), sketching design posters (Corel™, 2005), and annotating digital documents (GRAHL Software Design, 2005; Müller & Ottmann, 2000). As more electronic devices with pen interfaces continue to become available for entering and manipulating information, efforts have been made to ensure that supporting pen-applications are effective at leveraging this method of input. Handwriting is an input modality that is very familiar for most people since everyone learns to write in school. So, there is a high tendency for people to use this mode of input and control not only in the classroom scenario described previously, but for a great variety of different applications as well.

Ink traces and symbolic representation. The domain of the digital ink is unlike any others, such as text and graphics, that can have all its related information easily organized and cross-referenced, and be presented in front of users to allow them direct manipulation of the data. A *trace* refers to a trail of digital ink data made between a successive pair of pen-down and pen-up events representing a sequence of contiguous ink points—the *X* and *Y* coordinates of the pen's position. If the sampling property of the input device is not constant, it becomes advantageous to include timestamps for each pair of the sampled coordinates. A sequence of traces symbolically accumulates to meaningful graphics, forming what we humans perceive as characters, words, drawings, or gestures representing commands. Each trace can be categorized in terms of the timings noted for its *duration*, *lead*, and *lag* times.

The importance of digital ink has also been recognized by the Internet community, leading to the specification of the World Wide Web Consortium's Ink-Markup-Language (*InkML*) standard (Russel, Chee, Seni, Yaeger, Tremblay, Franke, Madhvanath, & Froumentin, 2004). InkML allows the description of precise digital ink information that is not only interchangeable between systems, but also allows the convenient "archival" and "streaming" of ink data between applications. Among many of its properties, it is important to note that:

- InkML provides a common format for the exchange of ink data between components such as handwriting and gesture recognizers, signature verifiers, and ink-aware modules;
- InkML supports the representation of hand-drawn ink with full attributed information, on top of capturing the pen positions over time;

- InkML allows the specification of extra information for additional accuracy such as pen tilt and pen tip force (pressure) for the enhanced support of applications such as character and handwriting-style recognition, and authentication;
- InkML provides the means for extension—by allowing application-specific information to be added to the ink files to support issues of compatibility.

Active digital ink in recordings and replay. One of the advantages of the usage of ICT in classrooms is the possibility to record and archive the live event for further usage and studying. Today, numerous systems exist for automatic lecture recording that automatically turn the live event into a multimedia document. These files are used, for example, by students to reflect a lecture. Others use them to deepen their understanding of particular topics. They can even be used as the core for building Web-based online courses.

Independent of the respective application scenario, the studies mentioned previously (Mukhopadhyay & Smith, 1999; Zupancic & Horz, 2002) highlight the importance of the development of thoughts through freehand writings. They also confirm the evidence that simply capturing the static end-result of the lecturer's annotations for recalling the subject at a later time is inferior to unambiguously maintaining the whole sequence and dynamics of those freehand annotations when recorded for interactive replay.

As a consequence, user interfaces that allow replaying of real-time multimedia documents usually include command buttons to quickly "fast-forward" and "rewind" their data sets for systematic browsing. We see this very often in many learning applications that try to cater to both students and teachers in assisting them to effectively retrieve desired segments of those documents. Random access navigation, that is, the ability to access any position along the time-line by using, for example, a slider interface, provides an additional advantage on top of this simple fast-forward and rewinding of real-time information. It gives users the ability to straight away focus on the intended portions of their documents without having to wait a second longer for these processes to arrive at the stipulated point of time, albeit the processes being a little faster than the normal replay mechanism. Hence, users should be able to navigate through digital ink recordings along the timeline. However, realizing such a *random visible scrolling* is a challenging task.

Summary. In this section, we introduced digital ink as a notion to describe pen-based input, which is used not only to model chalk or markers in the digital world, but also to interpret particular ink traces, which are the building blocks of digital ink, as gesture commands. In such a setup, we need sophisticated techniques, not only to represent, process, and manipulate traces of ink, but also to store, access, and replay them. The ability for random access navigation poses a particular challenge in this context.

In the following section, we first describe aspects about the personalization, archival, and streaming of digital ink. Subsequently, we introduce a new paradigm for interaction with electronic whiteboards via ink traces that are interpreted as gesture commands.

Personalizing Digital Ink for Archival and Streaming

In addressing the proper support interfaces for digital ink mediums that are to be stored and indexed in accessible archives or streamed in broadcast networks, appropriate tools are required for practical personal manipulation of the digital ink within multimedia and multivalent materials (Phelps & Wilensky, 1997). These tools are for the producing, capturing, and replaying of freehand writings, and should therefore contain features deemed to let users feel that their digital handwritings are acceptable substitutes for their normal ones when applied on digital documents.

We have identified six main feature-themes that relate to what users perceive in the contents of the formulated digital strokes and what they would expect when interfacing with them. These feature-themes refer to the personal flavor, manipulation in pixels, manipulation by objects, compactness of representation and scalability, replay and synchronization, and facilities for random-access.

1. **Personal flavor:** Every individual person has a unique and particular writing style. This is portrayed in the calligraphic output characteristics from their written works. A handwriting tool needs to allow the expression of this style, as accurately as possible. The recording samples and the replay stream of this tool should maintain all these personal calligraphic attributes. Various pen tip styles, such as coarse whiteboard marker-pens or fine pencil leads, and pressure-sensitive information should be supported during both recording (creation) and replay. Note that most currently available digital ink software offered in presentation tools is either nothing more than fixed-size pixel-traces on screen, or does not support the capture and replay of traces in a manner that maintains the dynamics of the generation process. That being mentioned, users should also expect simple anti-aliasing techniques on the interface tool to improve the stroke appearance of the traces rendered on screen (Klassen, 1991).

2. **Manipulation in pixels:** Removing traces, or parts of it, and inserting empty spaces on the grid-like digital screens are typical examples of pixel-oriented operations.

3. **Manipulation in objects:** Generating or selecting whole objects, stretching, contracting, reflecting, pivoting, copying, and pasting are typical examples of object-oriented operations applied to trace-objects. Arguably, the typical editing commands in modern graphics tools (insert, copy, paste,

and the like), however, may also be considered as pixel-based operations.

4. **Compactness of representation and scalability:** Extensive writing ultimately generates large volumes of data if the complete transcript of the raw digital ink is stored in an uncompressed form. Inevitably, eliminating any superfluous information will be a reasonable course of action. One way to ensure that the integrity of the data remains intact would be to try and symbolically represent the handwritten letters/alphabets as spline-curves that are independent of the screen resolution. That is, scaling such spline-curve-writings up or down would preserve and not deteriorate the rendering quality of the letters/alphabets during replay of the recorded traces.

5. **Replay and synchronization:** At this point, it should now be possible to replay all recorded handwritings in their best quality, the same way as they were first recorded/presented. Here, both the inter- and the intra-stream time constraints should be observed, such that the full dynamics of the generation process of handwritings are maintained in exactly the same way as they appeared at generation time. Furthermore, the interface must allow all (time-stamped) data streams to be synchronized with other recorded data streams, particularly with the audio stream of the lecturer's voice. The latter is usually considered to be the *master* stream in a master-slave synchronization model for replay (Müller & Ottmann, 2000), whereas the recorded ink traces are considered as the *slave* stream that is synchronously replayed with the master stream.

6. **Facilities for random-access:** Easy navigation, particularly "random visible scrolling" (cf. previous) through a recorded document, requires random real-time access to the entire data collection. Metaphorically, this ideology resembles the thumb-flipping of a book. Given an instance of time, the complete list of objects visible at this time instance must be made available for display almost "immediately." That is, it should be possible to compute and display all of these objects fast enough, so that the user gets the impression of immediacy, as opposed to making the user wait due to latency issues.

Table 1 summarizes the following discussion about how current enterprise tools fulfil these six requirements.

The Web tool *riteMail* (Pen&Internet® LLC, 2005) allows for handwritten messages in an interactive, electronic ink e-mail application. Users can create high resolution, fully interactive handwritten notes and drawings on hand-held devices, Tablet PCs, as well as on every Java-enabled desktop or laptop computer. The notes can then be sent to any e-mail address. The riteMail software employs unified Extensible Markup Language (XML)-based protocols for digital ink transmission between all components of the service. However, a replay facility is not included within (and, in order to be fair, not essential for its purpose).

Corel Grafigo™ (Corel™, 2005) targets pen-computers and is designed specially for the Windows XP Tablet PC Edition. It supports pressure-sensitive pens, allows the marking up of documents and images individually, and provides the features of shape recognition, and gesture-based commands. Data are saved in SVG format.

Painter™ *Classic*, marketed by Corel (Wacom, 2005), is an excellent paint program for graphic designers that simulates the various graphic markers and coloured pencils and pens, as well as water color and oil paints. As an image-editing program, it offers numerous high performance functions (edged and smooth drawing, distorting, cloning, etc.).

The *AOF-tools* and their commercial spin-off, *Lecturnity* (imc AG, 2003), fulfill many of the

Table 1. Summarized assessment of various tools on freehand writings

Criteria / Software	Writing style	Support of pixel-based operations	Object-oriented mani-pulation	Symbolic representation	Recording	Replay	Random access
riteMail	yes	yes	yes	yes	static	no	no
Corel Grafigo	yes	yes	yes	yes	static	no	no
Painter Classic	yes	no	yes	no	static	no	no
Tablet PC Software Development Kit	yes	yes	yes	yes	static	no	no
Lecturnity	no	yes	yes	no	dynamic	yes	yes

interface requirements discussed in the previous section, except that they do not fully preserve and regurgitate their user's personal style of writing. Moreover, the data volume on recorded documents with extensive handwritings is intolerable. The reason is its highly redundant storage method; for while Lecturnity offers a real-time random access facility during replay, it also computes the *entire* list of visible objects on the screen for every single time instance.

Using Digital Ink on Electronic Whiteboards

In the preceding discussion about input devices we already described different usage scenarios of electronic whiteboards in a ubiquitous computing classroom. Now we take a closer look at the actual applications running on those devices, how people are operating them, and what kind of interaction takes place.

Instructors and students in class do not only see the prepared course materials projected onto the electronic whiteboards, but also the "active" annotations made by the instructors using the digital pens as the lessons progress. Combined with dedicated software applications, the supporting whiteboard technologies can be made to

function more effectively with better pen control, and appropriately displaying both static and moving images at suitable resolutions. Among other things, these applications generally offer:

- "Flipchart" capabilities to save and print images as well as annotated ink-trace markings;
- A "blackboard" to manipulate primitive handwritten text and drawings;
- Integrated slides and blackboard "environment";
- "Movie screens" to showcase video and software demonstrations;
- "Tools" to facilitate discussions and group work; and
- Access to the network, where shared teaching resources may be available.

More importantly, the way the electronic whiteboards are utilized will shape the kind of impact they will have on the overall learning environment. The basic guidelines highlighted by Glover and Miller (2001) for good practices and outcomes of engaging classroom interaction and participation with the electronic whiteboards across the curriculum are:

- To increase efficiency by enabling teachers to draw upon a variety of ICT-based resources without disruption or loss of space;
- To extend learning by using more engaging materials to explain concepts; and
- To transform learning by creating new learning styles stimulated by interaction with the electronic whiteboards.

All of the previously mentioned technological and social benefits have positive indications from the wider observational point of view. Nevertheless, there are also subtle cases that can make instructors hesitant to change their pedagogy to incorporate the electronic whiteboards into their lesson plans, if practical considerations hinder their perspectives. We already pointed out that it requires effort in commitment to develop media-enhanced teaching contents for the electronic whiteboards, which could be considerably taxing on the teachers' initial workload. Also, according to the studies compiled by BECTA (2003), while the act of teaching with electronic whiteboards instills anxiety in the students to learn, it unduly places the pressure onto the teachers when it comes to delivering the contents. This is especially true if the writing environment of the electronic whiteboards is not sufficiently supported with the necessary interfacing tools. We have thoroughly discussed this in the preceding sections.

Good electronic whiteboard contents are generally those that can display themselves immediately in highly visual terms, which can be most effectively understood by a group of individuals (BECTA, 2003; Clyde, 2004). The ability to easily modify and change these content materials is all about the *personalization* of the electronic whiteboard environment. In relation to this, and in order to achieve good content presentation, there needs to be good software applications to manage and control the content data with enhanced features and functions. Currently, makers of the electronic whiteboards ship out accompanying software that is embedded into their systems for

use in classroom environments. Examples include those that are listed on Smart Technologies Inc.'s Web site such as *notebook whiteboarding software* and *SMART Board tools*. These intuitive programs support numerous operations that are categorized into many menu items under several options that teachers can use while delivering their lessons. So much so, that they tend to become more of a distraction to the teachers rather than an assistance to them in front of a live audience.

Writing and "feeling in control" of the board environment. Now, we are particularly interested in the part where the previous support interfacing software allows teachers to write on the electronic whiteboard freely as if it were a normal blackboard. The situation described previously may not necessarily pose as a problem if the screen-size of the electronic whiteboard is small. However, when these programs are maximized to full screen, then teachers will bump into the problem of "hand-and-eye coordination." This is a cross between uncomfortable peripheral views for the eyes, and awkward bodily positions to access the menus without disturbing the flow of the lesson, or blocking the audience. This problem for a single large screen worsens when we cascade the electronic boards in the learning environment in series next to each other as described in one of the previous case studies (cf. Figure 5).

Without investing in additional tracking devices such as motion-detectors or cameras, the large interconnected, high-resolution, wall-mounted, multiple displays are by themselves receptively sensitive to the teachers' touch. Properly configured, this electronic whiteboard environment offers an extended desktop metaphor quite unlike the ones that we presently know and have grown used to. Further incorporating the pen-input technology into this setup accords teachers a higher level of personal presentiment than a conventional monitor, in a way that it allows them to directly touch the active-screens and see immediate reactions through the digital pens. The electronic whiteboards are meant to be an active presentation medium for a congregation of audience in a large room. While there is always a desktop console that controls the electronic whiteboards, through the mouse and keyboard, freeing up this mode of interfacing lets teachers communicate directly with the screen using just a digital pen.

Judging by the dominant metaphor that what we have today is a mismatch for the computer environment we are dealing with tomorrow, it is difficult to place this huge screen scenario (alone) into any pronounced categories of user interface debates on concepts of adaptivity and adaptability (Shneiderman & Maes, 1997). For instance, the sphere of influence of the hand-and-eye coordination needs to be enlarged, and perhaps include the body, to follow the claims of direct manipulation of adaptable interfaces. Furthermore, while the audience have it easy watching from a distance, the teacher does not: standing so close to one part of the multiple huge screens often leads to the interface widgets he or she may require to be out of reach, or worse still, because the teacher cannot see those widgets, he or she may assume that such actions or commands represented by those widgets do not exist within the board application. We point out here that this may affect the flow of the delivery of the lesson contents. In this case, we may be left to rely on the adaptivity of the interface for the electronic whiteboards to proactively assist the instructor while at the same time ensuring that they still feel in control of the whole process.

Interacting with Electronic Whiteboards Through Gestures

In order to solve the problems previously described, we now describe an interaction concept that realizes a modeless interactivity by deriving gestures from digital ink traces. We define *modeless interactivity* for the digital ink environment on the electronic whiteboards as the seamless integration of both the "writing" and "gesture-command"

modes on a common, unified platform. On top of this, they further encompass the conventional on-screen widgets such as the fixed pull-down and pop-up menus as "interaction modes" that can be minimized on their usage or done away with completely when not needed in the most cumbersome of circumstances. They go by the notion that instructors should not always need to go between different sections of the boards in order to effect a menu action.

Deriving gestures from digital ink traces. It is possible to convincingly anticipate, based on the lead and lag times obtained, that the latest ink component is more of an instance of a trace, rather than a gesture. Advanced recognition techniques have been introduced to the digital ink domain, and while a number of works have gone into handwriting and sketch recognition (Rubin, 1991), there are among these works that use the same techniques to attempt to recognize hand-drawn pen gestures.

Hence, the "writing" mode as well as the "gesture" mode can help out with the current interface issues. "Gesturing to the system" refers to the actual gesticulated actions resulting from the pen movements that represent a command, and not merely the "tap-and-drag-the-icon" movements. The prospects of gesturing commands in ink-domain applications are encouraging. So much so that many authors think that this is the epitome of the final interface for pen-based applications. Although it is agreeable to a certain extent, that this mode of ubiquitous interfacing may form the fundamentals of future (more enhanced) hardware devices, we should not anticipate this to be the trend in this current context. The *perceptual user interface* (PUI) guidelines should be adopted and used to create the first steps of the bridging between fully packed screens of user interface widgets to that of a ubiquitous one (Shneiderman & Maes, 1997).

Deriving interfaces from gestures. For the same technique that a right-mouse-click can bring up a popup menu on documents that contain menu-items "generally" related to the application it serves, pen gestures have the relative capability to have this metaphor extended. They make it possible to provide more "specific" menu-commands that are currently in context. By this, we mean the placing of directed (or pointedly explicit) "context-specific" menu-items that should obviously take precedence on the front-most tier of the multi-cascading popup interface by virtue of what is currently being displayed on screen. The rest of the more "general" menu-items, however, are neatly tucked away in the lower-priority cascades to ensure that they are still accessible, as is required by the specifications of perceptual user interfaces. For example, right-clicking anywhere on a Word document (or most Windows applications for that matter) brings up menu-items generally affiliated to the *Edit*-menu on the application's main menubar. The advantage here is that users do not have to skit their mouse over a distance to access the main menus. This same advantage is magnified many times over when working in front of a series of large wall-mounted, hi-res digital screens where the pen is the primary input modal.

The extension we mentioned previously for this technique will involve additional information we can gather from the background environment, and is designed mainly for the convenience of the wall-mounted SMART electronic board users. We discussed this thoroughly in our previous work that deals with digital whiteboard-applications for classroom scenarios, where the sole objective is to assist lecturers in delivering their lessons comfortably and not worry about the support technology.

We incorporated an active program module called the Context-Assembler, running in the background of the main program application, that keeps track of all "items" that are visible on the digital board's writing area. These include all digital ink-entities that constitute drawings, writings, illustrations, and so forth, and other screen-related widgets like images, fonts, and the writing canvas itself. These "items" are ordered and cross-referenced with each other in an efficient way in the Context-Assembler to give optimal background support information known as "context-information." That is, if we ask the Context-Assembler about one particular trace that we wrote earlier on the writing canvas, it will tell us when and where the trace was created and located, which other "items" are its immediate neighbors, which are the other items' it is overlapping with, which group(s) of "paragraph" it is connected to, the probability of the trace being a gesture, and all other "items" that are similar to it in terms of appearance, size, color, and style. Based on this context-information that can be retrieved off any "items" in the Context-Assembler, we designed a "context-oriented" popup menu interface.

The mechanism that determines what menu-items receive higher priorities over others, in order to appear on the front-most tier of the cascading popup menu interface, is an application-defined mapping function that uses the context-information as its input parameters. For example, in Figure 7, the latest ink-element is queried for its context-information. Among other things, the Context-Assembler replies by telling that the ink-element in question is on top of another ink-element created at time (*t-m*), is on top of an image known as "slide p28," is on top of the writing area known as "p9," stretches horizontally across these three previous "items"—from left to right—and has a very high probability of being a "right-arrow" gesture. Putting these into the mapping function returns a list of thematically categorized menu-items that interprets the last ink-element as a command gesture. The top few high-priority menu-items in the list will suggest that the command gesture advance to the next "slide," or to the next "page," or to next "slide" and "page," or to move the overlapped ink-elements identified in the context-information to a new location.

To complete the visualization of the *on-demand* assistance, we bank-in on the last known coordinate position of that ink-element in-context. Popping up dynamic-content pie menus and/or

Figure 7. The latest ink-element in (a) is interpreted as a gesture that can have several interpretations. The current context of the board (writing area p9, slide p28, and ink@time(t-m)) is determined and assembled appropriately in (b). The output of the mapping function is then rendered onto the screen as support interface on-demand (c).

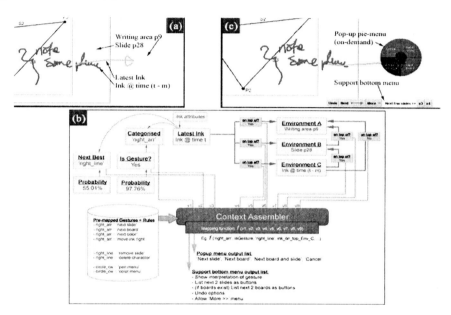

other static command buttons, with respect to the list of menu-items returned by the mapping function, in that vicinity seems most appropriate and serves as a convenience to the user. As said before, pie menus proved an advantage for users of digital screens as earlier research pointed out (Callahan et al., 1988). Our command button (toolbar) interface is logged to the bottom of the screens, appearing on-demand with only an array of anticipated widgets. The combined lengths of the number of widgets will not exceed the arm length of the user's to ensure that all widgets are within reach and within the user's line of sight.

CONCLUSION AND FUTURE TRENDS

Freehand writing is a natural way of exchanging viewpoints and communicating visual ideas between teachers and students in a classroom.

Motivated by this, we identified the value of pen-based computing for the usage of ICT in classroom teaching. By presenting an historical overview of the usage of pen-based input devices in classrooms and lecture halls and two case studies with currently available technology, we demonstrated that today's hardware equipment can be used to greatly improve the teaching experience. Using them, we are able to build a ubiquitous computing environment in the classroom that offers teachers full interaction with the respective technology using a pen while at the same time not interfering with the interaction between teacher and students.

As a trend of moving toward natural environments in the digital world, such a setup encourages freehand writings to become the bridging tool that encompasses portable and synchronizable standards of manipulating ink data between mediums and documents. Hence, we introduced the digital ink as a new "first-class" data type serving two purposes, first, the representation and preservation of information through freehand writing and annotations on the board. In this context we discussed issues about the personalization of digital ink as well as its archival, later access and streaming replay. Subsequently, we described the second purpose of digital ink—the operation and control of the classroom's ICT via pen-gestures. By interpreting ink traces as gestures, users can interact with the ubiquitous computing environment in a more interactive and intuitive way than with regular interface designs using traditional graphical user interfaces developed and optimized for desktop computing. This has also been proven to be the case for multi-user interaction on the horizontal table-interface: (cf. Figure 8) recognizing a gesture in its respective interpretation also tells us the side of the table it originated from, thus simultaneously identifying the user seated at that corner without having to install additional sensing devices.

For the future, we expect further improvements in the respective hardware and the development of new devices that might further improve the usage of ICT in the classroom. Although current devices and hardware configurations provide a real alternative to the traditional blackboard and overhead projector equipment, as we described in the hardware-related part of this chapter, there is always room for improvement in terms of size, quality, and production costs. At the same time,

new technology keeps evolving. Interesting developments with great potential for classroom usage include, for example, the so called electronic paper/electronic ink approaches (see Jacobson, Comiskey, Anderson, & Hasan, 2005 and Xerox Parc, 2005).

Wireless networks are more and more installed at universities, and although not directly related to input devices, this infrastructure will have great influence on the ICT usage in classrooms and thus on the HCI. For example, it is not clear how to seamlessly integrate different devices with different sizes into the overall communication and learning process. Lecturers write on large electronic whiteboards, while students connect mobile devices, such as laptops, Tablet PCs, or even very small PDAs and SmartPhones, to the wireless LAN. How to represent and exchange information between such devices that differ in size and processing power is an open research problem (MacIntyre & Feiner, 1996) where convincing solutions are still missing.

In addition, there exists an obvious trend toward computer-supported group work in classrooms. Instead of purely instructional presentations and lectures, which have been the focus of this chapter, other ways of teaching, such as seminars and group work, can benefit from the usage of ICT as well. Important research in this area has been done, for example, by the Interac-

Figure 8. An electronic whiteboard mounted horizontally in order to create an 'interactive table' for group-work

tive Workspaces Project at Stanford University (Johanson, Fox, & Winograd, 2002). In our own research lab, we are currently exploiting the usage of an "interactive table" where a data projector is mounted on the ceiling, projecting the content of a computer screen onto a horizontally mounted electronic whiteboard (cp. Figure 8). While the respective hardware to build such a table is already available, many open questions and problems remain regarding the design of the software side of the user interface, such as dealing with different orientations when people sit on different sides of the table, enabling people to reach remote objects on the virtual table's surface (i.e. the projected computer screen), and so forth. Such horizontally mounted interactive computing systems are an active research area, and we believe that classroom teaching can greatly benefit from the outcomes of the respective projects.

NOTE

Some of the notions for tools and devices described in this article are registered Trademarks of the respective companies or organizations. We kindly ask the reader to refer to the given references. All features and characteristics of these systems have been described to the best of our knowledge. However, we do like to mention that specific characteristics and technical specification frequently change, and therefore discrepancies between the descriptions in this article and the actual systems are possible.

REFERENCES

BECTA. (2003). What the research says about interactive whiteboards. *Becta ICT Research.*

Callahan, J., Hopkins, D., Weiser, M., & Shneiderman, B. (1988). An empirical comparison of pie vs. linear menus. In *Proceedings of the SIGCHI Conference on Human Factors in Computing Systems* (pp. 95-100).

Chong, N. S. T., & Sakauchi, M. (2000). Back to the basics: A first class chalkboard and more. In *Proceedings of the 2000 ACM Symposium on Applied Computing* (pp. 131-136).

Clyde, L. A. (2004). Electronic whiteboards. In *Teacher Librarian Toolkit: Information Technology 32*(2). Retrieved May 31, 2005, from http://www.teacherlibrarian.com/ tltoolkit/info_tech/ info_tech_32_2.html

Corel™. (2005). Corel grafigo 2—Create, annotate, collaborate. *Corel Corporation.* Retrieved May 31, 2005, from http://www.corel.com/grafigo

Cyber SIGN, Inc. (2005). Biometric signature verification—technology overview. Retrieved May 31, 2005, from http://www.cybersign.com/techoverview.htm

Glover, D., & Miller, D. (2001). Running with technology: The pedagogic impact of the large-scale introduction of interactive whiteboards in one secondary school. *Journal of Information Technology for Teacher Education, 10*(3), 257-276.

GRAHL Software Design. (2005). PDF annotator—Annotate, edit and comment PDF files. Retrieved May 31, 2005, from http://www.ograhl.com/en/pdfannotator

Griess, F. (2000). *Online signature verification.* Unpublished master's thesis, Michigan State University.

Grudin, J. (2001). Partitioning digital worlds: Focal and peripheral awareness in multiple monitor use. In *Proceedings of the SIGCHI Conference on Human Factors in Computing Systems* (pp. 458-465).

Hangai, S., Yamanaka, S., & Hamamoto, T. (2000).

Writer verification using altitude and direction of pen movement. In *Proceedings of the 15th International Conference on Pattern Recognition* (Vol. 3, pp. 483-486). IEEE.

Heer, J., Newberger, A., Beckmann, C., & Hong, J. I. (2003). Liquid: Context-aware distributed queries. In *Proceedings of UbiComp 2003* (pp. 140-148).

imc AG. (2003). Lecturnity—Create your content live and on the fly. *Information Multimedia Communication AG*. Retrieved May 31, 2005, from http://www.lecturnity.de/

Jacobson, J. M., Comiskey, B., Anderson, P., & Hasan, L. (2005). Electronic paper books and electronic books. *MIT Media Lab*. Retrieved May 31, 2005, from http://www.media.mit.edu/micromedia/elecpaper.html

Johanson, B., Fox, A., & Winograd, T. (2002). The interactive workspaces project: Experiences with ubiquitous computing rooms. *IEEE Pervasive Computing Magazine, 1*(2).

Klassen, R. V. (1991). Drawing antialiased cubic spline curves. *ACM Transactions on Graphics, 10*(1), 92-108.

MacIntyre, B., & Feiner, S. (1996). Future multimedia user interfaces. *Multimedia systems, 4*(5), 250-268.

Mukhopadhyay, S., & Smith, S. (1999). Passive capture and structuring of lectures. In *Proceedings of the 7th ACM International Conference on Multimedia (Part 1)* (pp. 477-487). ACM Press.

Müller, R., & Ottmann, T. (2000). The 'authoring on the fly' system for automated recording and replay of (tele)presentations. Special issue on 'multimedia authoring and presentation techniques'. *Multimedia Systems, 8*(3), 158-176.

Pen&Internet® LLC. (2005). riteMail—Product overview. *Pen&Internet® LLC*. Retrieved May 31, 2005, from http://www.ritemail.net

Phelps, T. A., & Wilensky, R. (1997). Multivalent annotations. In *Proceedings of the First European Conference on Research and Advanced Technology for Digital Libraries*.

Prante, T., Streitz, N. A., & Tandler, P. (2004). Roomware: Computers disappear and interaction evolves. *IEEE Computer*, December, 47-54.

Rubine, D. (1991). Specifying gestures by example. In *Proceedings of the 18th Annual Conference on Computer Graphics and Interactive Techniques* (pp. 329-337).

Russel, G., Chee, Y.-M., Seni, G., Yaeger, L., Tremblay, C., Franke, K., Madhvanath, S., & Froumentin, M. (2004). Ink markup language. *W3C Working Draft*. Retrieved May 31, 2005, from http://www.w3.org/TR/InkML

Shneiderman, B., & Maes, P. (1997). Direct manipulation vs. interface agents. *Interactions, 4*(6), 42-61.

Smart Technologies Inc. (2005). Retrieved May 31, 2005, from http://www2.smarttech.com

Wacom. (2005). Procreate—Painter classic. Retrieved May 31, 2005, from http://www.wacom-asia.com/products/intuos2/soft/painter.html

Weiser, M. (1991). The computer for the 21st century. *Scientific American, 265*(10), 71-72.

Xerox Parc. (2005). Project Gyricon. Retrieved May 31, 2005, from http://www2.parc.com/hsl/projects/gyricon/

Zupancic, B., & Horz, H. (2002). Lecture recording and its use in a traditional university course. In *Proceedings of the 7th Annual Conference on Innovation and Technology in Computer Science Education* (pp. 24-28). ACM Press.

Chapter III
Project Student Rescue:
Online Learning Facilitation in Higer Education to Improve Retention Rates for Distance Learners

Mandi Axmann
Open Universities Australia, Australia

ABSTRACT

This chapter reports on an ongoing trial project that is being conducted at seven Australian Universities. The chapter summarizes the project and suggests methods to facilitate effective online facilitation based on the preliminary findings, as well as findings from the literature. This chapter will provide a brief outline of elements that can be identified in an online facilitation system to help improve retention rates for distance learners.

INTRODUCTION

This research study will discuss an ongoing online learning facilitation project in higher education to improve to aspects such as student retention and unit completion (attrition rates), in distance learning. The discussion is based on a trial project that is currently being conducted at seven Australian Universities.

The availability of an online learning facilitator to support distance learning may address aspects such as student motivation and unit completion (London, 2004), and could contribute to student retention. This chapter will provide a brief outline of elements that can be identified in an online tutorial (facilitation) system to help improve retention rates for distance learners.

OVERVIEW OF THE CHAPTER

Open Universities Australia is a consortium of Australian Higher Education providers with the aim of providing distance-delivered open access to tertiary study education. Open Universities Australia is currently conducting an online tutorial support trial project that calls for a trial to measure the impact of providing additional tutorial support across all the skills units and a number of critical first-year units. The concept of "tutoring" has many diverse meanings within the online learning environment, and can imply stand-alone learning materials, the computer as tutor, intelligent tutoring design systems, and also the tutor (person) as a learning facilitator within the online learning classroom. For the purpose of this study, the tutor is a *person* that provides support to the students and assistance to the lecturer, within the online (Web-based) environment.

Studies on student retention can roughly be categorized into the following categories, depending on the emphasis they give to individual and environmental forces, namely psychological, societal, economical, organizational, interactional, and holistic theories. The focus of this study will be, however, not to determine the factors for student dropout, but to determine if a well-structured tutor support program will have an impact on student *motivation*, and thereby increasing student retention and throughput (persistence).

Effective online interaction will depend on how well the facilitator makes use of the online environment and the communication tools available. Certain elements of record keeping can help the online tutor structure the facilitation process. Conscientious record keeping may also benefit online learning facilitators themselves, by guiding them to plan and implement an appropriate course of learning support services, to review work as a whole, and to self-monitor more precisely.

Barriers to learning can cause learners to feel frustrated and isolated, and in turn have an impact on student retention. The online tutor can play an important role in eliminating or helping to relieve these barriers, which in turn can positively impact student retention. This chapter will report on the preliminary findings from the online tutor project conducted at Open Universities Australia.

BACKGROUND

Open Universities Australia is a consortium of seven Australian universities that was formed by the federal Australian Commonwealth Government as Open Learning Australia during 1993. After extensive market research, the name of the organization changed to Open Universities Australia in 2004 to better address the market needs. The aim is to provide distance-delivered open access to tertiary study, with the commitment to make higher education accessible and affordable for everyone who wants to study. Open Universities Australia consortium members hold shares in the company. The current shareholders are (Open Universities Australia, 2005):

- Curtin University of Technology, Western Australia
- Griffith University, Queensland
- Macquarie University, New South Wales
- Monash University, Victoria
- RMIT University, Victoria
- Swinburne University, Victoria
- University of South Australia, South Australia

The shareholders provide academic guidance, and the students obtain a degree from the provider, which is mainly responsible for the qualification, although students also have access to units from other providers. The largest segment of the Open Universities Australia market is defined as adult learners ranging from average ages of 25-50 years, although there are also students enrolled who are well into their sixties. Most students are full-time or part-time employed, and would find it difficult to attend on-campus classes.

Findings from the Student and Portal Members Online Survey Results (London, 2004) furthermore reported that past Open Universities Australia students identified "insufficient tutorial support" (47% of total population) and "staying motivated" (50% of total population) as their greatest concerns for studying with Open Universities Australia (students were able to select more than one option).

In order to address these concerns, Open Universities Australia proposed the implementation of the *online tutorial support trial project*. Approved by the Open Universities Australia Academic Board on September 24, 2004, this project calls for a trial to measure the impact of providing additional tutorial support across all the skills units and a number of critical first-year units, particularly in business subjects.

The purpose of the project is to find a level of tutorial support that both (a) makes a difference to student retention/attrition and motivation and (b) is as cost-effective as possible.

The online tutorial support trial project is aimed at addressing student concerns by providing additional online tutor support in order to facilitate the student's learning experience. The results of this effort will be analyzed, with recommendations then made regarding the impact of additional online tutorial support on student attrition and unit satisfaction.

Tutoring has many diverse meanings in the Web-based environment. The following section will discuss the role of the tutor in the online learning facilitation environment as understood within the context of this project.

TUTORING, TUTOR, AND ONLINE LEARNING FACILITATION

Association of the words *tutor, tutoring, online tutoring*, and *online learning facilitation* is varied and complex within the educational literature (Collison, Elbaum, Haavind, & Tinker, 2000; Gravett & Geyser, 2004; Salmon, 2000). Looking at the original meaning, the word *tutor* stems from the old French and Latin versions of tutus, variant past participle of tuēr, which means *to guard* (Encyclopedia Britannica, 2005). According to Roman legend, a tutor is seen as a treasurer or keeper, who guards, protects, watches over, or has care of some person or thing. The definition extends to one who has the charge of a child or pupil and his estate—*a guardian*.

To arrive at a satisfactory description of an online tutor within the context of this research study, it is first necessary to have a look at the complexity of settings in which tutoring may occur.

Tutoring can take place in the following environments:

- **Stand-alone learning materials** refer to learning materials that are set out in such a way that students can learn *without* the help of a lecturer or instructor. These materials are often known as *tutorials*, and the learning materials themselves act as the tutor. Contrary to popular belief, the concept of stand-alone learning materials is not a new phenomenon. Boyden (1965) observed that the first violin tutors were essentially *do-it-yourself* books. Such books flourished during the 17th and 18th centuries not only in music but in many other fields as well.

- **The computer as tutor:** The learning materials are set out as a computer-based learning package that guides learners through a specific course. Online tutorials are usually stand-alone learning packages, and the learner is supported by interactive activities and self-assessments. Many CD-ROM packages were developed during 1987-2000 as stand-alone instructional computer packages to train students in a wide variety of fields and software applications (Van der Westhuizen, 2004).

- **Intelligent tutoring design systems:** Systems such as these use a combination of delivery media (CD-ROM, Web site, Streaming media). Most of traditional intelligent techniques applied online learning environments can be roughly classified into three groups, which we will name as technologies:

curriculum sequencing, interactive problem solving support, and intelligent analysis of student solutions. All these technologies are aimed at supporting the *intelligent* duties of the human teacher, which cannot be supported by traditional non-intelligent tutoring systems (Brusilovsky, 1992, 1995).

- **The tutor as learning facilitator within the online environment:** For the purpose of this study, the tutor is a *person* that provides support to the students and assistance to the lecturer, within the online (Web-based) environment. The learning materials are delivered on a computer within a learning management system, and interactive activities and self-assessments may be part of the learning content, but the learner is also supported by means of asynchronous and synchronous online communication methods facilitated and facilitated by a tutor (Collison et al., 2000; Salmon, 2000).

Based on the previously mentioned descriptions, the 21st century concept of a tutor may vary from anything referring to a stand-alone computer-based package or a teaching assistant (also known as mentor, coach, or facilitator) that has the task of assisting the student with learning (Collison et al., 2000; Salmon, 2000; Van der Westhuizen, 2004). Irrespective, however, of the description of the concept *tutor*, the responsibility remains to instruct, support, facilitate, and in some instances assess the learner with regard to a specific set of learning tasks.

For the purpose of this study the tutor is seen as a *person* that provides support within the online environment by means of computer-mediated communication online (asynchronous and synchronous communication). Within the context of this research study, the lecturer provides academic content and moderation, and the tutor, similar to a teaching assistant, provides additional learning support (therefore working under the guidance and supervision of a lecturer).

One may argue that the tutor remains a modern-day version of a guardian, watching and guarding over the learning that is taking place in a specific learning environment, not unlike *Chiron,* the kindly centaur who tutored heroes (Encyclopaedia Britannica, 2005).

With this charge in mind, the tutor has an important role to play in terms of student motivation, retention, and attrition rates. The following section will focus further on student retention and the relation with distance education and tutorial programs.

Studies on Student Retention

Authors Berge and Yi-Ping (2004) made the following worrying observation:

In a recent review, the Institute for Higher Education Policy (IHEP, 1999) suggested that current research did not adequately explain why dropout rates in distance education are higher than with in-person education. Factors affecting retention or attrition decisions are complex and constantly evolving. In today's environment, the understanding of retention is becoming even more complex, particularly with the changing landscapes in learner demography, roles, and responsibilities; learning opportunity, needs and perceptions; and modes of instruction and learning. (p. 3)

While the study of retention in distance education is not new, the study of online learning retention is a relatively new area for research (Berge & Yi-Ping, 2004). Most of the existing models of retention were built on retention research of campus-based traditional learners and non-traditional learners (Bean, 1985; Boshier, 1973). *Student success* has become one of the primary factors in discussions of higher education quality, especially the quality of online programs (Devlin & Tia, 2003).

For the purpose of this study, the following terms are understood as follows (Bean & Metzner, 1985; Berge & Yi-Ping, 2004):

- Retention is continued student participation in a learning event to completion, which in higher education could be a course, program, institution, or system.
- Attrition is a decline in the number of students from the beginning to the end of the course, program, institution, or system under review.
- Persistence is the result of students' decisions to continue their participation in the learning event under analysis.

The following table represents some of the main models that were developed over recent years to grapple with the understanding of the problems associated with student retention.

Studies on student retention can roughly be categorized into the following categories, depending on the emphasis they give to individual and environmental forces, namely psychological, societal, economical, organizational, interactional, and holistic theories:

- **Psychological theories** on student persistence focus on individual personality traits, which distinguish those students who persist from those who do not complete their program of study. Retention is viewed as being dependent upon the individual's ability to complete successfully the requirements of the institution (e.g. Boshier, 1973; Powell, Conway, & Ross, 1990).
- **Societal/environmental theories** stress the roles of social status, race, prestige, and opportunity relative to student persistence, or they examine the barriers and hurdles that students have to overcome (Boshier, 1973; Kember, 1989; Spady, 1970. External forces are stressed in the process of student retention, as suggested by the Spady model (Spady, 1970).
- **Economic theories** of student departure emphasize the importance of individual finances and financial aid in student retention. There is little evidence to support the contention that financial forces are paramount to individual retention decisions. The financial situation was taken into account in the decision regarding entry, that is where and whether to attend in the first place (Manski & Wise, 1983). When students' experiences are positive they are more likely to accept greater financial burdens in order to continue their attendance (Kember, 1989).
- **Organizational theories** stress the impact of such variables as size of institution, stu-

Table 1. Main models on student retention

Explanatory Sociological Model of the Dropout Process (Spady, 1970)
A Model to Explain Adult Education Participation and Dropout (Boshier, 1973)
Longitudinal Model of Individual Departure (Tinto, 1975, 1993)
Conceptual Model for Research on Student-Faculty Informal Contact (Pascarella, 1980)
Conceptual Model of Dropout Syndrome (Bean, 1985)
Model of Dropout From Distance Education (Kember, 1989)
A Multivariate Framework for Analyzing Success and Persistence in Distance Education (Powell, Conway, & Ross, 1990)
The Model (Boyles, 2000)
A Model for Sustainable Student Retention: A Holistic Perspective on the Student Dropout Problem with Specific Attention to E-Learning (Berge & Yi-Ping, 2004)

dent/teacher ratios, institutional goals, and organizational structure on student departure rates. These factors appear to be more important in residential degree-granting institutions (e.g., Boyles, 2000).

- **Interactional theories** look at the fit between what a student expects from an institution and how well he/she integrates into the social and academic environment. Tinto's (1975) study is the major work in this area. Pascarella and Chapman in a 1983 study found that academic integration had an effect on institutional commitment for both four-year and two-year commuter post-secondary institutions, but social integration had no effect on persistence. Voorhees studied the social integration model on community colleges. He suggested that academic integration may be less important in explaining persistence of community college students compared to four-year University students (Voorhees, 1987).

- **Holistic theories** claim that reviewing the research and theoretical literature has shown the complexity and multi-dimensional nature of the retention phenomenon. Powell stated that *"even sophisticated multivariate studies have been hampered by the use of a limited range of measures and a lack of standardized measures, and the use of single items to measure broad concepts"* (Pascarella, Smart, & Ethington, 1986; Powell et al., 1990, p. 23). Holistic theories try to identify dynamic and customizable framework that take into consideration the significant variables and the interconnectivities among personal, institutional and circumstantial factors (Berge & Ya-Ping, 2004).

It has long been assumed that "completion of the program of studies undertaken" should be the goal of the student; however, in effect, especially the mature or adult student may have a different goal (Haiden, 2003; Hodges, 2003). The student's goal may be *to be able to find employment*; when they do, hence when the goal is achieved, they leave the program (Boyles, 2000; Darlaston-Jones, Cohen, Pike, Young, & Drew, 2003).

The focus of this study will be, however, not to determine the factors for student dropout, but to determine if a well-structured tutor support program will have an impact on student *motivation,* and thereby increasing student retention and throughput (persistence).

Reddy and Srivastava (2002) observe that distance education educators have tried to stimulate face-to-face communication through the development of instructional systems based on such technologies as audio conferencing, teleconferencing, audio graphic communication systems, videoconferencing, and computer-mediated communication between learners and teachers. There exists a recognized need to provide students with opportunities for human computer interaction (HCI) to support effective learning. The next section will discuss the role of online tutoring (facilitation) in respect to student retention.

ONLINE TUTORING AND STUDENT RETENTION

Mature or adult students probably leave higher education for reasons far different from those identified in Tinto's model of student attrition (Tinto, 1982, 1993a, 1993b). For example, social integration, important in Tinto's model, appears to have little empirical support as a reason for explaining non-traditional college attrition (Pascarella & Chapman, 1983).

As online learning moves from a marginal to an integral part of the overall educational and training arenas, questions and interventions related to learner success (however *success* is defined) are of both theoretical and practical importance (Berge & Yi-Ping, 2004; Powell et al., 1990). Personal interaction between learners and a tutor provides motivation, guidance, feedback, assessment, and support for learners.

The tutor's role in online learning includes moderating online discussions, facilitating group learning, problem solving, and guidance. However, there have not yet been practical proposals concerning *scaling up* online learning so that it can manage even current learner-tutor ratios handled by conventional distance learning, much less the usually large learner numbers facing open and distance learning providers (Lentell & O'Rourke, 2004; Salmon, 2000).

Since there are so many various ways of tutoring in the online environment, it became important to ensure some level of consistency amongst the various tutors and how they will be facilitating in the online environment, for the purpose of this study.

Therefore, included in the tutorial hours per study period would be participation in Open Universities Australia-provided training provided for the tutors in online learning facilitation, preparation of a facilitated introductory asynchronous discussion, facilitation of initial, mid-term (or around first assignment) contact, and pre-final-exam contact, as well as as-needed responses to individuals.

The identified tutors are expected to:

- Complete whatever professional development the university provides regarding how to teach online (how to conduct discussions, etc.).
- Complete a workshop on online tutoring with particular attention to adult student population.
- Provide 30 hours (3 tutorial hours×10) per study period of additional online tutoring above what would ordinarily be provided funded).
- Keep records of strategies they use and time devoted to additional tutoring (tutor log sheets).

Tutors are required to submit a log sheet of hours and online activities spent on tutor support (see Appendix A). All units will be surveyed at four intervals during the year to determine the students' overall unit satisfaction, and also asking specific feedback about tutor support. Student re-enrolment history for the various study periods will also be monitored.

Open Universities Australia conducts regular student unit satisfaction surveys on the unit offerings for each study period, completed as an online questionnaire. Relevant findings from these unit satisfaction surveys for the particular units will be incorporated in the quantitative data analysis of the study, to ensure further reliability and validity of the data.

Online Tutorial Support

Unlike in a classroom setting (face-to-face facilitation), the online tutor may never meet his/her students face to face. This absence of "faces" and lack of non-verbal cues is often the most important reason why students and facilitators may feel frustrated or isolated in this environment (Dewar & Whittington, 2000). A case study conducted by Bullen (1998) showed that some students felt disconnected from others in the online environment, citing lack of facial expressions and other features common to a traditional classroom environment.

Richardson and Swan (2003) furthermore argue that, not the lack of non-verbal communication, but a diminished *social presence* is the underlying reason for feelings of isolation. In an online environment, the rules for communication may be different from that of face-to-face facilitation, but the students can still benefit from facilitated discussion.

Effective online interaction will depend on how well the facilitator makes use of the online environment and the communication tools available. Table 2 highlights some of the immediate

Table 2. Differences between face-to-face and online tutorial interaction (Smith, 2000)

Face-to-face	Online
Emphasis on verbal skills	Emphasis on written skills
Summarizing "on the spot"	Time to reflect on summaries
Single conversation thread	Multiple conversations threads
Time and space limited	Time and space unlimited or variable
Content ephemeral	Content recorded
Managing equality of student contributions	Encouraging "lurkers" to participate

Table 3. Characteristics of effective online facilitators (Berge & Collins, 1995; Bruckman, 2002; Collison et al., 2000)

Characteristics of effective online facilitators	
Flexible	Modify learning and assessment activities before and during use to fit the learning objectives and learner profiles.
Adaptive	Adapt learning and assessment activities and techniques to changing circumstances.
Proactive	Plan learning activities proactively according to the learner profiles and the purpose of the activity.
Responsive	Be responsive to the learning and social needs of learners.
Resilient	Accept whatever happens during the learning activity as valuable in terms of the learning taking place.

differences between face-to-face and online learning facilitation interaction:

How do we distinguish between effective and not-so-effective online facilitation? From literature (Berge & Collins, 1995; Bruckman, 2002; Collison et al., 2000), effective online tutors demonstrate some distinctive characteristics as summarized in Table 3.

Following are some of the most important roles that an online facilitator would be expected to perform within the online learning environment (Richardson & Swan, 2003).

• **The online tutor as facilitator:** The online tutor should be able to point students to appropriate sources of information. The main aim is to enhance the learners' ability to search, find, integrate, and evaluate information from various sources, including textbooks, journals, online articles, subject experts, peers, and so forth.

• **The online tutor as coach and mentor:** There will be many times when the online tutor will need to act as a coach and mentor, helping to facilitate learning rather than presenting content directly. This role is especially important in an online environment where students may be working for long periods on their own initiative.

• **The online tutor as assessor:** With some self-paced online courses, assessment is integral to the study materials, and the online tutor is not required to conduct the assessment, but rather to facilitate students conducting their own reflective self-assessment and in some instances, peer-assessment, to develop their critical and analytical thinking skills.

Some academic courses, however, require the online tutor to conduct an assessment of the nature and extent of the learner's knowledge and skills.

These characteristics of the tutor often go hand-in-hand with the various roles that the online tutor performs, and may influence how these roles are executed. The role of the tutor can be altered to become more akin to a facilitator than a lecturer, while the role of students can be altered by allowing them to become active learners. Certain elements of record keeping can help the online tutor structure the facilitation process, as discussed in the following section.

ELEMENTS OF RECORD KEEPING

Once expectations have been discussed, they should be translated into an individual learning contract for each student. The contract defines the parameters for the way you work together.

This learning contract should be drawn up by both the facilitator and the learner. The learning contract may include the following (Berge & Collins, 1995; Bruckman, 2002; Collison et al., 2000):

- Learner's plan for the course
- Expectations of the online tutor—what can the student expect of him or her?
- Expectations of the student—what can the facilitator expect of him or her?
- Methods that will be used for communication and the basis for selecting each method
- Rules governing communication—times of day, frequency of communication, response

times (these rules should preferably be set within negotiation with the learners)
- Basis on which the learner's progress will be assessed

Records of tutor activities (tutor logs) allow the online learning facilitator to document and review the delivery of educational services. Conscientious record keeping may also benefit online learning facilitators themselves, by guiding them to plan and implement an appropriate course of learning support services, to review work as a whole, and to self-monitor more precisely. Maintenance of appropriate records may also be relevant for a variety of other institutional, financial, and legal purposes (Haiden, 2003).

In addition, well-documented records may help protect online learning facilitators from professional liability, if they become the subject of legal or ethical proceedings.

In these circumstances, the principal issue will be the professional action of the online learning facilitator, as reflected in part by the records:

- **Content of records:** Records include any information (including information stored in a computer) that may be used to document the nature, delivery, progress, or results of learning services. Records can be reviewed and duplicated.
- **Construction and control of records:** Records are organized in a manner that facilitates their use by the online learning facilitator and other authorized persons. Online learning facilitators strive to assure that record entries are legible. Records are to be completed in a timely manner. Records may be maintained in research purposes, so long as their utility, confidentiality, and durability are assured.

Following is an example of an overall course structure plan that includes the format, learner activities, tutor activities, as well as time frame

Table 4. Example: SSK12, Introduction to university learning (Murdoch University)

Overall learning objective: To apply the concept of culture to the university setting				
	Format	Learner Activities	Tutor activities	Timeframe/ Scheduling
Content	Lectures Text book Readers Website	Reading textbook, journal articles and reader Internet searches Library searches	Frequently Asked Questions Internet search guidelines	1 lesson / per week 1 topic / per month
Learning events	Online reflective journal Debates/ discussions on discussion forum Analyzing case studies Projects Reports	Writing learning log, essays Discussion: online and face to face	Guidelines for report writing Moderating and guiding discussion Provide examples	Indicate lessons in online calendar Set up forums on discussion board
Assessment: Continuous assessment tasks	Self-assessment after each lesson Peer-assessment after each topic Facilitator assessment	Essay questions Multiple-choice questions Short questions	FAQ for answering multiple choice Giving feedback on essay and short questions	Timely feedback upon assignment submission
Assessment: Final exam questions	Facilitator assessment	Exam essay questions	Final exam at end of study period	Timely feedback and marks for final exam

and scheduling. Integration of the tutor activities within the overall course structure is key to ensuring that these activities are coherent with the learning outcomes.

The best way to motivate adult students is simply to enhance their reasons for enrolling and decrease the barriers. A student evaluation sheet can be used to determine motivation and barriers to interaction in the online learning environment, as shown in the following example.

Records of education services minimally include (a) identifying student data, (b) dates of services, (c) types of services, (d) any assessment, plan for intervention, summary reports, and/or supporting data as may be appropriate, and (e)

any release of information obtained for research purposes (see tutor log page example).

In order to conduct a successful online discussion, it is important that the learning activity event should be planned. The next section will look at barriers within that adult learners may face within the online learning environment.

BARRIERS TO ONLINE LEARNING TUTORIAL SUPPORT

Online learning tutorial support occurs when the facilitation of the communication takes place in an electronic, Web-based, or computer-based environment (Collison et al., 2000). Elements that can be identified in an online tutorial (facilitation) system to help improve retention rates for distance learners are as follows.

An online tutor (facilitator) will, however, be entering a profession for which no clear-cut rules have been established. Online learning facilitation is mainly geared at achieving the following:

- Provide online opportunities, resources, and encouragement for the group to succeed in achieving its learning objectives.
- Empower students to take control and responsibility for their efforts, progress, and achievement.

Furthermore, there may be a variety of possible reasons why students would resist participating in an online discussion forum:

- Being unfamiliar or uncomfortable with using computers, e-mail, or e-mail lists. Some people may need time and experience to adapt; a little bit of training could be helpful.
- A fear of displaying one's writing abilities. It is very helpful to establish a norm where all writing styles are accepted, including

Table 5. Example of a student evaluation

Student Evaluation of discussion or learning event
Name:_____ Date: _____
Topic: _____
Your topic _____
When you initiated discussion: Who responded to your topic? Were the questions asked relevant to your topic? Did the questions build on your ideas and continue the discussion? Explain how you know whether or not your answer was comprehended.
When you were the participant: 4 – High, 3 – Medium, 2 – Low, 1 – No interest Rate your interest level   4   3   2 1 Rate your comprehension level 4   3   2   1 Rate your courtesy level   4   3   2 1 What were the most important questions you asked? Was your question answered to your satisfaction?
Assessment: What skills are necessary to become a productive member of the group? Explain in what way your group successfully discussed the topics. Which skills did you efficiently use to aid your group?

being casual and making errors in spelling and grammar.

- A fear of "going public." People may worry that someone might save their messages and later use them as "ammunition" against them. This anxiety may coincide with the worry that people outside the group may have access to the list or may be given e-mail by a group member.
- Anger, withdrawal, indifference. These emotional barriers are most likely a symptom of interpersonal dynamics within the group. The disinhibiting effect of e-mail communication may help people discuss and resolve these issues, but the lack of emotional cues may aggravate the problem.

Because of their varied responsibilities, adults also may have barriers against participating in learning. Some of these barriers include lack of time, money, confidence, or interest, lack of information about opportunities to learn, scheduling problems and problems with childcare, and transportation.

These barriers can cause learners to feel frustrated and isolated, and in turn have an impact on student retention. Further research can be conducted on how these barriers can be more effectively addressed and identified with additional online tutorial support. Following is the conclusion based on the preliminary project as well as the literature review.

CONCLUSION

The Latin word facilis means *to make easy, to remove obstacles, to lessen the labor of, to free from difficulties, to make easier, to help forward* (Encyclopedia Britannica, 2005). An online tutor, cast in the role of facilitator, will be required to lessen the burden of students in working with technology, and to make their learning experience as easy and *pain-free* as possible.

Bruckman (2002, p. 3) pleads: "Please don't have virtual classes where students sit behind virtual desks and teachers write on virtual blackboards. To do so combines some of the worst aspects of both traditional pedagogy and virtual worlds. Students learn better by working on personally meaningful projects than by being lectured to…"

Effective online tutorial will include the following:

- **Learning contract**, completed at the beginning of the unit, outlining previous difficulties with study and specific strategies to address these over the current semester
- **Tutorial worksheets,** based on exercises carried out in computer labs
- **Assessment records**, that is, self-assessment sheets, blogs, peer-assessment sheets, facilitator feedback
- **Evidence of online participation** (interaction on WebCT/Blackboard class discussion site)
- **Reflective statement** on students own learning and progress in the unit, to be completed toward the end of the semester
- **Tutor logs** for recordkeeping
- **Overall integration of tutorial activities** related to learning outcomes and learning activities in the course curriculum

Models describing student retention in distance education, the most prominent being Boyles (2000), Bean and Metzner (1985), Pascarella (1980), and Tinto (1975), usually try to identify the variables and attributes that may *cause* premature student departure. Not many models tackle the problem of how student retention may be addressed, and even fewer provide suggestions on how student dropout figures may be *prevented*. A well-structured online tutor support intervention may be a viable option to increase the retention and academic success of distance learning, online students.

REFERENCES

Bean, J. P. (1985). Interaction effects based on class level in an explanatory model of college student dropout syndrome. *American Educational Research Journal, 22*(1), 35-64.

Bean, J. P., & Hull, D. (1984). *Determinants of black and white student attrition at a major southern university.* Paper presented at the American Education Research Association, New Orleans, LA.

Bean, J. P., & Metzner, B. S. (1985). A conceptual model of nontraditional undergraduate student attrition. *Review of Educational Research, 55*(4), 485-540.

Berge, Z. L., & Collins, M. P. (Eds.). (1995). *Computer-mediated communication and the online classroom in distance education.* Cresskill, NJ: Hampton Press.

Berge, Z. L., & Yi-Ping, H. (2004), A model for sustainable student retention: A holistic perspective on the student dropout problem with specific attention to e-learning. *DeosNews, 13*(5), 1-26.

Boshier, B. (1973). Educational participation and dropout: A theoretical model. *Adult Education, 4*, 282-288.

Boyden, D. (1965). *The history of violin playing from its origins to 1761 and its relationship to the violin and violin music.* London: Oxford University Press.

Boyles, L. W. (2000). *Exploration of a retention model for community college student.* Unpublished doctoral dissertation, The University of North Carolina, Greensboro.

Bruckman, A. (2002). Co-evolution of technological design and pedagogy in an online learning community. In S. Barab, R. Gray, & J. Gray (Eds.), *Designing virtual communities in the service of learning.* Cambridge University Press.

Brusilovsky, P. (1995). Intelligent tutoring systems for World Wide Web. In *Proceedings of Third International WWW Conference* (pp. 42-45). Darmstadt.

Brusilovsky, P. L. (1992). A framework for intelligent knowledge sequencing and task sequencing. In C. Frasson, G. Gauthier, & G. I. McCalla (Eds.), *Intelligent tutoring systems. Lecture notes in computer science* (pp. 499-506). Berlin: Springer-Verlag.

Bullen, M. (1998). Participation and critical thinking in online university distance education. *Journal of Distance Education, 13*(2), 1-32.

Collison, G., Elbaum, B., Haavind, S., & Tinker, R. (2000). *Facilitating online learning: Effective strategies for moderators.* Madison, WI: Atwood Publishing.

Darlaston-Jones, D., Cohen, L.; H., S., Pike, L., Young, A., & Drew, N. (2003). The retention and persistence support (RAPS) project: A transition initiative. *Issues in Educational Research, 13*(2), 1-12.

Devlin, M., & Tjia, T. (2003). Beyond satisfaction surveys: The development of an evaluation process for a postgraduate transferable skills program. *Issues in Educational Research, 14*(1), 44-51.

Encyclopedia Britannica Online. (2005). Retrieved February 2006, from http://www.britannica.com/

Gravett, S., & Geyser, H. (Eds.). (2004). *Teaching and learning in higher education.* Pretoria: Van Schaik Publishers.

Haiden, G. A. (2003, July). *Students' perceptions of academic support designed to counter the effects of "underpreparedness".* Paper presented at the 7th Pacific Rim First Year in Higher Education Conference, Queensland University of Technology, Brisbane, Australia.

Hodges, T. K. (2002). *Linking learning and performance: A practical guide to measuring learning and on-the-job application.* Boston: Butterworth Heinemann.

Kember, D. (1989). A longitudinal-process model of dropout from distance education. *Journal of Higher Education, 60*(3), 278-301.

Lentell, H., & O'Rourke, J. (2004). Tutoring large numbers: An unmet challenge. *International Review of Research in Open and Distance Learning,* April. Retrieved January 2006, from http://www.irrodl.org/content/v5.1/lentell_orourke.html

London, J. (2004). *OLA Student and Portal Members Online Survey Results.* Unpublished statistical report, Open Universities Australia, Melbourne.

Macdonald, J., & Hills, L. (2005). Combining reflective logs with electronic networks for professional development among distance education tutors. *Distance Education, 26*(3), 325-339.

Manski, C. F., & Wise, A. D. (1983). *College choice in America.* Cambridge, MA: Harvard University Press.

Open University Australia. (2005). *Annual Report.* Unpublished document. Retrieved from http://www.open.edu.au

Pascarella, E. T. (1980). Student-faculty informal contact and college outcomes. *Review of Educational Research, 50*(4), 545-595.

Pascarella, E. T., & Chapman, D. W. (1983). A multi-institutional, path analytic validation of Tinto's model of college withdrawal. *American Educational Research Journal, 20*(1), 87-102.

Pascarella, E. T., Smart, J. C., & Ethington, C. A. (1986). Long-term persistence of two-year college students. *Research in Higher Education, 24*(1), 47-71.

Powell, R., Conway, C., & Ross, L. (1990). Effects of student predisposing characteristics on student success. *Journal of Distance Education, 5*(1), 20-37.

Reddy, V. V., & Srivastava, M. (2002). From face-to-face to virtual tutoring: Exploring the potential of e-learning support. In V. Phillips (Ed.), *Motivating & retaining adult learners online.* GetEducated.com, LLC. Retrieved January 2006, from http://www.geteducated.com

Richardson, J. C., & Swan, K. (2003). Examining social presence in online courses in relation to students' perceived learning and satisfaction. *Journal of Asynchronous Learning Networks, 7*(1), 68-77.

Salmon, G. (2000). *E-moderating: The key to teaching and learning online.* London: Kogan Page.

Smith, B. (2000). Teaching online: New or transferable skills. *The Higher Education Academy.* Retrieved January 2006, from http://www.heacademy.ac.uk/embedded_object.asp?id=21664&filename=Smith

Spady, W. (1970). Dropouts from higher education: An interdisciplinary review and synthesis. *Interchange, 1,* 64-65.

Tinto, V. (1975). Dropouts from higher education: A theoretical synthesis of the recent literature. *A Review of Educational Research, 45,* 89-125. University of Chicago, 1965-1969.

Tinto, V. (1993a). *Leaving college: Rethinking the causes and cures of student attrition.* Chicago: University of Chicago Press.

Tinto, V. (1993b). *Leaving college: Rethinking the causes and cures of student attrition* (2nd ed.). Chicago: University of Chicago Press.

Van der Westhuizen, D. (2004). The design and development of a Web-based learning environment. In S. Gravett & H. Geyser (Eds.), *Teaching and learning in higher education.* Pretoria: Van Schaik Publishers.

Voorhees, R. (1987). Toward building models of community college persistence: A logit analysis. *Research in Higher Education, 26*(2), 115-129.

Whittington, D., & Dewar, T. (2000). A strategy for studying learners using advanced learning technologies. In *Advanced Learning Technologies, IWALT Proceedings.* International Workshop, New Zealand.

Chapter IV
Enhancing Learning Through Mobile Computing

Marsha Berry
RMIT University, Australia

Margaret Hamilton
RMIT University, Australia

Naomi Herzog
RMIT University, Australia

Lin Padgham
RMIT University, Australia

Ron Van Schyndel
RMIT University, Australia

ABSTRACT

The mission of this chapter is to explore ways in which mobile computing via the employment of Tablet PCs can assist the human computer interaction in the design and project development process and thereby enhance learning. We follow the process of ethnographic action research and report on the learning, observations, and communications of students in a multimedia program who were given the use of a Tablet PC for their second year of their degree. We discuss the educational design and customized agent software developed for this project and draw conclusions for wireless networks, and benefits and issues involved in enabling mobile computing and encouraging group dynamics among students.

INTRODUCTION

It is interesting to consider how much people learn when mobile. When on the train traveling from home to university all manner of observations might influence the way a person thinks and reinforce some learning experience. It is also often a good time to revise notes before an exam or interview. Similarly, when walking from one lecture to another or over to the cafeteria, students may exchange information that contributes greatly to their learning. In the study discussed in this book chapter, we observe and analyze the learning experiences of students who were each given a Tablet PC for a semester of their course.

Ethnographic action research is a methodology for investigating the impact of technology on a community. It was first devised in 2002 to explore the use of computers on communities in India (Tacchi, Slater, & Hearn, 2004). Its principles are that one change rarely impacts on only one individual, and changing one aspect may affect many other aspects of a student's life within his or her community.

BACKGROUND

In this chapter we report our research into mobile computing and the design process. This research has been supported by HP Mobile Technology for Teaching Grant Initiative—2004 Higher Education, and we have undertaken exploratory ethnographic action research to explore and analyze to what extent Tablet PCs enhance learning within the context of students learning the design development process.

Formal RMIT student surveys (the top 10 student concerns are available through RMIT University) indicate that students would like to engage more fully with the University and fellow students in a manner that meets both their social and academic needs. Observations and conclusions drawn from this research indicate that students:

- undertake more hours of paid employment to support their study costs, resulting in increased pressure to maximize time and resources in academic hours;
- want to interact with the University in ways that best suit their personal circumstances and preferred learning practices; and
- have limited amounts of quality contact time with fellow students on campus.

Tablet PCs have the potential to facilitate students' engagement with the University and fellow students in a manner that does meet their social and academic needs, and our research explores the extent to which this may occur through the use of mobile computing devices.

We chose students from a multimedia design degree (Bachelor of Design [Multimedia Systems]) for this study because they spend considerable time engaged in group projects. It is also a challenging use of mobile technology as students spend time generating, analyzing, and collaborating around images. The students are diverse, with academic interests ranging from creative media design to software development. The aim of this study trial is to explore new methods for applying mobile technologies within both formal and ad hoc study groups. Students from the multimedia design program are generally expected to work in their groups both in and outside of the classroom on design projects. Interaction between students is not moderated; rather it is supported by a learning program that emphasizes team skills. Students enrolled in this program are typically local school leavers and have completed Year 12 Mathematics and English. A very small proportion is international students, mainly drawn from China and India. The students are enrolled in two design courses that require teamwork and collaboration for one semester.

Applications used in multimedia design are typically central processing unit (cpu) intensive and require a large display screen with keyboard, mouse, and WACOM (registered brand name) Tablet as input devices. The Tablet PCs with digitized screen, and pen and ink technology present an opportunity to explore the extent to which Tablet PCs may become an enabling technology for students learning design processes. A detailed description of Tablet PCs follows in Table 1.

The features we believe to be enabling are the digitized screen and ink technology, wireless capability, which means we can examine the use of enabling Web technologies such as blogs, and mobility, which means that students may capture inspiration as and when it occurs and store it locally on the hard drive or in a blog when in a wireless zone.

THE DESIGN PROCESS

The design process can be described as cyclical with iterative loops whereby an initial idea is developed into a concept. Feedback is sought and then the concept is expanded further into a proof of concept (in this case electronic) and finally manufactured into a product (in this case a Web site) that is ready for consumption with feedback sought and integrated at key junctures in the production process.

The participants in the study reported in this chapter were drawn from the students enrolled in a core second year design course of a Bachelor of Design (multimedia systems) degree program. In this particular course students engage in a group project where they design and build a Web site for a client so as to gain direct experience of working for a client with specific team role responsibilities. The student learning is scaffolded through a design and production process modeled on a simulated student-centered work-based learning approach that is described in the following section.

Workplace-Based Learning

Industry practice is often explored and tested in an educational institution via simulated projects that seek to meet specific and relevant learning outcomes. However, a simulated project can be less than effective as it often may lack critical detail and commercial imperatives to solve specific problems and challenges.

Central to the strategy of situated learning in the workplace is the direct experience and subsequent knowledge gained in the process. However, guided learning in the workplace can be limited due to commercial constraints and lack of mentoring skills and processes. In the absence of a structured pathway of learning, students are required to integrate the formal theory gained in a university and practical knowledge gained in the workplace.

Leaving learners, particularly novices, to piece together a picture of the complex workplace environment without guidance is more likely to result in incorrect and fragmented understandings. (Cornford & Beven, 1999)

The issue then is how to integrate the hands-on learning that occurs in industry and then bring that back into a formal learning environment that will assist in contextualizing their experiences and skills gained.

Guided learning can augment many of the strengths of learning through everyday activity, and also be able to address some of its weaknesses. (Billet, 2001)

As Billet proposes, a combination of strategies is required to achieve a meaningful outcome for students. An integration of the strengths of the workplace-based model, coupled with the benefits of a face-to-face learning environment (such as a tutorial seminar program) and underpinned by a lecture program would provide an effective structure in which to enhance learning outcomes.

In the absence of situated learning where students are located in the workplace, the structure of the curriculum focuses on the development of commercial projects over the duration of the semester within the educational institution. Students form small working groups within their tutorial classes and are provided with a commercial project and a client.

The design of this problem-based learning environment supports constructivist teaching and learning practices. Students are guided through a process that encourages, through the design process, a construction of knowledge and understanding based on direct experience. Savoie and Hughes (1994), outline several actions to put this into effect:

- Identify a problem suitable for the students;
- Connect the problem with the context of the students' world so that it presents authentic opportunities;
- Organize the subject matter around the problem, not the discipline;
- Give students responsibility for defining their learning experience and planning to solve the problem;
- Encourage collaboration by creating learning teams;
- Expect all students to demonstrate the results of their learning through a product or performance.

The forming strategies presented to the students are drawn from the Savoie and Hughes (1994) outline of actions. Students form work teams comprising of three to five individuals based on friendship groups.

MOBILE COMPUTING AND THE DESIGN PROCESS

Like those in the design industry, students often work together in concentrated patches, and then continue development largely on their own. They frequently juggle multiple projects and other concerns. Communication can be patchy and often is not centralized. Retrieval of communication items and files can also be unreliable. The result may take up valuable resources and development time and manifest in poor outcomes, frustration, and lack of momentum.

Development of a communication strategy and document retrieval process has been implemented to facilitate the design and development process. This is made possible by the use of mobile computing in the form of streamlining processes. The group members are asked to maintain a personal blog (Weblog) that is intended to provide a record of their research into their specific area of concern, and at the same time, also make this research transparent to the rest of the group. A Rich Site Summary (RSS) aggregate has been put in place to alert other team members that the new posts are up on the blog and can be viewed at their convenience. RSS is described in wikipedia as:

RSS is a family of Web feed formats, specified in eXtensible Markup Language (XML) and used for Web syndication. RSS is used by (among other things) news Web sites, Weblogs, and podcasting. The abbreviation is variously used to refer to the following standards:

- Rich Site Summary (RSS 0.91)
- Resource Description Framework (RDF) Site Summary (RSS 0.9 and 1.0)
- Really Simple Syndication (RSS 2.0)

Web feeds provide Web content or summaries of Web content together with links to the full versions of the content and other metadata. RSS in particular delivers this information as an XML file called an RSS feed, Web feed, RSS stream, or RSS channel. In addition to facilitating syndication, Web feeds allow a Web site's frequent readers to track updates on the site using an aggregator. (http://en.wikipedia.org/wiki/RSS_%28file_format%29)

RSS feeds allow people to remain up to date with changes that have been made to a blog or Web site that they visit regularly. An aggregator is a way of getting a customized and consolidated view of all the sites one regularly visits.

A group blog has also been set up to facilitate group communication. The groups use these in different ways:

- introduction of a new item of interest to the group overall;
- meeting minutes and actions to be taken;
- posting up documents, drafts, or approved designs;
- general considerations or concerns to the group;
- miscellaneous items such as notification of next meetings, introduction of new group members, and communication with tutor/exec producer.

Additionally, a client blog (now largely standard industry practice) has been put into place, with clients being given read and write access to monitor development and design of their project. This has been particularly useful in confirming outcomes and minimizing unnecessary client contact (usually in place to prevent clients from being uniformed).

Customized agent software has also been developed to facilitate document retrieval and assist in the process of design and programming. The agent is required to locate files on the server via a server agent and report back to the Tablet holder using a Tablet agent to notify updates to files and filing systems.

The overall intentions of these items are to:

- maintain communication across the groups and their clients;
- provide a map of next steps and actions;
- maintain momentum and focus throughout the design process;
- help members locate themselves within the framework of the group (particularly useful when they are involved in other projects or other commitments);
- aid group dynamics as lack of communication can contribute heavily to unsuccessful outcomes;
- enable contact maintenance with the client.

Tablet Personal Computers and the Wireless Network

Sixteen Hewlett Packard TC1100 Tablet PCs are given to the students, as well as three docking stations and two digital cameras for shared use. This creates an excellent opportunity to test two different aspects of mobility: wireless networking and the differences between the Tablet PCs and desktop computers.

The first aspect of mobility is the wireless ad-hoc networking made possible by the hardware. This enables two different kinds of interactions: person-to-person (via WiFi or Bluetooth—a short-range networking protocol chiefly used for wireless peripheral control or file transfer) and person-to-blog/server via WiFi—a longer-range networking protocol that is principally used for wireless network access.

As shown in the student comments later in this chapter, significant use is made of the wireless components, due partly to the communicative nature of the projects, and partly to the particular team assignment work.

One problem we encounter in implementing the system is the use of a specialized network protocol for the communication between agent and server (the agent system is described in more detail in the next section). A previously unallocated TCP/IP port (or channel number) is used as the communication port by default. Although the software allows any port to be chosen, it needs to be the same port for all tablets, as they must all use the same channel. In addition, the network needs to know that this port has been allocated for specific use, and all appropriate permissions need to be obtained. This effectively means that although the project can exist on a wireless network, that network has to be preconfigured to accept it.

While wireless networks exist that will accept any port (and thus need no such pre-configuration), they are generally insecure because of this blanket acceptance policy. The alternative is to allow the network packets of information to be encrypted on the Tablet PC and at the server end. This is effectively a virtual private network (VPN). The use within our University of a VPN as the wireless medium initially causes some concern because of the necessity to customize the VPN settings for using this port. In addition, our security policies do not directly allow access to the Internet (via port 80—the HTTP "channel") and prevent direct access to the internal wired network.

Students are required to access their blogs, which are installed on a server on the wired intranet. For this project, special provision and permissions are required to enable access to this server from the wireless network. This exposes the server to the wireless network, exchanging its internal security status for the wireless security arrangements. So the safety of a private intranet needs to be exchanged for that for a VPN. Because of the differing security models for these two configurations, we recommend that it would be preferable in future to have a wirelessly accessed server dedicated to this task alone, and any unrelated server activity be moved to a different separate internally wired server.

The second aspect of mobility that the students are exposed to is the user interface differences to a desktop computer. As seen in Table 1, the Tablet PCs have a keyboard, a screen that can be separated from the keyboard, a pen or stylus, and appropriate software to accept pen gestures, commands, and handwriting storage and recognition. For this Tablet PC, the keyboard is normally intended to be used only for extended text entry, and the pen used for normal Tablet functionality.

The tasks the students undertake often involve drawing and sketching (see the included software in Table 1), so it is encouraging to see some students using the pen in all activities, while others are content to use it only when appropriate.

The principal difference between a pen and a mouse depends on the dialog mode—input or selection mode. Neither pen nor mouse works in isolation as a positional input device. In both cases, these move a cursor, which is the positional input coordinate identifier. Herein lies the difference. A mouse moves the cursor using relative coordinates, which implies that the cursor's initial position is known to the user. So to press a button on the screen, the user must home in the cursor to the button, and then press the mouse button to select/activate. Moving the cursor is a necessarily interactive process, and any person who has experienced slow mouse response lag can appreciate the crucial dependence on interactivity that the mouse requires. Contrast this with a pen, where the user identifies the target button and using his/her hand positions the pen to the target. No intermediate interactivity is required to enable accurate positioning.

In input mode, the difference between pen and mouse is smaller, and more subject to personal taste. The benefit of the mouse is consistent hand positioning, support for the wrist and elbow, and having the hands away from the desktop so that it is always visible (note that these are all desktop-based advantages). While pen has direct positioning and given fast interaction can easily be used for drawing, the arm is usually not in a comfortable position for long duration detailed work. However, quick sketches in a mobile context are easily facilitated. Lastly, the direct positioning

Table 1. Work environment summary

Number and kind of Tablet PC's	16 Hewlett Packard TC1100 Tablet PCs
Hardware Configuration	• Tablet PC with builtin microphone • Detachable Keyboard • Pen/stylus • Earphones
Software Configuration (under University Licenses)	• Microsoft Windows XP Tablet Edition • Customised Agent Software • Microsoft Office (Word, Excel, Powerpoint, Frontpage); • Adobe Acrobat; • Macromedia products (Flash, Studio-MX2004); • Appropriate WiFi VPN network access software, including customised security and virus-checking software. This enables limited internet and university website access, but also allows wireless communication between Tablets; • Remote access to a personalised blog server for use in delayed project-related intercommunication and archiving. WordPress is installed on a server which is rendered visible to the WiFi network for student use.
Accessories for group use	3 docking stations, 2 digital cameras
Blog Server Hardware	Standard PC (Macintosh)
Blog software	WordPress
Number of students in whole class	80
Students involved in project	16 for individual work in semester 1, and team work for semester 2

of the cursor facilitates handwriting as easily as with a real pen, allowing text to be entered via handwriting recognition, a tool that some students have mentioned using in our study.

Customized Agent Software

Customized agent software has been developed, primarily for content synchronization between Tablets within each project group, and between Tablets and blog, or server-based data storage. Major check-points in content developments are stored on a communal server and could be accessed by participants and also the project coordinator(s) for progress verification and eventual project assessment.

We include an overview of the software model or architecture employed and the role each component plays in it. As will be explained in the next section, actual student usage of the software did not precisely follow the usage patterns envisaged by the previous design. However, this provides insight into the students' view of the environment, and how they adapt it for their own use.

Part of the process of designing a supportive environment includes the specification of the agent-based software. It must be able to provide automated support for a range of tasks such as proactive notification to students if the group files have been updated, to ensure that they check and access any relevant changes. This removes the tedium of repetitive manual checking. Intelligent

Figure 1. Team communication using three blogs

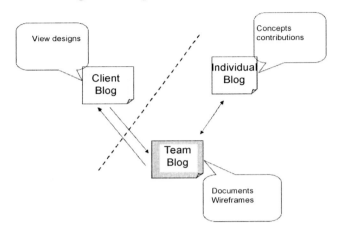

agents are a popular technology for open environments such as the Internet (Singh & Huhns, 2005). Small autonomous pieces of software (agents) can reside on different machines, and communicate with each other to achieve tasks. In this project we have an agent on each Tablet, which communicates with an agent on the central file server where files are located. Figure 1 shows the interaction between the agents that results in the user being notified if there are any updates.

While this initial task is quite straightforward, it is envisaged that there will be potentially a range of automated tasks that can be performed by the agent software on behalf of, or in support of the user. The intention is to interact with students to develop the particular support they will find useful. Observation of student behavior during the trial period indicates that the availability of the wireless network to the Tablets led to far less use of the central server and the file structure contained there than had been the case previously. Consequently we consider that it would be advantageous to adapt the agent software to better support the communication mechanisms the students actually use. For example they e-mail versions of their files to each other frequently. While this appears to have worked for this small project, this mechanism does not offer the same

level of backup and support as does storing files on the central file server. We could, for example, adapt the agent functionality to better support the way the participants end up doing things, by having the Tablet agent recognize when new files are sent to other team members, and automatically store these into the central server.

The agent approach used is what is referred to as *belief desire intention* (BDI) agents. This approach develops agents in terms of these mental concepts, as developed in philosophy, to explain how focused practical reasoning happens in humans (Bratman, 1987). Beliefs are the information that the agent has (or believes it has, as it may not always be accurate) about the world, other agents, or even itself. Desires are the goals the agent wishes to accomplish—which may arise based on information from the environment: for example, if a file is updated in the central repository, an agent managing that repository may then have a goal to ensure that all group members are notified of the change as soon as possible, potentially using various communication means such as e-mail or even sms, if the user is not accessible via the network. Intentions are the plans the agents has regarding how it *intends* to accomplish its goals. If, during execution of the plan, there is some problem, the agent will adapt

Figure 2. Specification of the customized agent-based software

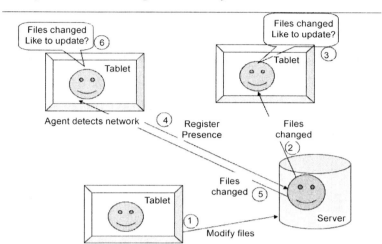

its intentions (or plans) to attempt to still achieve the goal. One advantage of this approach is the ease with which it can be adapted and evolved to manage an extremely large number of complex interactions regarding which decisions should be made. This enables the kind of support to be easily tailored to both very specific situations, and also to individual groups and/or users. For example the agent residing on a particular user's machine can build up beliefs regarding the way that user likes to work. Agent technology also facilitates pro-active behavior on the part of the system (to achieve *desires*, or goals). The agent software can persist in trying to achieve a particular goal (of which user notification of change is a simple example) using alternative approaches if attempts are unsuccessful. This makes it possible to build flexible and robust systems in dynamic environments.

Research Questions

In this research, we consider the question of how Tablet PCs help human computer interaction in the design and project development process. Our focus is on:

- The immediate circle of students in terms of how they are organized, how they carry out their work, and how the Tablet PC fits into their lives as students of multimedia design;
- The everyday lives of the participants, their ways of doing things, and the impact mobile technology in the form of wireless Tablet PCs has on this (if any);
- The construction of knowledge and meaning through the use of blogs and the impact mobile technology in the form of wireless Tablet PCs has on this (if any);
- The wider social context in terms of access to a wireless intranet, access to mobile computing, access to a personal blog.

Discourse analysis and ethnography provide the base for qualitative research into the contents of the blogs, structured interviews, and focus groups. Ethnography, in its literal sense, means "to write or represent a culture" (Tacchi et al., 2004). Ethnography is an approach that may encompass several methods rather than a specific methodology. The methods are integrated to provide a holistic account of a culture, in this case, students enrolled in the Bachelor of Design (multimedia systems) and their use of Tablet PCs in their everyday design studies. The structured interviews, informal feedback conversations with participants recorded as field notes by the researchers, questionnaires, blogs, and focus group conversations will be integrated so that the knowledge and experience gained through one method informs the other methods. This is in keeping with ethnographic and action research principles. This is in contrast to other studies where students used Tablet PCs only during their classroom learning, such as Tutty (2005; Tutty, White, & Pascoe, 2005, 2006). Our focus is on mapping the experience of the student participants in detail and to enable the use of the Tablet PC to become part of everyday life as ubiquitous computing. Therefore we did not use a comparison group of students who were not given Tablet PCs for their learning and personal use.

Our intervention is the introduction of the Tablet PCs, the wireless network, and the use of blogs. Students are provided with Tablet PCs for the whole semester and are able to carry them around with themselves wherever they go and to take them home. This allows the Tablet PCs to become a part of the students' normal daily living and learning routines.

WHAT THE STUDENTS SAID

In his discussion of the computer for the 21st century, Mark Weiser introduces his concept by suggesting that:

The most profound technologies are those that disappear. They weave themselves into the fabric of everyday life until they are indistinguishable from it. (Weiser, 1991)

In this study, we are interested in how the students have woven the use of the mobility afforded by the Tablet PC into their lives. To this end, we administer an initial survey to measure their initial use and experience of computers generally. We find that the majority of students consider themselves as novices and have no experience using pens with their computers. However, all indicate they believe they have average or expert Internet skills. All have computers at home, and all save one has Internet at home—most have broadband. The details of this questionnaire and the student responses have been published in Berry and Hamilton (2006). These results bear out our initial assumptions about the communicative ecology of the students. Our initial assumptions were that students would not have had extensive experience using pens and digitized screens.

The second part of the survey is designed to collect baseline information about the participants perceived skill levels in human computer interaction. The survey items fall into several categories: drawing skills, ability to use pens and Tablets or digitized screens, ability to use wireless networks, experience with handwriting recognition software, ability to use and maintain blogs, general use of the Internet to locate information, download and/or install software, ability to use mobile devices (specifically PDAs), and Web design and development skills. The snapshot that emerges from the survey response data indicates that a significant number felt themselves to be either novices or average users across most items except those dealing with use of the Internet to locate information, and downloading and installing software.

Students were asked to read each statement and circle the number that best suits their thoughts about their skill level at this time:

1   I am unsure of my skill level
2   I have no knowledge about this
3   I am a beginner/novice at this stage with a basic introductory skill level
4   I have intermediate skills
5   I am an expert user with highly proficient skills

Table 2. Baseline survey of students' skill levels

Responses – Skill Level Questions	5 Expert	4 inter	3 novice	2 none	1 unsure
Drawing with a mouse	14%	43%	43%	0%	0%
Drawing with a pen on a WACOM tablet	10%	19%	43%	24%	5%
Writing with a pen on a WACOM	5%	33%	38%	14%	5%
Using wireless networking	19%	43%	38%	0%	0%
Using the Internet	81%	19%	0%	0%	0%
Using a computer	71%	29%	0%	0%	0%
Installing software	57%	38%	5%	0%	0%
Downloading software from the Internet	62%	29%	0%	5%	0%
Using handwriting recognition software	10%	33%	33%	24%	0%
Using a PDA	10%	19%	29%	43%	0%
Using blogs	0%	10%	43%	43%	5%
Putting together my own blog	5%	10%	29%	43%	14%
Developing my own website	14%	38%	33%	5%	10%
Using chat software such as ICQ	52%	19%	24%	5%	0%
Using agent software	5%	10%	19%	43%	19%
Finding information I need using the Internet	62%	33%	5%	0%	0%

Next, we conduct focus group meetings so we can meet the students face to face and discuss how they initially use the Tablet PCs, what they intend to do, and any issues they currently have. The questions for these focus groups may be viewed at http://raws.adc.rmit.edu.au/~e01913/blog, and a discussion of the results is also in our earlier paper (Berry & Hamilton, 2006), as well as selected segments posted on a University Web site, http://www.lts.rmit.edu.au/mobcommec/index.htm.

For the first semester, the students mostly work individually; however, for the second semester, they are required to work in groups on an industry-based project as discussed previously. They are placed in groups regardless of whether they have a Tablet PC or not, as the majority of students in the class do not have a Tablet PC. Originally we had wanted all participants in a particular group to have a Tablet PC; however, in practice, this was not possible, as groups are composed of friendships, which are formed irrespective of how the Tablet PCs have been allocated. Each group of students has four or five members, and all have Tablets in the majority of groups; however,

there are two groups where only one student has a Tablet PC and one group where all except one member has a Tablet PC.

We analyzed the focus group tapes using discourse analysis and have selected the comments that best reflect the general trends. Discourse analysis is a technique that has its origins in linguistics and is also used in ethnography, which examines lived experience as its subject. We allow the students, our research collaborators, to speak for themselves. They become the experts in the uses and usefulness of the Tablet PCs. We adopted and maintained a nonjudgmental position and treated everything as valid. Sharp, Woodman, and Robson (2000) also used discourse analysis as part of their methodology to study software engineering practices. They follow the principle that "all views should be attended to, and given equal weight." We also adhere to this principle in our presentation of the student views. Ethnography is not empirical in its approach to phenomena.

In this section we present the student responses reflecting their lived experience and the impact possession of a Tablet PC has had on their learning and group work practices. We asked a very open-ended question that led to conversations about how the Tablet PCs fit into their work practices in their work groups. We chose to allow their voices to speak instead of overlaying their responses with an empirical set of categories. This is in keeping with postmodern anthropology and ethnography. Clifford (1986) foregrounds the dilemma of writing about lived experience and suggests possible ways of structuring and articulating the text:

Whatever else an ethnography does, it translates experience into text. There are various ways of effecting this translation, ways that have significant ethical and political consequences. One can "write up" the results of an individual experience of research. This may generate a realistic account of the unwritten experience of another group or person. One can present this textualization as the outcome of observation, of interpretation, of dialogue. One can construct an ethnography composed of dialogues. One can feature multiple voices, or a single voice. One can portray the other as a stable, essential whole, or one can show it to be the product of a narrative of discovery, in specific historical circumstances. (Clifford, 1986, p. 115)

Tyler (1986) discusses the multivocal or polyphonic nature of post-modern writing that aims to set down lived experience:

A post-modern ethnography is a cooperatively evolved text consisting of fragments of discourse intended to evoke in the minds of both reader and writer an emergent fantasy of a possible world of commonsense reality, and thus to provoke an aesthetic integration that will have a therapeutic effect. (Tyler, 1986, p. 125)

We asked the students the following question:

How are you Using the Tablets so far This Semester?

Their responses range from:

I have found the Tablet extremely useful in this scenario [work group]. I have used it in a way, so as a group, we can have lunch in the cafeteria and also discuss/browse relevant Internet sites—this makes it convenient and efficient instead of having lunch first then going over to the labs to discuss Web sites (since we are very busy students). Sometimes, when our lab is too packed, or fellow students use two computers at once to render images, and so forth, I take out my Tablet and use it instead. As a group, we did our proposal presentation to the client today; we had to use the Tablet to set up with the classroom projector to run our PowerPoints and Flash files. Without this, we would have had to do it in our client's office, which would have not been a terribly good experience.

And:

I have used the Tablet to create the Flash, and showing other team members and students the work. I have also used the Tablet to do other course homework.

From students who have the only Tablet PC in their group, to:

...really good, been using it to do the wireframes, site maps, and some other stuff. Also working on my blog banner with it, which I will be animating in Flash.

And:

I have been using the Tablet for all of my project work this semester. Some examples are using Flash to do some test animations, using Dreamweaver to put together some html docs, and we have all been taking notes using Windows Journal. We have been attempting to create a wireless network between our Tablets for easy transfer of files; I'm still working on that...

Both of these comments are from students who all had Tablet PCs in their group. Hence it would appear that while the majority of students are adopting the use of the Tablet in their immediate circle of friends, if their friends do not have one, they are becoming the note-taker, keeper of resources, and demonstrator of group work for the client.

Other responses include:

The Tablets are a great resource. When developing our proposal for our client, we took in mind that using a multimedia enriched presentation, especially for a children's writer, allows for the group to typically show where they are heading with the project. There is nothing easier than images and animation to describe the design flow of the group. The Tablets have allowed us to work with this content and to have it displayed on big projectors easily, knowing that it will work the way we want it to. We have been able to do designs on the spot for our client as well as take notes and even voice record our whole meeting so we know exactly what the client likes and dislikes about the project.

I am using my Tablet in every design class and also out of class for this project. It is very useful as when we have meetings we can view items on this Tablet and the work we have produced on this Tablet.

The use of Tablet PCs is becoming part of the everyday lives of the participants and their ways of doing things:

This semester I used my Tablet PC mainly for updating the blog and maintaining design research

in a folder stored on my laptop that can be easily taken from home to school.

The students are adopting it not just for their coursework, but also for their own construction of knowledge:

I have also been using the Microsoft Journal program to consolidate design ideas and do rough sketches (as I find Firework's FreeHand far too awkward because of its vectors), so essentially I just use it as good old 'butchers paper' in terms of sketching and making notes as design ideas come to me.

I use the Tablet to do a lot of writing as I'm a writer; I write on the train a lot thanks to the Tablet, and this writing often includes rationale for my designs to post on my blog. I use the laptop to connect to the RMIT wireless to send e-mails in the caf [student union cafeteria], and our group often meets in the caf so we can access the Internet and do any kind of research, e-mailing, or other Internet related tasks together whilst discussing our design project.

People have been using them for virtually every aspect of their studies, from note taking to sketching out designs.

This semester I have decided to use the Tablet PC for everything. This means any notes taken, and design ideas, Web page development, assignments, and so forth I am doing with the Tablet. Thus far it has been pretty good. We have tried to establish a wireless link between the Tablets, but have been so far unsuccessful.

Unfortunately access to the wireless network has been patchy:

I was having a great run with the wireless access, and was looking past the constant connectivity failures. Unfortunately what this meant was that

I am now getting the message that I have logged on too many times. Other than that, the Tablet has been a success and is most definitely a very good tool in the learning environment. In regards to using the imaging and graphics software on it, the small screen has been my major issue, as well as the processor not being able to handle images with a large file size.

And there have been issues with screen size. Some students have found the processing power slower, especially when they are using a large package like Photoshop:

I have decided to use the Tablet PC for everything: all note taking, all assignments, and most of my Internet research via the wireless network. This has been relatively successful, although I have had many complications with wireless connectivity and now with me getting the message saying that I have exceeded the maximum amount of logins. I have used the Tablet for a lot of the design development, and have basically transferred all of the usual things I would do on paper onto the Tablet. All of my note taking and assignment thoughts are now done on the journal software. More recently the PC has been running exceptionally slow. I am not sure, but I think it may be a virus. I have noticed a file labeled MediaGateway.exe, which should not have been there. I must have accessed it to view something on the Web. And it has rendered the Tablet almost unusable at the moment. I can still operate the PC in safe mode and have uninstalled that file following the Windows instructions. Anyway, I have backup plans in the interim, and will push on regardless. Other than this, the Tablet has been running exceptionally well and has been a brilliant asset to my development this year, and much more so this semester.

The majority of students have found using the Tablet PC enhanced their social context in terms of their access to the wireless intranet from the cafeteria, to their interactions with their clients:

So far this semester I have been using the Tablet PC in a number of ways. I used to the Tablet to construct the Home Hardware Web site proposal presentation. It was useful because I was able to carry it around anywhere, and my group members and I were all able to work on the presentation outside of class (e.g., the Cafe).

- I also used it to and from uni in the train to construct mock-ups for the Web site.
- The Tablet PC was also used after our client meetings to type up any notes, which were then uploaded onto my blog.
- I have also been using it to 'sketch' in ideas using the journal.

Some students are experimenting with the construction of knowledge beyond their immediate classrooms, to experimenting with various different new aspects provided by the mobility and wireless access to the Internet:

...sketching and listening to music. I bring it to meetings and use my handwriting to jot down notes. We haven't managed to set up MSN Meeting or use the agent, so it is like a laptop, to type up documentation.

I'm actually utilizing my Tablet quite a lot this semester. I'm currently using it for taking notes in lectures and classes, brainstorming, doing work on public transport, in the city, and at RMIT. I'm mainly using the programs Word, Photoshop, Illustrator, Journal, and Notepad on the Tablet.

Some light Flash work and using it as more of a tool to take down notes in class/lectures. More handy then a normal book that we write in, as we don't have to search through annoying papers, and so forth. Also use it sometimes in the cafeteria to research for our projects whenever other classes are taken. Very handy.

Other students are aware of these different options, but are busy enough adapting the technologies to their everyday needs as students:

So far we are using our Tablets like normal laptops, bringing them to class and working on them with Flash, Photoshop, and Illustrator. We haven't actually made use of the Tablet function in any way, as our project design is quite basic and comprised without the Tablet. It is good for us all to have one to bring and log on to wireless.

The Tablet goes everywhere; it's my test environment at home and at Uni. I keep the most up to date information on my Tablet, and I access it over a network to modify files stored on its Web server. I don't think I've rebooted it for about two weeks; it's great to turn on and off very quickly. I'm amused on the train with it, and wherever I go I can get work done. It's the Tablet's portability that's most valuable to me. It's very flexible in how I can use it (standing up/sitting down), and it's powerful enough to do my HTML/PHP/CSS work for the project.

During client meetings I am using the Tablet to take notes and track the meeting. I am also using it to check my e-mails at Uni and to transfer data from home to Uni.

Tablets this semester are really helpful! They have been great when working on my ideas for design and being able to show the other members in my group my work by simply turning on my computer. It almost works as a folio for me, in that I can transfer my work onto the Tablets (or even the work I have produced on the Tablets), bring it to Uni, and connect it up to the net to do simple things like update the blog and share my ideas with my teammates. I have been using the wireless connect a lot more this semester—once again really helpful, whereas now we can have meetings in the caf and not have to rely on computer rooms to be able to connect to the Internet to discuss our work and ideas during the meetings.

Of the 16 allocated to students in this design course, only one student found he was not using his Tablet PC, and his issues were:

To be totally honest, I haven't been using the Tablet at all this semester. I'm finding that the Tablets are extremely slow loading and laggy. Every time when you open up a browser, e-mail, or any application at all the system just hangs and you cannot do anything else until the application has opened. On top of that, because my role consists of using the keyboard a lot, the small keyboard makes things difficult to work with; therefore, I haven't used the Tablet at all.

We have the distinct impression that the Tablet PCs with their digitized screens and capacity for wireless networking have largely disappeared in to the fabric of the students' everyday life (Weiser, 1991). To check this impression we administer the final survey that contains items identical to the baseline survey. The results indicate that while their general abilities with the use of the Internet remained unchanged, the responses in the other categories at the beginning of this section are all now at the average and expert skill level, thus indicating that the participants feel their skills have definitely improved over the study period, especially with regard to using digitized Tablets with a pen and wireless networking.

Students were again asked to read each statement and circle the number that best suits their thoughts about their skill level at this time:

1   I am unsure of my skill level
2   I have no knowledge about this
3   I am a beginner/novice at this stage with a basic introductory skill level
4   I have intermediate skills
5   I am an expert user with highly proficient skills

Table 3. Exit survey of students' skill levels

Responses – Skill Level Questions	5 Expert	4 inter	3 novice	2 none	1 unsure
Drawing with a mouse	18%	55%	18%	9%	0%
Drawing with a pen on a WACOM tablet	27%	45%	18%	9%	0%
Writing with a pen on a WACOM	36%	45%	9%	9%	0%
Using wireless networking	18%	55%	18%	0%	0%
Using the Internet	73%	18%	9%	0%	0%
Using a computer	64%	36%	0%	0%	0%
Installing software	45%	45%	9%	0%	0%
Downloading software from the Internet	36%	45%	9%	9%	0%
Using handwriting recognition software	9%	73%	9%	9%	0%
Using a PDA	0%	18%	55%	27%	0%
Using blogs	27%	55%	18%	0%	0%
Putting together my own blog	18%	64%	18%	0%	0%
Developing my own website	45%	45%	9%	0%	0%
Using chat software such as ICQ	64%	18%	18%	0%	0%
Using agent software	0%	9%	45%	36%	9%
Finding information I need using the Internet	91%	0%	9%	0%	0%

CONCLUSION

Implementation of mobile computing effectively facilitates the establishment of a learning community among the students. Many of the structures initially set up seem to have broader application than originally anticipated. Mobile computing assists project groups by extending their communication beyond traditional methods.

Students are able to communicate with other groups effectively and solve a wide range of problems. Instant messaging and e-mail are a key component of contact over this semester and appear to be more prominent than previously observed. Additionally, alternate forms of record management such as document posting on secure sites to be retrieved seem to also be utilized. Weblogs are a key component in record keeping and are often linked to other student Weblogs recording a series of interesting or relevant information.

Many of the strategies set up to facilitate the mobile computing in fact benefit all projects.

Teaching staff are able to monitor project development with ease and often recognize issues that come up early in the piece, as the process is far more effectively documented. This has enabled early intervention and in many circumstances provided the group with clear direction to move forward and work through the challenges faced in each project.

The students are able to monitor their own work in relationship to their team members. Problems encountered in previous semesters do not appear to be the status quo with the presence of the mobile computing. There are often typical issues in the teaching and learning process such as:

- students being unprepared for meetings;
- leaving items at home and not available for discussion;
- technical difficulties of transporting files and data across platforms and via e-mail;
- lack of opportunity for meetings with each other out of class times due to work or study constraints;

- difficulties of interpretation or communication between group members and the client;
- progress slowed by weekly meetings.

The capability of the Tablet PCs and mobile computing allows students to communicate, review, and update their information and development strategies with fewer delays.

FUTURE TRENDS

So far our findings have been encouraging. However, our investigations have opened up further avenues to explore and have posed future research questions relating to allowing all students access to Tablet PCs for all their courses.

We note that the Tablet PCs provide a platform for the development of ideas and enable the centralizing of notes, sketches, various media, and drafts. This means that projects can move along faster, as more information and record keeping can be provided at meetings, more groundwork is covered in a more sophisticated way, and the progression of ideas can be seen more easily. It also results in less information being misplaced or lost, as might be the case with scraps of paper. However, memory storage can become an issue, and many students purchased memory sticks, both for the memory storage and faster transfer of files.

Tablet PCs can help students by providing a communication strategy to expand and support development processes and provide an immediacy to what students are doing, bypassing some pen and paper steps (as an aside: we noticed 40% of students in the cafeteria in Building 8, on Thursday July 28, at 10:30am were using notebook computers). In providing the means to show clients the current status of work, they also enable a clearer understanding of where the project is currently positioned. One student's final comments were:

The tablet has been very convenient for the year. It has assisted me with my design client work and everyday tasks. Thanks!

ACKNOWLEDGMENTS

The authors acknowledge the help and support of associate professor Jim McGovern, associate professor Vic Ciesielski, professors Mark Shortis, Evan Smith, Laurie Davies, and Matt Maddocks, and all members of the HP Mobility Grant team within our University. Also, this research is partially funded by HP by means of their HP Mobile Technology for Teaching Grant Initiative—2004 Higher Education.

REFERENCES

Berry, M., & Hamilton, M. (2006). Mobile computing, visual diaries, learning and communication: Changes to the communicative ecology of design students through mobile computing. In the *Eighth Australasian Computing Education Conference (ACE2006)*, Hobart, Tasmania, Australian Computer Society, Inc.

Billet, S. (2001). *Learning in the workplace: Strategies for effective learning.* Sydney: Allen & Unwin.

Bratman, M. (1987). *Intentions, plans, and practical reason.* Harvard University Press.

Clifford, J. (1986). On ethnographic allegory. In J. A. M. Clifford (Ed.), *Writing culture: The politics of ethnography.* G.E. University of California Press.

Cornford, I. R., & Beven, F. A. (1999). Workplace learning: Differential learning needs of novice and more experienced workers. *Australian and New Zealand Journal of Vocational Education Research, 28.*

Savoie, J. M., & Hughes, A. S. (1994). Problem-based learning as classroom solution. *Educational Leadership,* 54-57.

Sharp, H., Woodman, M., & Robson, H. (2000). Using ethnography and discourse analysis to study software engineering practices. *IEEE Software, 17*(1).

Singh, M. P., & Huhns, M. N. (2005). *Service-oriented computing: Semantics, processes, agents.* John Wiley & Sons, Ltd.

Tacchi, J., Slater, D., & Hearn, G. (2004). *Ethnographic action research.*

Tutty, J., White, B., & Pascoe, R. (2005a). Experiences from a wireless-enabled tablet classroom. In *Australasian Computing Education Conference.* Newcastle, Australia: CRPIT.

Tutty, J., White, B., & Pascoe, R. (2005b). Experiences from a wireless-enabled tablet classroom. In *Australasian Computing Education Conference* (pp. 165-172). Newcastle, Australia: CRPIT. 42.

Tutty, J., White, B., & Pascoe, R. (2006). Experiences from a wireless-enabled tablet classroom. In *The 8th Australasian Computing Education Conference.* Hobart, Australia: CRPIT.

Tyler, S. (1986). Post-modern ethnography: From document of the occult to occult document. In J. A. M. Clifford (Ed.), *Writing culture: The politics of ethnography.* G.E. University of California Press.

Weiser, M. (1991). The computer for the 21st century. *Scientific American,* 94-110.

Section II
Collaboration Learning Through HCI

Chapter V
Online Discourse:
Encouraging Active Student Participation in Large Classes

Sandra Jones
RMIT, Australia

ABSTRACT

This chapter explores how information and communications technology (ICT) can be designed to maximize human computer interactions (HCI) in order to create a student-centered learning environment within large classes by enabling small-group discourse. Through an empirical case study of student participation through computer-mediated-communication the chapter demonstrates how the flexibility created in the online environment enables students in large classes, particularly students from non-English speaking backgrounds, to participate at a pace that enables them to contribute considered opinions to a small-group discourse. The case study reiterates the argument that HCI is best achieved when ICTs and face-to-face classes are combined. It is argued that in so doing HCI assists the higher education environment to both meet the demands for mass-market, consumer-driven, globally accessible higher educational, as well as addressing industry demand for graduates with advanced problem-solving and analytical and reflective skills who are able to work collaboratively in teams.

TEACHING IN LARGE CLASSES

A recent Australian survey of 69 highly accomplished teachers and 21 academic developers employed in 23 Australian universities defined large classes as varying from between 70 to 500 students (AUTC, 2001). It found that the most common educational design for large classes was a weekly lecture for all students supplemented by weekly or fortnightly small group tutorials. The most common forms of assessment were written assignments, group oral presentations, and written examinations. Less common were formative assessments, group projects, marks for participation, and portfolio work.

The survey also found that in these large classes the most common issues and challenges identified were:

- relationship distance (psychological and physical) between the students and teacher
- assessment (including ensuring adequate and timely feedback, moderating assessment, checking for plagiarism)
- course design (including how to devise manageable yet flexible learning that is student-centered, and applicable across a heterogonous group)
- resource availability (including space/equipment requirements, training for tutors, and administrative assistance)

Since this survey, a further challenge for large class environments has been the increasingly cultural heterogeneity of students. This places further pressures on teachers and students in seeking to accommodate the diversity of language, cultural backgrounds, and experiences of education. For example, in Australia many international students come from Asian countries in which English is neither the spoken nor the educational instructional language and in which the educational process is steeped in a rich Confucian educational heritage of a teacher-centered learning approach. This has been described by Biggs (1999, pp. 131-132) as a *"conserving approach to knowledge"* and by Ballard and Clanchy (1997, p. 14) as placing emphasis on the *"extensive and accurate knowledge of the wisdom contained in authoritative texts or the sayings of earlier scholars and sages."* This has resulted, claims Tyson (1997, p. 77), in perpetuating a *"culture of dependent learners in a didactic, knowledge-focused classroom... [rather than] ...collaborative learners organizing and managing their own learning processes."* That is, many Asian students come from educational cultures in which they are used to deferring to authority, to not offering their views or questioning teachers during class (although they will approach the teacher individually at the end of class for clarification), and to participating only accordingly to clearly set guidelines (Yap, 1997).

It is within this educational environment that the next section discusses how ICT can be designed to assist large classes by maximizing HCI.

HCI LEARNING ENVIRONMENTS

The first wave of use of ICT for teaching purposes utilized an instructional design approach that tended to embed a teacher-centered learning environment focused upon content acquisition. Oliver (2004) states that much of the courseware management has been designed to support a content-oriented approach that focuses on what the teacher is doing rather than what learners are doing. Herrington, Oliver, Herrington, and Sparrow (2004) demonstrate how traditional content instruction is translated into online instruction, with the resulting interface described as:

generally text-based, and divided according to the scope and sequence of the content to be covered. The content is hierarchically organized and may follow the same sequence as the set textbook...the teacher controls the learning situation...weekly tasks may be set to enable students to practice what they learn...assessment is set as separate assignments apart from any activities that students may do throughout the unit. (Herrington et al., 2004, p. 4)

The second wave of use of ICT in higher education has adopted a more holistic, constructivist approach in which learners are provided the opportunity to engage in activities that simulate real-world environments that enable them to construct their own strategies, concepts, models, and knowledge. Oliver (2004) demonstrates how content-oriented courses can be designed on more constructivist principles through:

a syllabus with a number of discrete sections of content ...large amounts of information conveyed in Web pages for students to read...supported by group-based activities and tasks providing contexts for learners through application of the knowledge (and) assessment based on products and artifacts developed from the course material and content. (Oliver, 2004, p. 4)

That is, ICTs can be employed to maximize HCI such that collaborative learning environments are produced in which interactions between students provides the opportunity for knowledge sharing and development.

Oliver (2000) describes how HCI can be enhanced by providing opportunities for learners to access information (provided by the teacher), to participate in interactive learning (engaging the learner in activity, reflection, and decision-making and providing feedback), to communicate with other learners and teachers and to create and publish materials.

Creese (2003) goes further and discusses the outcomes of a number of recent pedagogical evaluations of the effectiveness of the new virtual space to enhance cognitive development (Andrews & Schwarz, 2002; McLoughlin, 2002; Stacey & Rice, 2002; Treleaven, 2002). Based on

these writings and her own experience, she argues that computer-mediated communication provides a new type of group space for social interaction between and within groups.

Building on Reeves' (1993) original argument that a well-designed multimedia environment can be used to provide a wealth of learning support activities through the design of situated learning environments, Reeves, Herrington, and Oliver (2002) argue that HCI can be designed to provide learners with situated learning environments that enable learners to:

move freely around the resources provided rather than move in a linear fashion that may not ape the complexities of real life. Problems presented to students can use the full capacities of the technology to present situations and scenarios in video clips, texts links and images to give meaning and purpose to the students' endeavours, and to provide motivation to complete the task. (Reeves et al., 2002, p. 566)

Jones (2005) and Jones and McCann (2004, 2005) describe how HCI can be enhanced through authentic learning environments in which students participate in experiential learning activities. They present examples of the design and use of *Virtual Situated Learning Environments* in which students access information through a virtual Web site and then become virtual practitioners in the organization, participating in a variety of professional practice activities that simulate authentic real-life business challenges. These fit McClelland's (1994, p. 8) suggestion that *"the context for a situated learning model may be a highly realistic or 'virtual' surrogate of the actual work environment."*

Many writers are also exploring the role that discussion tools can be used to enhance the HCI learning environment. Bradshaw, Powell, and Terrell (2002, p. 2) discuss how ICTs can be used to assist practitioners to engage in online discussion communities in which virtual discussion provides opportunities for *"reflection on experience, constructing understanding in work-based and social contexts, and basing learning on the learners needs and priorities."* Wozniak and Solveira (2004) discuss the flexibility of online discussion in which students can control when and where they post and reply to messages. They reference arguments by Vondervell (2002) and Geer (2003) that computer-mediated communication promotes a collaborative learning environment in which learners interact by negotiating, debating, reviewing, and reflecting upon existing knowledge and in so doing deepen their understanding of course content.

On the other hand, others highlight the limitations of computer-mediated communication such as the need for an e-moderator to ensure students do participate, do answer other students' communication, and do not simply *lurk* rather than participate (Ellis, 2001; Hara, Bok, & Angeli, 2000; Vonderevell, 2002). Understanding of these limitations led Salmon (2000) to devise a five stage model of teaching and learning online that required the e-moderator to include activities to enable students to familiarize themselves with the computer-mediated communication tools, engage in online socialization, exchange information, contribute to online conferences to construct knowledge, and develop a critical thinking capability.

In summary, literature upon the second wave of ICT use for educational purposes has focused on how to increase HCI as a means to engage students in a more student-centered, constructivist approach to learning. Despite this, there is little discussion in the literature on how this may apply in different learning environments with different mixes of students. Moreover, most of the studies present analysis of the HCI from the educator's perspective rather than the student's perspective. This chapter seeks to illustrate how the HCI can be improved by presenting an empirical example, from both the designer and educator perspective and the student participant

perspective, of how HCI can be used effectively in large classes. Of additional interest is how HCI may be used to assist in multi-cultural and multi-lingual classes. In so doing it is important to recognize that this case study used a blended approach in which HCI was first introduced in a face-to-face class, followed by computer-mediated communication. The particular tool used as the means for HCI was a discussion board provided as part of the University's distributed learning system, accessible to all enrolled students using either the University provided computer facilities, or student privately owned (or work related) computer facilities.

A qualitative methodology, using action-based, first person reflection by the author as the designer of the discussion board and as the academic seeking to establish a student-centered learning environment, is used to explore the issue. This first-person reflection is supplemented by feedback from student participants in the course.

THE CASE STUDY

The Student Body

The case study chosen for discussion is a class of 72 post-graduate students enrolled in a Master of Commerce (MCom) offered by a large Australian-based university. As the normal context for a post-graduate class in this faculty is 20 students, the class qualifies as a large class.

Sixty-five of the students enrolled in this course (over 90%) were from diverse international cultures in which English is often a second language. The largest groups of students (64%) were from China (23) and various Asia countries (Singapore, South Korea, Taiwan, Thailand, Vietnam), with the next largest (19%) from India (8), Pakistan, and Sri Lanka. Local (Australian) students made up the third largest group (11%). A smaller number of students also came from a variety of countries including Denmark, Columbia, Germany, Japan, Malaysia, Philippines, and South Africa.

In addition to the diverse country of origin, students were graduates of disparate disciplines including engineering, computer science, business, business information technology, hospitality, education, and health. Although all the international students were enrolled full-time, a number of local students were enrolled part-time. Few of the students had any significant work experience, with all the international students having recently completed either an undergraduate degree or a post-graduate degree in a specialized discipline. Several students had recently completed a master's degree (business information technology). Few students (with the exception of the computer science and business information technology students) had experience with the online learning environment, except in its use as a means to source secondary literature. None had experience with the University's online distributed learning system as a means to engage in asynchronous discussion.

The first (compulsory) course students undertake in the MCom is titled *Business and Government in a Global Context*. Given the combination of the large class and the diverse cultural mix (country of origin and discipline), this class provided an excellent opportunity to explore the contribution of ICTs that are designed and implemented to increase HCI in teaching large classes. The subject matter of the course made it possible to design experiential learning activity using computer-mediated communication that would not only test the challenges of the virtual learning environment, but also provide valuable identification of the advantages and challenges of using computer-mediated communication in a real-life global business environment. Given this, the next section assesses the effectiveness of HCI in terms of the challenges for large classes identified earlier in the recent Australian survey.

Addressing Challenges of Large Classes

Student-Centered Design: Supporting Relationships

As the academic responsible for design and delivery of this course I designed the course to address the issues earlier identified as challenges for large classes (that is to design the course to be student-centered, flexible, and heterogenous).

First, I divided the 72 students into 11 small collaborative learning networks of between six and seven; I randomly allocated students (although I did try to achieve a cultural mix). Students were asked to engage in a number of activities within these collaborative learning network groups, both in the face-to-face and the virtual environment (as described later) that required relationships to be established between the students. The online involvement was scheduled to occur between the third and sixth week of semester, sandwiched between face-to-face workshops.

Using the University's distributed learning system, I established group discussion boards for each collaborative learning network. Students were asked to discuss an issue of importance to global business over a period of three weeks (with no specified time period other than an end date by which discourse should be finalized) in which there was no *face-to-face* session.

The specific issue chosen for discussion was a contemporary one with which all students were familiar (viz: *the new demands on businesses operating in a global economy arising from the terrorist activity*). This provided an opportunity for private and personal ethical, emotional, and political views to be invoked; students were provided with a framework to be used as part of the critical analysis of their conceptual knowledge. As the educator I also had the ability to contribute to all discourses.

Resource Availability

Second, to ensure that students all had access to the University's distributed learning system it was demonstrated in class followed by an online announcement reiterating the exact steps to take. Students were asked to access the site, either from the University provided computer facilities or from remote locations (including student privately owned and work provided computer facilities, at any time of day or note from any locality). Technical assistance from a trained technical officer and me were also provided.

Assessment

Third, I designed cumulative assessment spread over the semester to ensure students received timely feedback before the next piece of assessment was due. The assessment required students to demonstrate both analytical and reflective capabilities using a combination of secondary sources and reflection upon their own experiences. Assessment had both a quantitative element (each student had to make three contributions of a minimum of 250 words each, or 750 words minimum, one of which was to start a new discussion thread, while the other two were to add to existing threads), and a qualitative element (the contribution of each student was to be assessed individually against criteria that required demonstration of both analysis and personal reflection upon the issue). Finally, a collaborative learning network verbal presentation of the main issues (to include assessment of the advantages and disadvantages of discussion on the online environment) was designed for the face-to-face class following finalization of the online discourse.

In summary, in seeking to address the issues associated with large classes identified by the Australian study, a student-centered learning environment was designed that incorporated a mix of technical and human resources to maximize HCI and face-to-face engagement. The focus was upon small-group discussion designed to assist relationship building. Paralleling this class design, assessment required both individual and group activities to demonstrate different types of skill development. The next section presents an assessment of the effectiveness of this design in practice from both the students and my own perspectives.

Assessment

Student-Centered Design and Relationships

All students were actively involved in the discourse, with more than one-third of students making more than the required number of contributions (indeed one student made 19 contributions). Most discourses occurred over an extended period of time varying from 9 to 24 days, with the average being around 17 days.

The asynchronous nature of the discourse was criticized by some students as frustrating, especially when trying to clarify what some contributions meant. This did lead to some misunderstandings and time wasting. On the other hand, some students (especially students less familiar with English) stated that the delay gave them time to reflect on the comments made by other students and to prepare a well referenced and thoughtful response. Comments made by students that reflect this included:

Compared with face to face discussion, the online discussion made it possible to form a well prepared argument, and for me, as an overseas student, the online discussion made me avoid the language expression problems in face-to-face discussion.

Another student stated:

We were able to share ideas, broaden our knowledge, and receive quick response via the Blackboard...I was able to contribute my ideas...while there was hardly a chance to do so in the classroom.

Students identified the positive flexibility of the interface as a major advantage in that they could both contribute and read the contributions of all students from anywhere, and at any time that suited them.

There was evidence that both student and teacher conceptual knowledge contributed to the discourse. In several collaborative learning networks students provided personal examples of how the topic under discussion had affected business in their country of origin. In others, students contributed examples of how their own industry had developed risk-avoidance strategies.

Many collaborative learning networks identified an increased exchange of information, although it was recognized that trust had to be established in different ways as the online environment removed the opportunity to read body language. There was some concern that any mistakes were written and thus could not be taken back.

Students also identified the ability to construct new knowledge from the discourse as ideas were shared and critical analytical capabilities developed from reading the different points of view of students.

In terms of new learning from, and adapting to, the global virtual environment, several collaborative learning networks and individual students reflected that participating in this online exercise had made them consider the effects of online communication for businesses operating in a global environment, particularly in regard to the functioning of virtual teams in a virtual global environment. One student commented:

I am glad that I was given the opportunity to take part in a virtual discussion because I understand that in today's globalized world, more and more companies are making use of virtual teamwork, and it is important to know how to effectively

communicate in different ways. The experience has shown me the advantages and difficulties of such work.

Another student stated:

Best part of the course was the online discussions and contributions...to put those three contributions on discussion board made me think, consider, and draw some inferences from those issues than I would otherwise.

An interesting reflection by a few students was that the discourse enabled them to consider the many different ways that an issue can be looked at as well as the many different interpretations people can have of the same thing. One student stated:

I was able to contradict views of my colleagues and their justification of them. This led me to further understand the ethical codes that they adhered to.

My own evaluation was that the HCI environment did enable all students to actively participate in the discourse and that over time all students became more confident in expressing their own opinions rather than relying on the written opinions of *experts*. As the exercise progressed, a number of students advanced from posting written comments that relied significantly on "expert" comments to personal comments that relied more on their own reflections.

Resource Availability

There were some resource problems identified by students. First, some students enrolled in the course after the discourse had begun, and thus it took time for them to identify the collaborative learning network to which they belonged and to learn how to access and use the distributed learning system. Second, the online environment was human resource intensive both in assisting students to technically identify how to contribute in the online environment, and in ensuring that the discourse did stay within the analytical framework. However, the major resource issues that arose concerned the assessment that required significant time and effort from the teacher (216 contributions had to be read and assessed).

This step reinforced the importance of ensuring that the technicalities of using the online environment are well addressed before students enter the Web sites. It also confirmed the need to ensure that students were familiarized with the online environment in a face-to-face environment where problems could be quickly addressed. Finally, it identified that the online environment is as resource intensive, if not more, as the face-to-face learning environment.

Relationship Distance

Student comments varied in regard to the effectiveness of an HCI environment for building relationships. Some students stated that the virtual environment was too impersonal. This impersonality was criticized for delaying the beginning of discourse and for leading to frustration when collaborative learning network members did not respond immediately to a discourse contribution, indeed a number of networks organized face-to-face meetings, before, during, or at the end of the online discourse. Comments made that reflected this limitation included:

There is a lack of a sense of community and dynamism that is associated with physical teamwork and face-to-face engagement and the presence of misunderstandings that were difficulty to clarify.

It would have been ideal to have met at least once or twice during the activity and thereby identifying the group members and also enabling them to create a bond and identify and read body language when it came to debating an issue.

On the other hand, collaborative learning network discourse activity was seen as constructive, as it limited the number of people involved in the discussion. Furthermore, especially for international students not used to offering their views, the discourse was seen as enabling them to develop the trust and confidence needed for them to express their individual opinions. One student claimed that he thought the online discourse provided opportunity for less confident students to participate, and at the same time, it was able to neutralize the contributions of the dominant personalities. Another student claimed that it provided the opportunity to criticize the views of other group members without hesitation. One student stated that the online environment:

removed the fear factor of not being accepted... people were more open with their views and also in expressing their feelings on a given subject or topic.

However, from my perspective, although there was evidence that students who had experienced a more didactic teacher-centered learning environment required more guidance in a face-to-face learning environment, the online environment did provide an effective platform for students to access at different times. The group presentations that resulted from the online discourse were all of a very high standard, and most collaborative learning networks demonstrated strong cohesion.

Assessment

The advantages of the cumulative assessment were that students received early feedback on their individual and group assessment. This assisted students more used to a teacher-centered environment to develop confidence in operating within a student-centered environment. One student stated:

Having learnt through the online discourse exercise how forms and functions of organizations influenced the outcomes of their business plan and strategy, I was more willing to put forth my views on the subject matter.

On the other hand, the extent of assessment caused timing difficulties for me as assessor, as I seemed to be continually marking papers in order to return them for student feedback.

CONCLUSION

This chapter set out to explore how ICTs can be designed to maximize HCI to assist the provision of a supportive student-centered learning environment in large classes. An empirical case study was used to explore this question from both a teacher and student perspective. This example demonstrated that ICTs can be employed to maximize HCI interactions that encourage student sharing of their conceptual knowledge and through this the development of critical analytical and reflective capabilities. The learning environment created is flexible, it enables students to consider and respond to different views over time, and it can lead to closer relationships if designed to enable small group discourse. However, the example reinforces discussion that has occurred since the first wave of ICT use for educational purposes, that is, the best HCI occurs in a mixed face-to-face and ICTs environment designed to create experiential learning opportunities. Accordingly, it is concluded that the best HCI will be seen where ICTs are utilized effectively to augment rather than replace the face-to-face learning environment.

REFERENCES

AUTC Project. (2001). A survey of large class teaching around Australia. *Teaching and Educational Development Institute.* Queensland: University of Queensland.

Andrews, T., & Schwarz, G. (2002). Preparing students for the virtual organization: An evaluation of learning with virtual learning technologies. *Educational Technology & Society, 5*(3). Retrieved November 24, 2003 from http://www.ifets.massy.ac.nz/periodical/vol_3_2002/andrews.html

Ballard, B., & Clanchy, J. (1997). *Teaching international students.* Deakin ACT: IDP Education.

Biggs, J. (1999). *Teaching for quality learning at university.* Buckingham: SRHE and Open University Press.

Bradshaw, P., Powell, S., & Terrell, I. (2002). *Online communities—Vehicles for professional learning?* Retrieved November 24, 2003, from www.ultralab.ac.uk/papers/bera2002paper.htm

Creese, E. (2003). Group dynamics and learning in an organisational behaviour virtual learning community: The case of 6 virtual peer-learning teams. *Ultibase.* Retrieved April 25, 2005, from http://ultibase.rmit.edu.au/articles/nov03/creese2htm

Ellis, A. (2001). Student-centered collaborative learning vs. face-to-face and asynchronous online communication: What's the difference? In *Proceedings of the 18ᵗʰ ASCILITE Conference.* Melbourne. Retrieved October 6, 2005, from http://www.ascilite.org.au/conference/melbourne01/pdf/papers/ellisa.pdf

Geer, R. (2003). Initial communicating styles and their impact on further interaction in computer conferences. In *Proceedings of the 20ᵗʰ ASCILITE Conference.* Adelaide. Retrieved October 6, 2005, from http://www.ascilite.org.au/conference/adelaide03/docs/pdf/194pdf

Hara, N., Bonk, C., & Angeli, C. (2000). Content analysis of online discussion in an applied educational psychology course. *Instruction Science,* 28, 115-152.

Herrington, J., Oliver, R., Herrington, T., & Sparrow, H. (2004). Towards a new tradition of online instruction: Using situated learning theory to design Web-based units. In *Proceedings of the 21ˢᵗ Ascilite Conference.* Perth. Retrieved October 6, 2005, from http://www.ascilite.org.au/conferences/pertho4/procs/herrington-J.html

Jones, S. (2005). Using IT to augment authentic learning environments. In A. Herrington & J. Herrington (Eds.), *Authentic learning environments* (pp.172-181). Hershey, USA: Idea Group Publishing.

Jones, S., & McCann, J. (2004). Virtual situated learning environments—The business education model for developing countries in a knowledge era. In *Business education and emerging market economies.* USA: Kluwer.

Jones, S., & McCann, J. (2005). Authentic virtual situated learning environments—The flexible learning alternative for peripatetic managers in a global, flexible workplace. *Journal of Workplace Learning Special Issue on E-Learning at the Workplace, 17*(5/6), 359-369.

McLellan, H. (1994). Situated learning: Continuing the conversation. *Educational Technology, 34*(10), 7-8.

McLouglin, C. (2002). Computer supported teamwork: An integrative approach to evaluating cooperative learning in an online environment. *Australian Journal of Technology, 18*(2), 227-254. Retrieved October 6, 2005, from http://www.ascilite.org.au/ajet/ajet18/mclouglin.html

Oliver, R. (2000). Developing and sustaining technology-based learning in higher education: The way ahead. In *Proceedings of the Higher Education Research and Development Society of Australia* (p. 23). Jamison: HERDSA.

Oliver, R. (2004). Moving beyond instructional comfort zones with online courses. In *Proceedings of the 21st Ascilite Conference.* Perth. Retrieved October 6, 2005, from http://www.ascilite.org.au/conferences/pertho4/procs/oliver-r.html

Reeves, T. (1993). Evaluating interactive multimedia. In D. Gayeski (Ed.), *Multimedia for learning: Development, application, evaluation* (pp. 97-112). Englewood Cliffs, NJ: Educational Technology Publications.

Reeves, T., Herrington, J., & Oliver, R. (2002). Authentic activities and online learning. In A. Goody, J. Herrington, & M. Northcote (Eds.), *Quality conversations: Research and development in higher education* (p. 25). Jamieson, ACT: HERDSA.

Salmon, G. (2000). *E-moderation: The key to teaching and learning online.* London: Kogan.

Stacey, E., & Rice, M. (2002). Evaluating an online environment. *Australian Journal of Education Technology, 18*(3), 323-340.

Students. (2005). *Feedback.* RMIT University, Melbourne, Australia.

Treleaven, L. (2003). Evaluating a communicative model for Web mediated collaborative learning and design. *Australian Journal of Education Technology, 19*(1), 100-117.

Tyson, T. (1997). Undergraduates in the deep end: First-year students as proactive experiential learners. In R. Ballantyne, J. Bain, & J. Packer (Eds.), *Reflecting on university teaching academics' stories* (pp. 75-88). Committee for University Teaching and Staff Development, DEETYA, AGPS.

Yap, C. (1997). Teaching overseas students: The case of introductory accounting. In R. Ballantyne, J. Bain, & J. Packer (Eds.), *Reflecting on university teaching academics' stories* (pp. 55-64). Committee for University Teaching and Staff Development, DEETYA, AGPS.

VonderVell, S. (2002). An examination of asynchronous communication experiences and perspectives of students in an online course: A case study. *The Internet and Higher Education,* 6, 77-90.

Wozniak, H., & Silveira, S. (2004). Online discussions: Promoting effective student-to-student interaction. In *Proceedings of the 21st Ascilite Conference*. Perth. Retrieved October 6, 2005, from http://www.ascilite.org.au/conferences/perth04/procs/wozniak.html

Chapter VI
Facilitating Social Learning in Virtual Communities of Practice

Rosanna Tarsiero
Gionnethics, Italy

ABSTRACT

This chapter introduces communities of practice as a means to explore human computer interaction in online collaborative environments. Through a wide review of the literature on communities of practice and their virtual counterparts, it argues that the focus for successful interaction design in these communities lies on those sociability and usability aspects that allow greater participation in social learning. It also argues that the facilitator assumes a fundamental role in guiding a virtual community of practice to accomplish work-related informal learning activities in a climate of trust and collaboration. The author hopes that understanding the special opportunities provided by virtual communities of practice will advocate for their widespread routine use.

INTRODUCTION

In these unsettled times, the capability of setting priorities, engaging in an activity, reflecting about such activity, welcoming feedback, accepting criticism, and changing one's course of action as a result of it, known as *continuous learning*, is highly prized in that it confers increased adaptability to the environment (Senge, 1990). At the same time, information and communication technology made knowledge creation, storage, and distribution easier. Such proliferating of new possibilities has led to a higher reliance on adult learning, both

in the form of distance education and workplace formal and informal online training. That, in turn, posed unexpected human computer interaction challenges (Salomon, 1991).

In the psychological and anthropological fields, theorists maintain that learning can*not* be separated from the practices and the contexts in which it occurs (Barab & Duffy, 2000; Lave & Wenger, 1991). Sustained discursive interactions with one another (Bielaczyc & Collins, 1999) as well as careful observation and reflection are pivotal for learners to collaborate and achieve new insights and generate, acquire, and share knowledge. Of the many tools that can be used to facilitate collaborative learning, communities of practice (CoPs) and their virtual counterparts are promising (Lesser & Storck, 2004; Liedka, 1999), especially in addressing *unstructured practices*, impossible to foresee, and too complex to formalize (Allen, 2003). Despite the interaction design acceleration that new forms of collaboration and/or cooperation have put on technology in general and software in particular, user-centered evaluations stress the role of the human factor (Preece, Rogers, & Sharp, 2002).

The remainder of this paper is structured as follows. The next *conceptual foundations section* provides background information on *communities of practice* and their virtual counterparts. Then, the *virtual communities of practice from an HCI perspective section* reframes such literature through the lens of interaction design and highlights the facilitator role in determining the success of these communities. Finally, the *future trends section* discusses the usefulness of this model and its future developments, while the *conclusion section* summarizes the main findings and their consequences.

CONCEPTUAL FOUNDATIONS

Communities of Practice (CoPs): Defining the Framework

When trying to define what a community of practice is, one stumbles into at least 11 definitions (Markestijn, 2004). Some of them even come from the same author or groups of authors (Lave & Wenger, 1991; Wenger, 1998; Wenger, McDermott, & Snyder, 2002), which has been interpreted as *contradictory* (Gourlay, 1999), *confusing* (Cox, 2004), and *hard to grasp* (Johnson, 2001). Nevertheless, the refinement of a concept through iterative cycles of definition, modeling, analysis, and reframing of the problem is consistent with the action research method (Argyris,

Putnam, & McLain Smith, 1985), a framework often mentioned in connection with epistemology of this field.

Many authors have tried to describe the characteristics of *communities of practice*. The *structural model* (Wenger et al., 2002) is the most widely adopted and defines a community of practice (CoP) as (a) a *community* composed of any number and type of members; (b) based on a shared *interest* that becomes the topic of most conversations among its members; and (c) engaging its participants into a collaborative *practice* regarding the aforementioned topic of conversation. Any domain of interest is possible, as long as it is related to a practice, intended as some form of *doing* in connection with a topic or an interest, and often but not always related to work (Wartburg, Rost, & Teichert, 2004). Participation in communities of practice is voluntary (Wenger et al., 2002), comes in different kinds (Lave & Wenger, 1991), from participants only engaging in observation to the ones heavily interactive, and is fostered by somebody facilitating the learning process (Johnson, 2001; Rogers, 2000). Opinions differ, even among practitioners, on whether a community of practice can be created via a formal initiative or only exist as a spontaneously emerging entity, most opting for the former (Allen, Ure, & Evans, 2003; Bourhis, Dubé, & Jacob, 2005; Brown & Duguid, 1991, 2001; Liedka, 1999; Wenger et al., 2002).

Communities of practice can be put to a number of uses, the main one being tacit-to-tacit knowledge conversion (Hildreth & Kimble, 1999; Preece, 2003) that allows learning of unstructured practices (Allen, 2003; Lesser & Storck, 2004). In this setting, a *community of practice* allows for the knowledge to flow from one member to another without being degraded through to conversion (from implicit into explicit and then from explicit into implicit), thereby having higher fidelity with the original. *Communities of practice* also are a tool to help employees become acculturated into an organization (Chao, 2001), develop a work-related identity (Hara, 2000; Yi, 2000), and learn skills and motivation to work from colleagues (Barab & Duffy, 2000). Finally, they can be used to foster workers' self-esteem and self-efficacy (Markestjin, 2004), as well as improve and support overall organizational performance and goals (Wenger & Snyder, 2000), while enhancing communication structure.

Members of a community of practice learn in assorted informal ways. They achieve new insights through sustained interactions with their peers (Bielaczyc & Collins, 1999) and through the observation of interactions among themselves, while attempting to extract and acquire from, as well as generate, knowledge and share it. Learning also comes from experience, without being de-contextualized from the situation and conditions in which it happens (Barab & Duffy, 2000; Lave & Wenger, 1991). Despite its cyclical and somewhat predictable motion (in terms of the learner's action in the environment, first proposition on the nature of the problem/situation, modelization of the *lessons learned*, testing and re-stating of the problem in a more accurate way), learning in these communities does not happen through formal training or education but is acquired through narrative and discourse (Brown & Duguid, 2000; Lesser & Storck, 2004; Orr, 1990). Finally, learning in *communities of practice* is continuous (Bielaczyc & Collins, 1999) yet demand driven (Brown & Duguid, 2000) and formative of identity, in that participants learn to *be* like their working peers (Brown & Duguid, 1991).

Despite the fuzziness of the definition and its boundaries, literature presents us with a clear portrait of communities of practice, their use, and the way learning happens within them, but the role played by ICT in supporting communities of practice is not systematically explored.

Virtual Communities of Practice: Extending the Metaphor

Despite the increasing adoption of virtual teams or communities by many firms and research insti-

tutes (Dubé, Bourhis, & Jacob, 2005), researchers have raised intellectual controversies on whether *communities of practice* could be successfully transposed into virtual environments (Hung & Nichani, 2002; Lueg, 2000), mirroring an analogue debate concerning virtual communities tout-court (Baym, 1995; Wellman & Gulia, 1999). The virtual community literature is basically split between two propositions: *virtual space is a real space in which communities may thrive* and *communities cannot thrive in absence of a shared physical space*. Usually, real life anecdotes are employed to support the former stance (such as Rheingold's experience with the Well community), while theories stressing the inadequacy of computer-mediated communication are used to support the latter view (for a review on both sides of the controversy, see Liu, 2002). However, although cyberspace is not a physical one, it is conceptualized as such (Tarsiero, 2006; Winograd, 1997), and research has shown how similarities do exist in the way people behave in these two *spaces* (Jeffrey & Mark, 1998).

Literature has presented us with a flurry of definitions involving groups of people meeting through the Internet for learning and/or working purposes through social interaction. Most research differentiates primarily between *virtual communities*, which are designed under a given technology and paradigm, and *virtual communities of practice*, which emerge within a virtual community through the differential use its participants make of the software (Johnson, 2001). Constructs somewhat related to *virtual communities of practice* have been described and explored from many different angles by many authors in several fields, mainly as learning communities sharing collaborative or cooperative practices (Dickinson, Graham, & Quinlan, 2005; Greif, 1988; Hildreth & Kimble, 1999; Lehtinen, Hakkarainen, Lipponen, Rahikainen, & Muukkonen, 1999; also see Figure 1 and Figure 2). *Learning communities* (Bielaczyc & Collins, 1999) focus on on-demand protracted informal learning,

Figure 1. Overlapping areas and concepts between computer-supported collaborative learning and virtual communities of practice

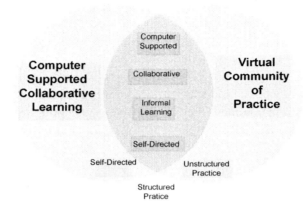

Figure 2. Overlapping areas and concepts between computer-supported cooperative/collaborative work and virtual communities of practice

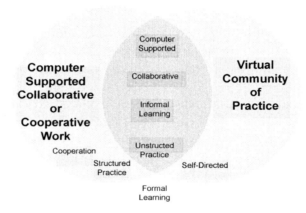

while *asynchronous learning networks* (Hiltz & Wellman, 1997) refer to the time modalities by which some types of formal learning happen. *Voluntary knowledge communities* (Carotenuto, Etienne, Fontaine, Friedman, Muller, Newberg, Simpson, Slusher, & Stevenson, 1999) stress voluntary motivation, while *collaboratories* (Kouzes, Myers, & Wulf, 1996) refer to researchers sharing collaborative practices online. All of these concepts are partially overlapping with distributed (Wenger et al., 2002), computer-mediated (Etzioni & Etzioni, 1999), online (Cothrel &

Williams, 1999), or electronic (Wasko & Faraj, 2000) communities of practice.

The very existence of *virtual communities of practice* has been questioned many times, and for this reason Hildreth and Kimble (1999) tested such hypothesis. They administered the same questionnaire to both co-located and distributed potential members, assessing five metrics deemed to be reflective of communities of practice properties: (a) regular talk with colleagues, (b) contact a colleague to solve a work-related problem, (c) sharing projects with colleagues, (d) anecdote sharing, and (e) learning from interactions with colleagues. The study found out that both face-to-face *communities of practice* and virtual ones could indeed exist and satisfy the aforementioned propositions. Hildreth and Kimble also discovered three ways of possible *virtual community of practice* formation: (a) initial formal or informal contact among distributed individuals, which would eventually constitute the members of a *virtual community of practice*; (b) members of a co-located *community of practice* contacting potential members in other locations and interacting all together through computer-mediated communication on a regular basis; and (c) members of a co-located *community of practice* contacting another distant co-located *community of practice* to start an ongoing dialogue via computer-mediated interaction. A surprising finding of this study was that legitimate peripheral participation, as defined by Lave and Wenger (1991), appeared not to be a key mechanism in a *virtual community of practice*, which might reinforce the proposition that *virtual communities of practice* are, in fact, not *real*. However, such a contradictory finding could also be explained by the fact that a survey is a description of conscious perceptions and behaviors, and therefore an unfit methodology to study implicit-to-implicit knowledge transfer. Such transfer occurs unconsciously, and its awareness can also be impaired by a lack of reflexivity on one's own learning.

Despite the intuitive difference between face-to-face and *virtual communities of practices*, literature often treated them as interchangeable (Dubé, Bourhis, & Jacob, 2003). Because they are two different things (Palloff & Pratt, 1999), Dubé et al. (2003) suggest keeping them distinct and revisiting both definition and literature before applying any of them. When referring to their differences, it is important to resist the temptation of de-contextualizing the comparison and think that one of the two is always better than

the other. *Virtual communities of practice* have a lesser number of cues with respect to face-to-face interactions, which to most are more *natural* and effortless (Ricketts, Wolfe, Norvelle, & Carpenter, 2000), but also overwhelming to others (Palloff & Pratt, 1999). Furthermore, being traditional group norms caused by physical presence reduced, they favor virtual *communities of practice* to emerge (Palloff & Pratt, 1999). From both a codification and a personalization perspective, *virtual communities of practice* also offer a more immediate form of knowledge management (Allen et al, 2003), because they use ICT. They need investments in terms of money and time allocation to build technological and social infrastructure, as well as some degree of organizational support, usually easier to get from organizations that rely more heavily on ICT (Lesser & Storck, 2004). *Virtual communities of practice* also tend to involve a higher number of diverse individuals from many regions and countries (Hiltz & Wellmann, 1997) allowing access to a broader expertise with far lower costs. Because the communication in them is computer-mediated, they have a fair number of advantages for their managers as well as for researchers on the topic: lower information sharing costs, easiness of storage of exchanges in their wholeness and depth, possibility of stricter rule setting and enforcement, and production of a higher range of qualitative and quantitative community metrics for result evaluation. Despite all the differences, however, many field studies so far have shown how *virtual communities of practice* are generally able to accomplish the formal and informal everyday operations of their face-to-face counterparts (Carotenuto et al., 1999; Dubé et al., 2003), even though this does not imply they accomplish the same tasks in the same way.

Defining *virtual communities of practice* ignites many controversies related to germane concepts as well as to the existence and characteristics of such communities, which point to the need for virtual communities of practice taxonomies.

Virtual Communities of Practice: Taxonomies

Because the *virtual community of practice* construct has been considered one-dimensional (Dubé et al., 2003), the field still lacks a taxonomy of these communities notwithstanding such a bulky literature. The one-dimensional stand implies a dichotomized classification of items into what *is* and *is not* a virtual community of practice, with no possibility of further exploration of the qualities *within* virtual communities of practice. A remarkable implication of such approach is the impossibility of studying the relationships among virtual communities of practice and their correlations with metrics. However, all community of practice taxonomies classify communities of practice as community of practice plus a series of adjectives (APCQ, 2001; Gongla & Rizzuto, 2001; Wenger et al, 2002), showing how all of these constructs suffer of the same limitations, which have the same consequences.

Capitalizing on previous work on *structuring characteristics*, Dubé et al. (2003, 2005) built a typology of virtual communities of practice. In order to define which characteristics can be deemed as structuring, these authors searched theoretical and empirical papers and books on face-to-face and *virtual communities of practice* whose focus was information sharing. They then selected the 21 most meaningful characteristics and subdivided these concepts into four main categories, namely:

1. demographics (intended objective, life span, age, and maturity level)
2. organizational context (top-down vs. bottom-up creation process, level of boundary crossing, organizational culture, organizational resources, the degree of institutionalized formalism, and governance structure)
3. membership characteristics (number, geographic dispersion, turnover, members' enrollment type, kind of selection process, degree of knowledge members had of one another prior to community experience, member usage of personal computer, cultural diversity, and the topic's relevance to the work and/or skills of the members)
4. technological environment (a virtual community of practice's overall degree of reliance on information and computer technology and the variety of ICT available to its members)

Using ethnography and social network analysis, Boud and Middleton (2003) analyzed four groups of informal work-related learning networks and discovered that only some of Wenger's (1998) 14 indicators that a community of practice has formed applied. These findings somehow match Dubé, et al. (2003, 2004, 2005) relative to their idea of a *virtual community or practice* as a multidimensional construct.

Despite the importance of structuring characteristics, human interventions are still the ones that can explain why similar communities with similar members, software, interventions, and tasks do not resemble one another and do not have analogous outcomes (Preece, 2001). Both the need for a specific kind of facilitation within *virtual communities of practice* (Kimball & Ladd, 2004) and the role distribution within face-to-face and *virtual communities of practice* have rarely been studied (Fontaine, 2001; Gongla & Rizzuto, 2001; Wenger et al., 2002; Wenger & Snyder, 2000), and in both cases in a non-systematic ways. When it comes to *virtual communities of practice* research, only Bourhis et al. (2005), Dubé et al. (2004), Tarmizi and Vreede (2005), and Tarmizi, Vreede, and Zigurs (2006) have explored roles within communities of practice, even if from different perspectives.

Dubé et al. (2004) analyzed 8 intentionally launched *virtual communities of practice* whose members had three roles assigned from the start. All of the *virtual communities of practice* were tagged with the structuring characteristics in Dubé et al.'s (2003) study. The authors identified three sets of management practices in these communities, each of which was able to modify the outcome of the community under study: (a) practices that foster extrinsic motivation; (b) practices that cultivate intrinsic motivation; and (c) enabling practices. In the same set of eight intentionally formed *virtual communities of practice*, Bourhis et al. (2005) studied leadership and discovered that in these communities success is linked to the leader's ability to foster trust and innovation as well as to make political alliances. In their elegant paper, Tarmizi and Vreede (2005) compare the *group support system facilitation* framework with the needs that arise in a virtual community of practice, aiming at understanding which tasks are required to properly facilitate the latter. The taxonomy they built revolves around the virtual community of practice as the focal center and two groups of tasks, one *outside* of the *virtual community of practice* (external source of information for the world about the *virtual community of practice*, a representative of the interests of the community and its members, and information collector for the community) and another *inside* of it (internal source of information for members, encouraging inspirator and counseling guide). Tarmizi et al. (2006) surveyed three groups of professionals in online facilitation, communities of practice, and facilitation and found that *virtual community of practice* facilitators rated encouraging participation, fostering group ownership and responsibility, and keeping a collaborative environment as the most difficult tasks to accomplish in their job.

Despite the analogies between face-to-face and virtual communities of practice, the reliance on ICT that characterizes the latter changes both their name and their essence. In fact, the very frameworks through which virtual communities of practice are conceptualized lead to a whole different set of problems and inconveniencies to resolve. The recent development of virtual communities of practice taxonomies, however, is of

help in analyzing these communities from a human computer interaction perspective.

Virtual Communities of Practice from a Human Computer Interaction Perspective

Before examining *virtual communities of practice* through HCI lenses, there is the need for a working definition of *virtual communities of practice* that enhances the understanding of the HCI requirements and issues. *Virtual communities of practice* are usually either analyzed from a reductionistic perspective or a-critically endorsed in mythological terms, in the attempt to overcome the fact that the degree of complexity that these communities and their inner dynamics have is very high. The analysis of their constituents cannot provide a predictable portrait of the whole set of properties a community has, because it assumes new properties while interacting with the environment. This feature is one of the characteristics of *living systems*, in which relationships among parts generate new properties for the whole (Capra, 1996). Two more properties are necessary for a living system to survive: *autopoiesis* (i.e., the capability of constantly self-generating) and *existence on the edge of chaos* (Allee, 2002). Face-to-face communities of practice also have an intrinsic instability that takes place when either diversity or seize increase and is responsible of adaptive changes to environmental challenges (Huberman & Hogg, 1995). If we look at *virtual communities of practice* as a set of interactions among their properties, and those properties and the environment, we get an idea of which additional challenges virtual communities of practice interaction design has. We can then analyze a *virtual community of practice* and its components, and also look at the process that links components to relationships and vice versa.

In her HCI framework, Jenny Preece (2001) proposed a model structured around sociability and usability as main pillars to consider when designing an online community. The framework is not specific to *virtual communities of practice* but is applicable to them in any part that does not conflict with their theoretical and practical characteristics and requirements. We therefore need to answer two questions:

1. What do we need in order to have a *virtual community of practice*?
2. How do we know if we are successful in our implementation?

Human Computer Interaction Needs in Virtual Communities of Practice

Sociability

Both taxonomies mentioned in the previous section (Dubé et al., 2003, 2004; Tarmizi & Vreede, 2005) are pivotal to understand why sociability is so important for virtual communities of practice. After having been neglected for 25 years in favor of usability (Preece, 2001), sociability can be looked at as composed of purpose, people, and policy (Preece, 2000).

Despite its apparent clearness, purpose is a fuzzy concept to define because most face-to-face communities of practice do not declare their purpose openly or clearly. Initially, they are *located* at intersections among departments (Allee, 2000), and then management leverages them through a formal initiative (Allee, 2002) whose purpose is reinforced through daily interactions. Because of the impossibility of having daily face-to-face interactions, a *virtual community of practice* needs to be built from scratch and declare, at least tangentially, a purpose related to a practice, such as on-demand collaborative learning and/or informal skill training without excluding or overlooking the social needs of its participants. Purpose, although not self-renewable, exists as an in-between of

goals and chaos, brought about and continuously challenged by events external and internal to the community and is responsible for virtual communities of practice adaptive behavior.

Likely, the way a *virtual community of practice* comes into existence and its own purpose also affect member motivation. Motivation is a construct germane to purpose whose relationships with general online communities are well known. Both ICT and online communities in general foster intrinsic motivation (Ardichvili, Cseh, Gasparishvili, Kristian, & Nemeskeri, 2003; Wasko & Faraj, 2000) that correlates with the success of *virtual communities of practice* as well, as shown by Dubé et al.'s (2004) experiment. Understanding the members' needs and marketing the community's successes are examples of intrinsic motivation fostering practices (Cothrel & Williams, 1999; Lesser & Everest, 2001) that have been validated in both theoretical (Tarmizi & Vreede, 2005) and practical studies on *virtual community of practice* facilitation (Tarmizi, et al., 2006). Intrinsic motivation has the interesting property of being self-renewable in that it fuels its own development and is both a determinant of and determined by social interaction (Ryan & Deci, 2000). Both purpose and motivation have relationships with the other constructs that refer to the definition of sociability in Preece's (2001) scheme, but also with the kind of tasks performed and the software used, that is, usability. They also can modify and be modified by facilitation.

Participation is pivotal to *virtual communities of practice* (Haythornwaithe, Kazmer, & Robins, 2000; Tarmizi & Vreede, 2005). Some of the intentionally formed *virtual communities of practice* studied by Bourhis et al. (2005) and Dubé et al. (2003, 2004, 2005) mandated participation, in striking contrast with the very definition of *community of practice* thereby risking to negatively affect the motivation to volunteer time and skills to the community (Stukas, Snyder, & Clary, 1999) in terms of contribution. According to Wenger's framework, a novice to the practice has to be free to decide at which pace and rate to interact with peers. All of the several degrees of participation are legitimate, and learning occurs via progressive engagement in observation, interaction, action, and reflection (Chao, 2001). In *virtual communities of practice*, an audience that appreciates contributions, especially if openly, provides a strong motivation to contribution (Craig & Zimring, 2000). Researchers tag members with different names according to their quantitative participation rate in the *virtual communities of practice* they are affiliated with (Fontaine, 2004). *Lurkers* are infrequent contributors that may amount to as much as 80-90% of members in an e-mail group, and they choose not to participate for a variety reasons (Nonnecke & Preece, 2001). However, it would be a mistake to frame lurking as an action without effects, because from a system thinking perspective both engagement and disengagement in public interaction contribute to community success or lack thereof, and no action (or inaction) is neutral. How to deal with the disengagement of previously active members is another participation concern matured from e-mail groups (Haythornthwaite, Kazmer, & Robins, 2000). It, too, happens for a variety of reasons (Nonnecke & Preece, 2001). In their extensive study of *communities of practice* at IBM, Gongla and Rizzuto (2001) have observed that face-to-face communities of practice tend to progress through several stages of development, as Wenger et al. (2002) reported in a less systematic way, characterized by quantitative and qualitative differences in member participation. However, to date, there are no studies identifying similar lifecycles in *virtual communities of practice*, let alone defining how such cycles might differ from their face-to-face counterparts. Frameworks like Haythornthwaite et al. (2000) invite managers of e-mail groups to use a variety of Internet communications technologies simultaneously to minimize participation dropout, and are generally accepted and used by online facilitators of *virtual communities of practice*. Participation is

a complex phenomenon also made up of complex parts, but when it reaches self-sustenance it allows for the capability *virtual communities of practice* have to respond to chaotic event without dismembering (Huberman & Hogg, 1995).

Policies are the characteristics of lowest complexity therefore the ones that can more easily be used for interventions and studied in their impact. In an online community, policies are needed in order to determine (a) membership requirements; (b) communication style; (c) acceptable and unacceptable conduct, and (d) role enforcement details (Preece, 2001). Interestingly, Lave and Wenger (1991) did not provide a framework for dealing with any of these issues, while Wenger et al. (2002) described snapshots of different communities without systematizing their policy implementations. Paradoxically, concerns about membership requirements, communication styles, and conduct are more evident in cyberspace than in face-to-face settings, probably because of the inhibiting role played by physical cues (such as voice tone, physical appearance, eye contact, etc.) on the individual with respect to the group norms. As for membership requirements in online learning communities, diversity of expertise among its members is as pivotal as their like-mindedness (Bielaczyc & Collins, 1999; Haythornthwaite et al., 2000) and communication style (Barab & Duffy, 2000; Johnson, 2001; Preece, 2001). Palloff and Pratt (1999) suggest that a community's purpose, norms, and code of conduct be defined before even finding a place to host an online learning community, and Allen et al. (2003) also insist in ensuring management and leadership support to the dawning *virtual community of practice*. Communication style can help establish common ground and foster cooperation and collaboration (Preece, 2001). For this purpose, requirements and examples can be inserted into the *virtual community of practice's* code of conduct, while breaching of the rules can be punished exactly as well as unacceptable conduct. It is very important for the rules to be clearly stated (Preece, 2003), have internal consistency, foster goals and behaviors consistent with *virtual community of practice* theory, practice, and outcomes, and specify who is in charge of producing and enforcing them. Some virtual community of practice members might achieve better understanding and subsequently higher compliance with the rules if in-depth explanations of the reasons behind a policy are provided. As works in *virtual communities of practice* suggest (Allen et al., 2003; Kimball & Ladd, 2004; Neus, 2001; Palloff & Pratt, 1999), the preferred method for establishing policies is to write a community *charter*. By doing so, a group of people with a shared interest and a common practice will undergo a *nucleation* phase in which the community will self-clarify its purpose, form a web of social bonds around a goal or a task, coalesce into a practice, take ownership of its rules and artifacts, foster collaborative behaviors and homogenous attitudes, and attract like-minded potential members.

Usability

Usability refers to the easiness and pleasantness with which software users can perform their tasks. This concept embeds the kind of tasks performed, the users, and the software used (Preece, 2001).

The practitioner literature abounds with recounts on which tasks *communities of practice* are able to perform and accomplish. Yet, no taxonomy exists reflecting which tasks characterize a *community of practice* and how they are (or might be) related to the community's outcome or performance, even in virtual settings. This is even more striking considering the relative easiness of storing, analyzing, and observing task execution in virtual groups. Because *virtual communities of practice* (a) are computer-supported; (b) focus on a practice; (c) have various degrees of informality; (d) revolve around continuous learning; and (e) use collaboration, they partially overlap with both computer-supported cooperative/collaborative work and computer-supported collaborative

learning, in characteristics and tasks. However, a *virtual community of practice* can be distinguished from these two constructs because of its prototypical characteristic: *informal learning* about *unstructured practices* (Allen, 2003). In Allen et al.'s (2003) study, *virtual community of practice* builders attributed informal learning in these settings to the fact it is situated, on-demand, and content-specific, while community members valued that it provides a broad perspective on a problem's solution increases. Interestingly, they both refer to increased interaction as another big learning factor.

Despite many doubts about the reliability of the *community of practice* paradigm in online settings where most interactions are text-based (Johnson, 2001), studies have shown that *virtual communities of practice* can exist (Carotenuto et al., 1999; Dubé et al., 2003; Hildreth & Kimble, 1999), and that written communication is very effective for transformative communication in that it requires extensive thinking processes (Cohen, 1994), and that computer-mediated communication can also foster openness under certain conditions (Walther, 1996). Although the topic of conversation in *virtual communities of practice* relates to practice, it does not imply excessive formality or focus on serious task-related conversations, because humor is notorious to have its place in learning (Gorham & Cristophel, 1990). Paying attention to conversational, coordination, and awareness mechanisms happening during conversations and to how they get modified in virtual text-based environments (Preece et al., 2002) helps fostering informal implicit-to-implicit knowledge transfer and healthy debate of issues at stake. *Virtual communities of practice* also qualify for the same tasks an online learning community (as defined by Bielaczyc & Collins, 1999) has, in particular: (a) seeking to continually advance collective and personal knowledge and skills; (b) emphasis on learning how to learn; and (c) sharing of what is learned. These are, however, complex tasks also impacted by sociability, especially for the ones depending on social interaction. The collaborative nature of tasks in *virtual communities of practice* can impact how they are managed temporally, because some of them can be scheduled (for example, a monthly brainstorming chat) while others can be defined only loosely or not at all (for example, rate of personal e-mails). In *virtual communities of practice* breaking down a task into subtasks can be impossible, because social tasks and the ones related to unstructured practices are too complex to be analyzed through the classical engineering paradigm. Furthermore, each task can be more or less complex at different moments in time, depending on the characteristics of the task itself, the situation faced, the user, and the software in use.

When it comes to users and their approach to computer-mediated communication and *virtual community of practice* dynamics, we are exposed to the whole range of possible human variation, from personal preferences to cognitive biases (Palloff & Pratt, 1999). There are age, gender, and cultural differences in online discourse, interaction styles, and use of paralanguage (Herring, 1992; Preece, 2001; Tarsiero, 2006; Wallace, 1999). Nevertheless, the increasing number of Internet users speaking English as a second language is facilitated by text-based computer-mediated interaction because it makes pronunciation mistakes irrelevant. While there are studies indicating how introverts prefer online collaborative environments (Palloff & Pratt, 1999), other researches point to the fact that learners who rely on interaction as oppose to reflection do not function well in virtual environments (Ricketts et al., 2000). Users of most *virtual communities of practice* are professionals, teachers, or adult students because these communities have been implemented in corporations, management consulting, or educational settings (Allen et al., 2003; APQC, 2001; Boud & Middleton, 2003; Bourhis et al., 2005; Dubé et al., 2003, 2004, 2005; Hildreth & Kimble, 1999; Markestijn, 2004; Wartburg et al., 2004). However, they all are learners.

When considering collective activity, major usability issues emerge, in that there is need of a fine balance between ease of use and versatility. Studies on software design for *virtual communities of practice* can be subdivided into two categories: (a) the ones regarding software as a *mechanism*, and thereby embodying a representation of a specific set of activities that are to be fostered, and (b) the ones regarding software as a *medium*, within and around which users are allowed to freely interact and experiment. Most institutions using *virtual communities of practice* as strategic tools forget how their users do not necessarily have or want to acquire deep information technology literacy. Because participation is driven by the user perception of balance between his/her efforts and the benefit s/he gets out of it (Bullen & Bennet, 1990), the software design has to be simple enough to allow engagement without intimidating the user or requiring too much training. On the other hand, the task needs are very convoluted, ranging from collaborative work-related tools to produce and exchange artifacts (such as a collaborative workspace tool, an artifact repository or file-sharing, and a task-related message archive) to satisfying social needs (asynchronous private messaging or e-mails, informal instant messenger, and more formal many-to-many online meetings). By using the *software as a medium* paradigm, greater flexibility can be obtained in supporting different preferences, behaviors, and learning and interaction needs and styles, all particularly useful when fostering situated implicit-to-implicit social learning. Software embedding a model of a complex interaction or task is doomed to fail whenever the practice is unstructured, that is, too complex to be represented. Some communities host their events using software that was not designed to be a part of a community: therefore, the message board looks different from the instant messaging and the Web site, and so on. Having a uniform look and many tools all in one software package are the main reasons for which many communities nowadays use groupware instead of multiple software packages. Only a few of the many software in use for *virtual communities of practice* have been studied in a rigorous way. Markestjin (2004) analyzed software encompassing both knowledge sharing and knowledge storage paradigm, plus some hybrid forms. He found out that only one allows personal communication, and it was the one that was ranked higher. For example, OntoShare, a Web-based ontology-based system for sharing files with one's *virtual community of practice* does not have any provision for personal communications (Davies, Duke, & Sure, 2003). However, the use of Web-based software allows features like user-control, file, database and document sharing, and computer conferencing, together with interaction.

In virtual communities of practice, human computer interaction barriers impair socialization and execution of tasks among individuals with the result that the virtual community of practice fails to meet the purpose for which it was launched. Furthermore, embodying a representation of an interaction into the software is responsible of excessive structure in the community, which may hamper success in dealing with unstructured practices.

Measuring Success

By measuring the right set of properties and community success metrics before and after implementing *human computer interventions* we can understand users' interaction needs as well as the impact the design had on the community, if any. However, while the aforementioned taxonomies (Bourhis et al., 2005; Dubé et al., 2003, 2004, 2005; Tarmizi & Vreede, 2005) can be used to inform community design, there is no consensus or guidelines on which set of metrics could be more representative of community of practice *success* (APCQ, 2001; Wenger et al., 2002). So far, the most rigorous metric studies involved *virtual communities of practice* (Allen et al., 2003; Bourhis et al., 2005; Dubé et al., 2003,

2004, 2005) probably because, as Cornejo Castro (2006) explains, *virtual communities of practice* can be easily monitored. The set of metrics he developed at Macuarium are the *first* in which usability measurement makes its appearance.

Quantitative metrics are the trickiest to interpret and rely upon because they are the hardest to give meaning to. In fact, the same value may mean and imply very different things in different *virtual communities of practice*, but also within the same one. For example, a high number of virtual communities of practice e-mails may mean good communication as well as inconclusive one; and a high time spent browsing a Web-based *virtual community of practice* may mean high and committed participation, as well as a complete waste of time in searching through bad repositories or inconclusive/useless artifacts. Of the few sets of metrics proposed in literature, some are quantitative while most are either qualitative or a hybrid of the two (Allen et al., 2003). Fontaine and Millen (2004) reviewed the various qualitative approaches to measuring the benefits of face-to-face communities of practice and categorized them as follows: (a) time savings consequent to knowledge management activities; (b) workplace ethnography; (c) social network analysis; (d) balanced scorecards; and (e) intelligible asset valuation methods, but they also mention subjective data collection through workplace surveys. In their review on metrics associated with *virtual communities of practice*, Allen et al. (2003) also include an in-depth assessment of repositories to check on the quality of exchanged information, as well as an evaluation on whether the *virtual community of practice* reached the purpose for which it was started or not (which only applies to intentionally formed ones). Unfortunately, all studies on metrics involved communities in organizational settings (Allen et al., 2003; Dubé et al., 2003, 2004, 2005). *Virtual communities of practice* involving students are usually encompassed in constructs like computer-supported collaborative learning and asynchronous learning networks, betraying the researchers' adherence with the paradigm that studying and learning are not practices.

All studies on *virtual communities of practice* metrics use either qualitative methods or a mix of quantitative and qualitative methods. In Dubé et al. (2005), the definition of *virtual communities of practice success* was in terms of two metrics, *existence* and *health*, the former defined as *existence of a leader and a core group around a work-related project* and the latter as *presence of ongoing group interactions*. Such evaluation, however, does encompass evaluation of repositories, back-channel private interactions, and qualitative characteristics of work-related exchanges. It could therefore be more representative of communities of interest, expertise, or learning, depending on the context. In another study (2004), the same authors considered *effectiveness* as a success indicator and conceptualized it as a mix of meeting the goals for which the *virtual community of practice* was launched, providing the organization with added value, and conferring benefits to its members. However, even though virtual communities of practice may have them, goals are not adequate to define purpose, although they may be related to it, while *added value* and *benefits* are hard to even define in a consistent fashion (Wartburg et al., 2004). Among the key findings, Dubé et al. (2005) found that all failing *virtual communities of practice* they studied had an obstructive management, while highly or moderately relevant discussed topics and the extent to which a *virtual community of practice* has been integrated into a company predicted success in, respectively, 8 and 9 cases out of 10. Decisions about leadership were also found to moderate the negative impact some structuring characteristics have on *virtual communities of practice*, with particular regard to poor ICT skills and low community experience (Bourhis et al., 2005), impacting on their outcome.

In research conducted for the Brigham Young University on *virtual community of practice*, Al-

len et al. (2003) conducted a qualitative study on the impact that *virtual communities of practice* can have in learning within organizations from both an individual and organizational perspective. Interestingly, they tended to ask usability questions to community builders, and sociability questions to users, even though they never labeled them as such.

Facilitating a Virtual Community of Practice

Online facilitation is what is left to do with a virtual community after *virtual community of practice* design is in place, and involves performing tasks related to sociability and usability concerns without overriding or micromanaging the *virtual communities of practice*. Fontaine and Millen (2004) view this role essentially as a sociability enhancer/optimizer, yet professionals in the field maintain it is more complex (Tarmizi et al., 2006).

It is pivotal for the success of virtual communities of practice that somebody assumes the facilitator role in helping the *virtual community of practice* stay on purpose (Bourhis et al., 2005), a relatively easy but important task (Tarmizi et al., 2006). The facilitator also helps old and new members clarify and transform purpose whenever the original one is not adequate to the actual situation.

Other important facilitation tasks involve fostering participation, both in direct and indirect ways. Professionals having facilitated a *virtual community of practice* for any length of time also agree in saying that engaging new members is the most difficult task, but differ in the relative importance they assign to this task as a function of their experience (Tarmizi et al., 2006). Direct engagement may be attempted by contacting new members privately, welcoming them in the community, and *seeding* discussion through purpose-related information and quotes. Indirect engagement involves dealing with those factors that enhance participation by fostering its antecedents, that is, trust and knowledge-sharing attitude (Ardichvili et al., 2003). Trust can be addressed through facilitation tasks like Tarmizi and Vreede's (2005) *create and reinforce an open, positive, and participative environment*, and *promote ownership and encourage group responsibility*, considered to be difficult by, respectively, 56.8% and 61.4% of professionals in the field and important for 56.8% and 47.7% (Tarmizi et al., 2006).

Policy interventions have to directly and indirectly improve cooperative behavior, known to be so important for the success of a *virtual community of practice* and yet so difficult (Tarmizi et al., 2006). Since *free riding* halts a face-to-face community of practice's intrinsic relational instability thereby hampering its adaptive reactions (Hubermann & Hogg, 1995), it is reasonable to think that it might worsen community performance in online settings as well, where anti-normative behaviors are even more frequent. In light of most recent findings on the evolutionary advantages of sanctionary institutions in inducing and keeping cooperation (Gurerk, Irlenbusch, & Rockenbach, 2006), it is advisable not to merely encourage participation, but to also directly discourage lack of cooperation. Meanwhile, encouraging trust and knowledge sharing is a way to indirectly foster collaboration, especially through the enforcement of communication, rituals, social norms, and symbolic actions (Ardichvili et al., 2003; Dubé et al., 2004; Wenger & Snyder, 2000). All of these findings confirm the validity of Tarmizi and Vreede's (2005) taxonomy.

Tasks in *virtual communities of practice* are very complex, for several reasons. For one, they are complex to begin with, pertaining to human socialization, implicit-to-implicit knowledge transfer, and the interaction of the two. They also can be differentially impacted by different combinations of structuring characteristics (Dubé et al., 2003), by the users' attributes, culture, and preferences, and by the software used. Finally,

their complexity is also relative to the observer who frames the task characteristics. While infrastructure will not automatically create community, and sharing artifacts will not guarantee that such artifacts will be used in the way they were intended (Johnson, 2001), legitimate tasks need to exist for the *virtual community of practice* to even begin to emerge in the first place. For these many reasons, and because of the lack of specific task taxonomy, designing tasks is basically impossible, and it is such impossibility to be the hallmark of facilitation in *virtual communities of practice*. The role of the facilitator is, paradoxically, very well described by Wenger et al.'s (2002) book titled *Cultivating Communities of Practice*, that is, creating the conditions for it develops by itself. In particular, the administration task is easier in e-mail-based settings, where collaboration can be organized, controlled, and tutored (Ahern, Peck, & Laycock, 1992).

Users' characteristics are one of the determinants of virtual communities of practice's higher complexity with respect to their face-to-face counterparts. Its membership relies on ICT and text-based communication (Schweitzer, 2003), is culturally diverse (Haythornthwaite et al., 2000), distributed, and often speaks English as a second language. The degree of ICT-friendliness and text-based communication are a matter of both personal (Palloff & Pratt, 1999; Ricketts et al., 2000) and cultural preference (Buragga, 2001; Gill, 1998; Hermeking, 2005), and the presence of members experienced and skilled in online communication benefits the whole community (Pawlowski, Robey, & Raven, 2000). In particular, cultural differences can act as barriers to communication (LeBaron, Pulkkinen, & Scollin, 2000). Geographical dispersion makes over-reliance on synchronous communication problematic, while voice communication can be a barrier to participation for people speaking English as a second language, because of pronunciation issues. If the *virtual community of practice* heavily relies on ICT, differences in ICT literacy can also be a barrier, but the facilitator has to overcome old prejudices toward computer-mediated communication due to early findings (Liu, 2002).

To date, there is no specific platform for *virtual communities of practice* that has been studied even if some are available, but Johnson (2001) noticed that a combination of content, scaffolding, and text-based communication is a suitable *milieu* for emerging *communities of practice*.

The key features software platform has to have in order for a virtual community of practice to develop are:

1.   information sources (such as search, news, or RSS feeds), to allow users to keep informed and current about the virtual community of practice purpose, domain and practice, and the *virtual community of practice* itself;

2.   participation spaces (such as bulletin boards, e-mail lists, or listservs), where members can interact within the community;

3.   administration features to be used to set and enforce rules;

4.   technical facilitation tools, allowing complex *virtual communities of practice* tasks without defining them in advance, both for private interactions (such as e-mail and private messaging software) and collaborative functions (virtual desktop or shared workspace, and document repository or file-sharing); and

5.   user customization, not just in terms of profiles, pictures, and languages, but also a user-controlled shared-space, like bulletins or private blogs.

A sample of Web-based self-identified *virtual communities of practice* more frequently offered: resources/links, *search* function, news, asynchronous communication tools, personal ID, and document exchange (Schweitzer, 2003).

Even when both sociability (purpose, people, and policy) and usability (tasks, users, and software) are correctly addressed, there is no guarantee that a given virtual community of practice

will have success, and there exists no consensus on which metrics to use in defining and refining such target. However, studies conducted on virtual communities of practice confirm the importance of the facilitator and his/her role in managing the technical aspects while providing leadership, rules, and models to members. Future studies on the interplay between technology and sociability will clarify these findings.

FUTURE TRENDS

HCI and the design of specific software for *virtual communities of practice* could impact the success of such communities' endeavors, but it needs broader theoretical concerns to be addressed, in particular the ones referring to cognitive frameworks of representation of online situated interactions. The field also needs more overall systematization about the kind of metrics to use (qualitative vs. quantitative vs. hybrid) and the reasons for such choices. Some concepts are particularly elusive when studied with a mismatched methodology, such as polling opinions about implicit-to-implicit knowledge transfer (that happens subconsciously) and behavioral experiments for assessing cognitive representations.

Since process facilitation skills are crucial to manage communities of practice (Yi, 2000) as well as groups that are not communities of practice, it could be useful for *virtual communities of practice* as well (Kimball & Ladd, 2004; Tarmizi & Vreede, 2005; Tarmizi et al., 2006). However, the field is still relatively unexplored (Bielaczyc & Collins, 1999) mainly because many practitioners resist the idea of structuring spontaneity (as per Brown & Duguid's definition, 2001).

A facilitator is a potentially very important role within *communities of practice* of any kind (Bielaczyc & Collins, 1999; Fontaine, 2001; Rogers, 2000); nevertheless, many discount or overlook it, interpreting the self-organizing properties of *communities of practice* to mean they could not need nurturing under any condition. A possible interpretation for the spontaneous emergence of communities of practice is the presence of a *spontaneous* facilitator in the autochthonous community population. A further development of this thread of thoughts would be about usability and sociability concerns from the perspective of the facilitator him/herself and his/her needs (Borges & Baranauskas, 2003; Damian, Eberlein, Shaw, & Gaines, 2003), with particular attention toward fostering the emergence of spontaneous facilitators.

Despite the potential pitfalls due to the lack of theory and systematization, the field still has much to be revealed, especially for what pertains to the interaction between the facilitator and the virtual community management software.

CONCLUSION

Despite the attention on continuous learning and the use of ICT for that purpose, *virtual communities of practice* are still relatively unknown, especially with respect to their face-to-face counterparts. Most knowledge conveyed through the Internet is still hard, job-related, and task-oriented, as a result of the first researchers' bias toward the new medium.

The literature review on *communities of practice* showed how most literature is a generalization of the social learning paradigm rooted in face-to-face communication as the *best* way to convey meaningful information and then extended to virtual settings as a way to cut costs. Of the studies on *virtual communities of practice*, most of them suffer from the usual limitations that studies on their face-to-face counterparts have. Some of those *communities of practice* have unrealistic engineered design, yet their findings are generalized as *scientific*, while others are apodictical case studies that do not analyze Wenger's works critically, or offer any new theory,

data, or metrics to build and generalize on top of. Nevertheless, the general attitude toward the medium is fairly balanced: in appropriate conditions, computers are seen as a means to facilitate human-to-human-mediated communication, and such communication has a number of interaction advantages recognized.

Researcher and practitioner literature on *virtual communities of practice* is spare and in desperate need of methodological robustness. In fact, the complexity of the field mandates a renewal of the epistemological approach, especially for what pertains to the assumed minor differences between virtual communities of practice and face-to-face *communities of practice*. In the few available studies, facilitation, management, and leadership appeared to be critical factors for the success of these communities, and yet the field of *virtual community of practice* facilitation is just at its beginning. It is mandatory to develop and validate a *community of practice* task taxonomy, so to incorporate it in bigger frameworks whenever appropriate.

HCI in *virtual communities of practice* is more and more a matter of user-centered interaction design because sociability and the representation of social learning in virtual settings are what determine success or failure of a virtual community of practice (Preece et al., 2002). If a *software as a mechanism* perspective is used, it does not begin to understand the complexity of *virtual community of practice* tasks. The alternative is to provide as many channels for collaborative informal learning as possible, by a comprehensive platform or an array of widely customizable software, and let the *virtual community of practice* organize around it with the help of a facilitator.

Neither design nor technical infrastructure may guarantee the effectiveness of human learning. However, looking at the human computer interface for *virtual community of practice* as a problem of social learning facilitation can be effective.

REFERENCES

Ahern, T., Peck, K., & Laycock, M. (1992). The effects of teacher discourse in computer-mediate discussion. *Journal of Educational Computing Research, 8*(3), 291-309.

Allee, V. (2000). Knowledge networks and communities of practice. *Organizational Development Practitioner, 32*(4), Article 0001. Retrieved November 1, 2005, from http://www.odnetwork. org/odponline/vol32n4/knowledgenets.html

Allee, V. (2002, November). *A value network approach for modelling and measuring intangibles.* Paper presented at Transparent Enterprise, Madrid, Spain.

Allen, S. (2003). *No formal training required: How an informal community of practice helps its members improve their individual performance.* Unpublished doctoral dissertation, Utah State University, Logan.

Allen, S., Ure, D., & Evans, S. (2003). *Virtual communities of practice as learning networks* (Research report produced for The Masie Center's e-Learning Consortium). Provo, UT: Brigham Young University, Instructional Psychology and Technology Department.

American Productivity and Quality Center International Benchmarking Clearinghouse (APQC). (2001). *Building and sustaining communities of practice: Final Report.* Houston, Texas: R. Mc-Dermott, C. O'Dell, & C. Hubert.

Ardichvili, A., Cseh, M., Gasparishvili, A., Kristian, B., & Nemeskeri, Z. (2003). Organizational culture and socio-cultural values: Evidence from five economies in transition. In S. A. Lynham & T. M. Egan (Eds.), *Proceedings of the Academy of Human Resource Development 2003 conference* (session 16-2, pp. 327-334). Bowling Greene, Ohio: Bowling Greene State University Press.

Ardichvili, A., Page, V., & Wenthling, T. (2003). Motivation and barriers to participation in virtual knowledge-sharing communities of practice. *Journal of Knowledge Management, 7*(1), 64-77.

Argyris, C., Putnam, R., & McLain Smith, D. (1985). *Action science: Concepts, methods, and skills for research and intervention.* San Francisco: Jossey-Bass.

Barab, S. A., & Duffy, T. M. (2000). From practice fields to communities of practice. In D. Jonassen & S. Land (Eds.), *Theoretical foundations of learning environments* (pp. 25-56). Mahwah, NJ: Erlbaum.

Baym, N. K. (1995). The emergence of community in computer-mediated communication. In S. Jones (Ed.), *Cybersociety.* Newbury Park, CA: Sage.

Bielaczyc, K., & Collins, A. (1999). Learning communities in classrooms: A reconceptualization of educational practice. In C. M. Reigeluth (Ed.), *Instructional-design theories and models: A new paradigm of instructional theory* (pp. 269-292). Mahwah, NJ: Erlbaum.

Borges, M. A. F., & Baranauskas, M. C. C. (2003). Supporting the facilitator in a collaborative learning environment. *International Journal of Continual Engineering Education and Lifelong Learning, 13*(1/2), 39-56.

Boud, D., & Middleton, H. (2003). Learning from others at work: Communities of practice and informal learning. *Journal of Workplace Learning, 15*(5), 194-202.

Bourhis, A., Dubé, L., & Jacob, R. (2005). The success of virtual communities of practice: The leadership factor. *The Electronic Journal of Knowledge Management, 3*(1), 23-34.

Brown, J. S., & Duguid, P. (1991). Organisational learning and communities of practice: Toward a unified view of working, learning, and innovation. *Organisational Science, 2*(1), 40-57.

Brown, J. S., & Duguid, P. (2000). *The social life of information*. Boston: Harvard Business School Press.

Brown, J. S., & Duguid, P. (2001). Structure and spontaneity: Knowledge and organization. In I. Nonaka & D. J. Teece (Eds.), *Managing industrial knowledge: Creation, transfer and utilization* (pp. 44-67). London: Sage.

Bullen, C. V., & Bennett, J. L. (1990). Groupware in practice: An interpretation of work experience. In *Proceedings of the Conference on Computer Supported Cooperative Work* (CSCW'90, pp. 291-302). New York: ACM Press.

Buragga, K. A. (2001). *An investigation of the relationship between national culture and the adoption of information technology*. Unpublished doctoral dissertation, George Mason University, Washington DC.

Capra, F. (1996). *The web of life*. New York: Anchor Books.

Carotenuto, L., Etienne, W., Fontaine, M., Friedman, J., Muller, M. J., Newberg, H., Simpson, M., Slusher, J., & Stevenson, K. (1999, April). *CommunitySpace: Towards flexible support for voluntary knowledge communities*. Paper presented at Changing Places workshop, London.

Chao, C. A. (2001). *Workplace learning as legitimate peripheral participation: A case study of newcomers in a management consulting organization*. Unpublished doctoral dissertation, Indiana University, Bloomington.

Cohen, A. (1994, April) *The effect of individual work on collaborative student activity in a CSILE classroom*. Paper presented at Computer Supported Collaboration for Scientific Inquiry: Bringing Science Learning Closer to Scientific Practice, Annual meeting of American Educational Research Association, New Orleans, LA.

Corrie, B., Wong, H., Zimmerman, T., Marsh, S., Patrick, A. S., Singer, J., Emond, B., & Noël, S. (2003, June). *Towards quality of experience in advanced collaborative environments*. Paper presented at the Third Annual Workshop on Advanced Collaborative Environments, Seattle, WA.

Cothrel, J., & Williams, R. L. (1999). Online communities: Helping them form and grow. *Journal of Knowledge Management, 3*(1), 54-60.

Cox, A. (2004). What are communities of practice? A critical review of four seminal works. In *Proceedings of the 5th European conference on Organizational Knowledge, Learning and Capabilities* (OKLC2004). Innsbruck, Austria: Know-Center.

Cornejo Castro, M. (2006). *The Macuarium set of community of practice measurements*. Retrieved from http://www.knowledgeboard.com

Craig, D. L, & Zimring, C. (2000). Supporting collaborative design groups as design communities. *Design Studies, 20*, 187-204.

Cross, R., Borgatti, S. P., & Parker, A. (2004). Making invisible work visible: Using social network analysis to support strategic collaboration. In E. Lesser & L. Prusak (Eds.), *Creating value with knowledge* (pp. 82-102). New York: Oxford University.

Damian, D. E., Eberlein, A., Shaw, M. L., & Gaines, B. R. (2003). An exploratory study of facilitation in distributed requirements engineering. *Requirements Engineering, 8*(1), 23-41.

Davies, J., Duke, A., & Sure, Y. (2003). OntoShare: A knowledge management environment for virtual communities of practice. In K. Tochtermann & H. Maurer (Eds.), *Proceedings of the 3rd International Conference on Knowledge Management* (I-KNOW'03, pp. 59-65): *(Virtual) Communities of Practice within Modern Organizations Special*

Track, Part 1. Group 2: Technical Support for COPs. Graz, Austria: Springer.

Dickinson, H. D., Graham, P. J., & Quinlan, L. (2005, September). *Understanding distributed communities of practice: Researcher perspectives*. Paper presented at the 2nd Workshop on Distributed Communities of Practice (DCoP), University of Saskatchewan, Saskatoon, Saskatchewan, Canada.

Dubé, L., Bourhis, A., & Jacob, R. (2003). *Towards a typology of virtual communities of practice* (Cahiers du GReSI nº 03-13). Montreal: HEC. Retrieved from http://gresi.hec.ca/cahier.asp

Dubé, L., Bourhis, A., & Jacob, R. (2004). *Structuring spontaneity: The impact of management practices on the success of intentionally formed virtual communities of practice* (Cahiers du GReSI nº 04-20). Montreal: HEC. Retrieved from http://gresi.hec.ca/cahier.asp

Dubé, L., Bourhis, A., & Jacob, R. (2005). The impact of structural characteristics on the launching of virtual communities of practice. *Journal of Organizational Change Management, 18*(2), 145-166.

Etzioni, A., & Etzioni, O. (1999). Face-to-face and computer-mediated communities: A comparative analysis. *The Information Society, 15*, 241-248.

Fontaine, M. A. (2001).Keeping communities of practice afloat: Understanding and fostering roles in communities. In E. Lesser & L. Prusak (Eds.), *Creating value with knowledge* (pp. 124-133). New York: Oxford University.

Fontaine, M. A., & Millen, D. R. (2004). Understanding the benefits and impact of communities of practice. In P. Hildreth & C. Kimble (Eds.), *Knowledge networks: Innovation through communities of practice* (pp. 1-13). Hershey, PA: Idea Group Publishing.

Gill, S. P. (1998). The cultural interface: The role of self. In C. Ess & F. Sudweeks, (Eds.), *Proceedings Cultural Attitudes towards Communication and Technology* (CATaC'98, pp. 246-251). Electronic Journal of Murdoch, Australia: Murdoch University.

Gongla, P., & Rizzuto, C. R. (2001). Evolving communities of practice: IBM Global Services experience. *IBM Systems Journal, 40*(4), 842-862.

Gorham, J., & Christophel, D. M. (1990). The relationship of teachers' use of humor in the classroom to immediacy and student learning. *Communication Education, 39*(1), 46-62.

Gourlay, S. N. (1999). Communities of practice: A new concept for the new millennium, or the rediscovery of the wheel? In M. Easterby-Smith, L. Araujo, & J. Burgoyne (Eds.), *Proceedings of the 3rd international conference on organizational learning: Vol.1* (pp. 479-495). Retrieved September 18, 2005, from http://ktru-main.lancs.ac.uk/pub/ol3.nsf/626e6035eadbb4cd85256499006b15a6/da7655c686292b288025676200449c99/$FILE/Gourlay.pdf

Greif, I. (1988). *Computer-supported cooperative work: A book of readings*. San Mateo, CA: Morgan Kaufmann.

Gurerk, O., Irlenbusch, B., & Rockenbach, B. (2006). The competitive advantage of sanctioning institutions. *Science, 7*(312), 108-111.

Hara, N. (2000). *Social construction of knowledge in professional communities of practice: Tales in courtrooms*. Unpublished doctoral dissertation, Indiana University, Bloomington.

Haythornthwaite, C., Kazmer, M., & Robins, J. (2000). Community development among distance learners: Temporal and technological dimensions. *Journal of Computer-Mediated Communication, 6*, Article 0001. Retrieved February 15, 2006, from http://jcmc.indiana.edu/vol6/issue1/haythornthwaite.html

Hermeking, M. (2005). Culture and Internet consumption: Contributions from cross-cultural marketing and advertising research. *Journal of Computer-Mediated Communication, 11*(1), article 10. Retrieved February 19, 2006, from http://jcmc.indiana.edu/vol11/issue1/hermeking.html

Herring, S. C. (1992). *Gender and participation in computer-mediated linguistic discourse.* Washington, D.C.: ERIC Clearinghouse on Languages and Linguistics (ERIC Document Reproduction Service No. ED345552).

Hildreth, P., & Kimble, C. (1999, March). *Communities of practice in the distributed international environment.* Paper presented at the Second Workshop on Understanding Work and Designing Artefacts: Design for Collaboration, Communities Constructing Technology. University of York, King's Manor, UK.

Hiltz, S. R., & Wellman, B. (1997). Asynchronous learning networks as a virtual classroom. *Communications of the ACM, 40*(9), 44-49.

Holsapple, C. W., & Whinston, A. P. (1996). *Decision support systems. A knowledge based approach.* Minneapolis, MN: West Publishing Company.

Huberman, B. A., & Hogg, T. (1995). Communities of practice: Performance and evolution. *Computational and Mathematical Organization Theory, 1*(1), 73-92.

Hung, D., & Nichani, M. (2002). Differentiating between communities of practices (CoPs) and quasi-communities: Can CoPs exist online? *International Journal on E-Learning, 1*(3), 23-29.

Jeffrey, P., & Mark, G. (1998). Constructing social spaces in virtual environments: A study of navigation and interaction. In K Höök, A. Munro, & D. Benyon (Eds.), *Workshop on Personalised and Social Navigation in Information Space*

(Technical Report T98:02, pp. 24-38), Stockholm: Swedish Institute of Computer Science.

Johnson, C. M. (2001). A survey of current research on online communities of practice. *Internet and Higher Education, 4*(1), 45-60.

Kamel, N., Narasipuram, M. M., & Toraskar, K. (1997). An approach to value-based modeling of information flows. *Information Society, 13*(1), 93-106.

Kaplan, R., & Norton, D. (1996). *The balanced scorecard: Translating strategy into action.* Boston: Harvard Business School.

Kimball, L., & Ladd, A. (2004). Facilitator toolkit for building and sustaining virtual communities of practice. In P. M. Hildreth & C. Kimble (Eds.), *Knowledge networks: Innovation through communities of practice* (pp. 202-215). Hershey, PA: Idea Group Publishing.

Kouzes, R. T., Myers, J. D., & Wulf, W. A. (1996). Collaboratories: Doing science on the Internet. *Computer, 29*(8), 40-46.

Lave, J., & Wenger, E. (1991). *Situated learning: Legitimate peripheral participation.* New York: Cambridge University.

Lehtinen, E., Hakkarainen, K., Lipponen, L., Rahikainen, M., & Muukkonen, H. (1999). *Computer supported collaborative learning: A review.* CL-Net Project. Retrieved March 30, 2006, from http://www.kas.utu.fi/clnet/clnetreport.html

Lesser, E., & Everest, K. (2001). Using communities of practice to manage intellectual capital. *Ivey Business Journal, 65*(4), 37-41.

Lesser, E., & Storck, J. (2004). Communities of practice and organizational performance. In E. Lesser & L. Prusak (Eds.), *Creating value with knowledge* (pp. 107-123). New York: Oxford University.

Liedka, J. (1999). Linking competitive advantage with communities of practice. *Journal of Management Inquiry, 8*(1), 5-16.

Liu, Y. (2002). What does research say about the nature of computer-mediated communication: Task-oriented, social-emotion-oriented, or both? *Electronic Journal of Sociology, 6*(1), Article 001. Retrieved December 21, 2005, from http://www.sociology.org/content/vol006.001/liu.html

Lueg, C. (2000, September). *Where is the action in virtual communities of practice?* Paper presented at the German Computer-Supported Cooperative Work Conference (D-CSCW), Workshop on Communication and Cooperation in Knowledge Communities, Munich, Germany.

Markestijn, J. (2004). *Communities of practice and supporting software.* Unpublished master's thesis, Vrije University, Amsterdam.

Neus, A. (2001). Managing information quality in virtual communities of practice. In E. Pierce & R. Katz-Haas (Eds.), *Proceedings of the 6th International Conference on Information Quality* (IQ '01, pp. 1-11). Retrieved February 16, 2006, from http://opensource.mit.edu/papers/neus.pdf

Nonnecke, B., & Preece, J. (2001). Why lurkers lurk. In *Proceeding of Seventh Americas Conference on Information Systems* (AMCIS'01, pp. 1521-1531). Boston: Omnipress.

Orr, J. (1990). Sharing knowledge celebrating identity: War stories and community memory in a service culture. In D. S. Middleton & D. Edwards (Eds.), *Collective remembering: Memory in society.* Beverly Hills, CA: Sage.

Palloff, R., & Pratt, K. (1999). *Building learning communities in cyberspace: Effective strategies for the online classroom.* San Francisco: Jossey-Bass.

Pawlowski, S. D., Robey, D., & Raven, A. (2000). Supporting shared information systems: Boundary objects, communities, and brokering. In

Proceedings of the 21st International Conference on Information Systems (ICIS'00, pp. 329-338). Boston: Omnipress.

Preece, J. (2001). *Online communities: Designing usability, supporting sociability.* New York: Wiley and Sons.

Preece, J. (2003). Tacit knowledge and social capital: Supporting sociability in online communities of practice. In K. Tochtermann & H. Maurer (Eds.), *Proceedings of the 3rd International Conference on Knowledge Management* (I-KNOW'03, pp. 72-78): *(Virtual) Communities of Practice within Modern Organizations Special Track, Part 1. Keynote closing speech.* Graz, Austria: Springer.

Preece, J., Rogers, Y., & Sharp, H. (2002). *Interaction design.* New York: Wiley and Sons.

Rheingold, H. (2000). *The virtual community: Homesteading on the electronic frontier* (Rev. ed.). Cambridge, MA: MIT.

Ricketts, J., Wolfe, F., Norvelle, E., & Carpenter, E. (2000). Multimedia: Asynchronous distributed education—A review and case study. *Social Science Computer Review, 18*(2), 132-146.

Rogers, J. (2000). Communities of practice: A framework for fostering coherence in virtual learning communities. *Educational Technology and Society, 3*(3), 384-392.

Ryan, R. M., & Deci, E. L. (2000). Self-determination theory and the facilitation of intrinsic motivation, social development, and well-being. *American Psychologist, 55*, 68-78.

Salomon, G. (1991). From theory to practice: The international science classroom. *Educational Technology, 31*(3), 41-44.

Schweitzer, S. J. (2003). *Discussion forums: The core of online communities of practice.* Retrieved March 24, 2006, from http://java.cs.vt.edu/public/classes/communities/uploads/schweitzer597_project.pdf

Senge, P. (1990). The art and practice of the learning organization. In M. Ray & A. Rinzler (Eds.), *The new paradigm in business*. New York: G. P. Putnam's Sons.

Stukas, A. A., Snyder, M., & Clary, E. G. (1999). The effects of "mandatory volunteerism" on intentions to volunteer. *Psychological Science, 10*(1), 59-64.

Tarmizi, H., & de Vreede, G. -J. (2005). A facilitation task taxonomy for communities of practice. In *Proceedings of the 11th Americas Conference on Information Systems* (AMCIS'05)*: Virtual Communities Minitrack* (paper #1570, pp. 3545-3554). Boston: Omnipress.

Tarmizi, H., de Vreede, G. -J., & Zigurs, I. (2006). Identifying challenges for facilitation in communities of practice. In *Proceedings of the 39th Hawaii International Conference on System Sciences (HICSS-39): Track 1. Virtual Work, Teams, and Organizations Minitrack* (p. 26a-10 pages). Los Alamitos, CA: IEEE Computer Society.

Tarsiero, R. (2006). *Linguistics of computer-mediated communication: Approaching the metaphor.* Manuscript submitted for publication.

Wallace, P. (1999). *The psychology of the Internet.* Cambridge, UK: Cambridge University.

Walther, J. B. (1996). Computer-mediated communication: Impersonal, interpersonal, and hyperpersonal interaction. *Communication Research, 23*(1), 1-43.

Wartburg, I. von, Rost, K., & Teichert, T. (2004). The creation of social and intellectual capital in virtual communities of practice. In *Proceedings of the 5th European conference on Organizational Knowledge, Learning and Capabilities (OKLC '04): Session E3*. Innsbruck, Austria: Know-Center.

Wasko, M. M., & Faraj, S. (2000). It is what one does: Why people participate and help others in electronic communities of practice. *Journal of Strategic Information Systems, 9*(2-3), 155-173.

Wellman, B., & Gulia, M. (1999). Net surfers don't ride alone: Virtual communities as communities. In B. Wellman (Ed.), *Networks in the Global Village* (pp. 331-366). Boulder, CO: Westview.

Wenger, E. C. (1998). *Communities of practice: Learning, meaning and identity.* New York: Cambridge University.

Wenger, E. C., McDermott, R., & Snyder, W. M. (2002). *Cultivating communities of practice: A guide to managing knowledge.* Boston: Harvard Business School.

Wenger, E. C., & Snyder, W. M. (2000). Communities of practice: The organizational frontier. *Harvard Business Review*, 139-145.

Winograd, T. (1997). The design of interaction. In P. J. Denning & R. M. Metcalfe (Eds.), *Beyond calculation: The next fifty years of computing.* New York: Springer.

Yi, J. Q. (2000). *Supporting business by facilitating organizational learning and knowledge creation in the MOT community of practice (CoP).* Unpublished doctoral dissertation, Indiana University, Bloomington.

Section III
Teacher and Student Use of HCI

Chapter VII
Design–Personae:
Matching Students' Learning Profiles in Web–Based Education

J. Martin
RMIT University, Australia

E. McKay
RMIT University, Australia

L. Hawkins
RMIT University, Australia

V. K. Murthy
RMIT University, Australia

ABSTRACT

Ever since the enthralling book Rethinking University Teaching: A Framework for the Effective Use of Educational Technology *(Laurillard, 1993) the literature has burst forth with a plethora of new and exciting ways for teacher and student use of information and communications technology (ICT) to enhance learning. Our chapter mirrors the enormous spread of professional practice involved in bringing about effective human-computer interaction (HCI) for Web-based education.*

SUMMARY

Designing effective and contemporary online learning environments presents major challenges for academic practitioners (Seagrave & Holt, 2003). This chapter is set within a social science context to convey a practical way to develop a flexible educational program. A theoretical case study situates our example of how to utilize a *design-persona* with characteristics that represent an individual student or a complete program cohort. We argue there are two issues involved in persona design. Firstly, educational designers need to know how to satisfy an ever diverse range of learners' needs for experiential learning. Secondly, the online developer needs to know how to implement satisfying instructional strategies with the complex tools that are offered by ICTs. While important developments such as the *semantic Web* (a *machine-dimension* of HCI that represents information as a combination of hypertext and the Internet technologies [Emonds-Banfield, 2006]) and agent technologies are emerging to assist educational designers (Anderson & Elloumi, 2004), we propose a practical way to implement instructional strategies through effective HCI. We apply the term HCI to reflect use and context (de Souza & Preece, 2004; Preece, 1994), to describe a combination of the social organization of work that occurs through the *human-machine* fit and adaptation of available ICT.

The chapter commences with an explanation of the diverse nature of teaching and learning in a technological age. Next there is a small discussion on the prominence of ICT tools that are emerging through multimedia resources to implement flexible education. The *student-centered* approach follows to progress the discussion from the *machine-dimension* of HCI within the education sector, to explain some of the more *human-dimensional* differences that occur in any student cohort.

We describe *design-personae* as a theoretical modelling technique that may reflect predicted students' characteristics. Courseware design is complicated (McKay & Martin, 2006). Many novice courseware designers are challenged when considering how to match individual characteristics of a learner to an appropriate learning context. Systems theory is then brought forward to highlight the importance of knowing how to synergize the *machine/human-dimensions* of HCI to initiate a basic courseware development plan.

Our *Getting Started: Case Study section* is presented as the hypothetical example of how to implement an online learning program using *design-personae* to capture the characteristics of a student cohort. There are four separate profiles or personae described in this section; two relate to the notions of having primary *design-personae*

to reflect the student cohorts, while the secondary *design-personae* are used to denote the university faculty management (for administrative functions) and the important external stakeholders (to denote employers and professional associations).

However, in looking toward the future of online learning environments, we also point to recent developments in the *semantic Web* and *software agents* (Murthy, 2005a), that are set to play an important role in an interactive and physical *(online)* sense, with their ability to *seamlessly* match each student's learning profile to meet their individual needs, thereby, broadening the flexibility of Web-based education. Our discussion closes with an overview of how the *design-personae* can be developed into an actual *software agent* tool, which is implemented as a physical electronic object (perhaps as an *e-persona*) that resides within an online learning environment.

INTRODUCTION

Teaching and learning in the new millennium require the integration of new technologies with aspects that will add value to the student experience and those that will detract from it. These decisions are made within the context of declining fiscal resources allocated to universities for teaching and learning, and with students being able to afford less and less time on-campus due to paid work commitments. As education is no longer universally free, a large proportion of students need to juggle paid work and study commitments along with other responsibilities and interests so they can afford to study. Fee for service creates another set of expectations with students considering value-for-money as part of their student learning experience. Universities have traditionally been seen as places of learning. However since education is no longer free, market forces threaten this tradition. Students are driven by different considerations to seek tertiary education. Accordingly, universities have to compete for students and in so doing, must design courses that accommodate the demands students make of them without compromising their tradition. An increasing number of students wish to complete their studies in a minimum amount of time with maximum learning and skills. They want to clearly see how these outcomes are going to maximize employment and career opportunities. ICTs can provide an effective solution. Animated *pedagogical agents* are emerging to facilitate interactive learning environments (Lester, Converse, Kahler, Barlow, Stone, & Bhoga, 1997).

It is tempting to embrace new technologies and put courses online. Web-based courseware provides students with flexibility as well as providing them with a wealth of information. Feedback from undergraduate students, however, reveals this is not what they really want. Education extends beyond reading copious amounts of materials online, chatting to lecturers and other students electronically, and meeting assessment requirements. Many undergraduate students complain about the amount of online learning that is being used in university courses and state a preference for *face-to-face* learning (Dennen, 2003). It is only a small minority who prefer this online learning (Hammond & Wiriyapinit, 2005). Students value quality learning experiences that meet their educational needs. This often includes flexible delivery (Hooks, 1994). Flexibility means that learners may retain the best combinations of instructional strategies to include instructor-led classroom sessions and practical activities that may be conducted elsewhere (Collis, 2004). One observation of a study commissioned by the Australian Department of Education, Training and Youth Affairs into the effectiveness of models of flexible provision of higher education was that the responses of both staff and student satisfaction were varied. Whilst both parties appreciated the flexibility, it was associated with a cost. "*For some students, staff contact was too limited; for others less flexibility was available than they anticipated.*

For staff flexible provision often involved a higher workload" (Ling & Arger, 2002, p. 27).

It is argued in this chapter that ICTs should be used as an adjunct to quality teaching and learning and not as a replacement for *face-to-face* contact. Flexible education is discussed, followed by consideration of a *student-centered* approach to teaching and learning. There are two important concepts relating to choosing the appropriate context for e-learning environments (McKay & Martin, 2006). *Instructional science* offers practical ways to identify appropriate e-learning designs (Schwier, 2001b), while there is a separate challenge to devise an appropriate instructional architecture in which to implement the learning materials. Differing *views-of-learning* relate to the cognitive processing that is expected by the learners and the learning task at hand (Clark, 2003). As such they set a *design view* for the type of *instructional architecture* to integrate the learning content and instructional strategies employed by the courseware developer. This activity is much the same as we experience in developing specifications with an architect when building a house. Added challenges for designing educational ICT resources relate to knowing how to capture the semiotic context or *human-dimension* of the HCI in an online educational program. In this context, we also briefly describe the role of the *semantic Web* and agent technology (Murthy, 2005c) in Web-based teaching and learning (Berners-Lee, Hendler, & Lassila, 2001).

The use of a *design-persona* as a hypothetical user provides a reference point for the relevance of content as well as for designing the means and methods of delivery. In this sense, the *design-persona* is useful for getting started in the use of ICTs as educational resource tools by providing a reference point for the design process (McKay & Martin, 2006). The hypothetical case study illustrates the application of a *design-persona* for courseware development. We present a composition of a number of features of different university courses in the human services sector including human services, social work, psychology, welfare studies, community work, and nursing. The case study provides a practical example for those who would like to use a *design-persona* for course and subject development.

FLEXIBLE EDUCATION

In comparison to traditional educational models, flexible education is broadly characterized by:

- Less reliance on *face-to-face* teaching
- Greater reliance on high quality alternate learning resources
- Greater opportunities to communicate—outside traditional teaching times
- An increasing use of ICTs
- The deployment of multi-skilled teams

(Martin, Hess, Hawkins, & Pitt, 2002)

Resource-based learning or flexible learning is often synonymous with the use of ICTs, including the electronic pasting of lecture notes and required readings, noticeboards, chat rooms, online exercises, and assessments (Moran & Myringer, 1999). This may be suited to students who live in rural and remote locations and students who cannot afford the time to attend classes (Cey, 2001). It may be appropriate for some courses to have high levels or total online delivery of content. However, process skills including interpersonal communication, teamwork, and conflict resolution cannot be taught electronically (Martin, 2002). Likewise, critical reflection and thinking is often stimulated through interaction with others (Beckett, 1998).

Flexible education encompasses a range of *multimedia* materials used for the design and delivery of the pedagogy and instructional resources that support learning. These include any combination of distance education, external/off-

campus studies, flexi-mode, min-conference, and extended campus mode (Seagrave & Holt, 2003). However, there is a significant body of literature that does not agree. Above all there is real concern for the lack of social interaction as the most severe barrier as perceived by students (Muillenburg & Berge, 2005). There are many types of learning environments, including the use of problem solving, experiential learning, practicum, video lectures, and so on that can also be used to provide flexibility for students. Experiential learning and practicum are examples of important interactive environments that promote individualistic educational ideology (Beckett, 1998). The application of flexible education in university policy focuses on a *student-centered* approach to flexible learning (Pond, 2002). In its broadest sense, flexible education recognizes that students have different teaching and learning needs. Flexible learning aims to meet individual needs by providing choices that allow students to meet their own educational requirements in ways that suit their individual circumstances.

Flexible education provides choices in time and/or place of study, including on and off campus, or combinations of both. It can cater for different learning styles and preferences by providing a range of learning resources and tasks to suit individual needs (McKay & Martin, 2006; Nicholson, 1995). Contextualized learning occurs through the ability to tailor some, or all, of the learning content, process, outcomes, or assessment to individual circumstances. However, this begs the question of what an individual's circumstances are and how universities can afford to meet these in an environment of funding cutbacks to higher education. Catering to individual student needs and differences is generally seen as resource intensive with universities increasingly adopting uniform processes to cut costs. How then can flexible education be delivered in a viable way that caters for individual needs, yet is not making excessive demands on resources? A collective view of *individual needs* is required with teaching and learning, *that meets the needs of a particular group of students, the emphasis being on negotiated times, places, and modes of learning and the combined use of face-to-face learning with communication by appropriate media and technology* (Hawkins & Sefton, 1989). Yet the question remains as to how we gain a sense of the collective needs of a particular group of students. We propose that implementing a *design-persona* during the process of courseware development strengthens a *student-centric* learning environment (Pruitt & Grudin, 2003).

STUDENT-CENTERED APPROACH

The *student-centered* approach underpinning flexible learning processes requires different teaching methodologies alongside a different type of relationship between teachers and students (Parchoma, 2003). A student-driven curriculum integrates theory and practice, providing students with the knowledge and skills required by employers without compromising the academic rigour of a university education. It is through comprehensive and flexible uses, that the latest in terms of teaching and learning strategies are responsive to student needs (Daniel, Schwier, & McCalla, 2003). *Student-centered* pedagogies empower learners (Hannafin & Land, 1997). Although educators have been working toward empowering

students, little understanding and research has been forthcoming (Sullivan, 2002).

According to Sullivan (2002), understanding the conception of power can be useful to examine empowerment in terms of *power-over, power-with,* and *power-to*. What students want from a university course is presented in Table 1, the *student empowerment model*.

Responsiveness to an individual student's needs and flexible education are central features of the *empowerment model*. The *design-persona* is a useful tool for the design and delivery of flexible education that is *student centered* and is responsive to the individual and collective needs of students in a way that is resource efficient (Pruitt & Grudin, 2003). Education for the *helping professions* challenges the individualism associated with traditional flexible delivery modes. Whilst flexible learning is based upon a *student-centered* approach, it is important to contextualize the student and factors identified in the *student empowerment model* within the broader community framework (Schwier, 2001a). The demand for access to and control of one's education (Ally, 2004), relating to time and space that is convenient to an individual, may risk isolating the student from the major parties and learning processes upon which the curriculum is based. A similar case may be argued for staff (Anderson & Elloumi, 2004). A comparatively small proportion of universities have researched flexibility

Table 1. Student empowerment model (Martin, 2002)

Wants, Desires, and Expectations—*Student-Centered* Empowerment	
Student-centered focus	Excellence
Sense of belonging	Flexibility
Currency in the marketplace	Learning community
Relevance	Value for money
Recognition of level of competency on entry into the degree	Range of methods used suited to the course being taught
Assessment needs to be clear and concise and aligned with individual student learning needs	Teaching and learning pitched at a level appropriate to educational and industry competencies, tasks, and outcomes
Community engagement	Student interaction

from a collective structural perspective, or have adequately mastered the human components of HCI to deliver Web-based instruction that suits the broad range of student learning styles.

When discussing flexible e-learning platform design, the range of students' cognitive processing should be taken into account (Preece, 1994). One effective way to describe how individuals process information taps into both cerebral hemispheres to attract benefits from both the analytical and visual orientation of the target users (McKay, 2000a). According to Riding (2002), researchers in general are aware of learners' cognitive or learning style differences—and the implications for instructional design. He describes a model of assessing the position of an individual on two basic dimensions of cognitive style. In the first, the *Verbal-Imagery* dimension depicts the way people prefer to represent information during thinking. This is the way many people refer to cognitive style. By drawing on Pavio's work Riding shows that some people think in terms of mental pictures *(the visualizers)*; while others think in terms of words *(the verbalizers)* (Riding, 2002). Riding points out that people are capable of utilizing either cognitive mode. He says that some people have a tendency to use only one mode—visual or verbal. Preferred cognitive style affects performance in both the perceptual and conceptual domains of the learning process. The more effective learning strategy would facilitate active integration of both these cognitive styles. According to Riding, it is the part of cognition that can change, according to the personal choice and the task at hand. People will naturally revert to the easiest thinking mode according to what they are doing at the time. Past experience may also play an important role in this dimension.

The second dimension Riding calls the *Wholist-Analytic* that identifies people's mode of processing information that is not changeable. Riding believes this cognitive dimension is inherent and may hold true over time. Cognitive style is therefore made up by the combinations of these

two basic dimensions, which Riding believes are independent. There is a common belief that imagers will learn better if offered visual material and that verbalizers will do best with text. However, common beliefs can lead researchers and courseware designers down the wrong path (McKay, 2000a, 2000b).

THE DESIGN-PERSONA

Providing a reference point for all aspects of educational design may safeguard against design elements that are inappropriate or not suited to the intended student population. A *design-persona* assists in understanding user information needs informing design and accessibility and ultimately suitability (Sinha, 2002). The *design-persona* represents the characteristics of a hypothetical student embodying the main features of the student cohort.

User profiles have been utilized for some time in marketing and project design, particularly since the late 1990s. Personae are seen to have replaced the so-called *elastic user* by replacing them with a caricature of a real person who becomes an integral part of the project design process. It was argued that designing a persona was better than designing for a vaguely defined group of users. The *design-persona* provides a conduit for transmitting a wide range of information about design and use. Representation of the user group is crucial, and this is the main advantage of using a *design-persona*.

A *design-persona* provides a lens that includes the socio-political context. By focusing attention on a particular user group, personae assist in identifying different kinds of users as well as those who are not being designed for (Pruitt & Grudin, 2003). Designing the right persona or set of personae can be challenging. A common mistake to avoid is choosing *flashy* technology over accessibility. Hourihan (2002) warns against the project team designing for themselves and losing sight of the intended user group.

A *design-persona* is developed through a number of quantitative and qualitative processes including interviews, observations, ethnographies, focus groups, brainstorming, market research, and usability studies (Sinha, 2002). Members of the project team ultimately direct any changes and modifications required to the *design-persona* throughout a courseware development project to ensure relevance and responsiveness to enact required changes (Sinha, 2002). It is essential that representative individuals from user groups are included in all aspects of project design including the development of the *design-persona*. It must not be seen as a replacement for active user involvement.

Slowly the *design-persona* comes to life as a real person when given a name. Empathic planning and decision-making can be made with this name and identity clarified. For instance, rather than thinking, *how would a student use this?*, this question can be personalized to reflect *how would Sally use this?* In this example, Sally's name is chosen as the representative of the intended user group to embody all of the personal features of the intended user group. These features might include age, gender, educational background, class, health, ability/disability, race, ethnicity and culture, sexuality, and spirituality (Giroux & Shannon, 1997). Cooper (2004, p. 53) comments, "*All things being equal I will use people of different races, genders, nationalities, and colours.*"

A common vision and commitment to the *design-persona* is essential for successful educational design and implementation. Communication processes will influence how the persona is included within the *design-team* at all stages of the project development. Communication is therefore an important aspect of project management, particularly for those who may be absent from meetings when the persona is being planned (McKay & Martin, 2006). Creative strategies are required to keep the design-persona relevant and the focus of the project's design activities. Detailed documentation that succinctly describes the main features of each *design-persona* is essential. For instance, the level of detail suggested by (Freydenson, 2002) includes *at least a first and last name, age, goals, background story, a telling quote, e-mail address, job title, and a photograph.* Overtime, the *design-persona* may change and develop along with the project. At times more than one persona may be required, particularly in instances of extreme diversity amongst potential user groups. Freydenson (2002) recommends the development of multiple personae with each given a status according to a hierarch of status. These categorized personae can therefore extend beyond a *primary-persona* defined for students to include others in a *secondary-persona* status, such as administration and management, professional associations, and employer groups. In the end, the *primary-persona* must be satisfied with the system you deliver (Hourihan, 2002).

Applied to an educational institution, this type of *design-persona* becomes a *hypothetical student* on a journey through a higher-degree or similar course of study. In this context, the challenge for an educational course *design-team* is to identify the routine tasks and procedures to create a personal and user friendly instructional environment. The use of such a *design-persona* in an educational environment may bring a student's profile to life as a reference point. In an educational setting the *design-persona* involves many contextual decisions.

Therefore, conducting a thorough *learning-task analysis* (Dick, Carey, & O'Carey, 2004) is useful in identifying the cognitive processes involved in gaining a university education. Often there are clear developmental stages that may include pre-entry, entry, engagement, and exit. Pre-entry includes consideration of marketing and promotion, study pre-requisites, and processes for applying, student selection, and enrollment. The pre-entry stage may also include consideration of credit transfers and pathways from other educational institutions, particularly in the *technical and further education distance (education) network* in Australia, known as TAFE. At times, there may be additional issues that impact upon a student's learning environment around access and equity, and special learning requirements for particular students. Entry into the TAFE sector includes orientation, preparation for success at *(Australian)* tertiary-level study, and a sense of focus and belonging. Engagement extends to maintaining and developing this focus in a *student-centered* environment that is responsive to student learning needs. Exit from TAFE requires adequate preparation for transition from university to the workplace including professional socialization as well as considering ongoing links and relationships with the university. Alongside the identification of learning processes and associated tasks at a university level, the expected learning outcomes should be aligned with the students' expectations (Dick et al., 2004), thereby identifying the personal and social features of the *design-persona*.

PROFILE MATCHING

The principles of instructional design define *fine-grained* ways to identify strategies that support effective HCI. It is very important to match the learning context with the target learners' profile and their specific needs (Merrill, 2002). Profile-matching, which is also called mapping, is useful for identifying personal and social factors that impact upon a student's ability to participate fully in tertiary education.

Mapping as it applies to the social sciences describes the process of identifying factors that will impact upon a person's ability to engage in university education to include the needs, interests, and concerns of the student *design-persona* that surround the main issues in her or his life. They may extend beyond the student's education to consider other aspects such as hours in paid employment, family responsibilities, and possibly health. In developing effective teaching and learning experiences, a key to success is the level of commitment by students and educators, for developing an understanding of how well students' needs are met and how much they have been considered in the design of an educational experience. Teaching and learning resources can then be developed to meet as many needs and concerns as possible. ICTs form an important part of the resources offered to students within a higher-educational environment. Because of this, it is considered important to take a social orientation toward technology use as a critical element of HCI (Preece, 2005). In matching a *learning-design* to specific students, it is useful to adopt a systematic strategy when investigating the plethora of issues involved (Dick et al., 2004).

SYSTEMS THEORY

Systems theory as it applies to the social sciences is critical in developing design-personae that are to be implemented within a learning environment that involves HCI. According to Payne (1997), explicit assumptions of systems theory applied to tertiary education involve:

- The university's obligation to ensure that students have access to resources, services, and opportunities that meet learning needs, to alleviate distress and realize their educational goals and aspirations.
- In providing services, the dignity and individuality of the student must be respected.
- Teaching and learning must maximize student's participation and self-determination.
- Students have a right to control their own education. As such, they should be encouraged to construct their own knowledge (Murphy & Cifuentes, 2001).
- Problems are manifestations of a breakdown in the interactions between students and the university.

Key concepts of systems theory as defined in a social science context are constant change, dynamic interaction, goodness of fit, and adaptation. The aim is to achieve a sense of balance or *steady state* that is conducive to a positive experience with change an integral component of this. Universities are viewed as complex, adaptive organizations that are continually changing and generating new patterns of actions, interactions, and meanings.

Systems theory as it applies to the components of HCI is very similar to the definition that the social science practitioners use. In computing, however, the origins were founded in computer science (Hawryszkiewycz, 1988). Emphasis is placed on the human-machine aspects of systems design for the fit and adaptation (Preece, 1994). Emphasis centers on the detailed description of the *(information)* system's design, the system's development cycle, the problem solving capacity of the algorithms, which underpin the system's functioning, the system's life cycle, a data dictionary that specifies attributes, data input, reporting or output, and the users' requirements. Systems analysis is central to an information systems design process. Over the years agreement is difficult to find on ways to implement the best analysis methods for which systems. Consequently, it has even been called a black art, due to the soft-nature or craft-like process, which relates to systems analysis that involves a set of multi-disciplinary skills (Whitehead, 1986).

ONE SIZE DEFINITELY DOES NOT FIT ALL

Personae have been criticized as a reductionist approach of *one size fits all* that does not allow for, or respond to student diversity (Perfetti, 2002). It is argued that by using a persona, individuals are stereotyped and characterized according to a predetermined set of characteristics. If the categories are not broad enough to be inclusive of the diversity within the student group, then discrimination is likely to occur. It is asserted that it is not possible to develop a persona that encompasses all of the features of the student body. Interestingly this argument is about exactly what a *design-persona* is designed to avoid. The aim of a *design-persona* is to be inclusive and non-discriminatory and to be responsive to the characteristics and needs of the student group, not the view or needs of the academics or learning facilitators. Perfetti (2001) explains that if a single or multiple personae are unable to capture the diversity of the student group, then its application is inappropriate. It is argued, however, that in the business sector, the use of multiple personae is quite well-suited. Furthermore, personae should not be used to stereotype personal characteristics (Spencer, 2000), but rather to capture the diversity of a student group. However, it is inappropriate to use the *design-persona* if it leads to discriminatory and exclusionary practice. As soon as a negative case occurs that does not resonate with the *design-persona*'s characteristics, the *design-team* needs to consider whether or not this is an extraordinary circumstance that is unlikely to be repeated or if it requires further development of the persona to build in these new features. Herein is the dynamic nature of a *design-persona*. As soon as the *design-persona* becomes static, particularly over prolonged periods, it loses credence. Thus an adaptive *design-persona* that has the ability to reflect the changes in a student population (Okonkwo & Vassileva, 2001) may improve the teaching and learning environments in an educational setting as well as the changing requirements of industry sector employers.

Many academics are adverse to the introduction of processes that streamline practices (Milanowski, 2003). It is somehow seen to be *non-student-centered*. Understandably, with the increase in full fee paying courses students are paying more and expecting more. The pressure is therefore on universities and academics in particular to deliver value added learning environments. However, the opposite is occurring around the world (nistudents.org, 2005), with students paying more and often receiving less in terms of their education. Alongside increased fees there have been cutbacks in the education budgets with academics being asked to do more for less. For some the response may been seen in terms of students' lives becoming increasingly complex—as they juggle paid work, family, study, and other commitments. Moreover, as academics are occupied creating individual course plans and responding to individual student needs for greater flexibility, the university is not to be seen as *student-centered* and responsive to individual student needs. It is argued in this chapter that within the current political and economic climate with ongoing cutbacks to tertiary education, it is not possible to sustain intensive *one-on-one* flexible student arrangements, without an effective ICT infrastructure that supports such activities (Fredericksen, Pickett, Shea, Peiz, & Swan, 2000).

HCI can promote many efficient and effective aspects of academia to enhance user friendliness. *Face-to-face* communication is not always necessary and at times can be an impediment to achieving desired outcomes. For many years, both academic and university administrative staff have debated the perceived benefits of online enrollments. As an example of this dilemma, some of the arguments for *face-to-face* contact at enrollments in the higher-education sector include student engagement with academics familiar with the course content, as well as interaction with the university's administrative staff that are familiar with enrollment processes, and the ability for students to ask questions and receive academic advice about their study requirements. However, due to limited administrative staff resources, this is generally not what occurs in practice. On enrollment day, students may be required to wait for long periods in a queue. In this type of enrollment process, particularly in the *higher-education sector*, administrative staff members have

little time to spend advising students due to the sheer volume of numbers of students enrolling. Moreover, flexibility to accommodate students' requirements is limited due to the requirement for students to attend the designated enrollment sessions in person. In circumstances when a student is unable to attend, they are required to send a proxy to attend on their behalf or risk jeopardizing their enrollment. The introduction of online student enrollments means that students can enroll anywhere at any time as long as they have access to the Internet; this is appropriate for the majority of students. For the minority who do require academic advice, this can still take place over the telephone, or via e-mail, or text messaging on a mobile phone. ICTs can assist in developing these types of individualized processes to increase efficiency.

COMMUNITIES OF LEARNING: EMBRACING DIVERSITY

The literature reveals a growing interest in online learning communities as a natural social interaction (Schwier, 2001a). A community's characteristics are usually as broad as the number of differing characteristics of the individuals involved (de Souza & Preece, 2004). Universities are challenged to develop new ways of developing communities that embrace diversity (Giroux & Shannon, 1997; Nicholson, 1995). However, as Doel and Shardlow (1994, p. 1) caution, *"Focussing on difference can lead to a neglect of similarity. The challenge for educators is to strive to find the most effective and efficient ways of promoting learning in partnership with their students."*

Utilizing a *design-persona* assists in creating learning communities that allow for students to embrace rather than suppress difference, and to value diversity whilst also recognizing and responding to similarities within the student group (Giroux, 1995; McLaren, 1995). According to Ramsden (1992, p. 114), teaching and learning is *"a process of working cooperatively with learn-ers to help them change their understanding."* Learning may occur by ensuring *"a context of learning which encourages students to actively engage with the subject matter."*

ICTs can provide the tools to assist in the de-sign and delivery of quality education (Schwier, 2001b). Most programs of study and careers in-volve *human-communication* as well as HCI. If universities are preparing students for professional practice, then both skill sets are required. There are many programs of study that require good communication skills, for example, medicine, psychiatry, law, psychology, social work, and the IT industry. Conflict resolution and negotiation skills are also particularly useful.

Problems may arise through poorly designed use of ICTs that does not appear to respond ap-propriately to issues of diversity. An outcome from a poorly designed system may mean there is further discrimination against those who already experience discrimination on a number of levels in the community. For instance, automated voice recognition systems do not allow for accents that are not considered within the mainstream. Thus people with different accents are often not understood by such voice recognition systems. Navigating one's way out of some systems is dif-ficult. At times the system's navigation pathway is dissimilar to the preferred pathway of the person using the system, like when an individual tries to do something that is not considered conven-tional. Fortunately, this occurrence is not likely in universities, given the emphasis on flexibility. Technological tools are required that provide numerous navigation pathways, which allow for the provision of required information that includes either electronic access, are implemented via a telephone, or *face-to-face*.

We propose that a *design-persona* can be used by courseware *design team*s for individual courses as well as or for university degree programs. The following discussion applies the concept of implementing a *design-persona* to the develop-

ment process of a hypothetical university's *human services degree*.

GETTING STARTED: HYPOTHETICAL CASE-STUDY EXAMPLE

The first step in developing a *design-persona* is for the academic program team and staff/stu-dent consultative committee to hold a meeting and brainstorm the main features of the student group. Main features identified are listed and then grouped together where connections seem evident. Groups of *design-personae* character-istics can then be refined and further developed. Electronic database repositories may provide supplementary student profile characteristics. It is interesting to see if staff and student perceptions of the dominant features of the student group match those identified in the student databases. One such example uncovered that the main fea-tures of the majority of degree students enrolled in an Australian vocational degree program in the human services sector are: age varies from late teens to early twenties, female, successful completion of secondary schooling or equivalent, middle class, Anglo-Saxon, proficient in English as first language, heterosexual and Christian, and in good physical and mental health. Students in the minority are: older students, particularly those aged 50 years and over, males, working class, possess physical and/or mental health dif-ficulties, gay, followers of non-Christian beliefs, and have English as their second language. From these demographics it is possible to form a design-persona or a series of personae to mirror such a student cohort. The system designer would need to be cognizant of these characteristics and take care with particular design specifications that would not be offensive to particular individu-als. In this instance, two *design-personae* were developed. For the purposes of this chapter, one *design-persona* named Jane was seen to be a *typical* student enrolled in a degree program at an Australian educational institution. The other is called Ali.

Primary Design-Persona 1: Jane – Typical Student

Jane is 19 years of age and has been working for one year prior to commencing full time studies in her degree. Jane is of Anglo-Saxon and middle class background and lives at home with her mother and siblings. She works part-time—10 hours per week—and has a computer at home with access to the Internet, and knowledge of basic programming. She is proficient in English. Her written and verbal skills are well developed. She is Christian, heterosexual, and in good physical and we assume mental health. Jane enjoys coming to university, class discussions, and meeting friends.

Primary Design-Persona 2: Ali – Atypical student

Ali is of non-Anglo and refugee background. His abilities with written and spoken English are limited. He suffers from physical and mental health difficulties. He is aged in his late forties. He struggles financially and is working 20 hours per week to support himself and his family. He does not have a computer at home and relies on computer access at the university and his local library. As the oldest male in the family, he has considerable responsibilities for his aged parents and younger family members. He is non-Christian and gay. Ali finds it very difficult to get to classes and is often absent due to family and work commitments. He is looking forward to completing his degree, so that he can work full time to support the family.

Both these *design-personae* are extremely valuable as they highlight the dominant features of a student cohort and those in the minority. Members of academic program teams can start to reflect on the composition of the student cohort and consider if this is the desired profile for this particular degree. In this hypothetical case, decisions can be made to support recruitment campaigns for students of more diverse backgrounds, given that these students will predominantly be employed in positions where they are working with members of minority groups.

Whilst Jane represents the majority of students, the *design-team* felt that both Jane and Ali were primary *design-personae*. It was considered essential that the needs of both personae would require adequate attention. Two secondary *design-personae* were developed—one representing employer groups and the professional association and the other representing university management. The *design-team* was mindful of the power and influence of these groups and debated whether or not to include them as primary *design-personae* as well. The decision to include them as secondary, rather than primary *design-personae* was based on the commitment to a *student-centered* approach. To include them as primary *design-personae* was seen as creating the potential risk of serving the university and other organizations rather than the students. In instances where this does occur, institutional practices can develop that can have devastating effects (Barnhart, 2000). Our *design-persona* is intended to avoid such dilemmas. As a secondary *design-persona* their characteristics are always considered, but the main focus remains on the students undertaking a degree program.

Secondary Design-Persona 1: Renee – Employer and Professional Association

Renee is the manager of a human services organization that is a main employer of graduates of the university's human services degree. She is also president of the professional accrediting association, as well as being a member of the industry advisory committee for the degree. Renee wants employees who are committed to the values and ethics of the profession. She requires staff that have the required knowledge and skills for practice as stipulated by the professional association. This profile includes direct practice, management policy, organizational development, and research. Employees are expected to have well developed communication skills—verbal, written, and computing. Effective teamwork skills are essential as well as the ability to work independently and use consultation processes as appropriate. Staff members are required to adhere to the professional code of ethics, as well as the organizational guidelines. Employees are encouraged to pursue ongoing professional education and to meet current professional accreditation requirements.

Secondary Design-Persona 2: Max – University Management

Max promotes the human services degree as a flagship degree for the university. This is due to excellence in teaching and learning as well as research and scholarly publications. Max, however, is under increasing pressures to increase academic output with reduced budget allocations. Max is now faced with having to cut staffing numbers through voluntary and forced redundancy packages. Sessional and casual staffing budgets have been cut. The remaining staff are required to do *more for less*, including increased hours of teaching, larger class sizes, and improved research outcomes. Increased efficiencies that are both administrative and academic are core features of the university's management plan. Excellence in teaching requires a *student-centered* approach, flexibility, creativity and innovation, and appropriate and effective use of ICT tools to support student learning. Once the *design-personae* have been identified, the mapping process occurs to link the needs, interests, and concerns of Jane, Ali, Renee, and Max, with their ability to engage in university education.

Mapping Needs, Interests, and Concerns

Maps are created individually for each *design-persona* according to the main needs, interests, and concerns in terms of quality education. Useful maps and summary documentation is developed to provide the point of reference for the academic program team. Mapping may concentrate on any issues that arise for the academic program team in the same way. For instance, mapping can be implemented on the use of ICTs, research, enrollments, course structure, and course content. Mapping can also occur on issues and/or stages of study and engagement with the university. For instance, mapping can proceed according to the stages of pre-entry, engagement, and exit. If not enough information is known about the *design-persona* to map needs, interests, and concerns, more information is required to further develop the personae. The mapping process is illustrated in Figure 1 to determine which of the ICT tools are appropriate.

Once the needs, interests, and concerns of all the *design-personae* have been considered, keeping in mind the primary and secondary status of each *design-persona*, appropriate responses to the ICT tools can be estimated by the *design-team*.

Developing Appropriate Responses

The first step in developing appropriate responses is looking at the commonalities in needs, interests, and concerns across all four *design-personae*. Whilst motivations may differ, there is common ground as all four express needs and interests in knowledge and practical skills in using ICT tools. Issues of access and equity are evident when it is noted that Ali expresses an interest in using these tools yet he is hindered by lack of access and familiarity with technology. ICT tools can be developed for administrative and academic pur-

Figure 1. Map of ICT needs, interests, and concerns

Primary Persona 1: Jane – *typical student*

Needs: appropriate ICT tools that promote an increase in efficiencies and add to the quality of the learning experience.

Interests: Interested in learning about and using ICTs that will enhance employability. Meeting people and making new friends and discussing ideas.

Concerns: That ICTs will be used in place of classroom learning and that classes will be put online.

Primary Persona 2: Ali – *atypical student*

Needs: Flexibility due to: need to work to support family financially; to help care for them; self-care due to health problems. Assistance with essay writing; especially due to English as a second language. Assistance is also required with ICT access and usability issues.

Interests: To learn and complete the degree quickly so as to gain employment as soon as possible. Interested in working with members of own ethnic community esp. refugees and asylum seekers. To learn how to use ICTs required by employers.

Concerns: Financial; no computer at home or Internet access; limited knowledge of computers and other ICTs.

Secondary Persona 1: Renee – *employer and professional association*

Needs: Staff who are familiar with a range of ICT including videoconferencing, teleconferencing, Internet search skills, e-mail, spreadsheets and basic computing and word processing skills.

Interests: Capabilities with basic statistical packages such as SSPS are also desirable as well as an ability to establish and use databases.

Concerns: Due to the interpersonal communication aspect of the Human Services degree that graduates may be lacking in knowledge and skills in ICTs.

Secondary Persona 2: Max – *university management*

Needs: ICTs that will increase efficiencies for staff and students and reduce costs. These need to be engaging for university students and are *user friendly*.

Interests: Rationalising administrative services and developing ICT systems that cater for large numbers of students. ICTs that will enhance classroom teaching.

Concerns: Staff and student dissatisfaction due to: loss of office staff who are familiar with students; possibility of ineffective engagement with students and lack of development of a student learning community due to rationalisation of services and increased class sizes.

---

poses to cater for Jane. She will experience little if any difficulty. However, in terms of concerns, she does not want to have ICT tools replace classroom activities such as discussions, skill development, and opportunities to make new friends. Whilst ICT may potentially make things easier for Ali in terms of his desire for flexibility, his access and user issues are limiting factors. All four want to maintain a quality student learning experience that is supported by administrative processes that are efficient and easy to use.

The staff in the human services program responded by developing a range of policies and practices to support the use of ICT tools for both administrative and educational practices. Online administrative practices adopted include enrollment and re-enrollment, enrollment in tutorials, timetable availability, results, and full enrollment record. It was recognized that for Jane it will be quite easy for her to use and access. Ali, however, may have difficulties associated with access to the information. Computers are made available at the university for enrollments and re-enrollments for those who wish to use them. Students can also vary their enrollments online. They can also do this with a staff member if they prefer this. Hard copies of timetables are also made available on student noticeboards. Discussions have focused on what is and is not appropriate to provide electronically. It was decided that all students would be provided with a hard copy of the Student Handbook on enrollment into the degree. This information is also provided electronically. However, the hard copy provides a record of the structure of the degree when the student first enrolled. Notification of meetings and minutes of meetings are sent to students electronically with hard copies posted on student noticeboards as well. Electronic communication to students occurs with e-mails to all students enrolled in the degree or according to individual subject enrollments. Assignments are submitted electronically or in hard copy if students prefer this. Staff student consultation processes are streamlined as much as possible with announcements in class rather than *one-on-one* communications with students. The result is that students have greater clarity around processes and therefore do not need as much administrative assistance from staff. The amount of time academic staff members spend with students on administrative matters is reduced. This has resulted in improvements in the quality of communications between academic staff and students with a far greater focus on issues related to learning. It has also freed up academic time to concentrate on other aspects of course development and research and to spend quality time with students like Ali who need it the most. With every development that has occurred, the program team has asked:

- What would Ali and Jane think about this?
- How would Ali access it?
- What backups are required?
- Is this initiative adding quality, and if so how?

- How can ICTs be used to develop and foster a student learning community?

In terms of teaching and learning, the academic program team has responded to the desire of all four *design-personae* to establish ICT as an integrated part of the curriculum. A focus has been to identify the most effective use of these technology tools to support student learning. A commitment has been made to include a learning component to introduce effective HCI in all subjects as appropriate. All subjects have an Internet site where the subject guide is available, lecture notes are available, and links are posted to relevant Web sites. The challenge has been to extend the use of ICTs as educational tools beyond the transmission of information. For instance, how to create a learning community online has been a main consideration alongside the development of reflective educational practice (de Souza & Preece, 2004). Several techniques have been used to date. These include e-journals, video feedback, online discussions and tutorials, case studies, role-plays, student supervision, and CD-ROMs containing course notes.

Some of these ICT tools do encourage reflection and engagement in ways that are more personal or different to those that occur in *face-to-face* classroom interactions. Responses to role-plays and journal entries are often quite personal and well considered rather than more spontaneous responses that occur in *face-to-face* interactions. Space is made for quieter students who may find a voice in online discussions that they have not had in *face-to-face* classes, particularly large classes. Video link ups allow for body language and tone of voice. Teamwork can also be achieved. Friendships and relationships develop between students as communication occurs outside of the boundaries of set class times. Whilst there are considerable advantages for integrating ICT into education for studies in human services, the main focus is on working and communicating effectively with people. ICT can only offer environmental tools to assist in developing quality education programs. Particularly due to the *human-dimension* of human services practice it is important that students do have appropriate amounts of *face-to-face* classes supplemented by technological tools. Where classroom time is replaced with online learning, sound pedagogical reasons must support this.

The discussion in this chapter has thus far been describing the *design-personae* as a theoretical modelling technique to reflect predicted student characteristics. We now move to describe the *design-personae* as technological tools, called agents, which are implemented as physical electronic-objects that actually reside within an online learning environment.

FUTURE TRENDS: AGENTS IN WEB-BASED EDUCATION AND E-LEARNING

A technological agent as it applies to computer science is a piece of software that runs without direct human control or constant supervision to accomplish goals provided by the user. Agents typically collect, filter, and process information found on the Web, sometimes with the help of other agents. Thus, agents play an important role in balancing exploitation with exploration in knowledge discovery and learning using Web-based systems (Murthy, 2005a). Consequently, the *design-personae* data that is captured online in a Web-based learning system can be reused as a personalized educational knowledge navigation tool.

Agents can be classified according to their high-level functionalities:

1. collaborative agents that compete or cooperate;
2. interface agents that act as personal assistants;

3. mobile agents that migrate among hosts to enhance the efficiency of computation and improve the network throughput;
4. information agents that manage, manipulate, and collate information from many distributed sources;
5. reactive agents that respond to stimulus and respond in an environment where they are embedded;
6. smart agents that learn from their actions.

Thus an agent is an *intelligent software program* that can be deployed through a computer network, to provide services to a user (Murthy, 2005b). Therefore, utilizing a smart agent's profile matching ability extends the high-level functionality of agent technology to enable an interactive dialogue between the user (the student) and the learning content. Moreover, collaborative agents are required to share data concerning student profiling and class-timetables. An interface agent can, however, take on a physical screen appearance through graphic representation as a screen-based object that a learner sees on the computer screen. Mobile agents (Murthy, 2005c) operate within the learning system, and as such they may not have a visible representation that a user will see. Nonetheless the high-level functionality means these agents, otherwise called software objects, react to interactive input from the learner while maintaining the integrity of the overall online learning system.

Production of this type of educational knowledge navigation tool requires a mixture of specialized information technology professionals, including an application architect to integrate the ICT tools into the existing learning system and a multimedia expert to develop the interactive computer screens and ICTs that interact with the learning system's application server. Engineering an interactive educational learning system can be a complicated process. In the initial stages of the learning system's development, a Web designer is required to consult on the user specifications, and act as the conduit between the architect and *multimedia* practitioner (McKay, 2006b).

Therefore, in taking a more technical view of agent technologies, in an online learning system they may be said to sit as a nexus between the Internet *server-side* and *client-side* functionality that include increased reach of the Internet to enhancing the learner's desktop computer with two-way communications platforms (McKay, 2006a). Consequently, agent technologies are useful for cross platform operation and in efficient management of communication and the consequent reduction in bandwidth requirements, as well as security enforcement, error-correction, transaction, and notification services. Agent technologies have the potential to add value to a learning environment through their adaptive abilities. Flexible education requires a range of instructional resources that are on call to support the learning event. We suggest that agent technologies that are adopted in Web-based pedagogies facilitate a *student-centered* approach to flexible learning.

An adaptive autonomous agent is characterized by:

1. interaction with the environment;
2. goal driven motivation;
3. intelligence;
4. adaptive dynamics.

In a Web-based online education system, agents can satisfy the basic requirements for flexibility in education such as changing course contents automatically, periodically adding assignment solutions, and promptly posting material and announcements. Also, agents enable us to reliably maintain the Web site. Flexible course material and dynamically changing course contents can improve the quality and effectiveness of teaching and learning, and ensure timely communication of personalized course materials for students (in multiple modes of delivery). It also helps to remove obsolete materials.

Agents can provide for integrating the two dimensions of cognitive styles *Wholistic-Analytic* dimensions (as mentioned in the *Student-Centered Approach* section of this chapter), since agents can be programmed to support learning and keep a watchful eye to discover patterns and react to pattern changes that usually occur in learning and teaching. Further, *software agents* can be personalized to provide appropriate services in Web-based education (Berners-Lee et al., 2001; Casati, Shan, Dayal, & Shan, 2003).

The Foundation for Intelligent Physical Agent Architecture (http://www.fipa.org) aims to improve agent interoperability by providing software usage standards for computer communications protocols and languages. Also, the Java 2 Micro-Edition (J2ME) programming language is targeted at devices that are known as *personal digital assistants* or PDAs. These developments provide a *software agent-based* execution environment in a PDA format that is important for applications in Web-based education. The literature on this type of *software agent* technology is growing rapidly and can provide us with a number of innovative ways to facilitate learning through knowledge navigation tools.

CONCLUSION

The main purpose of this chapter was to suggest a method for implementing *design-personae* as an educational systems development tool, which captures individual student characteristics or a complete program cohort. Educational resource developers are constantly required to integrate new technologies to improve the quality of the online learning environment. We have suggested there is an emerging acceptance for a more flexible approach to online education practice. Our *Student Empowerment Model* sets out the responsiveness to the educational needs that students seek from a university course. To ensure the *design-personae* are robust representations of the expected students' characteristics, we recommend that learning systems designers revisit the first principles of instruction as described by Merrill (2002). Returning to the foundations of instructional science is necessary, to ensure the profile matching process includes enough granularity to correctly reflect the target learners.

We drew on the systems theory as it applies to the social sciences to set the context for the discussion on achieving a balance or steady state to describe the dynamics of the continually changing nature of learning environments. However, we drew on the systems theory as it applies computer science to describe the interacting components of the *human-dimension* of HCI. In our opinion, educational systems developers need to be cognizant of the *systems development life cycle* as it relates to taking an organized approach with a structured methodology for any computerized information system development (Powers, Cheney, & Crow, 1990).

We urge educators to think creatively about how to utilize greater flexibility through the powerful relational databases that surround the *semantic Web* to achieve enhanced learning through effective HCI by using emerging ICTs to provide tools that may enhance quality teaching and learning, but cannot be seen as a replacement for existing resources. Educators need to think creatively about how they can best meet the changing needs of students, industry, and society in the design and delivery of courses (Caplan, 2004). We believe that a *student-centered* focus that creatively utilizes a range of teaching and learning techniques is essential. The *design-persona* as described in this chapter provides a personal focus for the planning and delivery of all teaching and learning experiences, which guards against institutional practices that lose sight of student needs. In mapping the needs, concerns, and interests of *design-personae*, we identified that developing appropriate responses achieved a collaborative process between team members involved in different aspects of the student teach-

ing and learning experience, including educators, administrative staff, and most importantly student representatives.

There is an emerging literature relating to online communities of learning. Problems can arise when diversity of the user characteristics is not managed well. To deal with this pressing issue we propose that educational resource designers may increase the effectiveness of their online instructional strategies if they adopt our *student-centered* model that incorporates *design-personae*.

More research is required to monitor and evaluate the practicalities and effectiveness of agent technologies and in particular, the developments of the *semantic Web*. We also suggest research needs to be conducted on the interactive effects of electronic agents that perform as personal Internet knowledge navigation tools.

REFERENCES

Ally, M. (2004). Foundations of educational for online learning. In T. Anderson & F. Elloumi (Eds.), *Theory and practice of online learning* (pp. 3-31). CA: Athabasca University. ISBN: 0-919737-59-5. Retrieved May 5, 2006, from http://cde. athabascau.ca/online_book/copyright.html

Anderson, T., & Elloumi, F. (Eds.). (2004). *Theory and practice of online learning*. Athabasca University. ISBN: 0-919737-59-5. Retrieved May 5, 2006, from http://cde.athabascau.ca/online_book/copyright.html

Barnhart, E. (2000). *Erving goffman: The presentation of self in everyday life*. Hewett. Retrieved March 10, 2006, from http://www.hewett.norfolk. sch.uk/curric/soc/symbol/goffman.htm

Beckett, D. (1998). *Disembodied learning: How flexible delivery shoots higher education in the foot, well sort of.* Retrieved February 22, 2006, from http://www.sociology.org/content/vol003.003/beckett.html

Berners-Lee, T., Hendler, J., & Lassila, O. (2001). The semantic Web: A new form of Web content that is meaningful to computers will unleash a revolution of new possibilities. *Scientific American, 284*(5), 28-37.

Caplan, D. (2004). The development of online courses. In T. Anderson & F. Elloumi (Eds.), *Theory and practice of online learning*. Canada: Athabasca University: ISBN: 0-919737-59-5.

Casati, F., Shan, E., Dayal, U., & Shan, M. -C. (2003). Business-oriented management of Web services comm. *ACM, 46*(10), 55-60.

Cey, R. (2001). Technology use in rural Saskatchewan: Opportunities and challenges—Occasional paper. *Educational Technology.*

Clark, R. C. (2003). Chapter 1. Expertise, learning, and instruction. In *Building expertise* (2nd ed.) (p. 256). MN: International Society for Performance Improvement: ISBN 1-890289-13-2; ISPI No.5103.

Collis, B. (2004, November-December). *Putting theories into practice: Technologies for flexible learning in universities and corporate settings.* Paper presented at the International Conference on Computers in Education—Acquiring and constructing knowledge through human-computer interaction: Creating new visions for the future of learning, Melbourne Exhibition Centre, Australia.

Daniel, B., Schwier, R. A., & McCalla, G. (2003). Social capital in virtual learning communities and distributed communities of practice. *Canadian Journal of Learning and Technology, 29*(3), 113-139.

de Souza, C. S., & Preece, J. (2004). A framework for analyzing and understanding online communities. *Journal, Interacting with Computers, 6,* 579-610. Retrieved March 4, 2006, from http://www.ifsm.umbc.edu/preece/Papers/Framework_desouza_preece2003.pdf

Dennen, V. P. (2003). *Designing peer feedback opportunities into online learning experiences.* The Board of Regents of the University of Wisconsin System. Retrieved March 7, 2006, from http://www.uwex.edu/disted/conference/Resource_library/proceedings/03_02.pdf

Dick, W. O., Carey, L., & O'Carey, J. (2004). *The systematic design of instruction* (6th ed.). ISBN: 0205412742: Allyn & Bacon.

Doel, M., & Shardlow, S. (1994, July). *Flexible learning and the practice curriculum.* Paper presented at the 27th Congress of the IASSW Social Work Education: State of the Art, Amsterdam.

Emonds-Banfield, P. (2006). *Building the semantic Web.* Orange Journal. Retrieved May 13, 2006, from http://orange.eserver.org/issues/3-2/emondsbanfield.html

Fredericksen, E., Pickett, A., Shea, P., Peiz, W., & Swan, K. (2000). Student satisfaction and perceived learning with online courses: Principles and examples from the suny learning network. In J. Bourne (Ed.), *Online education: Learning effectiveness and faculty satisfaction, proceedings of the 1999 Sloan Summer Workshop on asynchronous learning networks* (p. 288). Nashville, TN: ALN Centre, Vanderbilt University.

Freydenson, E. (2002). *Bringing your personas to life in real life.* Boxes and Arrows. Retrieved May 11, 2006, from http://www.boxesandarrows.com/archives/002343.php

Giroux, H. (1995). Border pedagogy and the politics of postmodernism. In P. McLaren (Ed.), *Postmodernism, postcolonialism and pedagogy.* Albert Park, Australia: James Nicholas.

Giroux, H., & Shannon, P. (Eds.). (1997). *Education and cultural studies; toward a performative practice.* New York: Routledge.

Hammond, M., & Wiriyapinit, M. (2005). Learning through online discussion: A case of triangulation in research. *Australasian Journal of Educational Technology, 21*(3), 283-302.

Hannafin, M. J., & Land, S. M. (1997). The foundations and assumptions of technology-enhanced student-centred learning environments. *Instructional Science, 25*(3 May), 167-202.

Hawkins, L., & Sefton, R. (1989). Flexible learning options for social welfare education. *Advances in Social Welfare Education,* 39-47.

Hawryszkiewycz, I. T. (1988). *Introduction to systems analysis and design.* New York: Prentice Hall.

Hooks, B. (1994). *Teaching to transgress education as the practice of freedom.* London & NY: Routledge.

Hourihan, M. (2002). Taking the 'you' out of user: My experience using personas. Retrieved June 2, 2006, from http://www.boxesandarrows.com

Laurillard, D. (1993). *Rethinking university teaching: A framework for the effective use of educational technology.* UK: Routledge.

Lester, J. C., Converse, S. A., Kahler, S. E., Barlow, S. T., Stone, B. A., & Bhoga, R. S. (1997). *The persona affect: Affective impact of animated pedagogical agents.* Paper presented at the CHI 97: Looking to the future, Atlanta, GA: ACM. Retrieved March 10, 2006, from http://www.sigchi.org/chi97/proceedings/paper/jl.htm http://research.csc.ncsu.edu/intellimedia/papers/dap-chi-97.pdf

Ling, P., & Arger, G. (2002). The effectiveness of flexible provision of higher education in Australia. *Journal of Institutional Research: South East Asia, 1*(1), 15-30.

Martin, J. (2002). *What students want from a university course: Empowerment model.* Paper presented at the RMIT University's Teaching and Learning Awards, Melbourne.

Martin, J., Hess, L., Hawkins, L., & Pitt, M. (2002). Flexible delivery mini-conference mode teaching and learning in tertiary education: Experiences in teaching and learning in mental health, field education and a cross-cultural study tour. *International Journal of E-Learning, 9.*

McKay, E. (2000a). *Instructional strategies integrating the cognitive style construct: A meta-knowledge processing model (contextual components that facilitate spatial/logical task performance).* Unpublished doctoral dissertation (Computer Science and Information Systems), total fulfillment, Deakin University, Australia.

McKay, E. (2000b). Measurement of cognitive performance in computer programming concept acquisition: Interactive effects of visual metaphors and the cognitive style construct. *Journal of Applied Measurement, 1*(3), 257-286.

McKay, E. (2006a). Editorial. *International Journal for Continuing Engineering Education and Life-Long Learning: Special Edition—The Effectiveness of Rich Internet Application for Education and Training, 16*(3/4), 151-155. Retrieved April 8, 2006, from http://www.inderscience.com/browse/index.php?journalID=6&year=2006&vol=16&issue=3/4

McKay, E. (2006b). Human-computer interaction passes on the wisdom: Intergenerational knowledge sharing. In M. Pivec (Ed.), *Affective and emotional aspects of human-computer interaction: Emphasis on game-based and innovative learning approaches* (Vol. 1, pp. 207-216). ISBN:1-58603-572-x. ISSN:1572-4794: IOS Press.

McKay, E., & Martin, J. (2006, in print). Multidisciplinary collaboration to unravel expert knowledge: Designing for effective human-computer interaction. In M. Keppell (Ed.), *Instructional design: Case studies in communities of practice.* UK: Idea Group, Inc.

McLaren, P. (1995). Introduction: Postmodernism, post-colonialism and pedagogy. In P. McLaren

(Ed.), *Postmodernism, postcolonialism and pedagogy*. Albert Park, Australia: James Nicholson.

Merrill, M. D. (2002). First principles of instruction. *ETR&D, 50*(3), 43-59. Retrieved January 11, 2006, from http://www.indiana.edu/~tedfrick/aect2002/firstprinciplesbymerrill.pdf

Milanowski, A. (2003). *The framework-based teacher performance assessment systems in Cincinnati and Washoe*. Consortium for policy research in education: CPRE-UW Working Paper Series—TC-03-07. Retrieved March 10, 2006, from http://www.wcer.wisc.edu/cpre/papers/CinciWashoe_TE.pdf

Moran, L., & Myringer, B. (1999). Flexible learning and university change. In H. Keith (Ed.), *Higher education through open and distance learning*. London: Routledge.

Muillenburg, L. Y., & Berge, Z. L. (2005). Student barriers to online learning: A factor analytic study. *Distance Education: An International Journal, 26*(1), 29-48.

Murphy, K. L., & Cifuentes, L. (2001). Using Web tools, collaborating, and learning online. *Distance Education, 22*(2), 285-305.

Murthy, V. K. (2005a). Agent-based software architecture for simulating distributed negotiation. *Springer-Verlag Lecture Notes in Computer Science, LNCS, 3681*, 212-218.

Murthy, V. K. (2005b). Agents in bio-inspired computation. *Springer-Verlag Lecture Notes in Computer Science, LNCS, 3683*, 799-805.

Murthy, V. K. (2005c). Contextual knowledge management in peer to peer computing: Applications to mobile-multiplayer games and robotics. *International Journal of Knowledge-Based and Intelligent Engineering Systems: IOS Press, Amsterdam, 9*(4), 303-314.

Nicholson, C. (1995). Teaching on uncommon ground: The idea of community. In P. McLaren

(Ed.), *Postmodernism, postcolonialism and pedagogy*. Albert Park, Australia: James Nicholson.

nistudents.org. (2005). *The future of higher education*. NUS-USI Initial Response to the UK White Paper. Retrieved March 10, 2006, from http://www.nistudents.org/sections/news/000240.php

Okonkwo, C., & Vassileva, J. (2001). *Affective pedagogical agents and user persuasion*. Paper presented at the Proceedings of the 9th International Conference on Human-Computer Interaction: Universal Access in Human-Computer Interaction (UAHCI), New Orleans, LA (pp. 397-401). Retrieved March 10, 2006, from http://bistrica.usask.ca/madmuc/emotions.htm

Parchoma, G. (2003). Learner-centered instructional design and development: Two examples of success. *Journal of Distance Education, 18*(2), 35-60.

Payne, M. (1997). *Modern social work theory* (2nd ed.). London: Macmillan Press.

Perfetti, C. (2002). *Personas: Matching a design to the users' goals. User interface 7 east*. Retrieved March 9, 2006, from http://www.uie.com;articles/personas

Pond, M. (2002). Distributed education in the 21st century: Implications for quality assurance. *Online Journal of Distance Learning Administration, 5*(2). Retrieved July 30, 2003, from http://www.westga.edu/967Edisstance/ojdla/summer952/pond952.html

Powers, M. J., Cheney, S., & Crow, G. (1990). *Structured systems development—Analysis, design, implementation*. Boston: Boyd & Fraser.

Preece, J. (1994). *Human-computer interaction*. Harlow, UK: Addison-Wesley.

Preece, J. (2005). Online communities: Design, theory, and practice. *Journal of Computer-Mediated Communication, 10*(4), Article 1.

Pruitt, J., & Grudin, J. (2003). *Personas: Practice and theory*. ACM. Retrieved January 9, 2006, from http://research.microsoft.com/research/coet/Grudin/Personas/Pruitt-Grudin.pdf

Ramsden, P. (1992). *Learning to teach in higher education*. United Kingdom: Routledge.

Riding, R. (2002). *School learning and cognitive styles*. London: David Fulton, ISBN: 1853466948.

Schwier, R. A. (2001a). Catalysts, emphases and elements of virtual learning communities: Implications for research and practice. *The Quarterly Review of Distance Education, 2*(1), 5-18.

Schwier, R. A. (2001b). *Web-based distance education: Pedagogy, epistemology, and instructional design*. Retrieved May 9, 2006, from http://www.usask.ca/education/coursework/802papers/boulton/boulton.pdf

Seagrave, S., & Holt, D. (2003). Contemporary learning environments: Designing e-learning for education in the professions. *Distance Education, 24*(1), 7-24.

Sinha, R. (2002). Creating personas for information-rich sites. Retrieved June 2, 2006, from www.rashmisinha.com/archives/02_07/creating-personas-for-informationrich-sebsites.html000036

Spencer, S. (2000). *Professor studies stereotypes and impacts*. University of Waterloo, USA. Retrieved March 10, 2006, from http://newsrelease.uwaterloo.ca/news.php?id=1438

Sullivan, S. (2002). *Pursuit of goals in partnerships: Empowerment in practice*. Paper presented at the Australian Association for Research in Education (AARE), Brisbane.

Whitehead, A. N. (1986). The changing nature of analysis. In G. E. Marshall (Ed.), *Systems analysis and design* (pp. 3-14). New Jersey: Reston.

Chapter VIII
Enlivening the Promise of Education:
Building Collaborative Learning Communities Through Online Discussion

Kuldip Kaur
Open University Malaysia, Malaysia

ABSTRACT

An important dimension in education is interaction, that is, the coming together of a number of people to discuss, debate, and deliberate about issues of common concern. In distance education, such social environments are as much present in online learning contexts as they are in face-to-face learning contexts such as tutorials. This chapter expands the notion of teacher-student interaction to focus on integrating human computer interaction in the curriculum. This is done through the use of online discussion forums at Open University Malaysia that help build collaborative online communities using common principles of teaching and learning. Citing a recent case in point, this chapter demonstrates how the Open University Malaysia-Collaborative Online Learning Model for online interaction helped cultivate learner-centric virtual discussions and supported an interactive online community that showcased characteristics of social interdependence and instructional support. This chapter takes a social constructivist view of human computer interaction by proposing an instructional model supported by collaboration, guidance, interdependence, cognitive challenge, knowledge construction, and knowledge extension. The Introduction section of this chapter provides the rationale for human computer interaction and gives an overview of current-day perspectives on the online classroom. This is followed by a trenchant review of recent research on online interaction with a view to outlining the theoretical premise for the use of computers to develop thinking and collaborative or team skills. This section also provides a rationale for the use of online forums and gives a frame of reference for the role of the instructor in this enterprise.

In the next section of this chapter, the Open University Malaysia-collaborative online learning model is described, with details on The Learning Context as well as Group Learning Outcomes, which may be seen as inherent parts of the model. Under the sub-section Knowledge Construction, the chapter carries a qualitative analysis of online interaction for one Open University Malaysia course using a comprehensive list of indigenous categories and sub-categories as well as examples of interactions that match each sub-category. The chapter ends with a Summary, a statement of Acknowledgement, a list of References, and an Appendix. The appendix contains the Task that was used for the course for which online interaction in this chapter was analyzed.

INTRODUCTION

In ancient Roman cities, a forum was an assembly place for judicial activity and public business. Such assembly often took place in a public square or marketplace. This is where orations were delivered, and public meetings and open discussions were held by various people. Similarly, in ancient Greece, a place of congregation—like a marketplace—was known as the agora. Such movements in history have given rise to the human need for discussion, debate and deliberation for the explication of ideas and facts before one can promote or dissuade an idea or event.

As extensions of the forum and the agora, today's online forums and online discussion groups have given rise to various discourse communities (Jonassen, 2002), collaborative learning groups (Dillenbourg and Schneider, 1995) and learning networks (Harasim, Hiltz, Teles, & Turoff, 1995). In these virtual classrooms (Hiltz, 1995), tutors, learners and experts come together to discuss content-related topics, debate on issues of common interest, share resources and deliberate on best solutions to various issues or problems. Such developments in educational practice have had an enormous impact on the way we teach, and on the way we interact with our students. We now view the online or virtual classroom as an extension of the traditional face-to-face classroom, and conversations begun in the latter are continued in the former, and so on. The role of the tutor or teacher has been redefined to include online facilitation, support frameworks and dialogue (Collison, Elbaum, Haavind & Tinker, 2000). In tandem to this, the learner is expected to play a constructive role in the knowledge s/he builds and in the online learning process s/he is engaged in (Jonassen, Peck & Wilson, 1999). In sum, the historical premise for discussion, debate and deliberation for the explication of ideas and facts remains significant in the classrooms of today.

The brief discussion above demonstrates the way the online classroom has become a significant part of educational practice today, and how human computer interaction has transformed current conceptions of the role of the teacher and the learner. In order to provide a framework for understanding these developments, the next section of this chapter presents a review of research on online interaction and outlines recent developments in the theory of online pedagogy.

(Note: In this chapter the term tutor also refers to a teacher, instructor or facilitator.)

ONLINE INTERACTION

Recent research on constructive pedagogy has drawn attention to the use of online networks to improve thinking and to develop team skills. The thrust of the work in this area comes from the social constructivist view of learning (Bruner, 1986; Shaw, 1994), where learning is perceived as a "personal, reflective and transformative process" leading to the co-construction of knowledge through collaboration, inquiry, invention and knowledge-building activities (Sandholtz, Ringstaff & Dwyer, 1997: 12-13).

One application of this perspective is the use of computers to develop thinking learners (Jonassen, 2002). Referring to selected applications as mindtools, Jonassen encourages learning with computers so that the whole enterprise of learning "becomes greater than the potential of the learner and the computer alone" (Jonassen, 2002 p. 4). Another perspective is forwarded by Anderson's (2004) theory of e-learning which espouses Bransford, Brown, and Cocking's (1999) four credentials of effective learning environments: learner-centredness, knowledge-centredness, assessment-centredness and community centredness. These perspectives recognize the power of collaboration, which is a critical component of interactive online learning.

The work of socio-psychologists who have researched constructive pedagogy (Bruner, 1986) and peer-led instructional support (Keefer, Zeitz, & Resnick, (2000) has shown that collaboration is a powerful learning tool. Research indicates that collaborative activity such as online peer tutoring and team projects increases the knowledge learned and the satisfaction derived from the process (Clark, 2000). Collaborative tasks in online forums are also effective learning tools as they involve discussion and debate, processes which are crucial to understanding the many elements that influence a situation (Laurillard, 1993) Other studies have shown that online collaboration strategies increase students' communicative ability (Andres, 2002), their self-efficacy and academic performance (Sandholtz, Ringstaff & Dwyer, 1997) as well as their motivation to work (Turoff, 1999). Online forums also facilitate discussion, which is significant to learning as it paves the way for the use of domain-specific language and allows learners to generate their own explanations of what is understood or learnt (McKendree, 2002).

Although the use of online forums for discussion and team skills is a relatively recent phe-

nomenon, it has become a part of many teaching and learning programmes in post-secondary education (Spatariu, Hartley & Bendixen, 2004). Many educationists (Collison, Elbaum, Haavind & Tinker, 2000; Kearsley, 2000; Liao, 1996) have extolled the value of online forums in the teaching-learning process because they facilitate transparent discussion, offer direct accessibility to learning resources or materials and utilize learner-centric instructional values. To understand the widespread use of online forums in delivering the promise of education, one must recognise their enormous potential as drivers of learning and as channels of meaningful communication.

To begin, online forums provide the space for individual contribution toward a topic of discussion in a way that traditional classrooms do not. Tutors or facilitators use online facilities to provide fodder for discussion, and learners access these forums as an anytime-anywhere learning facility (Twigg, 2001). Learners can also access the forum as many times as they wish and independently contribute to the discussion. Tutors can examine each and every learner's contributions and provide feedback to groups or to individuals depending on the nature of the task. Learner-led discussions in online forums give learners the latitude to say what they think (and what they mean) without feeling the pressure of adult presence (Johnson, Aragon, Najmuddin & Palma-Rivas, 2000). The teacher as a custodian of correctness or truth (Balester, Halasek & Peterson, 1992) phenomenon diminishes as learners exchange information in learner-led online forums. More importantly, one person's online contributions are accessible to all participants in the learning event, in a way that individual written products in an exercise book are not.

This, above all, is the most liberating influence of the forum: the ability to communicate in an unrestricted time and space, under less restrictive conditions, and to deliver one's thoughts to one or many as a matter of choice. For tutors, this offers an opportunity to exercise group activity and interaction in a way that they can help realise the learning potential of each participating member of the classroom.

Despite the learner-directed nature of online interaction, it is important to realize that the role of the tutor is not attenuated as more and more computer-mediated instruction is used in a learning programme. Tutors play a very active role in designing tasks that are appropriate for collaborative and constructive activity and in participating in online discussion by moderating, modeling, questioning and providing learning support. This active role played by the facilitator, as it were, is summed up by Anderson (2004:271) when he describes what an online teacher has to do: design and organise the learning experience; devise and implement activities to encourage discourse between and among students, between the teacher and the student, and between individual students and groups of students and content resources; add subject matter expertise through a variety of forms of direct instruction; and fulfill a critical credentialing role that involves the assessment and certification of student learning. Thus, while online forums have changed the landscape of teaching and learning in terms of space and process, especially in higher education, it is also significant that the role of participating individuals has been redefined to include meaningful interaction and knowledge construction.

The review of literature above sheds light on the social constructivist view of learning and the theory of e-learning with specific reference to human computer interaction. Of significance is the influence of socio-cognitive processes such as collaboration, discussion and learner-centredness, all of which may be imbibed through carefully selected online tasks and tutor-facilitated online activity. The next section of this chapter presents details of a model for collaborative online learning which was implemented at Open University Malaysia. The implementation of this model helped to realise the ideals of social constructivism and helped build an interactive online

learning community using online discussion and collaboration.

A MODEL FOR COLLABORATIVE ONLINE LEARNING

The theoretical premise for a constructivists' view on teaching and learning served as an impetus for the design of a model for online discussion at Open University Malaysia (OUM). This model, which is referred to as the OUM Collaborative Online Learning (COL) Model (Kuldip & Zoraini 2004), was developed to enrich the learning experience of Open University Malaysia's distance learners. Further, it was envisaged that computer-mediated communication would be the most effective way of providing instructional support for distance learners.

In the following sub-sections of this chapter, three aspects of the Open University Malaysia-collaborative online learning model are presented. These are: The Learning Context, which provides a description of how collaborative online learning was implemented; group learning outcomes, which outlines the learning design and the instructional outcomes of one course; and Knowledge Construction, which provides examples of online discussion utilizing principles of collaborative online learning pedagogy.

We begin with The Learning Context, a subsection that describes the learning environment at Open University Malaysia, and provides details of the five components which serve as interactive dimensions of the model itself.

The Learning Context

Learners at Open University Malaysia are required to participate in online activity as part of the total learning solution for a programme of study. For each course they are registered in, learners attend ten hours of face-to-face tutorials, engage in autonomous learning activity using a printed module and participate in online discussions. The online discussion forum is housed within Open University Malaysia's learning management system known as myLMS, which also serves as a repository for teaching-learning resources or sample tests and as a communication channel for all administrative matters. Throughout the year, Open University Malaysia tutors from various learning centres are trained in the finer points of online collaboration and online tutoring. Training of learners incorporates guidelines on the use of the forum to communicate with peers and tutors about academic matters, collaborative strategies, as well as access to online learning resources and notices on administrative matters.

Under the collaborative online learning model, online discussions may be led by a tutor or a learner, but the focus is on an assignment which carries 25% of the marks for the final grade. The assigned task is expected to be completed in six to eight weeks, and often requires extensive reading, deliberation, as well as some amount of research and application. Students are assigned to tutorial groups led by a tutor, and the same group functions as a virtual class in myLMS. Asynchronous discussions on the task begin at the beginning of each semester and learners access myLMS from their home, workplace or an Open University Malaysia learning centre. Either the tutor or a learner may begin a threaded discussion, but both parties are expected to play and active role in the online discussion forum. Using the assignment as a point of departure, tutors and learners focus on explication and inquiry leading to deliberation on best solutions, possible outcomes and findings of individual research. In this way, collaborative online learning helps to build an interactive online learning community aimed at providing instructional support to distance learners.

The fulcrum of the collaborative online learning model is collaboration, which may be defined as a communal process encouraging learners and tutors to work together as part of a larger system rather than as individuals (Kuldip & Zoraini,

2004). This interactive and recursive process draws on characteristics of four other components of the model, namely the task, instructional or learning support, discussion and knowledge construction. The following description of the five components of the collaborative online learning model illustrates its role in shaping the learning experience at Open University Malaysia.

1. **Online collaboration:** Learners and tutors using myLMS to work together toward common goals, which in this case is to co-construct understanding of the requirements of a task, deliberating on ways to perform the task, sharing findings based on task performance and evaluating outcomes of a task;

2. **The task:** An assignment such as a problem, a case study, a debate or a project, designed for learners to apply course content in a real-world situation, or to engage in critical examination of theory and findings of past research;

3. **Learning support:** Provision of online instructional support for the task from the tutor and subject matter expert, and encouraging participation from all learners and guidance on the use of online/printed learning resources;

4. **Discussion:** Active tutor and learner participation through asynchronous threaded discussions, a way for peers to help each other, and for the tutor to facilitate the collective solving of problems or work related to the assigned task; and

5. **Knowledge construction:** The intended outcome of a task which is characteristically (a) something the learner is unable to do independently and (b) represents new knowledge or new learning.

The above components are viewed as interactive dimensions in the Open University Malaysia collaborative online teaching and learning process. Thus a discussion group in Open University Malaysia's myLMS functions as a virtual classroom (Hiltz, 1995) where collaborative activity among tutors, learners and experts is encouraged, as well as deemed necessary. Using guidelines provided by Collison, Elbaum, Haavind & Tinker, (2000), collaborative online learning is designed for tutors to play a significant role in the facilitation of learner deliberations, provision of instructional support frameworks and modeling ways to engage in meaningful communication. In turn, the learner plays a direct role in the construction of knowledge and in gaining new learning experiences (Jonassen, Peck, & Wilson, 1999).

The sub-section above has described in detail the instructional environment that is part and parcel of the Open University Malaysia learning experience. It has also outlined the salient aspects of the implementation of the Open University Malaysia-Collaborative Online Learning Model. In the next sub-section, group learning outcomes for one course for which the model was implemented are described. Of particular importance are the four categories and 16 sub-categories of online interaction that were derived through a qualitative analysis of the data from the discussion forum, myLMS.

Group Learning Outcomes

After an initial round of pilot testing and evaluation (Kuldip & Zoraini, 2004), the collaborative online learning model was implemented for two teaching English as a second language (TESL) courses for in-service teacher trainees at the Open University Malaysia in the year 2005. This chapter uses data from one of the two courses, Introduction to Novels and Short Stories, which was conducted over a 15 week semester. There were 462 students registered in the course in multiple teaching sites. Each of the 21 student groups were led by a tutor and instruction was based on a prescribed module. Five tutorial sessions, totaling ten hours of face-to-face interaction, and self-regulated study were required for the course. In addition to the interaction during face-to-face tutorials, online discussions—another course requirement—related to the contents of the module and a take-home assignment contributed to the bulk of discussion that was held on the contents of the course. The assignment (Appendix A) required students to read and write reviews of texts assigned in the course and to hand in a bound portfolio based on their reading and reviews.

Although threaded discussions in myLMS were held by all 21 groups, this paper utilises data

Table 1. Analysis of selected group contributions in myLMS

Contributions	Number and Percentage of Contributions by Tutorial Group			
Total number of contributions analyzed: 288 (100%)	Group 1 total: 85 (29.5%)	Group 2 total: 82 (28.5%)	Group 3 total: 70 (24.3%)	Group 4 total: 51 (17.7%)
Number of tutor contributions analyzed: 117 (41%)	By tutor 1 30 (10.4%)	By tutor 2 37 (12.9%)	By tutor 3 26 (9%)	By tutor 4 24 (8.3%)
Number of student contributions analyzed: 171 (59%)	By 25 group 1 students 55 (19.1%)	By 16 group 2 students 45 (15.6%)	By 15 group 3 students 44 (15.3%)	By 10 group 4 students 27 (9.4%)

Table 2. Categories and sub-categories of online interaction

Category I: GUIDANCE	
Sub-categories	Description
i. Guidance on how to begin an assignment ii. Guidance on how to ask questions	Tutors work with learners to *show how* something is done
iii. Guidance on use of reference materials	Tutors help learners use printed and **online** resources
iv. Guidance on concepts related to course content	Tutors provide support through questions, leads, and simplification of difficult subject matter
v. Guidance on instructions by focusing learner attention	Tutors direct learners' attention to a particular point/topic or area of **discussion**

Category II: INTERDEPENDENCE	
Sub-categories	Description
vi. Peer coaching	Learners collectively answer questions, solve problems, or discuss solutions with assistance from the tutor
vii. Peer tutoring	Learners help each other by answering questions and providing direction without the assistance of a tutor
viii. Sharing	Learners share ideas and a variety of learning materials by telling each other what they know
ix. Utilizing learner expertise	Learners recognize and use each other as a knowledge source
x. Vicarious learning	Learners learn by reading, watching, or 'lurking' without directly contributing to a **discussion**

Category III: CHALLENGE	
Sub-categories	Description
xi. Designing tasks that require multiple skills	Tutors design tasks based on a broad idea of learning outcomes
xii. Pushing the boundaries	Tutors encourage learners to go beyond what they have done or what they think is sufficient for the task
xiii. Inspiriting learner ability	Tutors think of ways to inspirit learners' attempts at performing a task when the task proves too difficult
xiv. Redirecting to encourage greater autonomy	Tutors redirect learner attention to other resources in order to encourage autonomous learning

Category IV: EXTENSION	
Sub-categories	Description
xv. Recasting content learned in course	Learners recast, rephrase, or reformulate recently acquired content Learners seek feedback on content and ideas presented in their own words
xvi. Application of concepts learned in course	Learners use meta-cognitive strategies to analyze and apply theoretical views learned in course Learners view concepts from the social perspective or they relate real life experiences to course content

drawn from by the four most active groups. In addition, only contributions related to the assignment part of the course are used in the analysis. Thus, 4 tutors' (19 % of all tutors) and (their) 66 learners' (14 % of all students) contributions in the online forum related to the assignment were analysed. As shown in Table 1, a total of 288 contributions were analysed, of which 117 were from the 4 tutors while 171 were from the 66 students. The tutor-student ratio of contributions was 1:1.46; the average number of postings per tutor was 29.3 while the average number of postings per student was 2.9.

The 288 contributions from the four groups were analysed qualitatively to examine the nature of discussion during collaborative online learning. It was found that discussion threads could be classified under four categories of interaction: guidance, interdependence, challenge and extension. These four data-driven categories are not mutually exclusive, i.e., a single thread may present evidence for one or more categories of interaction. The analysis also revealed that the four main categories could be further divided into 16 subcategories as learners and tutors engaged in a lively discussion on the assignment. The descrip-

Figure 1. Interaction within the collaborative online learning model

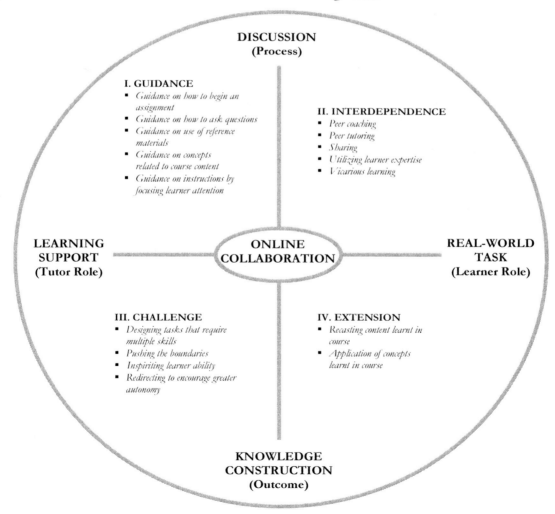

tion of categories and subcategories that emerged from the data is presented in Table 2.

The four categories and 16 subcategories categories are linked to all five components of the collaborative online learning model in terms of the specific thinking and learning processes that are brought to bear upon the discussion (Figure 1). In terms of collaboration, guidance was provided by both tutors and learners, and learners were interdependent in terms of their need for input on content, procedure and application of theory. Additionally, the assigned task appeared to have posed a challenge to learners, and learner activity provided evidence of skills extension. In terms of the four quadroons of the collaborative online learning model in Figure 1, guidance and challenge may be viewed in terms of an active tutor role while interdependence and extension may be viewed as an active learner role.

To summarise, the sub-section above has given the labels and operational definitions of the various categories and sub-categories of online interaction that are directly related to the Open University Malaysia-collaborative online learning model. These categories were derived from the analysis of online discussion during one course at Open University Malaysia. In the following sub-section, Knowledge Construction, vignettes taken from myLMS demonstrate the power of tutors' and learners' discussions in constructing meaning through co-construction and social interdependence.

Knowledge Construction

In order to demonstrate the viability of online interaction in creating a meaningful learning environment for distance learners, this sub-section is focused on discussion during the course Introduction to Novels and Short Stories. In the following pages, the analysis of online interaction is organised by category, vis. guidance, interdependence, challenge and extension (Table

1). Each category is then further explicated using descriptions and vignettes that fall under each sub-category. A 'cue' refers to the comment or contribution that triggers a threaded discussion, while cuer refers to the person who has triggered the thread. Unless otherwise indicated, all cues cited below were provided by learners.

(Note: The names of all contributors have been changed to protect their identity. Excerpts have not been edited for grammatical accuracy and italics in the data are the chapter author's.)

I. GUIDANCE

The collaborative online learning-based interaction showed that tutors play an active role in the discussion by providing instructional support or guidance to learners. This means that they show how a task can be done, help identify and glean information from printed and online resources, use questions and leads to direct understanding, simplify difficult subject matter, and model ways for learners to work together. In many classrooms or other educational contexts, this role of the teacher is oft-times not evident; teachers may get lost in a myriad of paperwork and evaluation-based activity, forgetting that they ought to play a role in showing how to do something—e.g., how to do a sum, write a paragraph or draw a diagram.

Below is a description of the tutors' role in providing guidance is illustrated with examples related to each of the five subcategories of guidance provided to include: how to begin an assignment, how ask questions, the use of reference materials, concepts related to course content, instructions by focusing learner attention.

i. Guidance on how to begin an assignment. In the following vignette, Aris seeks guidance on how she should begin the assignment on the novel The Pearl by John Steinbeck. Her tutor, John, tells her to begin by answering the given questions in sequence, and gives her pointers on what she should not include in her paper.

Cue 1.
Dear Sir, How do we begin the assignment? Should I start a little bit about the review of the Pearl or we just start by answering task 1. That is by just listing down the title, author...? Aris

Response from tutor.
Aris, just start by answering the questions in sequence. The second and third questions form the introduction to your who assignment. You are not required to write things not related to the assignment questions. Rgds., John

Feedback.
Dear Sir, Thank U for shedding some light to me. Aris

ii. Guidance on how to ask questions. In contrast to Aris, another student called Ravin asks a question that is rather vague (Cue 2). As shown in the extract below, the tutor responds by requesting for more specific information. This is an important move to encourage learners to learn how to communicate effectively, and to make students aware of the need to define a problem that they want resolved. Further, as Open University Malaysia assignments may be lengthy or contain several parts, online tutoring is effective if learners are more focused and concise when they raise questions.

Cue 2.
Dear Sir, Please explain about our assignment. Thank you.

Response from tutor.
Dear Ravin, Thank you for your attempt but you can't ask general questions like this. What or

which part of the assignment don't you understand? Be specific please so that I can be of help to you. John

iii. Guidance on use of reference materials. In the example below, the tutor, Tuan Hj. Idris, provides a reference and dictionary-based explanation for terminology used in the course. The tutor goes a step further by drawing attention to how the student can deduce the meaning of a concept. Initiatives such as these often benefit more than one student at a time, and have the effect of modeling study skills or information retrieval skills.

Cue 3.
Tuan Hj Idris. What is meant by using stylistic approach in teaching literature in the classroom?

Response from tutor.
Pari, My previous answer was a little hasty. Sorry.

Martin Grey's A Dictionary of Literary Terms, explain the term under style. Style = the characteristic manner in which a writer expresses himself... may be a combination of many different factors... describe by analysis of syntax, tone, imagery, point of view and linguistic features. As such we can always deduce that SA is like DA also Neo-RA i.e., looking at a literary work through the use of words.
Is that OK? Bye.

iv. Guidance on concepts related to course content. In response to questions posed by one student (Cue 4 & 5), a tutor explains concepts that are related to the course. Often such explanations are given when a concept is complex, or if it is new or difficult. If the term is found and well explained in the printed module, or if it is available in an online source, tutors may direct a learner to that specific source.

Cue 4.
Dear Sir, Please explain what the term 'generic conventions' is? Thank you.

Response from tutor.
Hi Nadine, Sorry for the late reply. Well, generic means the class origin - i.e belonging to a class and conventions means the basic characteristics. Therefore generic conventions would be the basic features of a certain type of writing or style or language used etc. For example what are the generic conventions of Shakespearean sonnet. So here you have to talk about the sonnet and what are the special conventions of the sonnets written by Shakespeare. Boleh faham kan? John.

Cue 5.
Dear Sir, What does the term 'contemporaneous appeal' mean when explaining short stories? Thank you.

Response from tutor.
Hi Nadine, Contemporaneous appeal refers to the current or present day readers/critics' appeal. As opposed to traditional or orthodox preferences. Rgds, John.

v. Guidance on instructions by focusing learner attention. Very often, students ask questions about a task because they have problems interpreting directions or instructions for the task. In the example below, the tutor focuses Salmah's attention on the language used in the directions for the task so that she better understands what she is required to do.

Cue 6.
For question no. 8, do I have to write an analysis of 3 reviews/ essays altogether OR do I have to write it separately thank you

Response from tutor.
Dear Salmah, The question specifically stated, Write a 300 word analysis on THESE reviews... so obviously you have to write on them as one. OK? Bye.

II. INTERDEPENDENCE

The analysis of the threaded discussions also showed that learners work interdependently on the task at hand. They do this by collectively solving problems, discussing solutions, sharing learning materials, answering questions and providing direction as well as by recognising and using each other as a knowledge source. In the case of this course, Introduction to Novels and Short Stories, learners appeared to have had difficulty with the critical review of assigned texts and in accessing material from the internet. Here is how learners demonstrated interdependence during their discussions.

vi. Peer coaching. In the following example, Cue 7 is a call for help on writing a critical review. The tutor responds by referring to an announcement he has posted. However, the students go further to take on the role of a coach or guide by making suggestions, as well as seeking and providing clarification on the task. In the threaded discussion below, four students (including the cuer) are involved in one such coaching event.

Cue 7.
Hai everybody!
I'm having problem to write my critical review of The Pearl. Does anyone has any tips on how to write a good critical review? TQ

Response from tutor.
Chong, Last night I posted an announcement concerning this kind of problem. Refer to the announcement, visit the web and then...? OK? Bye.

Response from peer 1 to cuer.
Saudari Chong, Voice your opinions at the end of every paragraph (6 paragraphs- 6 chapters)!
Suggestions:
Chapter 1- author constructs Kino as an eg. with concerns typical of persons of all social circles, couple symbolic of the Mexican-Indian community
Chapter 2- canoe as provider of income, describe to audience whether in reality will a diver find a big pearl coincidentally
Chapter 3-tempt the readers whether they want to be rich and famous, just like striking a gold mine in real life!
Chapter 4 -6: Request responses from readers by asking realistic Qs!

Response from peer 2 to peer 1.
I thought critical review is writing about the background of the author and the books he had produced. Someone please correct me if I'm wrong.

Response from peer 3 to peer 2.
Lai Fong, a critical review is to write the main events of a text. the ups and downs of life the main character faces. we may include the moral value behind the story; whether the book is worth reading or not; the background info. of the author can be included. hope it helps. all the best. Kim Wee

vii. Peer tutoring. In some instances, the tutor does not get involved in the discussion and learners assume the role of tutor. The analysis of the data showed that peer tutoring is evident in collaborative online learning as a number of learners' views are colligated to refine understanding of a concept. However,

it must be noted that peer tutoring does not always cover the full range of questions posed by a cuer as learners focus on what they know and on issues where they have some experience. In the following vignette, Chew, (cuer) gets a satisfactory response to only one of the two questions that he poses. The first question raised by Chew is addressed by a peer (peer 2) but this does not provide a solution to Chew's problem.

Cue 8.
Dear Tn. Haji Idris, 1. Q7 is a headache It requires us to find 3 book reviews on the selected text. I have searched the net but in vain. Must the book reviews be written by well-known critics or just anybody? 2. For our assignment, are we suppose to present the portfolio in an essay form or in point form according to the steps given as below? Eg. Title of book: The Pearl, Author: John Steinbeck, Year of Publication. 2. Plot Summary: The Pearl is a story......

Response from peer 1.
Answers Question 2: I think we can write both ways.

Response from peer 2.
Addresses Question 2 but does not give a satisfactory answer:
Saudari Chong,
Book reviews concern with research done on the book regarding the plot of the novel like what the researchers think and voice their opinions! Different researchers from different universities explain the contexts from various views! Haji Idris, pls correct me if I m wrong!

Response from cuer.
Thanks Selvam and Tek Boon. I still cannot find the book reviews.

viii. Sharing. In some instances, two or more learners facing the same problem with the task share their problem in the online forum. This is when multiple level communication and collaboration was evident showing a strong sense of group interdependence. As shown in the threaded discussion below, learners (Cuers 9 & 10) share information on how or where the cuers could get the information they need. For example, cuers trigger a discussion and other classmates exchange information on the topic, aiming to provide as much assistance as possible. Like tutors who use phrases such as have you tried…, learners help the cuers by giving directions e.g. with statements like Try typing in different keywords... However, it must be noted that as in this case, sharing does not always help every learner access the information needed, even though the discussion on this topic spanned four days.

Cue 9.
11 Oct 2004 02:52:36 AM
Dear Sir and friends,
I"m doing the assignment on short story, "The Pencil". I've tried looking for the book reviews as required but it seems that I"m not successful yet. Can someone help please?

Cue 10.
12 Oct 2004 10:01:33 PM
Hello Sir,
I'm doing the "The necklace" for my assignment but I'm facing problem searching for the reviews. Please give some tips on how to get the reviews. I 've tried using goggles and yahoo.
Eng L.P.

Response from cuer 10 to cuer 9.
12 Oct 2004 10:04:04 PM
Dear Philo, It seems that both of us are in the same boat as I can't find any reviews for the short story I'm doing. Hopefully, both of us will be able to find the reviews soon.

Response from tutor to cuer 9.
14 Oct 2004 03:13:00 PM
Hi there,
Have you tried another search engine, maybe Google? Type different keywords too - eg, Book review + The Pencil, etc. Give it a try.

Response from tutor to cuer 10.
14 Oct 2004 03:15:14 PM
Hi Lai Peng,
Have you tried the search engine recommended by Janice during T3? Try typing in different keywords - Book review of The Pencil, or the author's name, or Book review +Malaysian literature in English, etc.

Response from peer 1 to cuer 10.
15 Oct 2004 05:44:29 AM
Eng,
Just type 'Book Review: The Necklace'. I'm sure you'll see reviews there.

Response from peer 2 to peer 1.
15 Oct 2004 06:07:03 PM
For my case, I've typed book review: The secret life of Walter Mitty". The feedback is very disappointing. I just manage to access a few reviews on that particular story.

The three postings below (Cues 11-13) illustrate how learners shared resources among their peers and with their tutor—purely as a matter of personal initiative.

Cue 11.
Hi tutor and course-mates, I managed to get hold of the texts; Welcome and Return to Malaya. I don't mind making copies for all those interested but I have no idea how many copies to make. Enlighten me please. BTW I am still waiting for Hemmingway's text.

Response from tutor.
Hi Lily! You bring wonderful news. Hurray for you! Kindly make one set for me. I'll pay you later, thank you very much

Cue 12.
Dear all, I found this interesting story on this website: do read and let's enjoy the stories. http://reading.englishclub.com/short-stories.htm

Cue 13.
Dear sir,
http://incontinet.com/two_drugs_fail.htm
The above website is one the sites that offers critical review. What do you think of it. Is it ok enough for our assignment. TQ.

ix.   Utilising learner expertise. An important dimension of learner involvement in a discussion is the recognition of the learner as a knowing, able and knowledgeable individual who is capable of providing informed responses to a peer's questions. In the following exchange, the tutor raises this point by validating the ideas that have been put forward by two classmates and by acknowledging that their explanations were indeed 'good.' Learner involvement of this nature is necessary for learners to get feedback on the input they provide and to motivate them to take part in more discussions of this nature.

Cue 14.
Hello Mr Anthony and course-mates,
I'm quite confused and blurry on writing critical review of the text. Could anyone of you please elaborate more on the requirements of the question (3). What is the specific guideline/s needed to answer this question.
Thanks for your worth reply.

Response from peer 1.
Hello, Just to share what I understand about it. It is your respond toward the story. You can also tell what is it that you like in the story, the moral values and setting. You can also tell the part of the story that attract you the most and give reasons.

Response from peer 2
Can I add in some viewpoints here. You can also touch on why you like/dislike the characters in the story. Apart from that, you can also briefly elucidate on the author's writing whether his/her writing of the particular book awesome, breathtaking or even overwhelm. List out the interesting part/s you like most or may bring hatred to you.

Response from tutor.
Hi Marisa, Philomena & Jonathan have given a good explanation about this. Have their explanation helped you a little? It's giving your own personal response to the text and not writing a summary of the story.

x.   Vicarious learning. Learning in many contexts can occur when learners are not involved in the exchange, or are not providing input on a topic of discussion. This is something that may be present but is often not obvious in a traditional classroom. The threaded discussion below is an example of vicarious learning is evident as two classmates – Bob and Vimala – have benefited from a response from Mahera. As another facet of peer interdependence in myLMS, these learners learn from each other and express their satisfaction about the sharing of individual expertise.

Cue 15.
Hi there tutor and course-mates, I've chosen a short story "The secret life of Walter Mitty" for my assignment. Is it okay if I write these points for my blurb of the story. a. It portrays the stupidity and mild- mannered of a husband by the

name of Walter Mitty who merely dares to show his valiant only in his fantasy world. Read more to attain joyfulness and suspense of the story. b. The story is full of humorous and fantasy. c. The story is very entertaining and catchy. Readers are motivated and seemingly enjoy their reading entirely. [Bob]

Response from Peer 1.
Hello dear Bob, First of all, I would like to elucidate on blurbs which means a praising word/s to foster a novel or short story. Therefore, the word stupidity is not really recommended for writing blurb. Anyway, I do agree with your third viewpoint about the blurbs of the story. Nice of you selecting a Walter Mitty secret life for your assignment. Hope to meet your requirements. [Mahera]

Response from peer 2 to peer 1.
Hello Mahera, I was not sure on how to write the blurb a moment ago. At least your comment for Bob had given me some ideas. Thanks. [Vimala]

Response from cuer to peer 2.
Me too Vimala. Now, I've a picture on how to write the blurbs of the story. Hopefully our tutor will go along my path. [Bob]

III. CHALLENGE

At the Open University Malaysia, tutors are encouraged to design goals that challenge learners so that new knowledge is constructed, and learning is extended beyond current ability. The assignment for the course Introduction to Novels and Short Stories appeared to have been a challenging one as evidence by learners' deliberations on the many things that they were required to do for the submission of the portfolio. The subcategories below demonstrate the many areas in which learners were challenged, and how tutors helped by scaffolding the many demands of the task.

xi. Designing tasks that require multiple skills. In the following example, the tutor draws attention to the many skills that will be required to perform the assignment to satisfaction. The posting (Cue 16) was forwarded at the beginning of the semester, and appears to serve as an advance organizer for the tutorial group. It appears too that the tutor is making learners aware of the many cognitive skills that learners will have to exercise in undertaking the task.

Cue 16 from tutor.
After doing an internet search on a keyword form the selected text, choose 2 items about the keyword which you think are useful. Explain why it would be useful to the reader if he/she knows this information when reading the text or how it would help the reader understand the text better. For instance during T3, Nyet Fah gave us an example. She liked the word 'pearl' in The Pearl. So she did an internet search and came up with many things related to the word pearl. But she decided to choose only 2 items, that is, how pearls are formed and how people dive for pearls. Now ask yourself, if you were reading The Pearl, how would information on these 2 items help you understand the text better? You would be able to imagine the difficulty Kino goes through every time he dives into the sea to look for pearls. You would also know how he holds his breath, how he cuts the pearl from its shell, how long a diver can hold his breath, etc. Does this help you a little?

xii. Pushing the boundaries. Apart from assigning tasks that challenge learners, tutors also encouraged learners to work harder on their assignment. In the following example, Cuer 15 is told that he has done a good job with part of the task, but he has to do more. It must be noted that the tutor scaffolds the sub-tasks with the use of questions, which will indeed guide Nicholas in the presentation of the paper for the assignment.

Response from tutor to Cuer 15.

Dear Robert, These are nice blurbs you have written. But you can further improve on them. Be more specific. (b) It is humorous and full of fantasy. So what? Why should people read the story? (c) What is catcy? Do you mean catchy? How can readers be motivated and enjoy the reading? This is not clear. Try and improve them, Bob.

xiii. Inspiriting learner ability. For difficult tasks, learners sometimes need a great deal of encouragement and direction. In the example below, Rahim has a problem with part of his assignment and asks for help. His tutor responds by providing a set of guidelines Rahim can follow, and use to structure his answer. More importantly, the tutor uses a series of questions to inspirit Rahim's efforts by outlining the kind of information the examiner would like to see in the answer. Notably, Rahim also gets a response from his classmate something he gratefully acknowledges.

Cue 17.

Dear sir & fellow course-mate, Could explain a little bit more on question No.3 & 6. I'm still blurry about these two questions. TQ

Response from tutor.

Dear Rahim, Hi there. May I know what text you have chosen? Q3 requires you to write a critical review about the text which you have read. Writing a review is not writing a report about the story you have read. Notice the word 'critical' here. You should mention things like - what did you like/ dislike in the story? Do you think the story managed to convey its values/ message clearly to the reader? Which character did you like/ dislike? Were the characters effective in the story? What were the strengths/ weaknesses of the story? etc. Q4 requires you to write three 'blurbs' of the story which you have read. (to help promote, encourage other people to read the story) Please refer to the

module/ dictionary for the meaning of the word 'blurb'. We have discussed this before. Hope this has helped you a little.

Response from peer 1.

Hi Rahim, Critical review is about in simplest form what you have read, you try to summarise it according to your understanding (the context should be directly from the book) You suppose to sum up according to your own words. Just as Mr. Wong wrote, what you like/or dislike. The 200-250 will inspire you to write a well-compacted review (of course reading and understanding the book helps a lot, no short cut) After your critical review, you need to analyse which caption that fascinates you and see whether that caption were in the form of authorial or neo-rhetorical criticism and elaborate further. From, Sophia

Response from cuer.

Thanks for the replies. It helps a lot. TQ, again.

xiv. Redirecting to encourage greater autonomy. In the online forum, it was found that several postings were either repetitions or not very well thought out. Generally, questions in these postings had already been dealt with on another occasion by the same tutor. Thus, tutors sometimes redirected learners to sources where they could find the information, or to an earlier response by the tutor or student. This appeared to be a way to challenge learners to seek answers on their own, or to use more self-reliant measures in seeking answers to their questions, as demonstrated in the following examples.

Cue 18.

Dear Mr. Roshan. can you please explain what are the elements that i should put in this critical review? besides the author do i have to write about all the literary devices such as the theme, setting and mood of the text?

Response from tutor.
You may criticise on the use of literary devices, you may see some critical reviews on http://www. pinkmonkey.com/booknotes/ba4rrons/peqrl5.asp Regards, Roshan

Cue 19.
Sir, Can you please explain in detail how to to the assignment in our next tutorial? TQ

Response from tutor.
Got some techniques on writing a review from the forum. You may want to read them. It comes as an attachment. [Attachment]

Response from cuer.
Dear Sir, Thank you for the notes given on writing a review I am sure it will help me and others to write our assignment very well. Thank you Sir. That's all for now .Good bye.

Cue 20.
Sir, Can you please explain what is authorial criticism and neo-rhetorical criticism? Dear Sir,

Response from tutor.
Please refer to Janita's and Gerry's question on this forum Regards, Roshan

IV. EXTENSION

An important—albeit highly desirable—outcome of active learning is the extension of learners' skills or current thinking-learning ability. The analysis of the data showed that learners own attempts at extending their knowledge led to various ways of using course content. In this category, extension, the learner is in focus again as s/he works actively toward the recognition that s/he has to show his understanding of course content. The following examples illustrate learners' efforts at extending their cognitive reach through recasts and application, and their tutors' requests for extension of learner effort.

xv. Recasting content learnt in course. As learners came across new ideas, concepts and issues in their reading, they engaged in sense-making by way of rewording or restating what they read in their own words. Often these recasts, as it were, were accompanied by requests for feedback on their understanding of course content. In the following vignettes, Cuers 21 and 22 recast ideas to show what they have understood from their reading, and request for feedback from the tutor.

Cue 21.
Hi friends and tutor, Generally, the process of literary reading involves: a. pre-reading, b. while-reading, c. post-reading. Based on the process above, I would like to emphasize on pre-reading stage which involves identifying assumptions, interest and pre-conceptions. For this reason, I've chosen a questioning method activity that a teacher can carry out for literary learning.

Response from peer 1.
Jo, I agree with you about the process of literary reading. I also have the same idea like you. Me too state the pre-reading, while-reading and the post-reading as the process of reading literary text. Are we two right?

Response from tutor.
Hi Jo, Your answers are acceptable, but elaborate more in your paper. Be more descriptive. OK?

Cue 22.
Dear tutor and course-mates, A review of a novel is also a response since it normally includes an evaluation of the work. It requires analytic skill but it is not identical with an analysis. Some retelling of the plot is necessary, however, the review is primarily concerned with describing, analysing, and evaluating. Do you agree?

xvi. Application of concepts learnt in course. Another subcategory of extension is the application of theoretical concepts or approaches to what learners are reading or to matters related to their life. In the first case cited below, Putri seeks guidance on understanding the discursive approach to analysis literary discourse (Cue 23). Putri gets a response from the tutor, but another student, Rajesh, is unable to apply the discursive approach to the text he is reading, i.e. The Pearl by John Steinbeck. Rajesh's request on the same topic (Cue 24) is responded to by a peer, Yeo, who is from another OUM learning centre altogether. Finally Putri (and hopefully Rajesh too) is able to apply the discursive approach to The Pearl.

Cue 23.
01 Oct 2004 06:04:38 PM
Dear Tuan Haji Idris, according to question 5, we are suppose to give a brief definition of both criticisms. But it's not easy to understand about the discursive approach. Can you please explain it? [Putri]

Response from tutor to cuer 23.
01 Oct 2004 08:14:10 PM
Assalamualaikum Putri, Page 34 of the module, try to say something about discursive approach [da],but does not really make you understand it. Well I don't blame you. When you talk about da, you are actually looking at analysis of discourse in literature i.e. you want to see how sense, meaning, idea, fact, truth is built by language, produced by institutions, discipline—science, history etc. Every discourse is situated in an ideology/context; such as political, gender, class etc. When you talk about literary discourse, remember about imagination/ imaginative, rhetorical . Historical discourse has to be based on fact/factual. I hope this is easier to understand. Good luck. Wassalam.

Response from cuer 23 to tutor.
01 Oct 2004 08:31:04 PM
Thank you very much Tuan Hj. Idris, At least 1 have an idea what the da is.

Cue 24.
01 Oct 2004 09:04:33 PM
Dear Tuan Haji Idris, Can you give an example on how to view "The Pearl" according to discursive analyses. I think this examples will make me understand and apply the method [Rajesh]

Response from peer 1 to cuer 24.
04 Oct 2004 12:47:51 AM
Rajesh, Yeo again fr Seberang Jaya Centre! Discursive approach is classified under Neo-Rhetorical Approach according to the module which the second app. The first app. is the study of genres which consists of Poetry, Drama, Short stories & Novels as we have learned during Jan. semester (Intro. to Literature). For the module, it seems to me that discursive app. is regarding the possibility of the readers' perception. Thought & action that depends on the minds' structure of a certain meaningful field. It reflects as sense as opposed to incoherent nonsense of the literary texts!

Response from cuer 23 to peer 1 and to cuer 18.
04 Oct 2004 05:38:22 PM
Or can I say it in a simple way, discursive approach is the beauty of the language used in order to convey the message. For example, when the writer wrote 'Kino awakened in the dark night' -the first line of the first page tells you something sad or a tragic scene may happen through out the story as he was awaken in the dark -forwarding. While the last line in the last page mentioned 'And the music of the pearl drifted to a whisper and disappeared' is actually telling us the power of the pearl of the desire towards the pearl is no longer in Kino as it was thrown back to the sea. The author conveys message through his creativity

in playing with words and gives deep meaning to the reader. Am I right Tuan Hj Idris? [Putri]

Application of course content was also seen in relevance to matters beyond the classroom. In the following excerpts, we see how two students see the relevance of ideas picked up in the course in terms of personal experience (Cue 25) and in terms of metaphor (Cue 26) related to a short story with a Kelantanese setting (in the north-eastern part of West Malaysia).

Cue 25.
Dear Sir, as I discussed with you earlier I pick up the theme (no 10) caste in my assignment. As i go on doing, it is becoming a very sensitive matter to talk about. What you think? Can I continue with the same theme? I have almost towards the end of the product.

Response from tutor.
You don't have to worry. When we are discussing caste, we are looking at an academic point of view. Go ahead with the assignment. Regards

Cue 26.
Dear Sir, Here's what I understand of the title of the story of "Pak De Samad's Cinema". The word 'cinema' tells me of many things such as his life and struggles, entertainment, fantasy or maybe a place. Am I right? Thank you.

Response from tutor.
Wow! That's the way to go. You have the basic idea. Expand on that idea in your exam ok. John

The above sub-section on tutor-learner discussion has shown the many ways in which learners have benefited from participation in the online discussion forum. True to the historical premise of the forum, students in thus course (that was the focus of the analysis) engaged in a process that involved inquiry, debate and collaborative activity for the purpose of learning from their tutors and peers. The vignettes also demonstrate the authenticity with which the players approached the task, as well as the integrity that accompanies tutor feedback and peer-led interaction during online interaction. Below, the summary section presents an overview of the chapter, and links the aims of the chapter to the implementation of the model and related outcomes.

SUMMARY

This chapter is centred on the role of online discussion forums in creating meaningful learning experiences for learners in distance learning programmes. The use of a collaborative learning model that helped create an interactive online learning community at Open University Malaysia has been discussed. Within this model, task-directed collaborative activity provided authentic learning experiences and helped learners achieve specified learning outcomes. The chapter also presents exemplars of threaded discussions related to four categories: while guidance and challenge show how tutors play an active role in collaborative online learning, interdependence and extension demonstrate how learners play and active role in task-directed collaborative activity.

The Open University Malaysia-collaborative online learning model is premised upon the understanding that knowledge construction is a result of learners employing many skills simultaneously to carry out authentic, complex and less-structured tasks in culturally relevant learning environments. Thus, learners' skills are developed as they think of ways to resolve issues, define and solve problems, focus on ways to present newly acquired knowledge and actively strive to complete tasks and to achieve learning goals. As an instrument for learning, the discussion on the implementation of the Open University Malaysia-collaborative online learning model has shown how interactive online communities are instrumental in enlivening the promise of education in distance education programmes.

ACKNOWLEDGMENTS

The author thanks colleagues at Open University Malaysia for their help with the implementation of the collaborative learning model at the Open University Malaysia, especially Zoraini Wati Abas, for initial discussions on the collaborative online learning model, and David Lim Chong Lim for writing the task that was used in the course Introduction to Novels and Short Stories.

REFERENCES

Anderson, T. (2004). Teaching in an Online Learning Context. In T. Anderson & F. Elloumi (Eds.), *Theory and practice in online learning* (pp. 271-296). Athabasca: Athabasca University.

Andres, Y. M. (2002). Art of Collaboration: Awesome Tools and Proven Strategies. *Journal of Computer-Mediated Communication, 8*(1), Retrieved January 2005, from http://clp.cqu.edu. au/online_articles.htm

Balester, V., Halasek, K. & Peterson, N. (1992). Sharing authority: Collaborative teaching in a computer-based writing course. *Computers and Composition, 9*(1), 25-40.

Bransford, J., Brown, A., & Cocking, R. (1999). *How people learn: Brain, mind experience and school.* Retrieved April 2005, from http://www. nap.edu/html/howpeople1

Bruner, J. (1986). *Actual minds, possible worlds.* Cambridge: Harvard University Press.

Clark, J. (2000). Collaboration Tools in Online Learning Environments. *ALN Magazine, 4*(2). Retrieved August 2005, from http://www.sloan-c.org/publications/magazine/v4n1/index.asp

Collison, G., Elbaum, B., Haavind, S. & Tinker, R. (2000). *Facilitating Online Learning: Effective Strategies for Moderators.* Madison, WI: Atwood Publishing.

Dillenbourg, P., & Schneider, D. (1995, March 7-10). Collaborative learning and the internet. Paper presented at the *International Conference on Computer Assisted Instruction (ICCAI'95).* National Chiao Tung University, Hsinchu, Taiwan. Retrieved January 2005, from http://tecfa.unige. ch/tecfa/ research/CMC/colla/iccai95_1.html

Harasim, L., Hiltz, S., Teles, L. & Turoff, M. (1995). *Learning networks: A field guide to teaching and learning online.* Cambridge: MIT Press.

Hiltz, S. (1995, March 7-10). Teaching in a virtual classroom. Paper presented at the *International Conference on Computer Assisted Instruction (ICCAI'95).* National Chiao Tung University, Hsinchu, Taiwan.

Johnson, S., Aragon, S., Najmuddin Shaik, Palma-Rivas, N. (2000). Comparative analysis of learner satisfaction and learning outcomes in online and face-to-face learning environments. *Journal of Interactive Learning, 11*(1), 29-49.

Jonassen, D. (2002). *Computers as mindtools for schools.* Upper Saddle River, NJ: Merrill.

Jonassen, D., Peck, K., & Wilson, B. (1999). *Learning with technology: A constructivist perspective.* Upper Saddle River, NJ: Prentice Hall.

Kearsley, G. (2000). *Online education: Learning and teaching in cyberspace.* Belmont, CA: Wadsworth.

Keefer, M., Zeitz, C., & Resnick, L. (2000). Judging the quality of peer-led student dialogues. *Cognition and Instruction, 18*(1), 53-81.

Kuldip Kaur & Zoraini Wati Abas (2004). Implementation of a collaborative online learning project at Open University Malaysia. *2004 Southeast Asia Association for Institutional Research*

(SEAAIR) Conference (pp. 453-462). Wenzhou, China: SEAAIR.

Laurillard, D. (1993). *Rethinking university teaching: A framework for the effective use of educational technology.* London: Routledge.

McKendree, J. (2002). The Role of Discussion in Learning. Poster Presentation at *AMEE 2002,* 29 Aug-1 Sep, Lisbon, Portugal.

Sandholtz, J., Rngstaff, C., Dwyer, D. (1997) *Teaching with technology.* NY: Teachers College Press.

Spatariu, A., Hartley, K. & Bendixen, L. D. (2004). Defining and measuring quality in on-line discussion. *Journal of Interactive Online Learning, 2*(4). Retrieved January 2005, from http://www.ncolr.org/jiol/issues/PDF/2.4.2.pdf

Shaw, A. (1994). Neighborhood Networking and Community Building. In S. Cisler (Ed.), *Ties that bind: Building community networks.* Cuppertino, CA: Apple Computer.

Liao, T. T. (Ed.). (1996). *Advanced educational technology: Research issues and future technologies.* Berlin: Springer-Verlag.

Turoff, M. (1999). An end to student segregation: No more separation between distance learning and regular courses. *Telelearning 99 Symposium,* Montreal, Canada. Retrieved January 2005, from http://eies.njit.edu/~turoff/Papers/canadapres/segregation.htm

Twigg, C. (2001). Innovations in online learning: Moving beyond no significant difference. *The Pew Symposia in Learning and Technology 2001.* Retrieved January 2005, from http://www.center.rpi.edu/PewSym/mono4.html

APPENDIX A: THE TASK

This assignment aims to evaluate your grasp of the discussion in Unit 1 of the HBET4303 module and to facilitate hands-on experiential learning. To answer this question satisfactorily, you will need to (a) conduct library and/or internet-based research; (b) participate in online discussion to share resources and clarify ideas; and (c) apply the theories you have learned in Unit 1 on a literary text of your choice.

The specific aim of this assignment is to evaluate your understanding of the authorial and neo-rhetorical means by which a literary text is given coherence, that is, how we produce meaning from or weave it into a text. Online discussions based on steps (1) to (12) below are important to create an understanding of this task, as well as the process involved in putting together your portfolio.

Bear in mind that unacknowledged use of quotes or extracts constitutes plagiarism, the penalty of which will be severe.

To prepare a bound portfolio for submission to your tutor, follow these steps:

1.	Pick a literary text of your choice. List down the title, author, and year of publication. Choose a text discussed in your module or one that is used in the school where you teach. The text you select will form the basis of your research.

2.	Write a plot summary of the text you have selected. Your summary should be between 50-60 words.

3.	Write a 200-250 word critical review of the text as though you would submit it to a newspaper for publication. Don't just summarise the story in this section. Tell your readers something about the author and the place of the text in the author's oeuvre. Share with your readers your view on why it is worth reading (or not). Highlight standout moments in the text (if they exist in your opinion).

4. Produce three blurbs from your review to be used to promote (not disparage!) the text. Remember that while a blurb always says something positive, the full-text from which it is extracted need not be thoroughly so.

5. Write a brief definition of authorial criticism and neo-rhetorical criticism.

6. Reread your review of the selected text in (2) and analyse whether you have written an authorial and/or neo-rhetorical criticism. Substantiate your answer with appropriate quotes from your review. Your analysis should be between 150-200 words.

7. Conduct a library and/or internet search to find three book reviews (of reasonable length) and/or critical essays on the selected text. Marks will be given on the appropriateness of your choice, i.e. the reviews/essays should be scholarly and varied in response. Photocopy or print them out and compile them in your portfolio.

8. Study the three reviews/essays you have selected and photocopied or printed out. Write a 300-word analysis of these reviews/essays, in the same way that you analysed your own review in (2) above. Remember to think in terms of authorial and neo-rhetorical criticisms.

9. Decide on one keyword which, in your opinion, captures an important thematic aspect of your selected text. Examples: pearl, Mexico, imam, Malaya, colonialism, cross-cultural relationship, gedeber, modernism, love, evil, old age, Japanese occupation.

10. With that one selected keyword in mind, conduct a library and/or internet search for articles, essays, book chapters, and the like which not only revolve around the keyword you have selected but which also probes, unpack and shed light on it. From the mountains of material you are likely to find from various disciplines including history, sociology, psychology, philosophy, anthropology, cultural studies, and politics, select two items which best illuminate the fictional world of your selected text. Photocopy and/or print them out and append them to your portfolio.

11. Write a 400-word essay on the ways in which the two items in (9) are useful in adding depth to your appreciation of the literary text you selected in (1).

12. Provide a systematic bibliography of all works cited in your portfolio. Refer to guides like Joseph Gibaldi's *MLA Handbook for Writers of Research Paper* (6th edition) (New York: MLA, 2003) or *The Chicago Manual of Style* (15th edition) (Chicago: The University of Chicago Press, 2003).

Chapter IX

APEC Cyber Academy:
Integration of Pedagogical and HCI Principles in an International Networked Learning Environment

Chi-Syan Lin
National University of Tainan, Taiwan

C. Candace Chou
University of St. Thomas, USA

Carole A. Bagley
University of St. Thomas, USA

ABSTRACT

This chapter introduces how APEC Cyber Academy, an international networked learning environment designed for K-12 students, can foster global collaboration through the integration of sound pedagogy and human computer interaction (HCI). Pedagogical principles that encourage project-based learning, knowledge construction, collaborative learning, community building, and critical thinking are incorporated into the design of this human computer interface. Furthermore, HCI is enriched by 3D virtual reality, multi-player games, an intelligent agent, video/voice conferencing, text-to-speech technologies, and instructional modules that are rooted in constructivist and self-regulated learning. APEC Cyber Academy provides a platform for engaging students in global collaboration and increasing information and communications technology (ICT) skills.

INTRODUCTION

Web-based learning environments have become an integral part of both traditional face-to-face and online education. Most Web-based learning environments have such basic tools as content management, course delivery, discussion board, and assessment. The functionalities of a Web-based learning environment can either dictate or extend the instructional activities that a teacher can apply to the classroom. Over the past five years, the boom of e-learning has contributed to the creation of more course management systems that are designed to provide better accessibility to students. Although many of the systems claim to support pedagogical visions with good human computer interface that encourages peer collaboration, knowledge construction, mentoring, and community building, most systems are designed largely for college or adult learners and only manage syllabi and instructional content. Bonk and Dennen (2003) found most online courseware to be pedagogically and interaction negligent. Several sources have reported international standards for HCI and usability. Among others, these standards include guidelines on functionality, interface, interaction, and use of graphics and multimedia (Bevan, 1995; Nielsen, 2004; Shneiderman, 1998; UsabilityNet, 2006). Functionalities that assist the development of rich interaction, reflection, problem-based, or project-based learning are largely missing. Very few Web-based learning environments provide pedagogical tools and quality HCI to support good human computer interaction and collaboration among international K-12 learners.

APEC Cyber Academy, a networked learning environment, was originally designed for K-12 students of APEC (Asia Pacific Economic Cooperation) member economies and was developed to address the specific vogues in pedagogy and HCI that are essential for supporting international collaboration among K-12 learners (primary and secondary school learners). *APEC Cyber Academy* (http://linc.hinet.net/apec/) is built on a learner-centered paradigm that provides project-based learning programs and a rich international learning community. The original intent was to provide a place for students and teachers to communicate and engage in virtual learning experiences in international context. Launched in 2002, the project is hosted by APEC Digital Content Production Center currently under the auspices of APEC/EDNET and Ministry of Education of Taiwan. With its emphasis on active learning and creative digital content, *APEC Cyber Academy* has attracted a growing number of international users, including K-12 students and teachers. As of December 2005, there are more than 10,000 registered learners from countries around the world (see Table 5). This chapter will provide a framework for applying pedagogical and HCI principles in virtual learning environments appropriate for young learners.

THEORETICAL FRAMEWORK

Constructivism

Some constructivist schools of thought focus primarily on the individual learner, while others focus primarily on the social nature of knowledge construction. The consensus is that education is not the mere *transmission* of knowledge from the teacher to the student but requires that students be *active*. At one end is *radical constructivism*, which attributes its origins to Von Glasersfeld (1978, 1985), who proposed that knowledge is constructed from individual experience. On the other end is *cognitive constructivism* as suggested by Jean Piaget (1969, 1970), who proposed that knowledge is constructed through assimilation, accommodation, and equilibrium. In between these two extremes is the notion of *social constructivism*, which has its origins in the theories proposed by Lev Vygotsky. Social constructivism gives importance to cultural and social contexts in influencing learning, namely the role of the community and people.

The design and development of the *APEC Cyber Academy* is steeped in the tradition of constructivist (Vygotsky, 1978) and self-regulated learning theories (Bandura, 1997). Contextual learning and collaboration are strongly supported in the networked learning environment. Constructivism is a perspective that has tremendous influence on the design of emerging learning environments. According to Jonassen and Reeves (1996), constructivism explores the process of constructing meaning and knowledge in the world. They stipulated that:

how we construct knowledge depends on what we already know, our previous experiences, how we have organized those experiences into knowledge structures such as schemata and mental models, and beliefs that we use to interpret the objects and events we encounter in the world. (p. 695)

Constructivism theorists who are influenced by Vygotsky posit that knowledge is constructed through the appropriation of culturally relevant activities. In other words, knowledge is co-constructed with peers or experts and through immersion in a social context (Bonk & Cunningham, 1998). Through engagement in collaborative activities, learners could gain new insights or knowledge as a result of collaboration. Collaboration facilitates the acquisition of knowledge. Furthermore, greater learning takes place in a social process of knowledge construction than individual effort. In Vygotsky's view, the artifacts in the social and cultural environments play an important role in assisting the development of the mind (Cole & Wertsch, 1996). Learning does not exist only inside the head of an individual, but also through culturally mediated artifacts distributed in the environment. In a networked learning environment, representation of artifacts plays an even greater role in facilitating knowledge construction and collaboration (Suthers, Hundhausen, &

Girardeau, 2003). The constructivism theory has played an important role in the design of many learning environments (Lakkala, Rahikainen, & Hakkarainen, 2001).

Self-Regulated Learning

Self-regulated learning theory and constructivist theory complement each other well in fostering learner-centered learning. Self-regulated learning places strong emphasis in cultivating a learner's ability to be an autonomous learner. Self-regulated learning theory has also provided the theoretical basis in the content design of networked learning environments. Self-regulated learning refers to *"learners' abilities to understand and control their learning environments. Self-regulated learning involves a combination of cognitive strategy, meta-cognitive processing, and motivational beliefs"* (Schraw, Kauffman, & Lehman, 2002, p. 1067). In terms of the processes that help individuals to become self-regulated learners, Zimmerman (2001) proposed three phases: the forethought phase, performance phase, and self-reflection phase. The *forethought phase* involves task analysis and self-motivation. The *performance phase* encourages self-control and self-observation. The *self-reflection phase* promotes self-judgment and self-reaction. Research has indicated that learners who proactively set specific goals for their learning tend to pay more attention to their performance and display a higher level of self-efficacy than those who do not set goals (Bandura & Schunk, 1981). It is important to teach students to become self-regulated learners. It is equally important to design learning environments that encourage students to become self-regulated learners. The processes to become self-regulated learners are not through individual effort only. Zimmerman and Schunk (2001) suggested that a social network such as teachers, peer, coaches, or parents can all be part of the processes. Self-regulated learning is especially important in encouraging persistence in networked learning environments when learners are distributed in different geographical locations. Although self-regulated learners are goal-oriented, independent, and meta-cognitively active in their learning, the complex interaction between computer representations and human factors will influence the choices made in their learning processes.

The implications of self-regulated leaning in the instructional design of online learning environments have been discussed extensively (Azevedo, 2005; Kauffman, 2004). Azevedo (2005) suggested that a self-regulated learning framework for the design of hypermedia environments should include:

learner characteristics (e.g., prior knowledge, age), hypermedia system features (e.g., access to multiple representations of information, non-linear structure of information), and mediating contextual learning processes (e.g., metacognitive skills, strategy use), and considers how these interact during students' learning about complex systems. (p. 11)

The research implications of self-regulated learning and HCI have been incorporated into the online learning environment of the *APEC Cyber Academy* by:

1. Providing online prompts periodically for students to plan and activate their prior knowledge while learning a specific topic.
2. Engaging students in meta-cognitive monitoring activities such as relating the content to what they already know about a topic or verifying with the students that they have achieved certain sub-goals.
3. Providing prompts and feedback if ineffective learning strategies have been used by learners.
4. Including a monitoring system to indicate what goals have been met or not met with a clear time frame.

Azevedo (2005) recommended the use of a human tutor to provide more flexible scaffolding and monitoring for learners in hypermedia environments because of the limited capabilities of the current learning environments. The human tutor serves as an external regulating agent that *"monitors, evaluates, and provides feedback regarding a student's self-regulatory skills"* (Azevedo, 2005, p. 14). Azevedo's research also showed that young learners (middle school and high school) performed better when a human tutor was introduced.

The constructivist and self-regulated learning principles have been the theoretical foundations for the design of learning activities in *APEC Cyber Academy*. Computer-based agent and human tutors are both included in the facilitation of online collaboration. Learners are able to check their progress and compare their performance against the whole group. The learning modules will be elaborated in the later sections.

Pedagogical Principles

While most of the discussion on learning environments have focused on the emerging technologies and effectiveness of the systems, the research on the pedagogical applications of the systems have been scanty (Lakkala et al., 2001). Problem-based learning, reciprocal learning, and cognitive apprenticeship are often cited as some of the pedagogical models that are rooted in cognitive learning theories (Lakkala et al., 2001). Bonk and Reynolds (1997) provided specific examples of pedagogical activities for Web-based learning as summarized in Table 1.

While the system is not a course management system for instructors to store and archive online instructional materials, the *APEC Cyber Academy* serves as a venue for implementing innovative pedagogy that promotes motivation, creative-thinking, critical thinking, and collaborative learning as outlined by Bonk and Reynolds (1997). For example, the *8 Noun Introductions*

Table 1. Online learning pedagogical activities by thinking and learning model (Bonk & Reynolds, 1997)

Motivational and Ice-Breaking Activities	Creative-Thinking Activities
1. 8 Noun Introductions	1. Brainstorming
2. Coffee House Expectations	2. Role-Play
3. Scavenger Hunts	3. Topical Discussions
4. Two Truths, One Lie	4. Web-Based Explorations and Readings
5. Public Commitments	5. Recursive Tasks
6. Share-A-Link	6. Electronic Séances
Critical-Thinking Activities	**Collaborative Learning Activities**
1. Electronic Voting and Polling	1. Starter-Wrapper Discussions
2. Delphi Technique	2. Structured Controversy
3. Reading Reactions	3. Symposia or Expert Panels
4. Summary Writing and Minute Papers	4. Electronic Mentors and Guests
5. Field Reflections	5. Round-robin Activities
6. Online Case Analyses	6. Jigsaw and Group Problem Solving
7. Evaluating Web Resources	7. Gallery Tours and Publishing Work
8. Instructor- as well as Student-Generated Virtual debates	8. E-Mail Pals/Web Buddies and Critical/Constructive Friends

in the *Motivational and Ice-Breaking* category refers to the use of eight nouns to introduce oneself with an explanation on why the eight nouns are chosen. In the *Creative-Thinking Activities* category, the *Electronic Séances* is a synchronous process in which participants have to choose a character from books by famous dead people to participate in a chat to solve a present-day problem. Experts can be invited to participate in the process. Everyone will be debriefed at the end of the activity (Bonk, 2002).

HCI Principles

A good (HCI) user interface helps to reduce anxiety and fear of computer usage, assist the graceful transition for novice users, provide direct manipulation of objects, offer input devices and online assistance, and allow information exploration through easy navigation (Shneiderman, 1998, pp. 29-30). There have been abundant guidelines written on what constitutes good interface for various computer-based training and learning. Jakob Nielsen (2005) has been a leading figure in usability study. He has observed children's online

behavior and proposed child-friendly design. He compared the difference between age groups and presented the summaries in Table 2.

Children use the Web most often for fun or schoolwork, whereas adults use the Web for business purposes (Bernard, 2003; Gilutz & Nielsen, 2002). Dunham and Sindhvad (2003) summarized usability studies on children's behavior and concluded the following HCI elements are most important in the design of a kid-centered learning environment:

1. **Animation:** Children are attracted to animations and tend to click on them when available (Bernard, 2003). Gilutz and Nielsen (2002) found that the appropriate use of sound and animation can help children to stay focused on a Web site.

2. **Geographic navigation metaphors & minesweeping:** Children prefer metaphors of geographic representations such as rooms, villages, 3-D maps, or other emulations of real environment for a site entrance. They are willing to engage in *minesweeping* such

Table 2. Web design approaches for different age groups (Nielsen, 2005)

	Animation and sound effects	Minesweeping for links	Advertising	Scrolling	Reading
Kids	😊	😊	😊	☹	☹
Teens	😐	☹	😐	😐	☹
Adults	☹	☹	☹	😊	😐
Key					

😊 Enjoyable, interesting, and appealing, or users can easily adjust to it.

😐 Users might appreciate it to some extent, but overuse can be problematic.

☹ Users dislike it, do not do it, or find it difficult to operate.

as scrubbing the screen with a mouse to find clickable items or to enjoy a sound effect.

3. **Reading online:** Children are willing to read instructions before starting a game as long as the instruction is kept brief. Children usually do not scroll pages to seek information.

4. **Icons as recognizable symbols:** Children between 8 and 12 prefer icons that represent symbols or languages that they are familiar with from their real environments.

5. **Advertisements:** Children do click on advertisements and think that they are part of the content.

The *APEC Cyber Academy* learning environment is learner-centered and has followed many of the usability guidelines for young learners. The graphic presentations are children-friendly, and the symbols used are as universal as possible to all children. One of the main activities utilizes the metaphors of camping and provides a number of scavenger games for student adventure while engaging in collaborative projects. When students enter the learning space, the navigation buttons are animated with upbeat sound. The content and navigation buttons are accessible within the length of one screen (800 X 600 resolution). The online instructions are all brief and concise. The

following sections will provide more detailed information.

OVERVIEW OF *APEC CYBER ACADEMY*

Objectives

The main goal of the *APEC Cyber Academy* is to create an international learning environment for K-12 students to interact and collaborate on projects following the principles of social constructivism. The main objectives are: (1) providing a networked learning environment that follows the design principles of human computer interface to facilitate interaction for learning; (2) utilizing state-of-the-art technology to assist learning and assessment; (3) applying the pedagogical principles of collaborative learning into the design of online activities; (4) fostering international friendship among K-12 learners through online collaboration and computer-mediated communication; and (5) improving ICT skills through project-based learning. To accomplish these goal and objectives, it is essential that the design of the environment can facilitate human computer interaction and support the pedagogy that is steeped in constructivism and collaborative learning. The following sections explain how these objectives can be achieved.

APEC Cyber Academy Components

Although *APEC Cyber Academy* is much more than a course management system, many of the current course management systems for online learning have functions to support only static presentation of information. The *APEC Cyber Academy* was designed to create a dynamic and interactive learning experience for both instructors and learners. The metaphor of an academy was utilized with the implementation of many advanced computer technologies. The platform includes a lobby, playground, lecture hall, learning space (project-based learning programs), and communication systems that fully support human computer interaction as indicated in Figure 1.

The *Learning Space* is the place for accessing learning content that includes *Networked Collaborative Learning Program* and *APEC ICT Cyber Camp*. The *APEC e-library* is an electronic library that aims at helping K-12 teachers and students

to search appropriate learning resources on the Internet and share instructional materials. The *Lobby* provides a space for building learning community. The *PlayGround* has educational games for fun and entertainment. The *Lecture Hall* allows an instructor to engage students in learning activities through video-conferencing, whiteboard, text/slide presentation, Q&A, quizzes, and learner status. Learners will be able to experience a high level of instructor presence through sound and sight in the *Lecture Hall*. Each unit is designed with specific pedagogical goals as indicated in Table 3.

Human Computer Interaction (HCI)

The system is built to fully support the learner-computer interaction, learner-learner interaction, and learner-context interaction. Learners can find ample online and human support throughout the learning process. Learner-centered support is embedded in the systems under the category of the HCI and communication tools, which consist of various synchronous and asynchronous

Figure 1. APEC Cyber Academy components

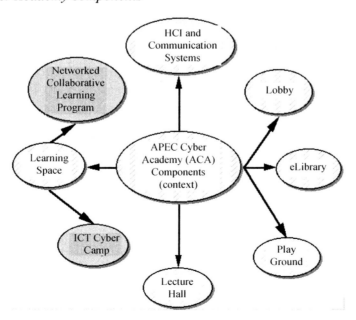

Table 3. APEC Cyber Academy components and pedagogical purposes

ACA Context	Content	Pedagogical Purposes
Learning Space	Networked collaborative learning program	Learning activities on holidays, money, a day in school, and convenience stores
	Cyber camp	Learning activities for community building, computer literacy, multimedia development, and language learning
APEC E-Library	Search engine, repository of learning materials	Databases on learning objects for K-12 instruction
Lobby	X-File	Motivation Community building Fact finding about learning status
	Journalistic kids	Collaboration Activity report of local communities
	Gallery	Global collaboration Individual artifacts publishing and sharing
	Forum	Opinion exchange
Play Ground	Online games	Online recreation Creative thinking
Lecture Hall	Slide and text presentation	Information-rich and interactive presentation
	White board	Creative thinking Brainstorming Live graphic presentation
	Q & A	Critical thinking Student feedback and questions about presentation
	Roster list	Online learner management
	Online quiz status	Instant feedback Pop quiz and summary data collection
	Video chat room	Community building Instructor and student video with voice

interpersonal communication tools as indicated in Table 4.

Building an international learning community and encouraging learners to interact with each other are two of the key principles in *APEC Cyber Academy*. Compared to other educational Web sites, *APEC Cyber Academy* contains rich communication tools such as synchronous text communicator, video conferencing, discussion forums, and learner profile. Learners could use these tools to interact with their international peers. Maintaining a consistent personal identity is the key to success in online interaction. *APEC Cyber Academy* requires learners to maintain and update their personal identities in their profiles. To participate in the activities, a teacher forms a team of students (5-20 students) and enrolls

the students in the learning programs. A team member mainly collaborates with teammates to complete the required projects. A participant can also utilize the HCI tools listed in Table 4 to interact with teammates or students from other teams. They can post in the Forum and send mail to each other through the built-in mailbox. They can also observe each other's progress in the learning programs using the Learner Profile in the WuKong agent. Online tutors also provide learning opportunities through video-conferencing, 3D virtual world chat, or asynchronous tools to interact with learners. Students are encouraged to evaluate projects posted by other teams and provide comments. Through the communication, online support, and assessment systems, human computer interaction is fully supported.

Table 4. HCI and communication tools of APEC Cyber Academy

Categories	HCI tools	Pedagogical purposes
Communication	Video chat room	Synchronous communication
	Forum (text)	Module-based asynchronous communication for each learning unit
	Bulletin board	Public announcement
	Mailbox	Correspondence with online learners
	Showcase	Digital portfolio of artifacts
Online support	Online tutor	Mentor, conference moderation, and forum facilitation
	Learning companion: WuKong agent	Provide scaffolding to learners with voice Show learner profile, notification of new mail, forum posting, hall of fame, buddy list, and help
	Learner profile	Provide information on: 1. Navigation 2. Ongoing assessment 3. Interpersonal communication 4. Personal information
Assessment	Peer evaluation	Rubric-based evaluation of artifacts by peer
	Expert evaluation	Criteria-based evaluation of artifacts and learning behaviors by experts
	Interpersonal communication	Online tracking of learner-learner interaction

The online postings are monitored by teachers, site managers, and online tutors to avoid possible abuse of the system.

APEC Cyber Academy System Architecture

The architecture of *APEC Cyber Academy* system is divided into three layers or tiers—client PCs, Internet Information Server 5.0 and Virtual Worlds Server, and Microsoft Exchange 2000 Server and Microsoft SQL 2000 Server as shown in Figure 2.

The *Internet Information Server* is the Web server that hosts all the digital content and application systems such as e-library, automatic learning activities tracking mechanism, and intelligent agents. Since the learning environment is built on a learner-centered pedagogy, the digital content is rich in interactive functionalities. From a technical perspective, the development of the digital content and the integration of the three-tiered system architecture required heavy coding with Web-based programming technologies such as Microsoft .Net and Component Object Model programming.

The *Virtual Worlds Server* is a 3D multi-user platform that provides immersive learning experiences to learners. The server is a robust, extensive application system. This team project is an ongoing virtual learning research project that uses numerous programming tools.

A *Microsoft Exchange Server* provides groupware services such as discussion forum, mailbox, and video conferencing. The storage of data, such as the learning activities, learner profiles, artifacts submitted by learners, and the e-library repository, are all recorded on an SQL 2000 Server.

Figure 2. The system architecture of APEC Cyber Academy

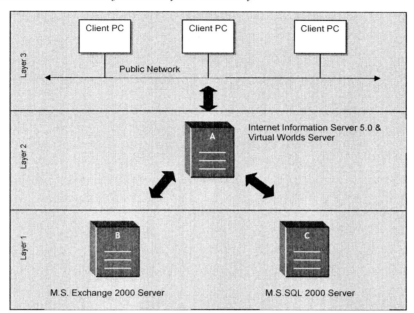

Pedagogical Applications and HCI Integration

Grounded in the constructivist and self-regulated learning, *APEC Cyber Academy* has incorporated the pedagogical principles of collaborative learning, project-based learning, creative/critical thinking, community building, and knowledge construction as indicated in Figure 3. The HCI was incorporated into the system to provide effective collaborative learning and project completion. Romiszowski (1981) summarized Bruner's (1966) theory on three levels of learning: enactive level (direct manipulation), iconic level (visual and mental image process), and symbolic level (manipulation of symbols via language). All three modes dominate one's learning all through life. Learning activities need to address all three levels to accommodate learner differences. Multimedia network learning environments are especially rich with functions to support all three levels if the activities fully utilize these features.

In *APEC Cyber Academy*, much of the instructional content is designed for K-12 learners. Students are strongly encouraged to browse and search the learning materials, conduct inquiry-based learning and assess their own learning performance, and communicate among each other in a networked learning environment. The activities of browsing and searching correspond to the enactive level of learning in the learning hierarchy. Ongoing assessment of learning performance such as creating artifacts or reflection activities corresponds to the iconic level of learning. Communicative learning activities such as discussing and consulting with each other among peers correspond to the symbolic or meta-cognitive level of learning (Lin, 2001).

In the design of the learning environment, content cannot be separated from the context. Context refers to the networked learning environment that is enriched with system platform, learning tools, and learning community. The learning content is the learning materials or activities that reside

Figure 3. APEC Cyber Academy pedagogical principles

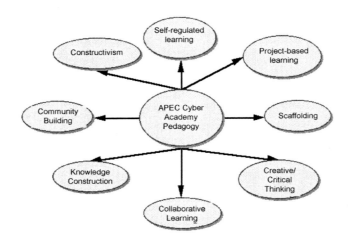

in the context. E-learning content should not be just about the provision of static information. The presentation of e-learning content in the networked learning environment or context must follow new pedagogical theories and HCI principles, and take advantage of computer network and multimedia technologies. Ideally, the content has to be integrated together with collaborative learning tools and the instructional management mechanism. In other words, the design of learning content and context go hand-in-hand together.

Above all, an e-learning environment should provide self-regulated learning content that allows learners not only to surf the information with their eyes, but also to pursue ongoing assessment and interpersonal communication learning activities meaningfully and purposefully. Also, the consideration of constructivism, sound HCI principles, and the nature of *information technology*, e-learning content, such as the content included in the *APEC Cyber Academy*, should focus on the incorporation of three learning activities: navigation, ongoing assessment, and interpersonal communication (Lin, 2001).

Navigation denotes that learners utilize their computers to surf learning resources on the Internet. This is to say that learners use their sense of *look* and *search* to obtain semantic knowledge or facts by browsing the information on Internet. It also implies that navigation is a specific learning activity that usually proceeds in a fast pace fashion. Usually, knowledge gained from navigation does not reach long-term memory.

In terms of a learning hierarchy, **ongoing assessment** is a higher learning activity than navigation is. Ongoing assessment might include each of the following: learners take an online assessment, perform assignments, or create artifacts in learning processes for gaining procedural knowledge and strategic knowledge. Therefore, ongoing assessment usually incorporates learning strategies such as presentation, evaluation, and reflection in assessing or examining learners' learning performance. The learning activity of ongoing assessment could also help learners to rethink the information they have just navigated and to plan further learning paths and objectives. It is ongoing assessment that really puts knowledge in learners' long-term memory.

Learning strategies such as discussion, emulation, collaboration, and exchange of ideas among people are related to the interaction of people and all are part of **interpersonal communication**. This could be the most significant cognitive activity in the learning processes as learners can construct meta-cognitive knowledge by means of interpersonal communication.

APEC CYBER ACADEMY LEARNING PROGRAMS

International Collaborative Learning Activities

APEC Cyber Academy has hosted an annual nine-week international online contest since 2002. A K-12 teacher who serves as a team leader forms a team of 5-20 students, and they attend the contest through the learning activities in both Networked Collaborative Learning Program and the ICT Cyber Camp. The teacher's role is to facilitate the learning process, not to complete the tasks for the students. Students collaborate with team members to complete the learning programs, which are described in the following sections. They could be working on projects face-to-face or online. Most teachers use after school hours or connect the activities with curriculum to facilitate students in completing the tasks. The learning programs can be accessed from any networked computers with Web browsers so a student could also login onto the site from home to engage in the collaborative learning process.

APEC Cyber Academy Awards are presented to winners of the contest. The winning teams receive recognition from the Taiwan's Ministry of Education and PCs as the award. This section introduces the learning modules in both programs.

Participants' Background

APEC Cyber Academy is a free site for all participants. Registration is required. Users can also enter as a guest with limited access to the site. However, to complete the online contest, a participant should be with a team to have access to certain functions that are essential to complete the learning activities. The participants need to have a basic command of English. Most of the participants are *English as a Second Language* students and view the activities as a great way to improve their English language writing and reading skills. As to the number of registered learners, there are 10,515 (95% of them are fourth grade ~ ninth grade kids) as of the end of 2005. The breakdown of countries and number of participants are shown in Table 5. The country that has the most participants is from Taiwan, and the students are mostly from the public school systems.

Table 5. Countries and number of registered APEC Cyber Academy participants

Country	Number of Registered Learners	Country	Number of Registered Learners
Australia	133	Papua New Guinea	7
Brunei	87	New Zealand	19
Canada	104	Peru	5
Chile	37	Philippines	299
China	112	Russia	2
Hong Kong	47	Singapore	153
Indonesia	67	Taiwan	7914
Japan	90	Thailand	140
Korea	438	United States	385
Malaysia	285	Viet Nam	13
Mexico	10	Others	168

Networked Collaborative Learning Program

Learning is moving beyond the recall of facts, principles, or procedural knowledge and into the areas of creativity, problem solving, analysis, or evaluation (the very skills needed in the workplace in a knowledge-based economy). Learners need the opportunity to communicate with their peers as well as with their teachers. This of course includes the opportunity to question, challenge, and discuss issues surrounding learners' daily life. It is claimed by many educators that learning is as much a social as an individual activity. Collaborative learning, constructive learning, and project-based learning seem best suited for fulfilling these needs.

APEC Cyber Academy advocates the project-based learning and learner-centered paradigm strongly. Under the *Learning Space*, there are four international collaborative online learning projects. The four projects are: *Money, Let's Go to Convenience Stores!, A Day in Our Schools,* and *Our Holidays* as summarized in Table 6. The Web portal of each project has the same structure as outlined in Figure 4.

In collaborative learning, the social context of the learning environment plays an important role. In *APEC Cyber Academy*, participants of the collaborative learning projects come from different countries with different native languages. In the projects, teachers are expected to provide scaffolding assistance such as offering learning support and guiding the discussion. As for the students,

Table 6. Project-based learning in the Networked Collaborative Learning Program

Networked Collaborative Learning Program	Objectives
Convenience store	Understand the cultural differences of convenience stores in different countries and currency conversion
Our holidays	Compare and contrast holidays in different countries thought cross-group collaboration
Money	Understand the monetary systems and discuss the value of money in APEC member economies
A day in our school	Enrich cultural diversity through the exchange of schooling experience in different countries

Figure 4. The structure of networked collaborative learning projects

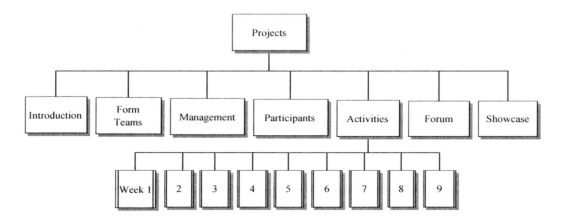

they are supposed to find resources in English, prepare and write their reports for assigned topics in English, use English to communicate with other participants, grade other teams' artifacts by providing comments in English, and even use video conferencing to talk with participants from other countries. Thus, English learning takes place in a meaningful, authentic context with these pre-designed collaborative learning activities and rich learning communities formed by communication tools. Here, learning becomes a social activity in which teachers, students, and peers work as members of a learning community to gain new experiences and knowledge and solve problems together.

Gallery is a digital portfolio for an individual learner; *Showcase* is a team or group digital portfolio applied in collaborative learning projects. Figure 5 is a *Showcase* screen shot that shows an artifact created by one of the participating teams in the collaborative learning program. This figure also shows the comments and grade of peer assessment. Participants and experts can evaluate each other's project using a checklist with five criteria in the Comment Assistant, which is a grading system for peer and expert evaluation. The system will list all grades that a project receives from peers.

A participant can evaluate a project and check off the criteria that a project has met. A project will receive points from all individuals who have reviewed the project, 5 points as meeting all five criteria and 1 point as meeting one criterion (see Figure 7 for the criteria and description of the Comment Assistant).

ICT Cyber Camp

Camping is a popular activity for most kids, and it could foster exceptional learning experiences that are not provided in classrooms. Virtual camping could be an alternative to the physical camping and create a new experience for all the kids, especially in the context of global education. Perspective campers are free from geographic distance and time zones restrictions, and they can participate in virtual camping activity at anytime and from anywhere. In essence, the rationale of virtual camping coincides with the concepts of project-based and collaborative learning perfectly. The *ICT Cyber Camp* demonstrates innovation by integrating information and communication technology with learning. Therefore, the *ICT Cyber Camp* will not only provide collaborative learning activities in gaming fashion, but will also guide the school

Figure 5. The Showcase and an artifact submitted by one of the teams participating in the Collaborative Learning Program

Table 7. Integration of pedagogy and HCI in the ICT Cyber Camp learning modules

ICT CyberCamp Modules	Pedagogy	HCI
APEC Traveler	Interactive games to understand the country names, food, currency, scenery, and national flags	Direct manipulation with arrow keys and mouse clicks, avatar for representation
APEC Challenger	Co-construction of knowledge and competition on quizzes	Agent base multimedia games
Magic House	Language comprehension in listening and speaking	Text-to-Speech and Speech-to-Text technologies
iHunter	Project-based learning	Student produced video presentation
Story Time	Round-robin activity, collaborative story-telling	Blog-type digital story telling
Icebreaker	Community building Virtual museum	3D virtual reality
E-Library	Teacher support and information sharing (refine search skills)	Institute of Electrical and Electronics Engineers Learning Object Metadata (IEEE LOM) Search engines Learning Material Repository
Campfire Party	Capstone activity Contest progress report	Student-produced video presentation

learners to explore the wonderland of information and communication technology while they are in the virtual camping site.

It is expected that campers are able to demonstrate the following skills when they pack their belongings and head for home in this nine-week virtual camping activity: (a) Collaborative and global problem-solving; (b) Apply multimedia software to creative development of artifacts, presentations, or written reports; and (c) Communicate with people at a distance and build a global learning community through the Internet.

In essence, the virtual camping focuses on applications of ICT and communication skills, as well as building international learning communities. Although, the program is open to K-12 schools, students and teachers who want to participate must first pass two online computer games before they are authorized to form teams of five including one teacher and four students. The *ICT Cyber Camp*

is composed of a sequence of two online games as the pre-requisite and six correlated learning modules designed with the pedagogical and HCI principles as summarized in Table 7.

The Prerequisites: APEC Challenger and APEC Traveler

In the reception booth of the virtual campsite, the perspective participants have to take on two games, APEC Challenger and APEC Traveler, before they are authorized to form teams and join the camp. Both of the games are designed with gaming genres to motivate kids to attain knowledge about APEC member economies and to fit into the English online learning environments.

Based on the quiz pool in information and knowledge about APEC member economies, APEC Challenger pops up questions randomly and allows students to compete with each other online as they complete the quiz. The game not only includes multimedia capability in editing and retrieving quiz items and feedback, but also is equipped with computerized assessment functionalities such as instant feedback and scoring. Most importantly, the game provides a sense of a learning community that could enhance and motivate active learning in a global networked learning environment.

APEC Traveler is a mission game that asks campers to complete five missions, which include spelling the names of countries, scenery puzzle, food court, gift shop (currencies exchange), and national flags collection. From the tasks that APEC Traveler provides, perspective campers can learn about the cultures and facts of the different countries, including geographic location, food, clothing, and currency, and so forth.

THE SIX LEARNING MODULES

There are six learning modules that make up the ICT Cyber Camp activities. The six modules are Magic House, Icebreaker, Story Time, iHunter, E-Library, and Campfire Party. All the camping activities are designed for campers to move forward collaboratively in a team, except the module of E-Library. The task in the E-Library module is specifically dedicated to the teacher of the team. The following is an introduction to each learning module:

1. **Magic House:** To guarantee the success of the camping, campers are expected to interact with each other using English. The module of Magic House is designed to help campers develop English capabilities in the aspects of listening comprehension and oral communication. The Magic House is a hotel with 10 floors, and each floor is equipped with different English learning materials that utilize Text-to-Speech and Speech-to-Text technology. Campers have to practice all the learning materials floor by floor and pass the quiz to get the best score possible.

2. **Icebreaker:** The goal of icebreaker is to build an online learning community and inspire interaction among campers in a 3D immersive learning space (Bronack, Riedle, & Tashner, 2005). The module is built on a 3D virtual world where campers are represented with avatars respectively. In the module, campers move their own avatars around the virtual world, which is a virtual world exposition. The module is implemented with the theme of a virtual museum: The Expo 2005. In the museum, campers are asked to appreciate the arts and cultures from different countries. Each team has to send voluntary narrators to introduce the works from their own countries to visitors. In addition, each team has to submit a Web page collaboratively to introduce their new friends made in the virtual museum and the impressiveness of the museum. In the end, campers are encouraged to review the Web pages submitted by other teams and provide grades and comments to the assignments.

3. **Story Time:** The module Story Time is designed following the instructional strategy of storytelling. The primary goal of the module is to excite imagination of campers in ICT applications in the future and to extend the interaction toward cooperation among teams. Digital storytelling is one of the most popular instructional strategies in the context of collaborative learning and language education.

    Story Time is a chain storytelling session in which the module initiates a scenario that is associated with the application of ICT. For the purposes of effectiveness and better practice, all teams in the camp will be grouped into several communities, each comprising four or five teams. In the module, members of the community will stay around a virtual campfire and take turns telling stories about how technologies affect the education or daily life in the future. The rule is that any camper in the community can be a storyteller who continues developing the stream of the story following the previous scripts. That is, each camper has to continue his/her story based on the previous story in the community and ensure the consistency of the story.

It is expected that each community will compose a unique set of stories about ICT at the end of the module. Furthermore, all teams have to design four comic pieces of their own to depict the story developed by the affiliated community.

4. **iHunter:** The goal of this module is to investigate and explore how information and communication technology (ICT) is being utilized in campers' local communities or school districts. Technology is changing the ways people do their jobs and changing the traditions of their lives. Campers have to work as a team and investigate how institutes or people in their communities are using ICT in their jobs or daily life and report what they have found in the investigation.

There are two activities for campers to pursue: Best Practice and Interview. In Best Practice, the investigating targets are organizations or institutes such as a school, a class, or even an office in the local community. The chosen target should demonstrate good practice of ICT in its field. In addition to text, it is encouraged to use photos to illustrate the information collected in the investigation. At the end, each team has to put all the information collected in a Web page and upload it to the camp site.

With the Interview, the investigating target here is people instead of organizations or institutes. Each team has to interview a teacher and a student who are using ICT in a unique way in their teaching and learning respectively. It is required to record the interview with a video camera. It is advised to edit the video with software before uploading it to the campsite.

5. **E-Library:** The E-Library system is implemented following the specifications of Learning Object Metadata (LOM) standards provided by the IEEE Learning Technology Standards Committee (2000). The learning module is designed specifically for teachers only. The primary goal of this module is to get teachers involved in the camp and develop skills of searching as well as evaluating online learning materials.

In other words, teachers who are participating in the camp have to surf the Internet and find good quality digital learning content inside their countries and then submit the information about the digital learning content collected through the recommendation system of the APEC E-Library. As such, people in the field of education could share the precious assets of learning materials. It is expected that this collective effort among teachers from different countries could create a rich warehouse of digital learning content.

6. **Campfire Party:** The campfire party is the farewell party for the campers and is held in the final week of the program. Prior to entering the party, each team in the camp has to shoot a short video of their music or art performance such as folk dancing, singing, or cultural illustration, and so on. After the completion of the video editing, every team must upload their video to the campsite and share with all the campers for review and evaluation.

In addition to the farewell party, the module also is the place to check on the status quo of each team in terms of learning performance. Furthermore, the result of the contest of the ICT Cyber Camp program will also be announced in this module. The virtual campsite map is shown in Figure 6.

Figure 6. The virtual campsite

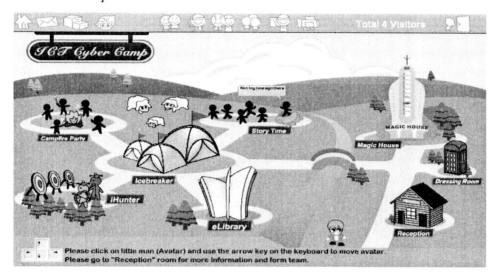

APEC Cyber Academy Assessment Rubrics

The participants of the Networked Collaborative Learning Program and ICT Cyber Camp are expected to complete all the modules in nine weeks based on the instruction in each module respectively. The performance assessment consists of three categories: peer evaluation on artifacts, expert evaluation on artifacts and learning behaviors, and evaluation on interpersonal interaction.

PEER EVALUATION ON ARTIFACTS

A peer evaluation grading system is embedded in *Showcase* within some of the modules. All participants are invited to grade or provide comments to all artifacts submitted by other teams. The score of each artifact will automatically be tabulated by the system.

EXPERT EVALUATION ON ARTIFACTS AND LEARNING BEHAVIORS

Several experts are invited to form an evaluation committee and review all the artifacts submitted by each team. The evaluation criteria are based on the artifacts' quality, creativity, and the timeliness of the submission. Furthermore, the committee will also look into the learning behaviors, including the quality of interpersonal interaction, of each team demonstrated in the contest. Bad and unacceptable learning behaviors could seriously damage the outcome of evaluation.

Automatic Evaluation of Interpersonal Interaction

Building up a versatile international learning community is one of the primary goals of *APEC Cyber Academy*. Therefore, participants of the camp are strongly encouraged to interact with their peers, especially with those who are in different teams or from different countries, by using forum and communication tools in the camp.

A tracking system is utilized to sum up the frequency of interpersonal communication automatically for each team. The mark assigned to a team in this category of evaluation will be based on its frequency of interpersonal communication recorded automatically by the learning behavior tracking system.

In short, the mark a team gets at the end of the virtual camping activities is based on its quality and quantity of interactions with other teams, artifacts, learning behaviors, and engagement in the collaborative learning process. The peer evaluation, expert evaluation, and evaluation of interpersonal interaction will count for 20%, 50%, and 30% of the final score respectively.

Preliminary Evaluation of *APEC Cyber Academy*

The underlying strategies in designing the learning content and modules are project-based learning and collaborative learning together with the expectation that HCI principles are incorporated. In this regard, the quantity and quality of interpersonal interaction in the learning processes is the primary indicator to demonstrate the performance of *APEC Cyber Academy* based on the pedagogical theories of project-based learning and collaborative learning and on HCI standards. In addition, the quantity and quality of interpersonal interaction is believed to be one of the indicators of learners' active engagement in learning processes (Luca & Mcloughlin, 2004). Furthermore, it is claimed that active engagement in the learning process enhances learning. The claim could lead to two fundamental principles in educational practice: (1) The amount of learning in any activity is directly proportional to the quantity and quality of student involvement; (2) The effectiveness of any

learning activity is directly related to the capacity of that activity to increase learning engagement (Barbara, Russell, Gabriel, James, Ronald, & Charles, 2005). These claims support the decision to use the quantity and quality of interpersonal interaction as the primary indicator on evaluation of learning performance in networked learning environments in this preliminary evaluation.

However, in the early phase of the project implementation it was observed that there were few interpersonal interactions (low quantity of interaction), including peer assessment, in the collaborative learning activities. This problem prompted the designers to conduct these two empirical studies with the aim at raising the quantity of interpersonal interaction in its collaborative learning activities.

Two empirical studies had been conducted focusing on evaluations of learning content and context. The first study reviewed the significance of the Comment Assistant in *Showcase*. The study designed a Comment Assistant for assisting peer assessment. The goals of the study were to examine whether the Comment Assistant could increase the frequency of peer assessment or not and to investigate the significance of the comment assistant on the quality of the peer assessment in networked collaborative learning activities. Figure 7 is the Comment Assistant that is embedded in the "Showcase" section of each networked collaborative learning project.

This study was conducted due to the poor quality and quantity of peer assessment in the *APEC 2002 Networked Collaborative Learning Program*. The problems were discussed, and solutions were provided by offering a Comment Assistant along with the new interface design of peer assessment modules. The solutions were implemented in the *APEC 2003 Networked Collaborative Learning Program*. The related data in the collaborative programs of both years were collected with learning activities tracking mechanisms and analyzed with statistical measures (Table 8). The z Test indicates a significant

Figure 7. The Comment Assistant of peer assessment

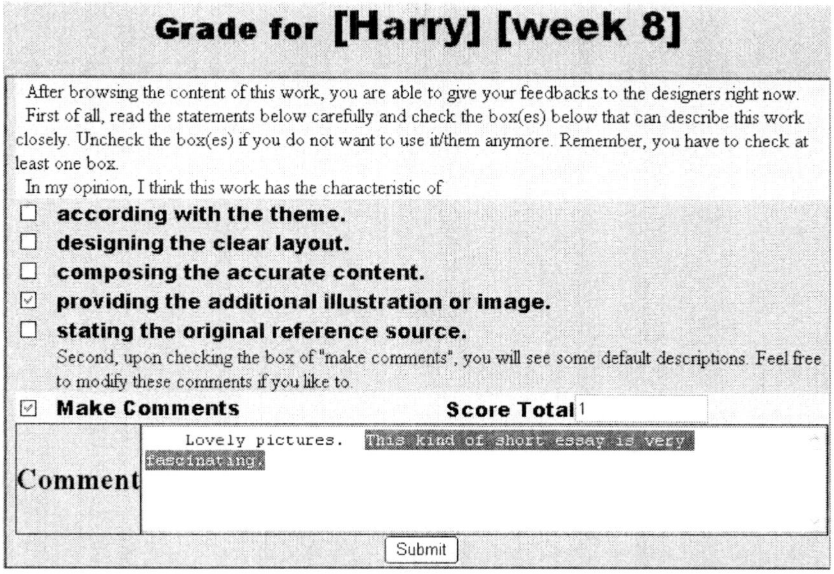

increase in the mean comments by the participants between 2002 and 2003 (p<0.001). The mean comments by the participants have increased from an average of 12.63 comments per person in 2002 to 18.88 comments per person in 2003. The results of the study revealed that the Comment Assistant has increased the frequency of comments and improved the quality of comments in peer assessment.

The second study focused on the impact of forum structure on interpersonal interactions in networked collaborative learning. The purpose of the study was to increase interpersonal interaction frequency by designing proper forum architecture in the networked collaborative learning environments. Furthermore, the study investigated the impact of forum architecture on interpersonal interactions. The study identified the factors contributing to low interpersonal interactions in *APEC 2002 Networked Collaborative Learning Program.* Solutions to the problem included a more user-friendly interface and more functions in the forum architecture for the *APEC 2003 Networked Collaborative Learning Program.*

The study aggregated data on the mean message postings and mean message responses per participant between 2002 and 2003. The z Test has shown a significant increase in the mean number of forum entries from an average of 2 entries per participant in 2002 to 29.76 entries per participant in 2004. The responses have also increased from less than 1 posting per person in

Table 8. z Test of the average of number of comments between 2002 and 2003

Year	Number of Participants	Mean of Comments	Standard Deviation	z
2002	640	12.63	17.47	-4.26*
2003	301	18.88	22.49	

*p<0.001

Table 9. z Test of the average number of postings and responses in forums between 2002 and 2003

Year	2002	2003	z
Number of Participants	149	340	
Mean of Postings	2.01	29.76	-7.326*
Mean of Responses	0.75	16.63	-7.132*

*p<0.01

2002 to 16.63 postings per person in 2003. The increase in postings and responses are both at a significant level (p<0.01) as summarized in Table 9. The significant improvement in forum interaction was due largely to system improvements that provided full text searching, personal information searching, individual performance ranking, online HTML editor, and hot-topic marking mechanism. In addition, the new installation of online facilitators in 2005 has also enabled more flexibility in interacting with the participants through editing capabilities.

Qualitative data such as participant comments that were collected from the forums and online surveys showed that most learners have responded positively in support of the collaborative learning environment. The students who participated in a recent survey have indicated what they liked about *APEC Cyber Academy*: interacting with participants from different cultures, improving English, gaining new knowledge, engaging in peer learning, and experiencing fun games. There were also suggestions for improvement: providing more interesting games, allowing more time for project completion, giving better instructions on activities, and supplying translation on some part of the Web activities. Although the studies are quite preliminary, we believe that we are in the right direction in the design of content and context for e-learning. More surveys of students' and teachers' attitudes toward the activities are underway. The data will yield more insight on the factors that contribute to learner interaction.

The statistical data from these two studies reveals that the quantity of interpersonal interaction has been achieved with the enhancement of communication and learning tools. Whereas, based on the observations of the messages posted in forums and comments provided in the Comment Assistant of peer assessment, the quality of interpersonal interaction is dismal and unacceptable. The messages were neither relevant to learning nor meaningful to social communication. It will be a great challenge in the near future to address the issue of the quality of interpersonal interaction due to its international context and English barrier of its learning community.

CONCLUSION

In this chapter, we have provided an overview of the *APEC Cyber Academy* learning environment and the connection with pedagogy and HCI. We have also elaborated on the specific pedagogical applications such as community building, knowledge construction, project-based learning, problem solving, critical thinking, authentic learning, and assessment that are rooted in constructivist and self-regulated learning. The HCI design including virtual reality, multi-user games, video conferencing, text-to-speech, and intelligent agents are appropriate for young learners. *APEC Cyber Academy* is flexible and adaptive for learners' learning needs. Many of the stand-alone features such as the video chat room and lecture hall are appropriate for both young and adult learners. The environment has also taken into account the diverse cultural backgrounds of the participating learners and encouraged global collaboration. Through the participation in the learning activities, learners are expected to achieve the following goals: (a) work collaboratively and authentically in solving problems; (b) apply computer skills and knowledge in locating information and creating artifacts; (c) communicate in English with international partners, and exchange ideas about global perspectives.

Based on three years of experience in holding international online contests, the design team has also experienced a few HCI issues. First, the system is only accessible from Windows computer using Internet Explorer. This has excluded all Mac users in North American schools, and this is a significant number. That could be one reason that explains the low participation from North America. The primary concern is that teachers and students are not able to participate in the learning programs due to platform incompatibility. Because the system architecture is built on Microsoft .Net and Component Object Model programming, this issue has yet to be resolved. Second, the complicated design can intimidate teachers who are not tech-savvy and reduce the willingness to bring students to participate. More intuitive design and online assistance should be provided to guide participants who need more assistance while navigating through the system. An evaluator who is not part of the design team is currently analyzing feedback from students on attitudes toward different learning programs. The data should provide information on factors contributing to student interaction.

The future plans for *APEC Cyber Academy* include adding more instructional modules, improving system performance, increasing participants from English-speaking countries, incorporating learning objects such as a learner profile to create the Intelligent Language Tutoring System, and utilizing *Automatic Speech Recognition* to enhance the communication interface. We believe that *APEC Cyber Academy* can be the model for the next generation e-learning system.

ACKNOWLEDGMENTS

The project is co-funded by Ministry of Education, Taiwan, Microsoft Taiwan, and LINC Digital Media, Ltd.

REFERENCES

Azevedo, R. (2005). Scaffolding learning with hypermedia: The role of self- and co-regulated learning during complex learning. *Annual Meeting of the American Educational Research Association*. Montreal, Quebec, Canada.

Bandura, A., & Schunk, D. H. (1981). Cultivating competence, self-efficacy, and intrinsic interest through proximal self-motivation. *Journal of Personality and Social Psychology, 41*, 586-598.

Barbara, P. H., Russell, L. H., Gabriel, G. L., James, H. R., Ronald, J. V., & Charles, R. W. (2005). Project Numina: Enhancing student learning with handheld computers. *Computer, 38*(6), 46-53.

Bernard, M. L. (2003). *Criteria for optimal Web design (designing for usability)*. Retrieved November 21, 2005, from http://psychology.wichita.edu/optimalweb/children.htm

Bevan, N. (1995). Human-computer interaction standards. In Y. Anzai, K. Ogawa, & H. Mori (Eds.), *Proceedings of the 6th International Conference on Human Computer Interaction*. Amsterdam, The Netherlands: Elsevier.

Bonk, C. J. (2002). *Motivational strategies for adult e-learning*. Retrieved April 5, 2006, from http://www.trainingshare.com/download/nebraska/motivation.ppt

Bonk, C. J., & Cunningham, D. J. (1998). Searching for learner-centered, constructivist, and sociocultural components of collaborative educational learning tools. In C. J. Bonk & K. S. King (Eds.), *Electronic collaborators: Learner centered technologies for literacy, apprenticeship, and discourse* (pp. 25-50). Mahwah, NJ: Lawrence Erlbaum Associates.

Bonk, C. J., & Dennen, V. (2003). Frameworks for research, design, benchmarks, training, and pedagogy in Web-based distance education. In M. G. Moore & W. G. Anderson (Eds.), *Handbook of distance education* (pp. 329-348). Mahwah, NJ: Lawrence Erlbaum Associates.

Bonk, C. J., & Reynolds, T. H. (1997). Learner-centered Web instruction for higher-order thinking, teamwork, and apprenticeship. In B. H. Khan (Ed.), *Web-based instruction* (pp. 167–178). Englewood Cliffs, NJ: Educational Technology Publications.

Bronack, S., Riedle, R., & Tashner, J. (2005). Teaching in 3D: Developing learning communities in a multi-user virtual environment. In C. Crawford et al. (Eds.), *Proceedings of Society for Information Technology and Teacher Education International Conference 2005* (pp. 2166-2170). Chesapeake, VA: AACE.

Bruner, J. S. (1966). *Towards a theory of instruction*. New York: Norton.

Cole, M., & Wertsch, J. V. (1996). Beyond the individual-social antimony in discussions of Piaget and Vygotsky. *Human Development, 39*, 250-256.

Dunham, T., & Sindhvad, S. (2003). *Exploring development & design of Web-based learning environments for children*. Paper presented at the Annual Conference on Distance Teaching and Learning, Madison, WI.

Gilutz, S., & Nielsen, J. (2002). *Usability of Web sites for children: 70 design guidelines*: Nielsen Norman Group.

Hakkarainen, K., Lakkala, M., Rahikainen, M., & Seitamaa-Hakkarainen, P. (2001). Pedagogical guidelines for designing ITCOLE CSCL. *D2.1 perspectives of CSCL in Europe: A review*. Retrieved November 13, 2005, from http://www.euro-cscl.org/site/itcole/D2_2_specification_design.pdf

IEEE Learning Technology Standards Committee. (2000). The learning object metadata standard. Retrieved November 28, 2005, from http://ieeeltsc.org/wg12LOM/lomDescription/

Jonassen, D. H., & Reeves, T. C. (1996). Learning with technology: Using computers as cognitive tools. In D. Jonassen (Ed.), *Handbook of research on educational communication and technology* (pp. 693-719). New York: Simon & Schuster Macmillan.

Kauffman, D. (2004). Self-regulated learning in Web-based environments: Instructional tools designed to facilitate self-regulated learning. *Journal of Educating Computing Research, 30*, 139-162.

Lakkala, M., Rahikainen, M., & Hakkarainen, K. (2001). D2.1 perspectives of CSCL in Europe: A review. *ITCOLE Project* (pp. 84-96). Retrieved December 1, 2005, from http://www.euro-cscl.org/site/itcole/D2_1_review_of_cscl.pdf

Lin, C. S. (2001). Implementation of the virtual school: Best cyber academy. In H. F. Shum, M. Liao, & S. F. Chang (Eds.), *Advances in multimedia information processing—PCM 2001 IEEE lecture notes in computer science* (pp. 316-323). Berlin, Germany: Springer-Verlag.

Luca, J., & Mcloughlin, C. (2004). Using online forums to support a community of learning. In *Proceedings of World Conference on Educational Multimedia, Hypermedia and Telecommunica-*

tions (EDMEDIA) 2004 (pp. 1468-1474). Norfolk, VA: AACE.

Nielsen, J. (2004). Kids' corner: Web site usability for children. Retrieved November 21, 2005, from http://www.useit.com/alertbox/20020414.html

Nielsen, J. (2005). Usability of Web sites for teenagers. Retrieved November 21, 2005, from http://www.useit.com/alertbox/20050131.html

Piaget, J. (1969). *Mechanisms of perception* (G.N.Seagrim, Trans.). New York: Basic Books.

Piaget, J. (1970). *Le structuralisme*. Paris: Presses Universitaires de France.

Romiszowski, A. J. (1981). *Designing instructional systems: Decision making in course planning and curriculum design*. New York: Nichols Publishing Company.

Schraw, G., Kauffman, D., & Lehman, S. (2002). Self-regulated learning. In J. Levin (Ed.), *Encyclopedia of cognitive science* (pp. 1063-1073). New York: Nature Publishing Group.

Shneiderman, B. (1998). *Designing the user interface: Strategies for effective human-computer interaction* (3rd ed.). Reading, MA: Addison-Wesley.

Suthers, D. D., Hundhausen, C. D., & Girardeau, L. E. (2003). Comparing the roles of representations in face-to-face and online computer supported collaborative learning. *Computers & Education, 41*(4), 335-351.

UsabilityNet. (2006). *International standards for HCI and usability*. Retrieved March 27, 2006, from http://www.usabilitynet.org/tools/r_international.htm

Von Glasersfeld, E. (1985). Reconstructing the concept of knowledge. *Archives de Psychologie, 53,* 91-101.

Vygotsky, L. S. (1978). *Mind in society: The development of higher psychological processes*. Cambridge, MA: Harvard University Press.

Zimmerman, B. J., & Schunk, D. H. (Eds.). (2001). *Self-regulated learning and academic achievement: Theoretical perspectives* (2nd ed.). Mahwah, NJ: Lawrence Erlbaum Associates Publishers.

Chapter X
Tangible User Interfaces as Mediating Tools within Adaptive Educational Environments

Daria Loi
RMIT University, Australia

ABSTRACT

This chapter proposes that, as approaches to human computer interaction (HCI), tangible user interfaces (TUIs) can scaffold rich classroom experiences if they are coupled and generated within multi-peda-gogical frameworks that adopt concepts such as Multimodality, Multisensoriality, and Multiliteracies. It overviews some necessary conditions for these tools to be effective, arguing that tangible user inter-faces and multi-pedagogies are efficient when they are conceptualized as part of adaptive educational environments—teaching and learning ecologies where learners and teachers are seen as co-creators of content and of new ways of interacting with such content.

INTRODUCTION

Information and communications technologies (ICTs) enable types of learning experiences involving HCI that other means do not easily achieve (Simon, 1987; Underwood & Under-wood, 1990). While digital spaces are tradition-ally manipulated via simple input devices (e.g., keyboard and mouse) that are used to manipulate representations displayed on output devices (e.g., monitors), *tangible user interfaces* remove this input-output distinction and connect physical and digital worlds using physical objects as interfaces to digital information (Ullmer & Ishii, 1997).

This chapter discusses the potential role of *tangible user interfaces* in scaffolding rich HCI classroom experiences and some necessary conditions for such tools to be effective. I argue that these interfaces can have a key role in con-temporary teaching and learning environments if they are coupled and generated within multi-pedagogical frameworks that adopt concepts such as Multimodality (Kress & Van Leeuwen, 2001), Multisensoriality (Ceppi & Zini, 1998), and Multiliteracies (Cope, Kalantzis, & New London Group, 2000).

Tangible user interfaces and *multi-pedagogies* are, however, effective when they are conceptualized as part of *adaptive educational environments* (Loi & Dillon, 2006)—teaching and learning ecologies where learners and teachers are seen as *co-creators* of content and of new ways of interacting with such content.

This chapter is divided into four sections. In the first part I overview why and how *tangible user interfaces* can enrich classroom experiences, while in the second I outline the importance of coupling them with multi-pedagogical frameworks. The third section overviews the notions of adaptive educational environments and proposes that *tangible user interfaces* can be conceptualized as mediating tools enabling a shift of such environments to become creative spaces. In the last section I offer a number of concluding remarks, highlighting future implications and the need for new ways of conceptualizing contemporary learning environments.

One of the key objectives of this chapter is to highlight the importance of designing *tangible user interfaces* for teaching and learning by considering them part of larger ecological HCI frameworks where pedagogy, people, and context play a crucial role.

TANGIBLE USER INTERFACES AND LEARNING ENVIRONMENTS

Ullmer and Ishii (1997) point out that while *graphical user interfaces* (GUIs) have proven to be "a successful and durable model for human computer interaction," the GUI approach to HCI "falls short in many respects, particularly in embracing the rich interface modalities between people and the physical environments they inhabit" (p. 1). Within this context, a range of alternatives

has been explored, from ubiquitous computing to augmented reality. However, these attempts often rely on exporting the GUIs paradigm to world-situated devices, failing in capturing the richness of physical-space interactions they want to enhance (Ullmer & Ishii, 1997).

This understanding was the basis on which the notion of *tangible user interfaces*—user interfaces that adopt surfaces, instruments, physical objects, and spaces as physical interfaces to digital information—was constructed through initial explorations by Fitzmaurice, Ishii, and Buxton (1995) and the original work of Ullmer and Ishii (1997). Tangible interfaces put emphasis on touch and physicality in both input and output and are often coupled to physical representations of actual objects (O'Malley & Stanton Fraser, 2004). Examples of *tangible user interfaces* include rehabilitation tools (Edmans, Gladman, Walker, Sunderland, Porter, & Stanton Fraser, 2004), drawing and designing tools (Ryokai, Marti, & Ishii, 2004), collaborative and management tools, browsers and exploratory tools (Piper, Ratti, & Ishii, 2002), multimodal interactive tools (Raffle, Joachim, & Tichenor, 2002), music creation and performance (Patten, Recht, & Ishii, 2002; Weinberg & Gan, 2001), and toys/educational tools (Mazalek, Wood, & Ishii, 2001; Vaucelle & Jehan, 2002).

O'Malley and Stanton Fraser (2004) stress the beneficial role of *physical manipulatives* in learning environments by highlighting that:

- physical action and concrete objects are important in learning;
- physical materials trigger mental images that inform future problem solving in the absence of physical materials;
- learners can abstract symbolic relations from a variety of concrete instances; and
- familiar physical objects are more easily understood by children if compared with more symbolic entities.

This suggests that children are capable of demonstrating their knowledge via physical actions (e.g., gestures) and can solve problems by working with given concrete materials even if they cannot solve them symbolically or *in their heads*. This is confirmed through the work of Bruner (1966), Piaget (1953), Church and Goldin-Meadow (1986), Goldin-Meadow (2003), and more recently Martin and Schwartz (2005).

Many thinkers have developed tools/environments that recognize the significance of children's interactions with the physical environment: Pestalozzi (1894) and his method; Dewey (1938) and his philosophy of experience and relation to education; Montessori (1917, 1949) and her method; Kamii & DeVries (1978, 1980) and their take on Piaget's theory; and Gardner and Hatch (1989) and their *multiple intelligences*.

The role of physical materials in triggering mental images useful for problem-solving has been discussed by several authors and teachers, including: Montessori (1917); Dienes (1964); Bruner (1966); Stigler (1984); Uttal, Scudder, and DeLoache (1997); and Chao, Stigler, and Woodward (2000).

The capacity to abstract symbolic relations from concrete instances is discussed by Bruner (1966) when he talks about *enactive, iconic*, and *symbolic* forms of representation and by Karmiloff-Smith (1992) and her theory of representational re-description where children's representations move from implicit to more explicit forms.

In synchrony with the previous body of literature, *tangible user interfaces* and *manipulatives* have a number of characteristics (O'Malley & Stanton Fraser, 2004) including:

- they allow for parallel input (e.g., two hands) improving the expressiveness or the communication capacity with the computer;
- they take advantage of well developed motor skills for physical object manipulations and spatial reasoning;

- they externalize traditionally internal computer representations;
- they afford multi-person, collaborative use;
- physical representations embody a greater variety of mechanisms for interactive control;
- physical representations are perceptually coupled to actively mediated digital representations; and
- the physical state of the tangible embodies key aspects of the digital state of the system.

There are a number of examples of *tangible user interfaces* that enrich HCI in classroom experience through these characteristics. O'Malley and Stanton Fraser (2004) have reviewed several of such examples, dividing them into three main categories.

The first category is that of digitally augmented paper and books, such as *Listen Reader* (Back, Cohen, Gold, Harrison, & Minneman, 2001), *MagicBook* (Billinghurst & Kato, 2002), the *KidStory* project (Stanton, Bayon, Neale, Benford, Cobb, Ingram, et al., 2001), which adopts the *KidPad* storytelling software (Druin, Stewart, Proft, Bederson, & Hollan, 1997), and *LeapPad®*. Another category of *tangible user interfaces* is that represented by *phicons* (physical objects—such as toys, blocks, and physical tags—used to trigger digital effects), such as the *CACHET project* (Luckin, Connolly, Plowman, & Airey, 2003), *Storymat* (Ryokai & Cassell, 1999), the *Tangible Viewpoints system* (Mazalek, Davenport, & Ishii, 2002), and *Chromarium* (Rogers, Scaife, Gabrielli, Smith, & Harris, 2002). There are also digital devices with embedded computational properties, such as *Triangles* (Gorbet, Orth, & Ishii, 1998), *Curlybot* (Frei, Su, Mikhak, & Ishii, 2000), *Topobo* (Raffle, Parkes, & Ishii, 2004), *Thinking Tags* (Borovoy, McDonald, Martin, & Resnick, 1996), and sensors and digital probes (tangible devices based on physical tools that act as sensors or probes of the environment), such as *Storytent* (Green, Schnädelbach, Koleva, Benford, Pridmore, & Medina, 2002), *I/O Brush* (Ryokai et al., 2004), and the *SENSE project* (Tallyn, Stanton, Benford, Rowland, Kirk, Paxton, et al., 2004).

Tangible user interfaces have a beneficial role in learning environments due to their physical and tangible characteristics and trigger HCI learning experiences that can have different qualities from those in which a learner can engage by using other digital resources such as the Web. Moreover, these tools can enable many different ways of integrating face-to-face and virtual learning, creating hybrid interactions via their tangibility and manipulability nature. However, *tangible user interfaces* cannot operate and should not be developed in isolation from other key factors, as discussed in the next section.

TANGIBLE USER INTERFACES AND MULTI-PEDAGOGIES

As mentioned, *tangible user interfaces* enable numerous ways of integrating face-to-face and virtual learning. However, I propose that to be effective in the classroom and to enhance rich HCI learning experiences, these media devices need to be coupled with *multi-pedagogical frameworks*. Failing to do so implies the development of *technology for technology sake* instead of rich ICT tools that can enhance, support, and scaffold rich HCI learning experiences. As Reimann and Goodyear (2004) highlight, *"technology is not so important in itself: what matters is how the technology is used"* (p. 2)—pedagogy and pedagogical choices in making good use of technology have crucial roles.

I define *multi-pedagogical frameworks* as scaffolds that refer to and integrate notions of Multiliteracies (Cope et al., 2000), Multimodality (Jewitt & Kress, 2003; Kress & Van Leeuwen, 2001), and Multisensoriality (Ceppi & Zini, 1998).

The term multiliteracies refers to the variability of meaning making in different cultural, social, or professional contexts and to the nature of new communications technologies (Cope & Kalantzis, 2005). Cope et al. (2000), drawing from a number of theories, generated the Multiliteracies model by merging four approaches to teaching and learning: situated practice, overt instruction, critical framing, and transformed practice. Deepening the notion of multiliteracies, Kalantzis and Cope (2003) look at pedagogy in terms of eight knowledge processes, which are selected and deployed by the teacher and define the mindful and premeditated use of such processes as learning-by-design (Cope, Kalantzis, & the Learning by Design project group, 2005). In the Learning-by-Design project, "the teacher becomes a reflective designer of learning experiences (teacher-as-designer), and classroom plans become shareable designs-for-learning" (Burrows & Loi, 2006, p. 2). In this model meaning is generated in the space where visual, audio, gestural, and spatial patterns of meaning interface written-linguistic modes of meaning (Cope & Kalantzis, 2005). To Kress (1999) the visual "is becoming more prominent in many domains of public communication" and is "taking over many of the functions of written language" while displacing the written language "from its hitherto unchallenged central position in the semiotic landscape" (p. 68).

Building on the preceding considerations, the notion of *multimodality* implies a paradigm shift in how the communication and representation of meanings can be interpreted. A multimodal text adopts several modes of communication (such as image, writing, and speech), and, while multimodality characterizes many modern texts, *"in the age of digitisation, the different modes have become the same at some level of representation, and they can be operated by one multi-skilled person"* (Kress & Van Leeuwen, 2001, p. 2). The notion of multimodality has been to date discussed by a number of authors from various disciplinary domains. Besides Kress and Van Leeuwen (2001), the works of Norris (2004), Levine and Scollon (2004), Kramsch, A'Ness, and Lam (2000), and Jewitt (Jewitt & Kress, 2003) represent key examples.

Ceppi and Zini (1998), when discussing the characteristics that learning environments should have, talk about *multisensoriality* and multisensorial spaces: complex environments *"made up of sensory contrasts and overlappings that are phenomenologically distinct"* (p. 17). To the author, the space should not simply be about *"being simply rich in stimuli,"* but it should have *"different sensory values so that each individual can tune into his or her own personal reception characteristics,"* implying that *"standard univocal solutions cannot be conceived"* (Ceppi & Zini, 1998, p. 17).

In multi-pedagogical frameworks teachers deploy a number of knowledge processes in a premeditated and mindful way (multiliteracies), becoming reflective designers of learning experiences where meaning is represented and unfolded in multimodal ways (multimodality) and enriched by different sensory values (multisensoriality). As already highlighted, pedagogy and pedagogical choices have crucial roles in making good use of technology in the classroom, and technology for the classroom should be conceived and developed *in light of* and *interlinked with* such pedagogical choices. Within this context, this chapter argues that the design and development of *tangible user interfaces* for the classroom should be coupled with multi-pedagogical frameworks.

TANGIBLE USER INTERFACES AND LEARNING ECOLOGIES

Tangible user interfaces have a key role in scaffolding rich HCI classroom experiences, and they should be coupled with multi-pedagogical frameworks. To amplify these notions, I suggest that *tangible user interfaces* and multi-pedagogical frameworks are in fact part of *learning ecologies*,

together with learners, teachers, and context, and, of course, the relationships among all actors (refer to Figure 1). These five actors are interrelated similarly to how context, people, practices, and relationship interact within collaborative workspaces (Loi, 2003). Reggio Emilia schools offer an exemplary instance of how HCI can be part of the learning ecologies (Project Zero & Reggio Children, 2001).

This model of learning ecology describes a situation where actors are deeply interrelated and co-dependent—there is a sense of wholeness and rich complexity. This implies that *tangible user interfaces* cannot be developed in isolation from other key actors, but rather conceived in light of their users (teachers and learners), contexts of HCI use, and designed learning experiences (multi-pedagogical choices).

Previous work (Loi & Dillon, 2006) discussed how ideas about collaborative workspaces (Loi, 2005) and integrativism (Dillon, 2006) can be incorporated and extended to look at the ecological nature of learning environments and to unfold notions of *adaptive educational environments*— spaces that accommodate changing relationships between people and resources—and *creative spaces*—environments that have been modified through *designed interventions*. Creative spaces I suggest that *tangible user interfaces* could be employed as HCI *mediating tools* within learning ecologies that are conceptualized as adaptive

Figure 1. A complex web of relationships

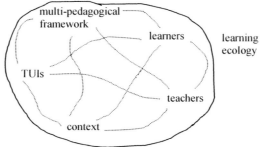

Figure 2. Tangible user interfaces as HCI mediating tools

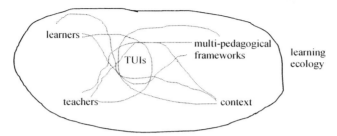

educational environments. This implies that the dynamic flow underpinning the previous model (in Figure 1) requires a refinement (refer to Figure 2). This model maintains the ecological nature of Figure 1, while underlining the possibility to consider *tangible user interfaces* as mediating HCI agents (or brokers). This role and its positioning within educational environments impact how *tangible user interfaces* can be conceived, developed, and adopted. In line with Loi and Dillon (2006), the notion of *tangible user interfaces* as HCI mediating tools can be extended to re-conceptualize them as *designed interventions* that can trigger the development of creative spaces. These concepts will be explored in future work.

To address the development of *tangible user interfaces* in the described HCI context, I suggest that a participatory design approach (Sanoff, 1990; Schuler & Namioka, 1993) should be adopted to ensure that all parts of the whole are active participants in the design process. This proposition implies that teachers and learners must be involved in the design process; designers and technologists must operate in multidisciplinary teams together with teachers and pedagogy experts; and the contexts where technology will be adopted/embedded must be considered at all times. There are a number of examples of teams currently developing *tangible user interfaces* within these participatory paradigms. An interesting example within the educational context is offered by the *Children as Design Partners* project.

As previously mentioned, Reimann and Goodyear (2004) propose that in educational environments, *"technology is not so important in itself: what matters is how the technology is used"* (p. 2). Their statement, which implies that pedagogical choices in making good use of ICT have crucial roles, should be amplified because when considering HCI learning ecologies, the design of ICT has an equally crucial role, as it strongly impacts what pedagogical choices can be conceived and enacted. The interrelations and co-dependencies of technology and pedagogy should not be underestimated. In light of this, I suggest that *tangible user interfaces* can offer significant opportunities for effective use of HCI within the classroom if:

- they are conceptualized as actors within learning ecologies, together with multi-pedagogical frameworks, learners, teachers, and contexts;
- there is a strong appreciation of the deep interrelationships and co-dependencies existing among learning ecologies' actors;
- they are conceived as mediating tools within learning ecologies;
- the learning experiences that are mediated by *tangible user interfaces* are designed adopting multi-pedagogical frameworks; and
- they are developed adopting a participatory design approach.

The adoption of a participatory design approach can be extended to the development of rich HCI learning experiences. When looked at through such lenses, teaching and learning practices can be expanded to notions of teachers-creators, learners-creators, and teacher-student as space for content emergence (O'Malley & Stanton Fraser, 2004); teachers as author-publishers and project-consultants (Burrows, 2005a, 2005b); teacher-as-designer (Brown & Edelson, 2003); and teachers and learners as co-researchers (Loughran, Mitchell, & Mitchell, 2002; Phelps, Graham, et al., 2004).

Tangible user interfaces offer some significant benefits to classroom activities, in particular from (1) creativity, (2) diversity, and (3) collaborative perspectives. These are discussed in the following paragraphs.

Creativity is an "essential life skill, which needs to be fostered by the education system(s) from the early years onward" (Craft, 1999, p. 137). In her literature review on creativity, technology and learning, Loveless (2003, p. 13) overviews the characteristics of learning environments that are conducive to creative developments, including opportunities for exploration and play with materials, information and ideas (Craft, 2000), flexibility in time and space for the different stages of creative activity (Claxton, 1999), and opportunities to take risks and make mistakes in a non-threatening atmosphere (Davies, 1999). These are in synchrony with some characteristics typical of *tangible user interfaces*, such as their physicality, manipulability, concreteness, and familiarity (O'Malley & Stanton Fraser, 2004).

Tangible HCI enables learners to combine and recombine the known and familiar in new and unfamiliar ways (Hoyles & Noss, 1999) and to unfold the world through discovery and participation (Soloway, Guzdial, & Hay, 1994; Tapscott, 1998). As Hoyles and Noss (1999) stress, "it is this dialectic between known and unknown, familiar and novel, that provides a motor for creativity" (p. 19). Moreover, combining familiarity with unfamiliarity can promote reflexiveness (Rogers et al., 2002; Scaife, 2002), stimulating awareness and enhancing learning (Ackerman, 1996; Piaget & Inhelder, 1967).

Green, Facer, Rudd, Dillon, and Humphreys (2005) have suggested that as mobile, tangible, and networked technologies are increasingly deployed in facilitating creative work, educational environments will be characterized by a high degree of personalization where individuals will have greater influence over how they choose and use learning resources. The education system is constantly challenged by diversity issues, and researchers/educators are regularly looking for ways to enable learning for diverse learners (refer, for instance, to Cope et al., 2000). Through his work on the Internet generation, Prensky (2001) argues there is a need to radically rethink teaching practice to mirror current ways of learning. The *diversity issue* implies a need to change the education system so that it can conform to learners. Interestingly, learners are already shaping their own learning outside the classroom, using digital resources to create personalized learning environments for themselves outside of school. As a matter of fact, it has been suggested that by the age of 21 the average person will have spent 15,000 hours in formal education, 20,000 hours in front of the TV, and 50,000 hours in front of a computer screen (International Futures Forum, Futuribles, European Journal of Education, & Université de Paris Dauphine, 2005). Various studies provide practical example of this tendency (for instance, Ba, Tally, & Tsikalas, 2002; Marsh, 2004).

The preceding data reiterates the need to find ways to shift the educational system so that it can conform to learners, better addressing their diversities. As Green et al. (2005) observe, *the logic of education systems should be reversed so that it is the system that conforms to the learner, rather than the learner to the system*. Thanks to *tangible user interfaces*, their intrinsic characteristics (physicality and active-oriented nature; sensory engagement; accessibility; concreteness and stimuli to abstract symbolic relations; capacity to trigger mental images that inform future problem-solving; familiarity) could offer interesting possibilities to this needed shift, enabling interactive HCI classroom activities where diverse learners can be in charge of how they choose and employ available learning resources.

A third significant benefit to classroom activities offered by *tangible user interfaces* is represented by their capacity to encourage collaboration as they afford multi-person, collaborative use (O'Malley & Stanton Fraser, 2004). A number of researchers have discussed and tested the benefits of: children working together (Rogoff, 1990; Stanton et al., 2001; Wood & O'Malley, 1996); collaborative practices on learning (for instance, Brandt, 1990; Hurley, Boykin, & Allen, 2005; Johnson, 1994; Johnson, Johnson, & Scott, 1978; Johnson, Maruyama, Johnson, Nelson, & Skon, 1981; Slavin, 1987); information technologies in peer and cooperative learning (for instance, Anderson, 2005; Chen & Morin, 2006; Topping, 2005); and that of tangible media in collaborative classroom practice (Africano, Berg, Lindbergh, Lundholm, Nilbrink, & Persson, 2004).

CONCLUSION AND FUTURE WORK

Although ICTs are already integrated into teaching across the curriculum, *more encouragement might be given to teachers in terms of incorporating everyday technologies* into the classroom, and the development of physical and multisensory activities, increasingly part of the curriculum, should occur with regard to the use of ICT (O'Malley & Stanton Fraser, 2004). In particular, *tangible user interfaces* could be considered and designed as mediating agents between pedagogy, teachers, learners, and context. This can occur only if more emphasis is placed on learners' practices and teachers' pedagogical choices and if teachers and learners are co-designers in the development of tangible HCI for learning.

There is a need to expand the ways in which tangible HCIs are researched, developed, deployed, evaluated, and implemented, and it is necessary

to bridge the gap between technologist, designers, researchers, and teachers as their technical, pedagogical, and methodological knowledge and skills differ while complementing each other. A way to translate, mediate, and share ways of doing, thinking, and creating effective HCI must be developed.

As O'Malley and Stanton Fraser (2004) stress:

More research is needed on the benefits of tangibles for learning—so far the evaluation of these technologies has been rather scarce. More effort is also needed to translate some of the research prototypes into technologies and toolkits that teachers can use without too much technical knowledge. Teachers also need training in the use of non-traditional forms of ICT and how to incorporate them into teaching across the curriculum. And finally, new forms of assessment are needed to reflect the potential of these new technologies for learning.

The notion of *tangible user interfaces* as mediating agents within educational environments implies a shift in how the learning process is viewed, a shift in the roles of teachers and learners, and a shift in how learning spaces are shaped and interacted with.

O'Malley and Stanton Fraser (2004) express their hope that teachers will *take inspiration from the whole idea of technology-enhanced learning moving beyond the desktop or classroom computer by, for example, making links between ICT-based activities and other more physical activities.* I share this hope, and this chapter aims at nurturing this notion by linking technological aspects of HCI with pedagogical, ecological, and methodological considerations under the same holistic framework. The proposed HCI scaffold fosters a different way of looking at technology-design and technology-deployment, while promoting the opportunity to re-conceptualize roles, practices, and the relationships among key actors.

As discussed in this chapter, *tangible user interfaces* offer some significant benefits to classroom activities that involve HCI, in particular from creativity, diversity, and collaborative perspectives. However, these benefits imply a need for educational institutions to re-consider and re-address how they view the professional development of teachers, the classroom space, and how curriculum development and learning resources should be designed and deployed.

In the next phase of this work and building on current work around creative educational spaces, I propose to investigate the opportunities to re-conceptualize *tangible user interfaces* as *designed interventions*. Future research in this field might also include longer term qualitative studies to (1) test *tangible user interfaces* in specific HCI contexts—living laboratories—with particular emphasis on their capacity to scaffold collaboration, creativity, and diversity; (2) further explore their agency in learning ecologies and (3) their impact on the HCI classroom space; (4) investigate specific benefits and challenges for instructors that decide to use the proposed model, coupling multi-pedagogical framework with *tangible user interfaces*; (5) look at how teachers can be scaffolded from a professional development perspective in their deployment of HCI tangibles; and (6) what type of learning resources can be designed for *tangible user interfaces* to deeply enrich the HCI classroom experience.

ACKNOWLEDGMENTS

My special thanks go to Prof. Patrick Dillon for sharing with me the *adaptive educational environments* journey. Thank you also to Mary Featherston for her contagious spaces-for-learning-enthusiasm. Finally, many thanks to Dr. Peter Burrows for our discussions and shared visions, which truly enrich my work.

REFERENCES

Ackerman, E. (1996). Perspective-taking and object construction: Two keys to learning. In Y. Kafai & M. Resnick (Eds.), *Constructionism in practice: Designing, thinking and learning in a digital world*. NJ: Lawrence Erlbaum.

Africano, D., Berg, S., Lindbergh, K., Lundholm, P., Nilbrink, F., & Persson, A. (2004, April). *Designing tangible interfaces for children's collaboration*. Paper presented at the CHI 04, Vienna, Austria.

Anderson, L. S. (2005). A digital doorway to the world. *T.H.E. Journal, 33*(4), 14-15.

Ba, H., Tally, W., & Tsikalas, K. (2002). Investigating children's emerging digital literacies. *The Journal of Technology, Learning and Assessment, 1*(4), 3-50.

Back, M., Cohen, J., Gold, R., Harrison, S., & Minneman, S. (2001). *Listen reader: An electronically augmented paper-based book*. Paper presented at the ACM SIGCHI Conference on Human Factors in Computing Systems (CHI01), Seattle, WA.

Billinghurst, M., & Kato, H. (2002). Collaborative augmented reality. *Communications of the ACM, 45*(7), 64-70.

Borovoy, R., McDonald, M., Martin, F., & Resnick, M. (1996). Things that blink: Computationally augmented name tags. *IBM Systems Journal, 35*(3), 488-495.

Brandt, R. (1990). On cooperative learning: A conversation with Spencer Kagan. *Educational Leadership, 47*(4), 8-11.

Brown, M., & Edelson, D. C. (2003). *Teaching as design*. Detroit, MI: The Center for Learning Technologies in Urban Schools.

Bruner, J. (1966). *Toward a theory of instruction*. New York: WW Norton.

Burrows, P. (2005a). The emergence of pedagogical mentors: The project-consultant. In M. Kalantzis, B. Cope, & the Learning by Design project group (Eds.), *Learning by design* (pp. 177-196). Melbourne: Common Ground Publishing.

Burrows, P. (2005b). The role of the teacher as theory-enactor and author-publisher. In M. Kalantzis, B. Cope, & the Learning by Design project group (Eds.), *Learning by design* (pp. 197-216). Melbourne: Common Ground Publishing.

Burrows, P., & Loi, D. (2006). Learning-by-design: Combining a pedagogical framework and epublishing medium to create, plan and share teaching practice. *The International Journal of Learning, 13*.

Ceppi, G., & Zini, M. (1998). *Children, spaces & relations—Metaproject for an environment for young children.* Reggio Emilia, Italy: Reggio Children S.r.l. & Domus Academy Research Center.

Chao, S., Stigler, J., & Woodward, J. (2000). The effects of physical materials on kindergartners' learning of number concepts. *Cognition and Instruction, 18*(3), 285-316.

Chen, L., & Morin, M. (2006). Trading files or learning? Exploring the educational potential of instant messaging. *Orbit, 36*(1), 18-21.

Church, R., & Goldin-Meadow, S. (1986). The mismatch between gesture and speech as an index of transitional knowledge. *Cognition, 23*, 43-71.

Claxton, G. (1999). *Wise up: The challenge of lifelong learning.* London: Bloomsbury Publishing.

Cope, B., & Kalantzis, M. (2005). *Multiliteracies.* Retrieved November 11, 2005, from http://www.cgpublisher.com/publishers/1/web/index.html

Cope, B., Kalantzis, M., & New London Group. (2000). *Multiliteracies: Literacy learning and the design of social futures.* London; New York: Routledge.

Cope, B., Kalantzis, M., & the Learning by Design project group. (2005). *Learning by design.* Melbourne, Australia: Common Ground Publishing.

Craft, A. (1999). Creative development in the early years: Some implications of policy for practice. *The Curriculum Journal, 10*(1), 135-150.

Craft, A. (2000). *Creativity across the primary curriculum: Framing and developing practice.* London: Routledge.

Davies, T. (1999). Taking risks as a feature of creativity in the teaching and learning of design and technology. *The Journal of Design and Technology Education, 4*(2), 101-108.

Dewey, J. (1938). *Experience and education.* New York: Collier Books.

Dienes, Z. (1964). *Building up mathematics* (2nd ed.). London: Hutchinson International.

Dillon, P. (2006). Creativity, integrativism and a pedagogy of connection. *International Journal of Thinking Skills and Creativity, 1*(2), forthcoming.

Druin, A., Stewart, J., Proft, D., Bederson, B., & Hollan, J. (1997). *KidPad: A design collaboration between children, technologists and educators.* Paper presented at the ACM SIGCHI Conference on Human Factors in Computing Systems (CHI97), Atlanta, Georgia.

Edmans, J., Gladman, J., Walker, M., Sunderland, A., Porter, A., & Stanton Fraser, D. (2004). *Mixed reality environments in stroke rehabilitation: Development of rehabilitation tools.* Paper presented at the 4th International Conference on Disability, Virtual Reality and Associated Technologies, Oxford.

Fitzmaurice, G., Ishii, H., & Buxton, W. (1995). *Bricks: Laying the foundations for graspable user interfaces.* Paper presented at the SIGCHI

Conference on Human Factors in Computing Systems (CHI95), Denver, Colorado.

Frei, P., Su, V., Mikhak, B., & Ishii, H. (2000). *Curlybot: Designing a new class of computational toys.* Paper presented at the SIGCHI conference on Human Factors in Computing Systems (CHI00), The Hague, Netherlands.

Gardner, H., & Hatch, T. (1989). Multiple intelligences go to school: Educational implications of the theory of multiple intelligences. *Educational Researcher, 18*(8), 4-9.

Goldin-Meadow, S. (2003). *Hearing gesture: How our hands help us think.* Harvard University Press.

Gorbet, M., Orth, M., & Ishii, H. (1998). *Triangles: Tangible interface for manipulation and exploration of digital information topography.* Paper presented at the ACM SIGCHI Conference on Human Factors in Computing Systems (CHI98), Los Angeles, CA.

Green, H., Facer, K., Rudd, T., Dillon, P., & Humphreys, P. (2005). Personalisation and digital technologies. Retrieved January 11, 2006, from http://www.futurelab.org.uk/research/personalisation/report_01.htm

Green, J., Schnädelbach, H., Koleva, B., Benford, S., Pridmore, T., & Medina, K. (2002). *Camping in the digital wilderness: Tents and flashlights as interfaces to virtual worlds.* Paper presented at the ACM SICGHI Conference on Human Factors in Computing Systems (CHI02), Minneapolis, MN.

Hoyles, C., & Noss, R. (1999). *Playing with (and without) words.* Paper presented at the 7th European Logo Conference - Eurologo '99, Sofia, Bulgaria.

Hurley, E. A., Boykin, A. W., & Allen, B. A. (2005). Communal versus individual learning of a math-estimation task: African American children

and the culture of learning contexts. *The Journal of Psychology; Provincetown 139*(6), 513-527.

International Futures Forum, Futuribles, European Journal of Education, & Université de Paris Dauphine. (2005). *Futures of learning seminars, future learning practice* (Seminar report). Glasgow.

Ishii, H., & Ullmer, B. (1997). *Tangible bits: Towards seamless interfaces between people, bits and atoms.* Paper presented at the ACM SICGHI Conference on Human Factors in Computing Systems (CHI97), Atlanta, GA.

Jewitt, C., & Kress, G. (Eds.). (2003). *Multimodal literacy.* New York: Peter Lang.

Johnson, D. W. (1994). *The new circles of learning: Cooperation in the classroom and school* (Report): Association for Supervision and Curriculum Development.

Johnson, D. W., Johnson, R. T., & Scott, L. (1978). The effects of cooperative and individualized instruction on student attitudes and achievement. *Journal of Social Psychology, 104*, 207-216.

Johnson, D. W., Maruyama, G., Johnson, R., Nelson, D., & Skon, L. (1981). Effects of cooperative, competitive, and individualistic goal structures on achievement: A meta-analysis. *Psychological Bulletin, 89*(1), 47-62.

Kalantzis, M., Cope, B., & et al. (2003). Assessing multiliteracies and the new basics. *Assessment in Education, 10*(1), 15-26.

Kamii, C., & DeVries, R. (1978). *Physical knowledge in preschool education: Implications of Piaget's theory.* Englewood Cliffs, NJ: Prentice-Hall, Inc.

Kamii, C., & DeVries, R. (1980). *Group games in early education: Implications of Piaget's theory.* NAEYC Publication.

Karmiloff-Smith, A. (1992). *Beyond modularity.* MIT Press.

Kramsch, C., A'Ness, F., & Lam, W. (2000). Authenticity and authorship in the computer-mediated acquisition of L2 literacy. *Language Learning and Technology, 4*(2), 78-104.

Kress, G. (1999). 'English' at the crossroads: Rethinking the curricula of communication in the context of the turn to the visual. In G. E. Hawisher & C. L. Selfe (Eds.), *Passions, pedagogies, and 21st century technologies.* Utah State University Press.

Kress, G., & Van Leeuwen, T. (2001). *Multimodal discourse: The modes and media of contemporary communication.* London; New York: Arnold; Oxford University Press.

Levine, P., & Scollon, R. (Eds.). (2004). *Discourse and technology. Multimodal discourse analysis.* Washington, DC: Georgetown University Press.

Loi, D. (2003, April). *Shared work environments as ecologies: New ways of working and designing.* Paper presented at the Techné—5th European Academy of Design Conference, Barcelona, Spain.

Loi, D. (2005). Piazzas where to meet: Organisational settings and their un-manageable spaces in-between. *International Journal of Knowledge, Culture and Change Management, 4.*

Loi, D., & Dillon, P. (2006). Adaptive educational environments as creative spaces. *Cambridge Journal of Education—Special Issue: Creativity in Education, 36*(3).

Loughran, J., Mitchell, I., & Mitchell, J. (2002). *Learning from teacher research.* St Leonards, N.S.W.: Allen & Unwin.

Loveless, A. (2003). *Literature review in creativity, new technologies and learning.* Bristol: NESTA Futurelab.

Luckin, R., Connolly, D., Plowman, L., & Airey, S. (2003). Children's interactions with interactive toy technology. *Journal of Computer Assisted Learning, 19*, 165-176.

Marsh, J. (2004). The techno-literacy practices of young children. *Journal of Early Childhood Research, 2*(1).

Martin, T., & Schwartz, D. (2005). Physically distributed learning: Adapting and reinterpreting physical environments in the development of fraction concepts. *Cognitive Science, 29*(4), 587-626.

Mazalek, A., Davenport, G., & Ishii, H. (2002). *Tangible viewpoints: A physical approach to multimedia stories.* Paper presented at the ACM Multimedia Conference, Juan-les-Pins, France.

Mazalek, A., Wood, A., & Ishii, H. (2001). *genieBottles: An interactive narrative in bottles.* Paper presented at the SIGGRAPH 2001—Special Interest Group on Computer Graphics, Los Angeles, CA.

Montessori, M. (1917). *The advanced Montessori method.* New York: Frederick A Stokes.

Montessori, M. (1949). *The absorbent mind.* New York: Dell.

Norris, S. (2004). *Analyzing multimodal interaction. A methodological framework.* New York & London: Routledge.

O'Malley, C., & Stanton Fraser, D. (2004). Literature review in learning with tangible technologies. Retrieved August 5, 2005, from http://www.nestafuturelab.org/research/reviews/reviews_11_and12/12_01.htm

Patten, J., Recht, B., & Ishii, H. (2002). *Audiopad: A tag-based interface for musical performance.* Paper presented at the New Interface for Musical Expression (NIME '02), Dublin.

Pestalozzi, J. (1894). *How Gertrude teaches her children*. London: Swan Sonnenschein.

Phelps, R., Graham, A., et al. (2004). Teachers and ICT: Exploring a metacognitive approach to professional development. *Australasian Journal of Educational Technology, 20*, 49-68.

Piaget, J. (1953). How children form mathematical concepts. *Scientific American, 189*(5), 74-79.

Piaget, J., & Inhelder, B. (1967). The coordination of perspectives. In J. Piaget & B. Inhelder (Eds.), *The child's conception of space*. New York: Norton and Company.

Piper, B., Ratti, C., & Ishii, H. (2002). *Illuminating clay: A 3-D tangible interface for landscape analysis*. Paper presented at the ACM SIGCHI Conference on Human Factors in Computing Systems (CHI02), Minneapolis, MN.

Prensky, M. (2001). Digital natives, digital immigrants. *On the Horizon, 9*(5).

Project Zero, & Reggio Children. (2001). *Making learning visible: Children as individual and group learners*. Reggio Emilia, Italy: Reggio Children.

Raffle, H., Joachim, M., & Tichenor, J. (2002). *Super cilia skin: An interactive membrane*. Paper presented at the ACM SIGCHI Conference on Human Factors in Computing Systems (CHI02), Fort Lauderdale, FL.

Raffle, H., Parkes, A., & Ishii, H. (2004). *Topobo: A constructive assembly system with kinetic memory*. Paper presented at the ACM SIGCHI Conference on Human Factors in Computing Systems (CHI04), Vienna, Austria.

Reimann, P., & Goodyear, P. (2004). ICT and pedagogy stimulus paper. In *Review of national goals: "Australia's common and agreed goals for schooling in the twenty-first century"* (pp. 1-42). Sydney: Ministerial Council for Education, Employment, Training and Youth Affairs (MCEETYA) Task Force.

Rogers, Y., Scaife, M., Gabrielli, S., Smith, H., & Harris, E. (2002). A conceptual framework for mixed reality environments: Designing novel learning activities for young children. *Presence: Teleoperators & Virtual Environments, 11*(6), 677-686.

Rogoff, B. (1990). *Apprenticeship in thinking: Cognitive development in social context*. New York: Oxford University Press.

Ryokai, K., & Cassell, J. (1999). *StoryMat: A play space for collaborative storytelling*. Paper presented at the ACM SIGCHI Conference on Human Factors in Computing Systems (CHI99), Pittsburgh, PA.

Ryokai, K., Marti, S., & Ishii, H. (2004). *I/O brush: Drawing with everyday objects as ink*. Paper presented at the ACM SIGCHI Conference on Human Factors in Computing Systems (CHI04), Vienna, Austria.

Sanoff, H. (1990). *Participatory design: Theory & techniques*. Raleigh, NC: Henry Sanoff (distributor).

Scaife, M. (2002). External cognition, innovative technologies and effective learning. In P. Gardenfors & P. Johansson (Eds.), *Cognition, education and communication technology*. Lawrence Erlbaum Associates.

Schuler, D., & Namioka, A. (1993). *Participatory design: Principles and practices*. Hillsdale, NJ: Lawrence Erlbaum Associates.

Simon, T. (1987). Claims for LOGO: What should we believe and why? In J. Rutkowska & C. Crook (Eds.), *Computers, cognition and development* (pp. 115-133). Chichester: John Wiley & Sons.

Slavin, R. E. (1987). Cooperative learning and the cooperative school. *Educational Leadership, 45*(3), 7-13.

Soloway, E., Guzdial, M., & Hay, K. (1994). Learner-centered design: The next challenge for HCI. *ACM Interactions, 1*(2), 36-48.

Stanton, D., Bayon, V., Neale, H., Benford, S., Cobb, S., Ingram, R., et al. (2001). *Classroom collaboration in the design of tangible interfaces for storytelling.* Paper presented at the ACM SIG-CHI Conference on Human Factors in Computing Systems (CHI01), Seattle, WA.

Stigler, J. (1984). Mental abacus—The effect of abacus training on Chinese children's mental calculation. *Cognitive Psychology, 16*(2), 145-176.

Tallyn, E., Stanton, D., Benford, S., Rowland, D., Kirk, D., Paxton, M., et al. (2004). *Introducting e-science to the classroom.* Paper presented at the UK e-science All Hands Meeting, EPSRC.

Tapscott, D. (1998). *Growing up digital: The rise of the net generation.* New York: McGraw Hill.

Topping, K. J. (2005). Trends in peer learning. *Educational Psychology; Dorchester-on-Thames, 25*(6), 631.

Ullmer, B., & Ishii, H. (1997). The metaDESK: Models and prototypes for tangible user inter-faces. In *10th Annual ACM Symposium on User Interface Software and Technology (UIST'97)* (pp. 223-232). Banff, Alberta, Canada.

Underwood, J., & Underwood, G. (1990). *Computers and learning: Helping children acquire thinking skills.* Oxford: Basil Blackwell.

Uttal, D., Scudder, K., & DeLoache, J. (1997). Manipulatives as symbols: A new perspective on the use of concrete objects to teach mathematics. *Journal of Applied Developmental Psychology, 18*(1), 37-54

Vaucelle, C., & Jehan, T. (2002). *Dolltalk: A computational toy to enhance children's creativity.* Paper presented at the ACM SIGCHI Conference on Human Factors in Computing System (CHI02), Minneapolis, MN.

Weinberg, G., & Gan, S. (2001). The squeezables: Toward an expressive and interdependent multiplayer musical instrument. *Computer Music Journal, 25*(2), 37-45.

Wood, D., & O'Malley, C. (1996). Collaborative learning between peers: An overview. *Educational Psychology in Practice, 11*(4), 4-9.

Chapter XI
Building the Virtual into Teacher Education

Gloria Latham
RMIT University, Australia

Julie Faulkner
RMIT University, Australia

ABSTRACT

This chapter describes how two lecturers in teacher education (with the assistance of critical friends) developed a virtual primary school as a digital tool to help preservice teachers at the theory/HCI practice interface. The development and future directions of their online virtual environment will be discussed and will detail how scenario building in online learning communities fosters an alternative way of thinking about teaching and learning. Developing the virtual primary school was not based on a course requiring flexible delivery in distance education. The primary school was created to provide a place of learning not often available to preservice teachers on their professional practice placements. While the concept for a virtual school is not a new one, our goals for its design were different, and application was specifically oriented toward inquiry learning and new learning philosophies involving HCI. We will explore how a narrative-based scenario approach has been assisting our work at the edge of the traditional and the new.

INTRODUCTION

The process of restructuring and revisioning our teaching and students' learning was given prominence with the reconceptualization of the Bachelor of Education program, in line with the principles of new learning. New learning ideals have been filtering into educational debates and challenging what is worth knowing. The proponents assert that schools need to prepare students for jobs/careers that are yet to be created; that jobs/careers will change every five years; that information and communication technologies impact upon the way we think and learn. According to the Australian Council of Deans of Education (ACDE, 2001), schooling must reflect the notion of New

Learning: that schooling in the 21st century must embrace the need for learners to be interdisciplinary, navigate change and diversity, to learn as they go, to solve problems, collaborate, and be flexible and creative. The challenge for teacher education programs is to excite beginning teachers to think deeply and critically about teaching and learning in the 21st century, that is, to encourage critically reflective teaching (Zeichner & Liston, 1996). Our challenge as lecturers is how to make the prospects and needs for change tangible in our teacher education program.

Too often our preservice teachers are unable to experience New Learning practices in their professional practice sites. As novice teachers enter the teaching profession they have had at least 12 years of being a learner in schools and have intimate knowledge of the practices of schooling. Understandably, teachers tend to trust what they experience, which in turn confirms their expectations and prior experiences (Orlofsky, 2001). We wanted to contest these expectations and prior learning experiences, offering alternative ways of conceiving practice (Crocco, 2001).

Learning occurs most effectively when it is authentic, situated, and meaningful to the learner (Duffy & Cunningham, 1996). To allow for effective learning and 21st century needs, we created a virtual primary school that we named Lathner Primary. Preservice teachers have a placement in this school in a Year 4/5 classroom with a teacher mentor, Anna Jones. Through this virtual school we pose scenarios that seek to challenge outmoded ways of teaching. Simulations as learning environments are often being used in teacher education (Ferry, Kervin, Cambourne, Turbill, Puglisi, Jonassen, & Hedberg, 2004; Gibson, 2002; Risco, 1995). Existing simulations seek to replicate school settings in order to have preservice teachers study them in some detail through role-plays. However, as these simulations are pre-programmed, they often become static representations of schools. Our virtual primary school differs in that it is a dynamic environment that seeks to reflect what schools might become in response to new learning challenges.

Advances in educational software in the past decade are allowing educators to develop simulations that provide new kinds of learning experiences in an evolving context. Thus the introduction of information communications technologies (ICT) in schools over the past 20 years has offered educators rich opportunities to rethink curriculum and pedagogy, or what we teach and how we teach it (Loveless & Ellis, 2001; Papert, 1993; Snyder, 1997). The potential of digital technology to transform learning has yet to be realized for a range of pragmatic and human reasons. Developing and maintaining up to date digital infrastructure is costly; the technology and software programs are challenging to learn; their reliability can be frustrating; and teachers (not unlike other professionals) can be resistant to change. However, the imperative *to* change grows. The massive social and economic upheavals of the past decades, largely wrought by technological change, have become embedded in our lives and must precipitate change in our learning institutions. We cannot continue maintaining 19th century classrooms and teaching practices while new generations enthusiastically explore the powerful learning and creativity offered by ICT (Heppell, 2001; Papert, 1993). Moreover, we need to acknowledge the shift in young people's use of digital technology from emphasis on information to communication. However, the ultimate value of ICT in education remains heavily contingent on the ways that curriculum and pedagogies work through the new technologies (Brennan, 2001; Lankshear, Snyder, & Green, 2000).

The design of the Web site is a school with a building over 100 years old, housing a new addition. From the outside, the building looks much like a school our preservice teachers may remember from their Primary School days. Yet we confront the familiar by deliberately fashioning elements of the future with environments and students and teachers learning in new ways. We began by using

Table 1.

The Evolving Context: Technology and Scenario Building	
The development of the virtual school	
2002	Conception of idea of virtual primary classroom. Profiles of 25 virtual students constructed and introduced to BEd students at RMIT using Blackboard. Preservice teachers have a placement at the virtual primary school.
2003	Virtual primary classroom concept evaluated and expanded to a virtual school. Preservice teachers and staff add to existing student profiles and build scenarios (for example, classroom dilemmas and writing parent/teacher interviews around the virtual students)
2004	The emerging concept of the virtual classroom becomes integral to ongoing action research. Twenty-five students were reduced to 20 due to preservice teacher feedback.
2005	Digital representations of 4/5F students are added online and enhanced with audiotaped sound of primary children and teachers and folders containing additional information. Wider context of the school is developed with additional teachers at the school. The graphic design of the school and classrooms continues to grow.
2006	An interactive Web site is designed and created to house the Virtual Primary School and contents. This concept is trialled.

Figure 1. A view of the playground at Lathner Primary

Blackboard for our virtual primary school, and the content was mainly text-based. Since then we have had assistance in the design and construction of an interactive Web site that reflects some of the tenets of New Learning. Adding digital dimensions in turn adds choices for the preservice teachers. The preservice teachers are positioned as active leaders and critical thinkers reflecting on how they might proceed as embryonic teachers and why. Further critical framing invites preservice teachers to consider how their decisions work to shape their "coming to know" processes. As the virtual classroom evolves, so too does our sense of working with new technologies as an integral concept to New Learning.

Through ongoing discussions, a graphic designer and a programmer from the Educational Media Group at RMIT University built the architecture for the virtual environment. We used a number of design and development applications to create the Lathner Virtual School. Our main tools were Macromedia Studio 8, which includes Flash and Dreamweaver, plus Adobe Creative Suite 2, specifically Photoshop and Illustrator. We started out with some photo shoots that were treated in Photoshop and VR software to help create the 360 degree surround experience. Most of the design work was created in Illustrator. As the prime tool for making rich media Web sites, Flash was used to build the interactive environment, hosting the rooms and all their contents. All the interactive and animated elements were also built in Flash. Other Flash-related technologies were also applied—Zoomify and FlashPaper. We added surprises at every turn to awaken new views of learning. They have employed multiple content objects using flashpaper and additional interactives. Some of the elements appear over time as the user visits each room, rather than all at once. This assists in making the environment dynamic, encouraging participants to revisit the places again and again.

There is no site map provided as the preservice teachers navigate through the virtual primary school environment. On their travels they discover a range of information housed in filing cabinets and cupboards, drawers, and on classroom walls. The information they find (text based, audio, and visual) and the order in which it is discovered is arbitrary, yet the paths they take on their tour frame their attitudes and expectations about the rest of the school environment. For example, it is Responsibility Week at the school, and the Year 5/6s have taken over the school positions of administrative staff, teachers, and support staff. The preservice teachers entering the virtual site are greeted by two students in the office who invite them to take a tour of the school. If the novice teachers navigate their way into a classroom first, they might encounter a traditional teaching space with a teacher still resistant to change. The preservice teachers are encouraged to roam the school grounds, classrooms, and hallways in order to get a feel for the environment where they will be teaching. They continue to be met with a range of familiar and unfamiliar classroom environments, including one classroom surrounded by windows and outside courtyards.

There are often several adults in each room, people of all ages and abilities, and the atmosphere has the feeling of a workshop where all members are participants—all are learners sharing their knowledge and skills.

Thrown into this foreign territory, our preservice teachers are anxious to discuss teaching and

learning in this environment and how they might best meet the needs of these students. They form a teaching and learning community by talking face-to-face in and outside of university tutorial sessions, and writing online about the same school, the same classroom, and the same students. Currently, the preservice teachers are planning curriculum for the Year 4/5F class on the novel *Dragonkeeper* by Carole Wilkinson, and we invited the author to come online for a couple of weeks and interact with our preservice teachers.

Preservice Teacher: Can you share how the idea for Dragonkeeper *emerged?*

Carol Wilkinson: I developed an interest in dragons early in my writing career ... I was intrigued by the universality of the dragon myth and kept researching it long after the project finished ... Much of the dragon's lifecycle and habits stem from ancient Chinese writing.

Inviting "experts" into the virtual environment adds a rich layer of learning. Preservice teachers' interactions with the author provide understanding about authors' work and the research undertaken while writing a text. It also deepens understanding about some of the complexities inherent in the text. These discoveries are discussed and interrogated in some detail both online and in face-to-face tutorials.

We began creating content for this virtual primary school through an English course we were both teaching for fourth year preservice teachers. We wanted to provide the preservice teachers with a class teacher who is moving her teaching toward *new times*, a phrase coined by Stuart Hall (1996) to describe social and cultural conditions characterized by new technologies. The term conceptualizes the shift toward globalization, complex cultural and social transformations, and a sense of uncertainly about the future. We also wanted to provide the opportunity for novice teachers to have a placement in this virtual classroom so

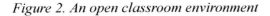
Figure 2. An open classroom environment

that they could realize new practices as they got to know and work with the students.

In order to study the effectiveness of the Virtual Primary School we employed an action research model involving planning, acting, reflecting, evaluating, and initiating additions and improvements that have assisted in expanding and strengthening our virtual school over time (Burns, 1999; Kemmis & McTaggart, 1988). As a process-oriented approach, Action Research helps us to contexualize our research knowledge by monitoring our teaching and students' learning over time and making informed and systematic decisions about change. Its growth in scope and complexity over the past few years has encouraged us to continue developing the concept, believing that it has the potential to offer rich learning and teaching understandings to other disciplines. While our concept is a populated classroom set in a primary school, the details of the space and texture of responses could transfer to a myriad other environments where more reflective practices are sought by critical educators from all sectors.

To complement the virtual, we introduced "real" face-to-face elements. A blurring of the

"real" and the virtual enhanced the preservice teachers' understanding of the structure and functions of the workplace. For example, we invite the Principal in role to talk about ongoing curriculum issues in Lathner Primary School. A president of the Parent/Teacher Association arrives (in role) to discuss the virtual primary school's policy on homework and offers parental perspectives on learning. Their presence provides a tangible sense of Lathner Primary School, connecting our digital tool to professional practice sites known to our students, while extending theory/practice links.

Lathner Primary School is an environment in progress and is "growing in," as past and current preservice teachers with digital skills add content and animate the classroom, augmenting the Web site with children in conversation audiotaped from actual primary classrooms. In this sense, the virtual school is far from a static concept. Over the past three years since its initiation, it has evolved, and will continue to evolve according to our analysis of need through our future ideas in relation to the resources available and educational change.

In our first year of developing the virtual school we concentrated on the creation of 25 students in the Year 4/5 classroom. The preservice teachers were provided with a description of the primary school (Lathner Primary School), the composite Year 4/5 classroom of 25 students, and a brief profile of each student. To familiarize themselves with the virtual students, the preservice teachers held mock parent/teacher/student reading and writing and viewing conferences and planned curriculum for them.

Since then we have focused far more on the class teacher, Anna Jones, and the ways in which she was moving her teaching to new times. We built her profile in lectures, tutorials, online through her professional journal, and in her interactions with the preservice teachers, other colleagues, parents, and students. From her professional journal Anna Jones explains some of the tensions she experiences daily.

I realize that most of the questions are coming from me lately—I'm slipping back a little as I try and take the students on to where I want them to go, not where they are interested in going. I don't feel I can always relinquish that control. Tomorrow I'm going to consciously try a different starting point from their questions, and see where that goes. ...

We deliberately created a teacher who keeps facing her traditional past, slipping back to traditional modes of operating but still seeking needed change. Anna Jones is a highly reflective practitioner and a teacher/researcher. She became the kind of questioning reflective teacher we encourage our preservice teachers to become. Anna asks new kinds of questions about teaching and learning.

Recently we reduced the number of students in the virtual classroom to 20 in order to help our students hold onto and get to know these virtual people. We further developed their profiles as well as their learning folders on the online site. Along with this we built and strengthened the school and community around the school to give

credence to the pedagogical and physical shifts in this school and in this classroom. We recognized the influence and importance of the wider context for understanding and accepting change. It is often when there is instability or threat, when backs are up against the wall that change is sought. The authors purposefully made Lathner Primary a school on the edge.

AN ENDURING TEACHER NARRATIVE

Often a single story has guided views of teachers and teaching. Because of this single view, preservice teachers find it extremely difficult to conceive of teaching and learning in ways other than those they have experienced as learners or what they are exposed to on professional practice. This story shapes our world, and this story or narrative becomes an embedded or intrinsic feature of our lives. Soap operas, serial programs, and reality television take people's lives and reshape them into stories through editing. Characters are stereotyped and made identifiable as "good" or "bad"; mundane or everyday material is cut, and interesting or intriguing events are highlighted. However, even more than this, incidents and relationships are tailored and sequenced to fit a classical western narrative structure. This structure is one that we all recognize implicitly from our earliest reading and viewing experiences: a beginning, middle, and end or, as termed by literacy genrists, orientation, complication, and resolution. Shaping stories in this way becomes fundamental and, eventually, "natural" to our way of seeing the world. Part of learning to read encompasses the process of fitting textual material into frameworks we already know, and story becomes a very familiar and, thus, influential framework.

A persistent popular culture teacher narrative involves a young, idealistic (and usually attractive) teacher entering a hostile school environment and being confronted by almost insurmountable challenges. He or she endures apathy, rudeness, and aggression, often from low socioeconomic background students, and it takes all the teacher's forbearance and resourcefulness to manage the assault. Within the space of 100 minutes, the determination of the young idealist has won through, and even the most hardened student is misty-eyed as Lulu sings "To Sir with Love" over the credits.

Films such as *To Sir with Love, Dead Poets Society, Dangerous Minds*, and *Mona Lisa Smile* are genre films—they follow predictable narrative conventions and are designed to evoke predictable emotional responses. As stories, they are often effective, but as teaching models, they limit our ways of interpreting (and thus, acting upon) experience.

A NEW NARRATIVE CALLING

We wondered how we might reframe enduring teacher narratives to create alternative stories of teaching. In the past two decades there has been increased recognition from a range of disciplines with respect to the power and usefulness of stories to enact change. For instance, in medicine, Robert Coles (1989) and Oliver Sachs (1984) use stories to connect people in the medical profession to immediate human experiences. Stephen Brookfield (1990) and Jack Meizrow (1990) use critical incidents in adult education to explore learner assumptions. In business, Ulrich Goluke (1999), Tom Reamy (2002), and Stephen Denning (2000) among others utilize storytelling for future actions.

Plausible and appropriate narratives have the power to draw readers in and make them feel a part of the present in ways that a theoretical approach cannot accomplish. Strong narratives can also present alternative views of a situation one faces, along with creating a picture of the future and helping to visualize how to get there. Goluke (1999) from *The Global Scenarios of the World Business Council for Sustainable Development* offers narratives that provide a view of another direction. He believes that story-building scenarios can help us to look 5-10 years into the future in order to determine what changes need to be made now to shape that future. Story building typically results in two to four contrasting visions of the future. Scenario building provides the freedom to look at new paths by understanding the structure and behavior of a community and causes of events, rather than studying the chronology of the past. By creating a series of carefully constructed scenarios about Lathner Primary, we are attempting to provide another view of education.

Reamy (2002), author and information architect, suggests an awareness that authors have always known. Stories are a fundamental form of knowledge, he argues, a means that humans use to structure the world. Our brains seem to be wired to easily and almost automatically organize information into stories.

Denning (2000), former director of the World Bank's knowledge management program, devises Springboard Stories. Denning says:

A springboard story is a story that can communicate a complex idea and spring people into action. It has an impact not so much through transferring large amounts of information, but through catalyzing understanding. It can enable listeners to visualize from a story in one context what is involved in a large-scale transformation in an analogous context. It can enable them to grasp the idea as a whole not only very simply and quickly, but also in a non-threatening way. It works like a metaphor—you tell a story about the past where something has already happened and invite the audience to imagine a future where this isolated example happened much more widely.

With deeper understanding of the power of narrative, we set forth to construct alternative classroom narratives that would allow novice teachers scope for taking the big theoretical ideas about New Learning into the everydayness of a school and into a classroom.

A PORTRAIT FOR SCHOOL CHANGE

One scenario, for instance, plants the seeds for needed change and begins building alternative stories for how schooling can be conceived in this school. The preservice teachers learned that several converging circumstances prompted the need for some radical rethinking about the direction of Lathner Primary. For the past several years the teachers at the school had been informally annotating changes in students' behavior and general attitudes toward learning. They often spoke about children's shorter attention spans, incessant comments about being bored, tired, and unmotivated. The teachers also felt that the students were far less compliant—often refusing to do what they were told. The staff members at the school were finding more students disruptive and noisy while others just tuned out. The rewards and punishments given out were not working. They were creating even greater divisions between students. The staff generally agreed that the abilities and knowledge base of the students in recent years were greater than ever before, but the students were not performing to their potential and were increasingly difficult to manage. The job of teaching was becoming highly stressful.

The demographics of the school population were also shifting. A once middle class predominantly Anglo Saxon population became a far more multicultural community with greater mobility, and quite varied economic levels. There were larger numbers of rental properties in the area than ever before and more families in financial need. There were also fewer children in the area, and the population of Lather Primary was rapidly declining. So, this once stable and somewhat predictable school community was in the midst of a sizable change.

Along with these two major shifts, five teachers at the school retired or transferred schools. Two of these teachers admitted they had become unable to cope with the daily student demands. A new group of beginning teachers was hired along with one more experienced teacher, each bringing their unique orientations and personalities to teaching and learning and new challenges to existing staff. These teachers breathed life and energy into a somewhat tired and troubled school. One of these new teachers was Anna Jones. At staff meetings Anna Jones, in particular, kept asking questions—important questions about some of our existing and enduring beliefs and practices at the school. It became apparent that staff did not always know why they were perpetuating particular philosophies and practices. Clearly many of the school practices were no longer effective, and yet staff members were clinging to them because these practices were what they knew. A few teachers started to read some current research on new pedagogies.

Slowly, yet purposefully, needed change was underway. Representatives from teachers, students, families, and the wider community formed part of a reference group and created a five-year plan. A new school Mission Statement was created, and a curriculum innovation committee was started. Other teachers and experts were consulted as critical friends; teachers in the school worked together in learning communities; and change was underway in a wider community sense. Teachers are aware that new and daring thinking, designs, and transformations of schools, classrooms, and repertoires of practice are needed to accommodate for learners' needs. Therefore we created a model from narrative knowing to transform educational practice. Further, one of the dimensions of new learning involves moving away from the known into the possibilities of the future. Established accounts, routinized basic skills, and standard texts may serve classrooms in a static world, but in an accelerating world of change we need to equip preservice teachers with knowledge, attitudes, and thinking for the future. Educating for the unknown as well as the known can, however, be a threatening prospect. We needed to negotiate the tensions between the familiarity of prior experience and the uncertainty of untried directions. A virtual community assisted and scaffolded this process.

SHIFTING LEARNING ENVIRONMENTS AND CONVERSATIONS

It has been claimed that, characteristically of the postmodern era, we have shifted from face-to-face to symbolic communities (Olalquiaga, 1992; Smith & Wexler, 1995). Meyrowitz (1985) argues that electronic media have the potential to create a feeling of sharing and belonging as well as one of exclusion and isolation. The relationship between group identity and group territory is tied to the traditional relationship between place and information access. Electronic and now digital media, by severing the traditional link between physical location and physical settings, blur previously distinct boundaries and allow for new ones to form. For first generation computer users, traditional sites of socialization, such as the school, have shifted to the agencies of digital culture and popular entertainment. Meyrowitz's (1985) theories predate the Internet, but the rapidly-expanding sense of context and genuinely connected relationships through e-mail, SMS, and chat rooms attest to his observations.

To explore such ideas, preservice teachers frequently shared and built on their plans and strategies for these students through online discussions. For instance, Ahmet, one of the Year 4/5F students, was not engaging with the class novel

Dragonkeeper, and a few preservice teachers were discussing how to arrest his interest.

Carolyn: Perhaps Ahmet could make up a chart that advises other students about what computer games he has played and how he rates them. He could source suitable games...such as quest games and this could lead him willingly into the genre.
Catherine: Ahmet may be persuaded to give Dragonkeeper a chance if he sees his peers taking an interest in the book. These students need critical literacy skills. I have found that when a few students get excited about a book, the enthusiasm spreads.

Kylie: Once Ahmet begins to discover what other kinds of texts can bring him, hopefully his enjoyment will take over. As Cath said, it is important for all children to develop critical literacy skills. Ahmet needs to be exposed to the feelings that text can bring him. I don't believe visual imagery has to only come from computer games.

Belinda: I like what you suggested Kylie and I thought that an activity that would be beneficial to Ahmet ...would be to read a story and then watch the film on that particular text to see whether the written text gave the same feeling as from the media text and if so why and how. I think we just need to find an appropriate text which will entice him.

The preservice teachers also discussed challenges (hopes, fears, and expectations) as they worked through and planned for and with these students.

Carmela: There are many obstacles and challenges but they are all worth it. ...have the courage, like me to be a teacher and a student as well...

James: I agree with you Carmela, nothing replaces the feeling of being with a group of learners, the excitement, the connections, the sense of satisfac-

Figure 3. Virtual playground environment

tion of building worthwhile relationships. Just one of the things I have learnt is that we must always bring a sense of courage with us into the classroom.

The participants were, and continue to be, presented with unfolding scenarios and uncharacteristic environments that made the life of this school dynamic.

REFLECTING ON THE STRENGTHS AND LIMITATIONS OF THE VIRTUAL ENVIRONMENT

This chapter advocates the strengths of the virtual primary school as a powerful and relevant teaching tool. Its evolving, open-ended potential offers education students rich opportunities to move beyond the school life they have known and take risks in an environment that is moving teaching and learning forward. Carefully constructed scenarios pose new kinds of questions about what knowledge is worth having and the new role of the teacher in challenging times. Preservice teachers are also sharing and interrogating teaching and learning stories about the same school, and in particular, the same classroom one teacher and one group of students. These shared narratives give novice teachers opportunities to wrestle with new learning pedagogies in a supportive and non-threatening environment. Becoming a preservice teacher in this school supports preservice teachers' efforts to leave their comfort zones and experiment with the concepts of new learning.

We also recognize the limitations in this virtual experience. Although preservice teachers can take risks in this school, it is not possible to give them a real sense of how these risks play out with respect to the students and their learning. As well, a virtual primary school can never mirror the moment-to-moment dynamics of a school environment. It is our awareness of these limitations that has caused us to continue to combine both face-to-face and virtual modes of delivery.

Using ICT to create a multifaceted but student-friendly teaching scenario that embodied the principles of new learning has been an ongoing challenge for us as educators. We are aware that many preservice teachers enter teacher education programs with beliefs that are not consistent with new learning, and need to be engaged in processes that help them rethink traditional instruction. Courses within teacher education programs must therefore assist preservice teachers to consider their place in the classrooms of tomorrow in light of their own educational experiences and learning. In order to bring about purposeful change, preservice teachers need to become aware of their own beliefs, deconstruct them, and reconceptualize the kind of teacher they hope to be (Yero, 2002). We want to better understand and help our students understand how the theories of new learning might play out in the everydayness of a classroom. We want preservice teachers to increase their capacities to network, incorporate diverse learning needs, adapt to changing circumstances, and initiate inquiry-based learning. The virtual classroom has emerged as a creative means through which we can explore our educational objectives through digital technologies.

We acknowledge the assistance of The Educational Media Group and in particular Russell Bywater from RMIT University for describing the digital design elements of the virtual classroom.

REFERENCES

ACDE. (2001). *New learning: A charter of Australian education.* Canberra: ACDE.

Burns, A. (1999). *Collaborative action research.* Cambridge, MA: Cambridge University Press.

Brennan, M. (2001). *The futures we have to have or the futures we might stand up for?* Keynote address presented to the biennial Home Economics Institute of Australia conference, Canberra.

Brookfield, S. (1990). Using critical incidents to analyze learners assumptions. In J. Mezerow (Ed.), *Transformative dimensions of adult learning* (pp. 177-193). San Francisco: Jossey-Bass.

Coles, R. (1989). *The call of stories: Teaching and the moral imagination.* New York: Houghton Mifflin.

Crocco, M. (2001). Leveraging constructivist learning in the social studies classroom. *Contemporary Issues in Technology and Teacher Education.* Retrieved May 4, 2006, from http:www.citcjournal.org/Vol1/iss3/socialstudies/article2.htm

Denning, S. (2000). *The springboard: How storytelling ignites action in knowledge era organizations.* Boston: Butterworth: Heinemann. Retrieved August 10, 2006, from http://www.knowledgebusiness.com/knowledge-business/projects/Knowledge_Library_Read.asp?site=1&sitesect=3&cat=18&subcat=&content_Id=2248

Duffy, T., & Cunningham, D. (1996). Constructivism: Implications for the design and delivery of instruction. In D. Jonassen (Ed.), *Handbook of research for educational communication and technology.* New York: Simon & Schuster Macmillan.

Ferry, B., Kervin, L., Cambourne, B., Turbill, J., Puglisi, S., Jonassen, D., & Hedberg, J. (2004). Online classroom simulation: The next wave for pre-service teacher education? In R. Atkinson, C. McBeath, D. Jonas-Dwyer, & R. Phillips (Eds.), *Beyond the comfort zone: Proceedings of the 21ˢᵗ ASCILITE Conference* (pp. 294-302). Perth, December 5-8. Retrieved April 10, 2006, from http://www.ascilite.org.au/conferences/perth04/procs/ferry.html

Gibson, S. (2002). Using a problem based, multimedia enhanced approach in learning in the social studies classroom. *Australian Journal of Educational Technology, 18*(3), 394-409.

Golike, U. (1998). Future. *The Hoechst Magazine.* Manager Scenario Unit, World Business Council for Sustainable Development.

Hall, S. (1996). The problem of ideology: Marxism without guarantees. In D. Morley & K. Chen (Eds.), *Stuart Hall: Critical dialogues in cultural studies* (pp. 25-46). London; New York: Routledge.

Heppell, S. (2001). Preface. In A. Loveless & V. Ellis (Eds.), *ICT, pedagogy and the curriculum: Subject to change* (pp. xv-xiv). London and New York: Routledge/Falmer.

Kemmis, S., & McTaggart, R. (1988). *The action research planner.* Victoria: Deakin University.

Lankshear, C., Snyder, I., & Green, B. (2000). *Teachers and technoliteracy.* Sydney: Allen and Unwin.

Loveless, A., & Ellis, V. (Eds.). (2001). *ICT, pedagogy and the curriculum: Subject to change.* London and New York: Routledge/Falmer.

Meizerow, J. (1990). (Ed.). *Transformative dimensions of adult learning*, 5-12. San Francisco: Jossey-Bass.

Meyrowitz, J. (1985). *No sense of place: The impact of electronic media on social behaviour.* New York: Oxford University Press.

Olalquiaga, C. (1992). *Megalopolis: Contemporary cultural sensibilities.* Minneapolis: University of Minnesota Press.

Orlofsky, D. (2001). *Redefining teacher education.* New York: Peter Lang.

Papert, S. (1993). *The children's machine: Rethinking school in the age of the computer.* New York: Basic Books.

Reamy, T. (2002). Imparting life through storytelling, part 1 & 2. *KMWorld, 11*(6), 1-9 and *11*(7), 1-9.

Risco, V. (1995). Using videodisc based cases to promote preservice teachers problem solving and mental model building. In W. Linch & E. Stutevant (Eds.), *Growing literacy* (pp. 173-187). Pittsburgh, PA: College Reading Association.

Sachs, O. (1984). *A leg to stand on.* New York: Summit Books.

Smith, R., & Wexler, P. (Eds.). (1995). *After postmodernism: Politics, identity and education.* London: The Falmer Press.

Snyder, I. (1997). *Page to screen: Taking literacy into the electronic era.* Sydney: Allen and Unwin.

Yero, J. (2002). *Teaching in mind: How teacher thinking shapes education.* Hamilton, MT: MindFlight Publishing.

Zeichner, K., & Liston, D. (1996). *Reflective teaching: An introduction.* Mahwah, NJ: Lawrence Erlbaum Associates.

Chapter XII
Integrating Human Computer Interaction in Veterinary Medicine Curricula

Gale Parchoma
University of Saskatchewan, Canada

Susan M. Taylor
University of Saskatchewan, Canada

Jonathan M. Naylor
Ross University School of Veterinary Medicine, West Indies

Sameeh M. Abutarbush
University of Prince Edward Island, Canada

Katharina L. Lohmann
University of Saskatchewan, Canada

Kathy Schwarz
University of Saskatchewan, Canada

Cheryl Waldner
University of Saskatchewan, Canada

Sharon Porterfield
University of Saskatchewan, Canada

Cindy L. Shmon
University of Saskatchewan, Canada

Lydden Polley
University of Saskatchewan, Canada

Chris Clark
University of Saskatchewan, Canada

ABSTRACT

This chapter discusses contemporary global challenges facing veterinary educators and summarizes some of the economic, social, political, and technological pressures underlying curricular and pedagogical change initiatives. Integrating human computer interaction (HCI) into veterinary medicine curricula, as a strategy for implementing pedagogical transformation, is reviewed. Computer-assisted learning (CAL) projects recently developed at a veterinary college are described. Results of studies evaluating the effectiveness of CAL approaches to HCI integration within the veterinary medicine curricula are reported. Future research directions are proposed.

INTRODUCTION

Contemporary veterinary medical education is in a transformative state. Veterinary educators are responding to public demands for the expansion of veterinary roles, for specialized veterinary care, and increased concern for animal welfare, global demands for standardization of veterinary curricula, and veterinary teaching hospital practice in the context of coping with a diminishing pool of academic veterinary researcher/educators who must manage a rapidly expanding knowledge base. Increasingly, veterinary educators are seeking human computer interaction (HCI) solutions to addressing these emergent challenges. This chapter examines these emergent challenges and describes international initiatives focused on integrating HCI into veterinary medical curricula. The chapter includes an in-depth examination of technology-enhanced learning (TEL) research and development program at the Western College of Veterinary Medicine in Canada.

EMERGENT CHALLENGES

Contemporary veterinary educators are responding to a series of emergent challenges. Increasing public demands to expand veterinary roles into public health-assurance issues are at the fore of these challenges. Veterinary responsibilities for ensuring a secure, sustainable food supply and managing industrial-scale food animal production—within a climate of public fear of pandemic disease outbreaks—have globalized these issues within veterinary colleges, regions, and governance bodies. Animal welfare concerns, as well as ecological and environmental, issues are affecting not only what is taught in veterinary school, but also the way in which it is taught. Public demand for access to specialized veterinary care and expanding pressures on veterinary teaching hospitals to train specialists and increase caseload have resulted in a predominance of secondary and

tertiary cases (referrals from practicing veterinarians) being evaluated at veterinary teaching clinics, decreasing the access of veterinary students to "general practice" cases.

Meanwhile, the pool of veterinary educators is diminishing as more financially rewarding opportunities abound in private practice and the corporate sector. All veterinary colleges cannot secure, in a timely fashion, candidates for open positions in veterinary teaching. Therefore, student access to inter-institutional experts and specialists is an emerging necessity. The veterinary knowledge base is rapidly expanding, so that it is no longer realistic to teach veterinary students "everything they need to know" within their four-year curriculum. Debates about the merits of traditional broad-based curricula versus early specialization, the appropriateness of national and regional versus global credential standards, and even pedagogical approaches to veterinary teaching and learning are recurrent themes in current veterinary literature. The combined effects of these challenges for change in veterinary teaching methodologies have resulted in calls for HCI alternatives to traditional lecture-based pedagogy and to invasive animal use in veterinary educational laboratory exercises (Association of American Veterinary Medical Colleges, 2005; Fernandes, 2004).

Globalization of the Veterinary Profession

The veterinary medical profession is increasingly expected to contribute to the development of solutions for global problems. This new responsibility makes the teaching and practice of veterinary medicine a global concern. Societal expectations that the veterinary profession should "undertake roles relevant to the re-assurance of human well-being, in terms of public health," and address "the increasing consciousness in issues of animal welfare, sustainable animal production and environmental protection" (Rodriguez-Martinez, 2004,

p. 30) are driving this change. Animal disease crises with implications for human health, such as Bovine Spongiform Encephalopathy (BSE; mad cow disease), Avian influenza, West Nile virus, and Chronic Wasting Disease have brought issues of "food safety, public health, food animal health, and food animal production" (Walsh, 2004, p. 9) to the fore of public attention. As food security, environmental sustainability, and biodiversity (Edwards, 2004) are not subject to national or regional boundaries, veterinary education curricula and credentialing standards have become subjects of international interest.

Concerns about global educational standards in the health science professions in general (Clarkson, 2005; Jackson & Callman, 2006), as well as in veterinary medical education in particular (Edwards, 2004; Hammick, 2005a) have influenced the adoption of evidence-based evaluation of teaching and learning effectiveness. Initiatives, such as the formation of the Best Evidence Medical Education (BEME) and Campbell collaborations, focus on systematic reviews of medical science education for the purpose of "providing teachers, institutions and all concerned with healthcare education" with evidence to support curricular and pedagogical decision-making (Hammick, 2005b, p. 339). Computerized collection, analysis, and dissemination of evidence supporting educational effectiveness have come to the fore in these efforts.

Veterinary Teaching Hospital Challenges

The clinical veterinary profession has dramatically changed during the last 20 years, with increasing public demands and willingness to pay for a higher standard of care and veterinary expertise. The role of specialists has increased, not only within particular species, such as small animals, horses, food animals, exotic animals, and so forth, but also within the disciplines, such as epidemiology, internal medicine, surgery, cardiology, dermatology, dentistry, ophthalmology, neurology, and oncology. Most clinicians teaching at veterinary teaching hospitals are board-certified specialists. Despite the need for veterinary students to "handle routine cases typical of those seen in veterinary practice," in most teaching hospitals, "the majority of the caseload is based on referrals, and most cases could be classified as receiving secondary or tertiary care" (Brown, 2003, p. 227).

There are many different diseases affecting wildlife, exotic, companion, and food animal health. It is not possible to discuss all of the conditions and their possible clinical presentations within the current veterinary curriculum. Ensuring that all interested students see examples of each condition during their clinical rotations is also not feasible. As a result, learning opportunities are often "hit or miss" with respect to specific case scenarios to which the students are exposed. Computer-assisted learning resources provide one method of addressing this problem by maximizing the use of current and historical case materials to expose students to the "typical clinical presentations" of many common or important diseases in each species (Abutarbush, Naylor, Parchoma, D'Eon, Petrie, & Carruthers, 2006; Clark, 2005).

Information Expansion

Veterinary information has rapidly expanded (Naylor, 2005), making it impossible for veterinary educational programs to teach students everything they will need to know for their career during a four-year veterinary program (Rodriguez-Martinez, 2004). In addition, current information is constantly being updated and changing. As a result, veterinary curricula and the expected competencies of veterinary graduates require constant review (Edwards, 2004). It is a challenge to balance the demands for a broad based curriculum to support professional licensure and provide the "basic training that should be broad enough to warrant the graduate to practice, in principle, in any field of veterinary medicine" while also satisfying the increasing demands for specialized knowledge and expertise within the limited timeframe of undergraduate study (Rodriguez-Martinez, 2004, p. 31; see also Fernandes, 2004). Furthermore, preparing students for clinical practice is only part of the picture. Veterinary curricula are also expected to prepare graduates for potential careers in epidemiology, pharmacology, public health, or basic science research. The futility of trying to "teach it all" is clear (Rodriguez-Martinez, 2004, p. 31). Veterinary curricula must make choices, and, above all, veterinary graduates must have the skills, attitudes, and dedication that promote life-long learning and continuing education after graduation.

Veterinary Educator Shortages

While the need for access to veterinary learning opportunities is expanding, the pool of veterinary educators is diminishing. Veterinary colleges "worldwide are facing numerous challenges including increasingly limited resource allocations, difficulties on enrollments, gender changes, keeping up with advances in information and other technologies, remaining aware and responsive to … [learners] and the need to aggressively globalize their teaching, research and outreach programs" (Fernandes, 2004, pp. 9-10). Difficult economic situations in developing countries further exacerbate efforts to meet these challenges. In developed countries, attracting potential faculty clinicians away from fiscally rewarding private specialty practices and positions in the veterinary corporate sector (e.g., food sector, feed, and pharmaceutical industries) into an under-resourced and increasingly demanding academic work environment is a pervasive concern (De Castrol & Zucconi, 2004). "[A]mong veterinary establishments worldwide [there] is [a] worrying lowering number of veterinary graduates enrolling in postgraduate veterinary

training" (Rodriguez-Martinez, 2004, p. 36). Most veterinary colleges are actively struggling to replace their retiring professoriate as well as their young faculty who are being lured into non-academic careers.

The Pedagogical Shift

Undergraduate veterinary education in Europe (and perhaps worldwide) is probably still considered one of the most traditional university educations, with extensive formal teaching, based upon rigid curricula, most often teaching facts rather than principles (Rodriguez-Martinez, 2004, p. 32).

Teaching veterinary students the processes of independent and collaborative "problem-identification, problem-solving and decision-making" and transforming pedagogical praxis from traditional fact-based lectures and demonstrations into "active, student-centred learning environments" has become a priority in many veterinary curricula (Rodriguez-Martinez, 2004, pp. 31-32). Computer-assisted learning (CAL) plays an important role in this change initiative. CAL has the capacity to link dispersed veterinary specialists in knowledge-sharing and collaborative teaching ventures, and to provide students with independent and collaborative case analyses and problem solving opportunities.

The use of CAL in veterinary education is expanding, and a range of tools supporting problem-based learning in virtual environments has been developed (Dhein, 2005; Hines, Collin, Quitadamo, Brahler, Knudson, & Crouch, 2005; Schoenfeld-Tacher, Bright, McConnell, Marley, & Kogan, 2005). Based in the United Kingdom, the Computer-aided Learning in Veterinary Education (CLIVE) consortium involves 14 colleges of veterinary medicine around the globe dedicated to developing and sharing electronic resources for CAL. A range of veterinary CAL initiatives have also developed in North America. Examples include Cornell University's *Consultant*, a diagnostic database "designed to link over 500 clinical signs and symptoms to nearly 7,000 possible diagnoses or disease conditions (White, 2005); the integration of HCI into pharmacology instruction (Kochevar, 2003); large animal veterinary education (Dascanio, 2003), antimicrobial resistance and animal welfare (Bernardo & Malinowski, 2005); systemic pathology (Hines et al., 2005), and an introduction to anesthetic and surgical principles and techniques (Howe, Boothe, & Hartsfield, 2005). The *Animal Behaviour Learning Environment* (ABLE), developed in Australia, uses virtual case studies and Web-based resources to support veterinary students in their efforts to diagnose and prepare treatment plans (McGreevy, Della Torre, & Evans, 2003). The *Virtual Veterinary Medicine Learning Commons*, a Canadian collaboration among the Atlantic, Ontario, and Western Colleges of Veterinary Medicine, has resulted in the sharing of high quality case-based clinical instruction by advanced broadband Internet technology (V2VLC, 2001). The University of Montreal has produced multilingual bovine medicine CD-ROMs, (Carriére, DesCôteaux, Durocher, & Harvey, 2005; Desrochers & Harvey, 2002).

INTEGRATING HCI INTO VETERINARY MEDICAL EDUCATION AT THE UNIVERSITY OF SASKATCHEWAN

The Western College of Veterinary Medicine (WCVM), established in 1964 at the University of Saskatchewan, provides undergraduate and graduate veterinary education to students from the four western Canadian provinces, as well as to national and international students. WCVM is accredited by the *Council on Education of the American Veterinary Medical Association*. The stated aim of the Doctor of Veterinary Medicine Program at the Western College of Veterinary Medicine is "to provide an excellent education

in animal health that meets society's needs, now and in the future" (WCVM, 2006, Mission statement, para. 1). The WCVM undergraduate veterinary program currently provides a fairly traditional education. In the first three years, a strong foundation in the basic sciences is followed by clinical courses, while the final year consists of clinical rotations through various clinical specialty areas. Within the next three years, however, the WCVM will be moving to a new core-elective curriculum whereby the core content (required to be taken by every student) will be decreased in order to expand elective opportunities available to students. This will allow each student to modify the curriculum to meet his or her own needs. The broad-based core curriculum will encompass the common knowledge, skills, and behaviors that veterinary students need to acquire, regardless of their ultimate career objectives. This approach will provide students with a basic understanding of the common problems facing veterinarians and prepare them for the national licensing examination. Elective opportunities will complement and enhance the knowledge, skills, and behaviors acquired in the core, allowing students to gain the additional knowledge, ability, and experience necessary for confident and successful entry in their chosen career path.

Computer-assisted learning has been a component of the veterinary curriculum at the WCVM for many years, and it is anticipated that it will play an even more important role in the new curriculum. Some courses (Virology and Clinical Pharmacology) have used WebCT to provide students with electronic lecture handouts, copies of PowerPoint slide lectures, quizzes, and interactions with faculty. Other courses, including Small Animal Medicine and Surgery, have made case materials (photographs and videos) available to students prior to case-based or modified problem-based class discussions. A few case-based CD-ROMs and DVDs have also been developed to supplement lecture-based discussions. In the Department of Small Animal Clinical Sciences two clinical faculty members (one surgeon and one internist) spent a sabbatical leave at CLIVE developing two interactive DVDs for teaching clinical neurology to veterinary students (Shmon & Taylor, 2003; Taylor & Shmon, 2003). In the Department of Large Animal Clinical Sciences, a series of CAL initiatives began in late 1990s. Results included interactive case simulations using the problem-oriented format: *Diseases of Calves* and *Diseases of Horses* (Naylor, 1996) and more recently CD-ROM-based learning modules concentrating on the skills of auscultation, *The Art of Equine Auscultation*, 2nd edition, (Naylor, 2001) and *The Art of Bovine Auscultation* (Naylor, 2003), and bovine foot care: *Cattle Claw Care* (Clark, 2004).

Provincially Supported Technology-Enhanced Learning Initiatives in Veterinary Curricular Development and Educational Research

Funding support from the province of Saskatchewan's *Technology Enhanced Learning* (TEL) initiative from 2001 to the present has extended the scope of CAL development and evaluation of CAL projects undertaken at the WCVM.

In the Department of Veterinary Microbiology, a Web-based learning resource in veterinary parasitology is being developed. The key element of this resource is a searchable database containing information on the taxonomy, morphology, geographic and host distributions, life cycle, pathology, clinical signs, diagnosis, epidemiology, treatment, control, and public health significance of approximately 100 parasites important in domestic animals in Canada. The text material for each parasite is complemented by a set of images and by animations summarizing the life cycles. For veterinary students, probably the primary users, the database can be accessed through WebCT, which provides opportunities for discussions and quizzes, together with the potential to use the database as an integral component of the students'

learning experiences in parasitology. Practicing veterinarians, animal health technicians, and students in other veterinary programs will also be able to access the database directly through the Web, although it is password protected. To assess whether this WCVM parasitology resource has wider application in veterinary education, parasitologists at the School of Veterinary and Biomedical Sciences at Murdoch University in Western Australia are participating in its development and evaluation. Information and expertise sharing initiatives, such as this parasitology database, provide HCI-based collaboration opportunities for learners, educators, researchers, and practitioners.

In the departments of Small and Large Animal Clinical Sciences, a number of TEL projects have been developed including interactive, self-learning CD-ROMs, and DVDs, developed as alternatives to traditional laboratory manuals and live-animal teaching demonstrations. To date, this resource set includes *Passing a Nasogastric Tube in the Horse, Canine and Feline Medical Exercises, Medical Imaging,* and *Basic Anesthetic and Surgical Principles. Equine Medicine* and *Canine Orthopedics* resources are in development, and a proposal for the creation of a case-based interactive electronic learning environment for bovine disease diagnosis has been funded. In addition to meeting the needs of undergraduate students, the clinical science CAL resources have been designed to support learners enrolled in other veterinary colleges, the veterinary technology program at the *Saskatchewan Institute of Applied Science and Technology,* for continuing education credit options for practitioners and foreign graduates seeking practicing licenses in Canada, as well for workers in the beef-ranching community. Many of the completed instructional resources have been the focus of educational effectiveness research projects.

A major goal of many of the clinical science CAL projects is to reduce the number of live animals used in teaching, thus promoting ani-

Figure 1. Active learning model (Adapted from Dale, 1969)

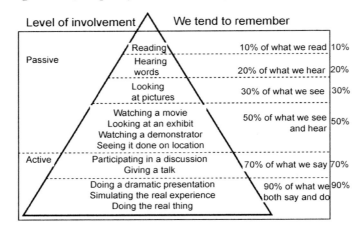

mal welfare, while continuing to provide highly relevant clinical material. To confirm that the approaches to creating and implementing these CAL modules were educationally sound, project members adopted a stance of research-based educational practice. Team members investigated current literature on veterinary education, active learning, and problem-based learning. While problem-based and active learning have become buzzwords in teaching-oriented journals (Hines et al., 2005), the instructional designers and WCVM faculty (Naylor, 2005) specifically employed Dale's active learning model (see Figure 1).

Learning effectiveness studies suggest that knowledge retention improves with the number of senses stimulated and the degree of active involvement in the learning process (Dale, 1969; Peal & Wilson, 2001). Older methods of teaching often score poorly on the active-passive scale. Traditional lectures, where the professor verbally recites a synopsis of facts that the student copies, stimulate few senses and provoke little mental involvement. The degree of complexity in this task can be increased if the student has to mentally summarize the information before transcribing; however, new technologies make more effective learning methods possible. Computer-based presentations provide a method for accessing and displaying different types of material so that a

variety of sensual stimuli can be used to improve retention. In addition, computer-based presentations offer a means of establishing relevance by incorporating actual recorded clinical case material into the presentation. Another benefit of computer-based models is the ability to add specific active learning exercises, which challenge the student, focus the learning, and give immediate feedback.

Accurate characterization of visual, auditory, or tactile phenomena is difficult using purely verbal or text-based descriptions. With paper-based books, this can be partially rectified by inserting annotated diagrams or images, but traditional books cannot reproduce sound or movement. As a result, meaning is lost, and learning may be misdirected. For example, an evaluation of the ability of veterinarians to describe and interpret common equine heart sounds found a lack of a common vocabulary, but not a lack of vocabulary. In other words, wide varieties of words were used in an inconsistent and sometimes contradictory fashion (Naylor, Wolker, & Pharr, 2003); in addition, there was a lack of interpretive skills when the clinicians were played recordings of heart sounds from horses with common clinical arrhythmias (Naylor, Yadernuck, Pharr, & Ashburner, 2001).

Text, audio, still photos, medical illustrations, and video demonstrations are incorporated into the clinical science CAL projects. Active learning is stimulated with interactive case simulations or technical problem solving exercises. Veterinary students are asked to work through these materials and complete formative evaluation exercises before performing these techniques on live animals in the teaching hospital. This is regarded as both an example of good learning practice and of attention to animal welfare.

The emergent pedagogical foci on problem-based and active learning were also considered in some modules. This was done by first presenting a clinical case, accompanied by the usual "ill structured" problems, "similar to tasks a student will face in real world" veterinary practice (Schoenfeld-Tacher et al., 2005). Student learning was supported by access to textual and visual information describing the indications and contraindications of a specific technique, as well as demonstrations of common errors and their consequences.

Research-Based CAL Development: Equine

A self-learning computer module, How to pass a nasogastric tube in the horse, was developed by a team of veterinarians, along with instructional designers, and multimedia specialists. The computer-based learning module includes sections on indications for the technique, needed equipment, relevant anatomy, detailed instructions for performing the procedure, and common errors and complications. Each section consists of learning objectives and instructional text, supplemented with a combination of synchronized video clips of endoscopic and external camera views, audio, still photographs, and medical illustrations. The module concludes with an electronically scored student self-test, in which test questions are based upon both text and images (Naylor & Abutarbush, 2004).

The development of this module occurred over a two-year time-period. First, a WCVM faculty member and a resident (clinical graduate student) conducted an extensive literature review and clinical review of anatomy. From this basis, an initial project concept was developed. An exploration of ways to teach nasogastric intubation (NGI) resulted in the selection of synchronous video endoscopy of the internal and external passage of the stomach tube in living horses and dead horses, as well as photography of clinical specimens and medical illustrations.

A clinical resident, with the support of a WCVM faculty member, developed the first draft of the written content for the module. At this point, an instructional designer was added to the team to construct a project blueprint. In collaboration with media specialists, the team expanded the instructional design blueprint into a detailed storyboard, which identified text, visual, audio, and video components and sequences, as well as interactive elements. Illustrations were collaboratively developed by the faculty member, the resident, and a medical illustrator. Instructional objectives were aligned with student performance expectations and evaluation techniques. Media specialists collaborated with the team to select appropriate technologies, add to the overall concept of the project, gather, compile, and edit the video clips, and produce the visual design and navigation of the CAL learning environment. A multimedia programmer used Macromedia Director MX and Macromedia Flash MX to bring each of these elements together in an interactive learning experience. Throughout this process, the instructional designer tracked the overall progress of the project, adjusted the project blueprint and milestones, as required, and distributed updated documentation to group members.

Prior to the release of the CD-ROM for student use, a double blind, monocentric study involving 52 third-year student-participants in the Doctor of Veterinary Medicine program was conducted. The objective of this study was to evaluate the effectiveness of the NGI self-learning computer module compared with the effectiveness of traditional demonstration-based instruction (Abutarbush, Parchoma, Petrie, & Naylor, 2004). Participants were randomly assigned to control (traditional demonstration) and experimental (CAL) groups. Both groups received the same amount of instructional time.

In the NGI study, quantitative and qualitative data were collected and analyzed. Quantitative data were collected via student self-reports on a 5-point Likert scale (5-strong preference for CAL to 1-strong preference for traditional instruction). Twenty-six percent of participants reported either a preference or a strong preference for traditional instruction; 26% reported a preference for CAL; and 48% reported no preference. A comparison of the groups showed that within the control group the mean preference for CAL was slightly lower (2.57) than in the CAL group (3.29). However, the independent samples *t-test* showed no significant difference in preference between groups.

Learner confidence in mode of instruction received was measured using three questions. The overall quality of instruction was rated as high by 42.6% of all participants and very high by 57.4%. There was a mean rating of 4.6 on the 5-point scale for organization of instruction in the control group and 4.5 in the experimental group. High (46.8%) and very high (57.4%) levels of student-participant confidence in their preparedness to perform the nastogastric intubation procedure were reported. The group means for their level of confidence were 4.39 and 4.67 on the 5-point scale for the control and CAL groups respectively. Again, *t*-test results showed no significant difference between groups.

Encouragingly, the audio and visual clips on the CD were rated as being significantly better than the live horse demonstration in helping students learn to perform the procedure. Median values were 4 and 5 for the control and CAL groups respectively.

Participant achievement levels were measured by student scores on a knowledge quiz and during practical evaluations of performance of the technique. Each student-participant performance of the technique was videotaped from two camera angles. Two evaluators reviewed the videotapes and assessed student performances. Proficiency of technique performances was measured using an evaluation rubric (see *Appendix A*). Evaluators had no knowledge of which group individuals had been assigned.

Data collected from the knowledge quiz results and evaluation rubric were analyzed using descriptive statistics, non-parametric tests: the *Wilcoxon Rank Sum* and *Chi-square*, with the help of a computerized statistical package, *Student Statistix 7* (Abutarbush et al., 2004). Quantitative results showed students in the CAL group performed better on the test of knowledge (median scores out of 10 were 9.67 for the CAL group and 8.1 for traditional demonstration group; analysis of significant difference resulted in $P<0.001$) (Abutarbush et al., 2004). In the assessment of the students' practical ability, there was no significant difference in the number of attempts or number of times assistance was required during the performance of the procedure. The number of technical errors between the two groups was found to be consistent by both evaluators. However, the students in the CAL group needed significantly less time to perform the procedure than did the traditionally instructed group (Abutarbush et al., 2004). A reduction in time to complete the performance of the procedure reduces stress to the horses, and therefore, contributes to improved animal welfare.

Following the experiment, student comments on their experiences in the evaluative study were gathered via conducting two semi-structured focus group debriefing sessions: one for volunteers from the control group, and one for volunteers from the experimental group. The focus groups were facilitated by the instructional designer, rather the faculty from the WCVM in order to ensure students felt able to comment freely, without concern for faculty members' responses to individual comments.

Focus group transcripts were made anonymous, coded, and analyzed prior to results being shared with faculty members. The results of these focus group sessions contributed to refinements of the NGI CAL module, as well as to subsequent educational research directions.

As a follow-up to the pilot use of the NGI resource, a faculty member who was not yet involved in either the CAL development or the associated research study was interviewed after using the CD-ROM to teach the technique. A summary of the interview follows:

As a new faculty member at WCVM, I had not participated in development of the CAL module and had not taught the laboratory previously. I had reviewed the module prior to teaching the laboratory and compared it to my own experiences with the procedure.

I purposely limited instruction to the students reviewing the CD module without additional verbal instruction or demonstration of the procedure. It was intended to have each student review the CD individually; however, due to technical problems in the computer laboratory, several students had to share computers and review the CD as a group. Following review of the CD, I only provided logistical information, such as how many students were to work on any one horse, and gave instructions pertaining to safety measures. The students then proceeded to pass nasogastric tubes, with instructors present to answer questions and provide help as needed.

The students reviewed the CD module very willingly and completed most of the module in the time given. Most students had not reviewed the CD module prior to the lab. Several students volunteered positive feedback pertaining to the quality of the module. It was interesting to observe students reviewing the module as a group or individually; while students reviewing the module individually tended to complete it step by step, much discussion arose in the groups sharing one module and students explained to each other what was unclear to them and highlighted important points.

During the practical portion of the laboratory, all students were able to pass a nasogastric tube successfully in the time allotted, and no major problems, such as significant bleeding in the teaching horses arose. I was pleasantly surprised by this outcome as I had expected problems and remembered my frustration of not being able to complete the procedure as a veterinary student myself. The students approached the procedure without much hesitation and appeared to recall most of the instructions given on the CD. Help was needed mostly when problems arose with restraint of horses, or to reassure students that they had completed the procedure successfully.

It was again very interesting to observe interactions between students. Five to six students worked on one horse and took turns completing the procedure. Students who had already completed the procedure could be overheard recounting their experiences and providing advice to their peers. The quality of their explanations was as good, if not better, than that I could have given myself, especially as students could relate to the initial insecurities much better than a more experienced person. Following the laboratory, several students asked to check out the CD module for additional review.

This was my first experience using a CAL module for student instruction and it was a very positive experience. I have since become involved with development of additional modules to teach equine procedures, and am looking forward to using them in future medical exercises laboratories.

Documentation of the learning benefits of CAL in the NGI study and continuing student and faculty enthusiasm for the use of the NGI resource prompted faculty interest in developing more CAL modules. The Department of Large

Animal Clinical Science has undertaken a new and more ambitious project, *Techniques in Equine Medicine*. This project is slated to include modules on performing a number of diagnostic techniques including transtracheal wash, pleurocentesis, liver biopsy, abdominocentesis, urine collection, and cerebrospinal fluid collection from atlanto-occipital and lumbosacral sites.

The *Techniques in Equine Medicine* project completion date is projected for 2007. While this project is much greater in scope than the NGI project, the lessons learned in the NGI development, as well as elements, such as the learning environment's structures, functionalities, and visual design will be reused, thus creating time and cost efficiencies.

Research-Based CAL Development: Canine and Feline

A self-learning computer module, *Canine and Feline Medical Exercises*, was developed by a veterinarian at the WCVM who was not involved in the NGI module in conjunction with a University of Saskatchewan team of instructional designers and media specialists. The development of this project took place over the course of three years, and an educational study is underway to evaluate the modules. The canine-feline medical exercises CAL modules were structured similarly to the NGI design, but a series of adaptations were made to accommodate multiple exercises. Five systems were identified (respiratory, gastrointestinal, urinary, dermatology, joints), and the important diagnostic and sample collection techniques taught to veterinary students for each system were determined. Each of the 28 technique modules was designed to include the following components:

- A list of indications and contraindications for performing the technique
- A link to a case description to illustrate where the technique was successful in obtaining a diagnosis or influencing therapy

- A list and photographs of the specialized equipment necessary to perform the technique
- A step-by-step written description of the technique paired with digital photographs (with anatomic landmarks labeled) and/or drawings illustrating each important step of the procedure; the written description was then followed by a narrated videotape of the procedure as it was performed, re-emphasizing the important points already discussed
- A description of appropriate sample handling, submission for analysis, and (where appropriate) interpretation of results
- A list of possible complications of the technique
- Self-tests emphasizing key anatomic landmarks or details of the techniques

A detailed list of the digital still photos and video requirements needed was prepared for each technique. Instructional designers formatted all of this information into a course design map. This map clearly defined the learning objectives, and the content, activities, and media requirements for each objective. The design map was then circulated among the development team for approval.

Following the development of the design map, the faculty member met several times with an instructional designer to blueprint each procedure. The blueprint provided the media team with the information it needed to produce the final product. Each screen of the final product was sketched. The media team knew exactly what was required to appear on each screen and the written text to accompany it. The completed blueprints were sent to the media team and the design team.

Video footage and still digital photos were taken during two days of demonstrations of the techniques. Once the raw material had been gathered, the media team began to edit and assemble the pieces. Errors and omissions were discovered and corrected. A multimedia programmer used Macromedia Director MX and Macromedia Flash MX to bring each of these elements together in an interactive learning experience.

Five fourth-year veterinary students and two veterinary technicians, under the guidance of an instructional designer, user-tested the set of two CD-ROMs. User testing resulted in a series of revisions and improvements to the modules. These revisions included additional feedback to learners on their performance in interactive exercises and self-tests.

As an extension of the NGI research study into the educational effectiveness of WCVM's CAL resources, the research study into the *Canine and Feline Medical Exercises* modules will investigate student learning styles, student preferences, and module effectiveness as a learning tool. This direction has been taken, in part, because student-participants in the NGI study reported individual learning style as a variable in learner preferences for traditional or CAL-based instruction. A literature review was undertaken, and peer-reviewed articles that support the student reports were identified (Buchanan, Carter, Cowgill, Hurley, Lewis, MacLeod, Melton, Moore, Pessah, Roberson, Robertson, Smith, & Vadenplas, 2005; Dale, Nasir, & Sullivan, 2005; Schoenfeld-Tacher, McConnell, & Schultheiss, 2003). The Canine-Feline study compares traditional versus CAL instruction. In addition, research team members want additional insight into the effect of learning styles on student responses to CAL resources and will attempt to discover if individual learning-style preferences are a significant variable in instructional mode preference or in student achievement.

Fifty-eight third-year veterinary students agreed to participate in the Canine-Feline research study. The research design included quantitative and qualitative research methodologies. The research team assigned all participants numbered codes to insert in the identity portion of the online version of the *Felder-Silverman Index of Learning Styles* (ILS) measurement instrument, and all student participants completed the ILS questionnaire to establish their learning style. Participants were assigned to experimental (CAL) and control (traditional laboratory manual) groups using block randomization. Participants were divided into four groups based on their learning styles and then randomized within groups. No member of the faculty of Veterinary Medicine knew which students or codes had been assigned to control or experimental groups.

The ILS measurement instrument has been rigorously tested via multiple studies across post-secondary disciplines and institutions for reliability and validity. Reliability and validity results have been published in peer-reviewed, scholarly publications (Litzinger, Lee, Wise, & Felder, 2005). Results of the ILS measurement instrument are only considered valid and reliable when the instrument is used to help instructors "to achieve balanced [learning-style] course instruction" and to "help learners understand their learning strengths and areas for improvement" (Felder & Spurlin, 2005, pp. 110-111). In this study, the researchers will use participant scores on the ILS for the purpose of seeking further information on the comparative effectiveness of traditional and computer-assisted modes of instruction for students with different learning styles as well as evaluating the impact of learning styles on learning-mode preference. It is anticipated that the results of this study will have an impact on the design and development of future products to support student learning in HCI environments.

Participants were asked to complete a short survey, including mode-of-instruction-preference questions with responses selections on a Likert scale. Likert scale results will be compared to ILS measurement results in order to investigate potential linkages between learning styles and learning mode preferences. The correlation between learning styles and learning mode of instruction preference will be examined using Spearman's correlation coefficient.

The association between learning styles and achievement will be assessed using regression analysis. Learning styles will be measured along the visual versus verbal continua (Felder & Spurlin, 2005) in order to determine the degree of polarity (or lack of polarity) of individual visual versus verbal learning styles within the participant group. Data analysis will include measures of potential combined effects of self-reported learning preferences and ILS scores. Achievement will be measured using student performance on a standardized practical oral examination.

The question of whether multimodal instruction using the CAL modules results in better achievement in students of particular learning styles will be assessed via regression analysis. The study will specifically examine whether use of the CAL modules or the traditional laboratory manual worked differently for students with different learning styles. Data will be analyzed assessing whether or to what extent instruction modules designed to support individual learning styles might interact with learner achievement.

The results of the Canine and Feline Medical Exercises CAL study will post-date the publication of this chapter. The research team hopes to use the evidence gathered to identify ways to improve future instructional design and development to better meet WCVM learner needs.

CONCLUSION

Given the significant challenges and pressures influencing veterinary colleges, teaching hospitals, and educators, new strategies for providing high quality learning must be considered. CAL is an effective tool that can be used to enhance the veterinary curriculum and provide increased student access to clinical material while reducing the unnecessary use of live animals in teaching. The CAL-based veterinary medical learning resources developed at the WCVM represent a collaborative effort between the veterinary clinicians and researchers who conceived each project and served as content experts and the instructional designers, media specialists, and multimedia programmers who fine-tuned each project as it was developed. The results of educational research performed on the CAL modules as they have been implemented in the curriculum have already directly influenced the development of future projects integrating HCI into the WCVM curriculum and future directions for research focused on these projects. It is hoped these efforts will contribute to the globalization of the veterinary profession through evidence-based approaches to innovation in the use of HCI in veterinary education.

ACKNOWLEDGMENTS

Research and development projects described in this chapter have been supported by the Government of Saskatchewan's *Technology Enhanced Learning* (TEL) initiative, and the *Association for Media and Technology in Education in Canada* (AMTEC) Trust.

Lily McCaig, a WCVM student, contributed to the literature review and the development of the equine medicine CAL modules.

Juliana Deubner, medical illustrator for the WCVM, prepared all medical images for the CAL learning modules, as well as the figure for the chapter.

Frank Bulk, Gabe Ng, and Wayne Giesbrecht, multimedia developers at the University of Saskatchewan, have contributed their talents to many projects described in the chapter.

REFERENCES

Abutarbush, S. M., Naylor, J. M., Parchoma, G., D'Eon, M., Petrie, L., & Carruthers, T. (2006). Evaluation of traditional instruction versus a self-learning computer module in teaching veterinary students how to pass a nasogastric tube in the horse. *Journal of Veterinary Medical Education.*

Abutarbush, S. M., Parchoma, G., Petrie, L., & Naylor, J. M. (2004, June). *Evaluation of traditional versus a self-learning computer module in teaching how to pass a nasogastric tube in the horse.* Paper presented at the Annual American College of Veterinary Internal Medicine Forum, Minneapolis, MN.

Association of American Veterinary Medical Colleges. (2005). The use of animals in veterinary medical teaching: Replacement, reduction, refinement. Retrieved November 8, 2005, from http://aavmc.org/meetings_events/2006EducationalSymposium.html

Bernardo, T. M., & Malinowski, R. P. (2005). Progress in the capture, manipulation, and delivery of medical media and its impact on education, clinical care, and research. *Journal of Veterinary Medical Education, 32*(1), 21-30.

Brown, C. M. (2003). The future of the North American veterinary teaching hospital. *Journal of Veterinary Medical Education, 30*(3), 197-202.

Buchanan, M. F., Carter, W. C., Cowgill, L. M., Hurley, D. J., Lewis, S. J., MacLeod, J. N., Melton, T. R., Moore, J. N., Pessah, I., Roberson, M., Robertson, T. P., Smith, M. L., & Vadenplas, M. L. (2005). Using 3D animations to teach intracellular signal transduction mechanisms: Taking the arrows out of the cells. *Journal of Veterinary Medical Education, 32*(1), 72-78.

Carriére, P., DesCôteaux, L., Durocher, J., & Harvey, D. (2005). *Ultrasonography of the reproduction system of the cow* [CD ROM]. Montreal, Canada: Université de Montréal.

Clark, C. (2004). *Cattle claw care*, Ed. 1.1[CD ROM]. Saskatoon, Saskatchewan, Canada: Vet Visions, Inc.

Clark, C. (2005). Diseases of feedlot cattle. Retrieved November 9, 2005, from http://tel-web.sasked.gov.sk.ca/Members/View-Loi.aspx?id=840

Clarkson, J. J. (2005). Global developments in dental education. *Oral Health Care Report, 15*(1), 8-10.

Dale, E. (1969). *Audio-visual methods in teaching* (3rd ed.). Orlando, FL: Holt, Rinehart, and Winston.

Dale, V. H. M., Nasir, L., & Sullivan, M. (2005). Exploring student attitudes to directed self-learning online through evaluation of an Internet-based biomolecular sciences resource. *Journal of Veterinary Medical Education, 32*(1), 129-137.

Dascanio, J. J. (2003). The use of information technology in large animal veterinary education. *Journal of Veterinary Medical Education, 30*(4), 326-330.

De Castrol, P., & Zucconi, S. (2004). Development of European educational strategies: Design of veterinarian profiles identified by market needs for the year 2020 [Electronic version]. *Veterinary Research Communications, 28*, 13-28. Retrieved November 8, 2005, from the Springer database.

Desrochers, A., & Harvey, D. (2002). *Surgeries of the abomasum in cattle* [CD ROM]. Montreal, Canada: LITIEM.

Dhein, C. R. (2005). Online small animal case simulations, a.k.a. the virtual veterinary clinic. *Journal of Veterinary Medical Education, 32*(1), 93-102.

Edwards, J. (2004). Global perspectives of veterinary education: Reflections from the 27th world veterinary congress. *Journal of Veterinary Medical Education, 31*(1), 9-12.

Felder, R. M., & Spurlin, J. (2005). Applications, reliability and validity of the index of learning styles. *International Journal of Engineering Education, 21*(1), 103-112.

Fernandes, T. (2004). The role of Vet2020 project on quality of European veterinary Education [Electronic version]. *Veterinary Research Communications, 28*, 9–11. Retrieved August 8, 2005, from the Springer database.

Hammick, M. R. (2005a). Evidence-informed education in health care science professions. *Journal of Veterinary Medical Education, 32*(4), 339-403.

Hammick, M. R. (2005b). A BEME review: A little illumination. *Medical Teacher, 27*(1), 1-3.

Hines, S. A., Collin, P. L., Quitadamo, I. J., Brahler, C. J., Knudson, C. D., & Crouch, G. J. (2005). ATLes: The strategic application of Web-based technology to address learning objectives and enhance classroom discussion in a veterinary pathology course. *Journal of Veterinary Medical Education, 32*(1), 103-112.

Howe, L. M., Boothe, H. W. Jr., & Hartsfield, S. M. (2005). Student assessment for the educational benefits of using a CD-ROM for instruction of basic surgical skills. *Journal of Veterinary Medical Education, 32*(1), 138-143.

Jackson, M., & Callman, K. (2006). Medical education past, present and future. *Medical Education, 40*(3), 190-192.

Kochevar, D. T. (2003). Information technology in veterinary pharmacology instruction. *Journal of Veterinary Medical Education, 30*(4), 331-337.

Litzinger, T. A., Lee, S. E., Wise, J. C., & Felder, R. M. (2005). A study of the reliability and validity of the Felder-Soloman Index of Learning Styles. *International Journal of Engineering Education, 21*(1), 103-112.

McGreevy, P. D., Della Torre, P. K., & Evans, D. L. (2003). Animal behaviour learning environment: Software to facilitate learning in canine and feline behaviour therapy. *Journal of Veterinary Medical Education, 30*(4), 308-317.

Naylor, J. M. (1996). *Diseases of calves: A series of simulations* [CD ROM]. Saskatoon, Saskatchewan, Canada: Vet Visions, Inc.

Naylor, J. M. (2001). *The art of equine auscultation* [CD ROM]. Saskatoon, Saskatchewan, Canada: Vet Visions, Inc.

Naylor, J. M. (2003). *The art of bovine auscultation* [CD ROM]. Saskatoon, Saskatchewan, Canada: Vet Visions, Inc.

Naylor, J. M. (2005, May). Learning in the information age: Electronic resources for veterinarians. In G. Parchoma (Guest Ed.), *Large Animal Veterinary Rounds, 5*(5).

Naylor, J. M., & Abutarbush, S. M. (2004). *Passing a nasogastric tube in the horse: A self–learning module* (1st ed.) [CD ROM]. Saskatoon, Saskatchewan, Canada: Vet Visions, Inc.

Naylor, J. M., Abutarbush, S. M., & Parchoma, G. (2005, March). *Using technology to improve animal welfare. Results of a randomized controlled trial comparing knowledge, preference and proficiency of students taught by traditional instructor demonstration or a multimedia CD.* Paper presented at the Association of Veterinary Teachers and Research Workers Conference, Scarborough, England.

Naylor, J. M., Wolker, R. E., & Pharr, J. W. (2003). An assessment of the terminology used by diplomats and students to describe the character of quine mitral and aortic valve regurgitant murmurs: Correlations with the psysical properties of the sounds. *Journal of Veterinary Internal Medicine, 17*(3), 332-336.

Naylor, J. M., Yadernuck, L. M., Pharr, J. W., & Ashburner, J. S. (2001). An assessment of the ability of diplomates, practitioners, and students to describe and interpret recordings of heart murmurs and arrhythmia correlations of clinical diagnosis with the physical properties of the sounds and the underlying cardiac problem. *Journal of Veterinary Internal Medicine, 15(*6*)*, 507-515.

Peal, D., & Wilson, B. G. (2001). Activity theory and Web-based training. In B. Khan (Ed.), *Web-based training.* Englewood Cliffs, NJ: Educational Technology Publications.

Rodriguez-Martinez, H. (2004). Quality assurance: The key for amendments of the EU-directives regulating veterinary training in Europe [Electronic version]. *Veterinary Research Communications, 28*, 29-44. Retrieved November 8, 2005, from the Springer database.

Shmon, C. L., & Taylor S. M. (2003). *Solving neurological problems (Dogs and Cats)—An interactive DVD.* CLIVE: University of Edinburgh.

Schoenfeld-Tacher, R., Bright, J. M., McConnell, S. L., Marley, W. S., & Kogan, L. R. (2005). Web-based technology: Its effects on small group "problem-based learning": Interactions in a professional veterinary medical program. *Journal of Veterinary Medical Education, 32*(1), 86-92.

Schoenfeld-Tacher, R., McConnell, S. L., & Schultheiss, T. (2003). Use of interactive online histopathology modules at different stages of a veterinary program. *Journal of Veterinary Medical Education, 30*(4), 364-371.

Taylor, S. M., & Shmon, C. L. (2003) *Cases in clinical neurology (Dogs and Cats)—An interactive DVD.* CLIVE: University of Edinburgh.

V2VLC. (2001). Project summary. Retrieved November 8, 2005, from http://www.ovc.uoguelph.ca/CARNARIE/PROJECT/summary.html

Walsh, D. (2004). Global perspectives of veterinary education. *Journal of Veterinary Medical Education, 31*(1), 9.

White, M. E. (2005). *Consultant.* Retrieved November 8, 2005, from http://www.vet.cornell.edu/consultant/Consult.asp

M. S. (2003). A contribution to validation of score meaning for Felder-Soloman's index of learning styles. In *Proceedings of the 2003 American Society for Engineering Education Annual Conference & Exposition* [Electronic version]. Retrieved April 25, 2006, from http://www.ncsu.edu/felder-public/ILSdir/Zywno_Validation_Study.pdf

WCVM. (2006). *Mission statement.* Retrieved December 1, 2006 from the University of Saskatchewan Web site: http://www.usask.ca/wcvm/about/mission.php

APPENDIX A: RUBRIC USED FOR EVALUATION OF STUDENT PERFORMANCE OF NASOGASTRIC INTUBATION

_____

Student # _____

Tape # / Angle _____/_____ (overhead / floor views of camera angle and tape number)

Time frame on tape # _____ / _____ /_____ to _____/_____/_____ (OH or FL time-stamp: circle your initials)

Time taken to complete the procedure (minutes)						
Number of times the student asked for assistance (circle one below)						
0	1	2	3	4	5	6

1. Technical Errors in NGI procedure	Yes	No
Failed to evert the false nostril		
Occluded the nostril		
Left the free end of the tube unattended		
Incorrect restraint		
Failed to do measurements		
Failed to lubricate the tube		
Failed to stimulate swallowing		
Failed to kink the tube		
Bleeding occurred with tube passage		
Failed to flex the neck/left the neck stretched		
Failure to perform 3 checks of tube position		
2. Tube position checking procedures		
Ensured correct resistance on the tube		
Checked whether air could be sucked back		
Checked whether the tube could be seen moving on the outside of the neck		
Inflated the esophagus		
Rattled trachea to see if can feel the tube		
Checked for sound or smell of stomach gas		
Had an assistant use a stethoscope to listen for stomach sounds		
Checked whether the tube could be felt moving on the outside of the neck		
Coughing not elicited		
3. Number of times to successful completion		

Section IV
HCI in Educational Practice

Chapter XIII
Problem–Based Learning at a Distance:
Course Design and HCI in an Environmental Management Master's Programme

Ralph Horne
RMIT University, Australia

Jon Kellett
University of South Australia, Australia

ABSTRACT

A case study approach is taken to illustrate a design approach to the development of a Masters course. Over a 10-year period, the course was developed from traditional delivery and teaching modes, through the introduction of problem-based learning, and the incorporation of human computer interaction (HCI) elements. The latter development coincided with a shift from classroom-based teaching to distance learning mode, and the resource and design issues in this dual transformation are discussed. Pedagogic principles of problem-based learning were applied along with a range of other case conditions in framing the design intent. It is concluded that the design process in HCI and problem-based learning applications is central in ensuring that appropriate learning environments are established. While there is no single formula for designing problem-based learning or integrating HCI into learning programmes, the application of appropriate principles and methods is essential.

INTRODUCTION

It is commonly accepted that people can learn more effectively when they *"own"* parts of the learning process, by having some control over how, when, and what they do. Online learning resources appear to offer benefits in these respects.

This term is subject to multiple definitions, which may include e-learning, Internet learning, tele-learning, distributed learning, virtual learning, computer assisted learning, Web-based learning, and distance learning. Ally (in Anderson & El-loumi, 2004, p. 4) notes that the common factor is that the learner is at a distance from the tutor, obtains tutorial support, and uses some form of technology to interact.

Students vary widely in their preferred learning styles. Anderson and Elloumi (2004) provide a thorough exploration of the theory and practice of online learning and in particular examine the different ways in which students learn. Learning programs that incorporate a variety of learning techniques, tools, and materials, and allow students to exercise choice as to how they utilize them, offer potential advantages in flexibility and effectiveness across a range of learning styles. However, direction may be required within *student-centered* learning programs if learning outcomes are to be maximized across the cohort. Issues such as the organization of materials on screen, the use of advance organizers to provide a framework for learning, prerequisite testing, chunking of information provision and strategies that promote application, synthesis, and evaluation of knowledge are all important aspects in design for effective learning (Ally in Anderson & Elloumi, 2004, pp.11-12).

Diversity in learning modes and materials is not effective *per* se. HCI technology allows diversity, but unless each element is integrated within a coherent structure and directly linked with meeting learning outcomes, their effectiveness will be limited. This is a case for design, and central to the course design process are both student needs and the interplay of these needs with curriculum, learning outcomes, and appropriate selection from the suite of HCI and other learning tools available (Anderson & Elloumi, 2004; Koschmann, Myers, Feltovich, & Barrows, 1994). Online learning places a greater onus upon students to generate and maintain motivation. Students who are physically distant from their tutor lack the discipline of scheduled classes and immediate peer support, so the course materials themselves need to provide intrinsic motivation in their design. For example, Ally (in Anderson & Elloumi, 2004, p.6) comments that capturing learners' attentions at the outset; establishing

relevance of materials to learners' experiences or aspirations; making explicit statements of expected outcomes; and regular reinforcement of progress by testing and review are all relevant attributes of good design. Rapid engagement with learning materials is helpful in all learning situations, and, in the case of online learning at a distance, it may prove crucial. Popper's (1999) description of the essential nature of problem solving as a path to knowledge acquisition and understanding is informative in this regard. He argues that trial and error, undertaking a process of *problem—attempted solution—elimination (of unsuccessful solutions)* mirrors the natural evolutionary process and intimates that, perhaps as a consequence, it represents a natural approach to learning (Popper, 1999).

The approach to course design and the use of HCI is the central topic of this chapter. A wide and growing literature indicates both the complexity and importance of this issue, building on seminal work in the field (Barrows & Tamblyn, 2000; Koschmann et al., 1994; Koschmann, Kelson, Feltovich, & Barrows, 1996). The context for this chapter is the application of group-centered *problem-based learning* within a distance mode. A case study approach is adopted in order to demonstrate development and evolution of the use of HCI in course delivery through the application of design principles over a 10-year period. The aim is to illustrate how HCI can help bridge the gap between distance learning modes of learning and the essential group interaction associated with problem-based learning-based approaches in multidisciplinary studies. In progressing toward this aim, the following objectives will be outlined and discussed:

- An overview of developments in knowledge and techniques in the area;
- An historical account of the phases in the development of the course case study;
- Analysis of the challenges, successes, and problems encountered;

- Recommendations drawn from the experience;
- Conclusions and comments on future trends.

BACKGOUND

The rapid development of computer and Internet technology and applications allied to progressively more user-friendly systems has offered fertile ground for educational designers over the last two decades. *Computer-based learning* has become widely established as a valid mechanism for using technology to assist in realizing effective knowledge and learning development. Developments have occurred across a range of disciplines, and again, notably in the medical sciences (for example, Koschmann, 1999). HCI has now largely replaced *computer-based learning* as a term that also reflects a rapid development path in the theory and use of computers in learning. Other terms exist, relating specifically to collaborative learning (see for example, Dimitracopoulou & Petrou, 2003). These trends have followed alongside rapid technology developments, so that much greater depth and range of interactions are now possible using the computer interface. While the software has diversified and specialized, a major strand of educational software has emerged around the concept of the *virtual learning environment*, where a range of resources are made available to students in a more-or-less integrated form, often using a single primary software platform. Despite these technological advances it remains crucial that the process is driven by the pedagogical design and not by the technology (Juwah, 2004).

A crucial aspect of pedagogical design is interaction capacity and variety, and specific educational software generally facilitates this. Establishing a community that stimulates sociability and usability is noted as an important aspect of online learning by Preece (2000). The design

decision to opt for synchronous or asynchronous teacher-student or student-student interaction is important in this respect. The freedom to participate in learning at a pace determined by the learner is often a noted benefit of distance or online learning as opposed to attendance at formal classes. There is a potential conflict here with a community-based approach requiring synchronous communications between student and teacher. Anderson points to the design choice to be made between temporal freedom and synchronicity, which may place undesirable time constraints on learners (Anderson & Elloumi, 2004).

Should the design approach be to create learner, knowledge, assessment, or community centered processes? Interaction is central to this debate. Anderson (Anderson & Elloumi, 2004) presents a model for online learning design that illustrates the range of potential interactions between learners, teacher, and materials. Appropriate design of online materials demands consideration of where the interactive emphasis is placed and, furthermore, how the right choice and range of types and modes of interaction can be incorporated into the final product.

Turning to *problem-based learning*, we can now consider the design possibilities of incorporating this approach into online materials. In the late 1990s, the literature on problem-based learning was expanding (White, 1996; Glasgow, 1997). Developments in a range of disciplines, notably the medical sciences, were taking place, and Rhem (1998) noted how the concept had permeated other discipline areas. Applications were often associated with problem solving in small groups of approximately five students who must agree on how to define the problem and to divide up their efforts to address solutions. The concept of structuring a course around a project and making the learning contingent on the project was further supported by the ideas of Barrows (see endnote), who identified the following as characteristics of problem-based learning:

- Students must have the responsibility for their own learning;
- The problem simulations used in problem-based learning must be ill-structured and allow for free inquiry;
- Learning should be integrated from a wide range of disciplines or subjects;
- Collaboration is essential;
- What students learn during their self-directed learning must be applied back to the problem with reanalysis and resolution;
- A closing analysis of what has been learned from work with the problem and a discussion of what concepts and principles have been learned is essential;
- Self and peer assessment should be carried out at the completion of each problem and at the end of every curricular unit;
- The activities carried out in problem-based learning must be those valued in the real world;
- Student examinations must measure student progress toward the goals of problem-based learning;
- Problem-based learning must be the pedagogical base in the curriculum and not part of a didactic curriculum.

Now, problem-based learning has matured into a widely recognized valid instructional method that challenges students to *learn to learn*, working cooperatively in groups to seek solutions to real world problems (Duch, 2005). A wide literature has also emerged on the evaluation of problem-based learning effectiveness. Although this is not the main topic of this chapter, it is important to note that, in general, student skills outcomes are consistently good, and while some studies report that students in problem-based learning gain slightly less knowledge, there is evidence that they remember more of the acquired knowledge (Dochy, Segers, Van den Bossche, & Gijbels, 2003). Such evidence supports Popper's (1999) views on the logic of scientific problem solving

and, in particular, his distinction between truth and certainty. He asserts that through a trial and error approach to problem solving we can achieve truth—a result that provides a satisfactory explanation or resolution of the problem *for the moment*, although such truth will always fall short of absolute certainty. Recognition of the role of uncertainty and the qualification that this attaches to our problem solving is a valuable aspect of education in any discipline. This is especially true in the social sciences and is particularly relevant to the multidisciplinary project centered course, such as in the case study described in the next section. Problem solving more readily mirrors real life situations than more abstract or academic exercises, and the key approaches to problem solving and outcomes are likely to be retained in the learner's memory as a result.

Reported problems with problem-based learning include dysfunctional group dynamics, superficial research, and lack of support for problem-based learning and frustration with tutors who lack content expertise (Houlden, Collier, Frid, John, & Pross, 2001), although these problems can be expected to be effectively managed through effective tutor training and design. More fundamentally, problems of set up and maintenance cost, time, induced stress, and reduced basic knowledge retention are reported (Finucane, Johnson, & Prideaux, 1998). Access to sufficient resources and a clear view of likely participant student numbers and staff workloads are vital prerequisites to success.

The last decade has seen rapid change in higher education institutions, with a general shift away from *elitist* highly selective courses toward larger cohorts. The globalization of the higher education market has seen rapid changes in the number of international students entering higher education in the University systems of the United Kingdom, United States, Australia, and other countries. Pressure on resources and funding for domestic students has also been a feature across much of the sectors in these countries, with a resulting increasing emphasis on recruiting overseas students. The effects of these changes at the level of course design, curriculum delivery, and learning outcomes have been varied, although a common feature has been increased use of Virtual Learning Environments as a means to assist in management of large and diverse student cohorts. This is seen as a way of providing greater market flexibility, particularly in respect of students who are unable to attend university during conventional daytime teaching periods. It is also seen as a means of opening up potential for international students to undertake study at a distance.

These considerations represent important market drivers of importance to university management. However, the extent to which HCI utilization can be used to meet the dual needs of these drivers and pedagogical requirements of learning outcomes at the same time is questionable. Effective design of problem-based learning material is important in this, and both design and implementation are resource intensive, with delivery also placing potentially heavy demands on academic time. Increasing the mobility of students and courses through HCI assisted delivery has implications for university work planning and resourcing. The following case study investigates one means by which, using theory and evidence of the pedagogical benefits of HCI and problem-based learning techniques, and a team approach to course planning and development, such potentially competing issues can be balanced through appropriate course design.

THE CASE STUDY

The authors developed a master's program in environmental management for business in 1995, comprising eight taught courses and a major research thesis. One of the courses, titled Environmental Liability for Redevelopment, forms the case study. This course has undergone four main phases of development, from theory-centered

(1995-1997) to problem-based learning-centered (1998-2003), to problem-based learning-centered using HCI technology (2003-2004), to problem-based learning-centered using HCI technology in distance mode (2005).

The subject matter is rapidly developing and highly topical, and includes an important liability problem facing western democracies, namely, the issue of land that has previously been used for industry or other purposes, is potentially contaminated, and occurs in an area where there are potential environmental or human risks as a result. In England, where the case study was developed, thousands of hectares of land have been damaged by industrial activity in the past. Much of this land is now surrounded by high value development, thus creating a demand for redevelopment, if only the liability issues can be managed effectively. Issues of hazard risk assessment, redevelopment potential and value, as well as financial responsibility for cleanup, are all pertinent. Solutions involve input from a range of professions and rely on both a variety of available data and evidence, but also require assumptions to be made where information is lacking. In essence, several disciplinary inputs are required, including planning, environmental science, engineering, property and land valuation, financial appraisal, law, and risk assessment and management.

Early Design and Development

Phase one of the course design involved a series of lectures, each linked to workshops, and arranged in a chronologic order to mimic the typical process of site redevelopment, as follows:

- Introduction to environmental liability and redevelopment issues;
- Project management and the professions;
- Desk study;
- Legal issues and standards;
- Planning issues and end-use potential;

- Site investigation (including on-site sampling and laboratory analysis);
- Contamination characterization (including calculation of volumes of contaminated material);
- Risk assessment;
- Risk management plan (including considerations of risk transfer—insurance—and other options);
- Remediation (including contamination removal/treatment);
- Valuation (including build costs, clean-up costs, and calculation of net present value and internal rate of return);
- Developments in the subject area.

These 10 topics indicate the breadth of subject matter, and teaching was led by a total of five lecturers from different disciplines. In each case, the lecturer also provided workshops and exercises to illustrate the subject matter, and there was a project site used at various points through the course. Evidence both from student feedback questionnaires suggested that the course lacked the coherence required to allow integration of these diverse areas. It should be noted that this course could be considered ambitious and experimental in its attempt to bridge areas normally dealt with by different professions and consultants. The course was *traditional* in that it consisted of lectures and workshops, yet represented a shift that has been documented as a widespread trend of the last decade or so toward *contextually applied transdisciplinary, highly reflective, experience-based knowledge* (Bridges, 2000). The team worked from the standpoint that successful resolution of the liability problems demands such an approach and that unique advantages flow from it.

To underline these advantages, a short discussion of the UK approach to land redevelopment is required. Since the Contaminated Land Regulations 2000, the UK has formally pursued a system of land redevelopment where the contamination clean-up standard required is set according to the future use—the so-called *suitable for use* approach. If the contamination will not leach or migrate, and a hard development end use such as a car park is to be developed, depending on the case, the contamination may be left in the ground, rather than removed, with attendant transport risks and costs, to a facility, which would fill up precious landfill space. On the contrary, where housing and gardens are planned, a very high level of site cleanup is required. The system is therefore economically, socially, and environmentally sustainable. However, it requires that environmental scientists undertaking risk assessment and designing site clean up know what the property development experts are planning for the site, and this requires a level of professional integration, which is not common and not covered in traditional single discipline-based courses on the subject. Hence, the integrated approach taken here is extremely valuable in learning outcomes terms, and the course team have therefore prioritized the maintenance of this multi-disciplinary format through successive developments, including the integration of HCI.

External examiners valuable input at this stage. The consensus was that the course as a whole was ground breaking in the way it attempted to integrate material from diverse disciplines, but it required some changes in delivery. To address the coherence problem, the course team held a series of staff workshops to exchange views and knowledge of their own perspectives and assumptions, and to seek a vehicle that would provide the cohesion required. The essential nature of the course was discussed, as a complex problem solving exercise to which there is more than one credible solution and certainly no single *right answer*. Uncertainty in terms of some aspects of site related data and uncertainty in respect of potential solutions is a key theme. It was concluded that the nature of the liability problem as originally defined, closely mirrors Dennen's description of problem based learning as a scenario that, "assesses student performance on tasks that go beyond requiring just knowledge, comprehension, and application, and that involve demonstration of analysis, synthesis, and evaluation, all of which are more complex abilities. Students must define these problems before they may solve them, and typically there is no set solution." (Dennen, 2000, 329)

Structuring the course around the project and making the learning contingent upon it reflects Popper's views on the fundamental place of problem solving in all aspects of life, and was informed by the work of a number of problem-based learning developers (Barrows & Tamblyn, 2000; Rhem, 1998). A design based on a series of goals, derived from analysis of previous educational practice, reflects the theoretical development framework set out by Koschmann et al. (1994). Whilst the educational goals or outcomes remained as originally expressed, the design specification changed to:

- Give central place to the problem as opposed to the support materials;
- Package the problem and support resources in an attractive manner in order to engage interest;
- Allow students to address the problem from a variety of standpoints, moving away from sequential delivery, which was seen as a major constraint;
- Provide students with a flexible framework for analysis of the problem;
- Make the learning experience internationally relevant;
- Provide resources and information about the problem in a "real world" format.

The challenging problem of cohesion and integration, which began life as conventional piece of assessment, now formed the centerpiece of the course, and the cohesion problem appeared to be solved. Instead of sequential lectures, the main course content was provided in the form of a course text written specifically for the course by the course team, and comprising a chapter

(with exercises) on each of the topics. A further document, the Holbrook Colliery Brief, was also distributed at commencement of the course. This provided information on the (real) case study site, which students used throughout the course for their problem-based learning group project and assessment.

While the switch to problem-based learning undoubtedly improved outcomes (as recorded in an upward trend in marks, positive comments in student feedback questionnaires, and comments by external examiners), over the phase of two years (1998-2003), there is also continuing evidence from the external examiner reports and student feedback questionnaires of a recurrent problem. With a problem-based learning-based course based around a complex group project, the majority of the assessment was conducted on a group basis. Some students felt that their high effort and attainment was not adequately reflected within their marks obtained, as these were *moderated* by the involvement of average and below average performers within the group. Minor adjustments were made in order to alter the balance and provide individual elements. However, the course team, with joint responsibility for design, was of the opinion that the learning benefits of the group problem-based learning model outweighed the problems of reflecting attainment at the margins. This opinion was largely shared by the external examiners, who praised the course, especially during 2000-2002, and by students *ex ante*—anecdotal evidence from alumni suggests that as the immediate experience of the group work faded; students recognized the unique value of the course and found it extremely valuable in their subsequent dealings with other professions.

During 1998-2003, then, the course was highly valued by the classroom-based students in terms of topicality, skills development, and applicability to the world of work, but undertaking it was a painful process that tended to result in a very high and intense problem solving/presentation preparation period in its latter stages. Respondents in successive annual student feedback questionnaire surveys likened the pressure felt during the last two or three weeks of the project to the pressure they had experienced during undergraduate final examinations. The pressure period was viewed as *bad* whilst it lasted, but once the final presentation and report were delivered, this uncomfortable experience tended to be viewed in a more positive light, the level of pressure and the reaction to it being interpreted as indicating the value of the project as a learning experience.

With the problem-based learning structure, timetabled sessions were student-led, in that the topic was pre-set (due to tutor availability constraints) in the chronological order of topics, but within the three hours available to the student group, it was for students to determine how best to utilize the input from the tutor. Students generally chose to read and work with the course materials in advance, and use the time to develop project work with the tutor, although the choice was theirs. The availability of staff assistance, however, remained an issue. If the student project team needed tutorial help, for example on development appraisal and valuation issues, they could read up the notes provided by the teacher in the workbook. But if they required further explanation and guidance they would have to wait until the timetabled appearance of that tutor. Worse, if they needed to refer back to the tutor after their timetable workshop, they would need to schedule extra time with the tutor, which presented difficulties for both.

Design Approach to Incorporate HCI

During 2002-2004, there was a marked and sustained rise in the number of students from international backgrounds in the cohort. These students had varying needs, and it became clear to the course team that a variety of approaches to learning should be offered to the students to cater for these diverse needs. Partly as a response

to this, the team introduced a virtual learning environment in the form of *Blackboard* software. The virtual learning environment was used as a basic learning support tool, providing exercises, notes, links, and an online discussion forum, all of which the student could access any number of times, at their own pace, and in their own order of preference.

The introduction of HCI provided another major development in the course. However, of importance here is the fact that the benefits did not simply arise with the international students. United Kingdom-based students began providing positive anecdotal feedback on the benefits to learning that this facility had provided them. These students tended to be those who had felt the course was a struggle. Evidence in course assessment outcomes is not clear, due to the masking effect of group marking. Indeed, on reflection, this masking effect may have prevented course staff from previously identifying the fact that some United Kingdom students would benefit from the more flexible learning mode provided by the integration of HCI.

Given the *win-win* outcome for both United Kingdom and overseas students within the cohort upon the introduction of HCI, the course team began to look beyond the *Blackboard* interface. The full range of available HCI options was then contemplated, and it was determined that an appropriate design approach be adopted, as with previous course developments, based on established principles, and that the adoption of HCI should be fully resourced and planned. Funding was sought from third parties, and the proposal to develop a *distance-learning* mode to allow students who could not attend the University regularly to participate in the course was developed in detail.

With funding secured, the course team embarked on the design process in detail. One of the authors chaired this course team, and had some previous experience of developing HCI-based course materials for the property profession.

However, given the complex, multidisciplinary nature of the course, and the clear, proven benefits of the problem-based learning-centered approach, it was inevitable that the new HCI-based distance-learning version of the course would need to be designed carefully, and "tailor made." The design approach taken was:

- Set out the learning outcome requirements;
- Undertake a literature review of current practice regarding HCI and achieving the pedagogic goals;
- Develop content and course elements according to the review outcomes;
- Develop HCI mechanisms appropriate to the technology, local and student requirements, and resource limitations of the course administration and management.
- The key learning outcomes remain the same as for the pre-existing problem-based learning-based course, namely, at the end of the course the student should be able to:
- Identify important environmental liabilities that may threaten a business;
- Recognize the need for a coherent and coordinated approach to containing the problem of environmental liabilities;
- Operate effectively within a team and practice project management in addressing the problems of environmental liabilities;
- Demonstrate basic understanding of current legislation as it applies to environmental liabilities;
- Apply the principles of risk assessment and management to environmental liabilities;
- Demonstrate a basic understanding of asset valuation and the measurement and role of environmental impairment within it.

Some literature review had already been undertaken, although this was updated in line with the rapid developments in interest and research in HCI. It was noted that the issue of aligning pedagogic principles in good design strategies is essential (Hubscher & Frizell, 2002), and that design support for HCI applications is recognized as an important part of effective HCI implementation across various situations (Barab, MaKinster, & Scheckler, 2004; Gao, Baylor, & Shen, 2005).

The design process then got underway, by setting out each of six principles for effective learning for complex subject areas (after Koschmann et al., 1994, p. 233), and developing course elements to satisfy each:

1. **Multiplicity:** Multiple perspectives are brought to the course through the various tutors and the inherent multi-disciplinarity of the course subject;
2. **Activeness:** Active learning is encouraged by setting an assessment-based major project, requiring students to solve problems—low cognitive Web browsing modes, and so forth are therefore avoided in favor of complex problem-led online research (high cognitive);
3. **Accommodation and adaption:** Ongoing modification of student understanding and the need to accommodate new views is ensured through the group-based project (and discussion therein) as well as the chronologic development of successive new study areas within the subject;
4. **Authenticity:** The real world nature of the cases and the main project, avoiding contrivances in key learning areas, provides this for students;
5. **Articulation:** Student commitment through the project allows them to practice their learning and apply abstraction, thus providing confidence in learning relevance, and learning enhancement through application;
6. **Termlessness:** The project explicitly demonstrates that there is *no single right answer* to the problem of land redevelopment, and

that knowledge development of both process and outcomes is never complete, only enriched—while the project has clear outcomes, the subject is termless and a matter for lifelong knowledge advancement.

Thus, the detail of the format and structure of the new HCI-based course was developed in application of these principles and the design approach, and this is discussed further later. Given the history of the preceding course, there was a sound basis for retaining the learning outcomes and the key known success factors as far as possible in the transition of modes. For each, an appropriate HCI *solution* was sought. However, for sound pedagogical reasons, as well as the practical reasons of variable Internet cost and access for international students, and varying abilities and aptitudes with technology, HCI elements were selected on the basis of simplicity as well as appropriateness, and designed for learning effectiveness rather than *because the technology allows*. Following Bentley and Dourish (1995), the aim was to provide a framework within which activity could take place, rather than structuring the activity prescriptively. The course development process was student needs-driven rather than technology-driven. At the same time, the course team members were conscious of the need for clarity and user friendliness in the presentational structure.

Format and Structure

Following the design intent, the structure devised for the Distance Learning mode mirrors the previous classroom mode in many ways, as indicated in Figure 1, which also shows the progression in each key element from classroom to distance to HCI mode. There are three basic course material types in the package:

- A *compact disk (CD)* containing interactive text and multimedia material, including video clips and various interactive audio-visual information (see screen print of mainpage, Figure 2);
- A Reader containing course info, background reading (a course text) and assessment schedules;
- A *Blackboard* Web site containing a chat room and e-mail facility, plus auto-choice tasks, assessments, references, reading Web links (all hot-linked to the CD).

The lecture notes are replaced by Unit spines on the course CD. These are written as chapter summaries, in a format that brings approximately 100 words onto the screen at time. Links are provided to the other elements throughout (see Figure 3). On the basis of past experience with aspects that students found hard to conceptualize or understand, video excerpts are used to illustrate certain points. Reading materials are also provided for reference. This reading material is supported by multiple-choice tests as a backup for learners to reinforce understanding.

Through the Virtual Office (Figure 4), the problem-based learning project remains central, and is provided as an attractive simulation, almost like a computer game, based on the participant(s) occupying and exploring a virtual office that contains a range of resources for their use. These include the project brief, a computer to access the Internet, a filing cabinet of project related materials, relevant background material on video, and a virtual site visit with expert commentary. This base is sufficient to allow the learner to explore problem-based solutions and, in the process, acquire skills and knowledge in respect of contaminated land liabilities. The visually appealing nature of the simulation represents an explicit attempt to foster a deep learning experience (Marton & Säljö, 1976) by encouraging repeated office visits.

Small groups of four to six students are tasked with preparing a strategy for the owners of the designated contaminated site and preparing a written report and PowerPoint presentation, set-

Figure 1. Course and HCI elements

Classroom course element	DL element	HCI element
Establishment of student groups and working relationships	Kick-off week with intensive project work, discussions, and presentations	Tutorials to demonstrate and develop IT and HCI user skills
Lecture notes	Units (approximately 2,000 words)	CD-based unit spines with links to Web and other elements, and clear learning outcomes (see Figure 2)
Workshop exercises and lecturer explanations of key points	"Stop and Think" exercises	"Stop and Think" exercises embedded within unit spines and "Example" audio-visual clips and related hot-linked illustrations and explanations
Class questions and interaction	Question and answer tasks (c. 150 questions)	Q&A tasks online with automated marking and feedback
Guided further reading	Guided further reading provided in a reader	Guided further reading provided in a reader, supplemented with further Web links and student group coordinated further reading via *Blackboard*
PROBLEM BASED LEARNING large project assessment	Extensive project brief with supporting documents and "virtual" group via group chat facility	The Virtual Office, containing visual user interface with animated office elements and links to project files, videophone advice clips, virtual site visit, site maps, and the Web facility
Group working	-	Virtual group working via assessment led PROBLEM BASED LEARNING and *Blackboard* chat and e-mail

ting out their analysis of the nature and extent of the liability arising from the contamination and putting forward a strategy to mange the resulting risks along with a viable development scheme.

International students may not possess the latest computer hardware and software and may have unreliable links to the Internet. The HCI package was therefore designed to run successfully at varying screen resolutions; it incorporated software requirements such as *QuickTime* and was placed on a CD rather than on a Web-server to facilitate access and minimize time spent online. The intention of designing the CD to have a life of three years before requiring updating demanded a careful analysis of which material was relatively stable and could be committed to CD and which

was volatile or liable to require change. Web links and multiple-choice tasks are therefore stored on the Web site, which is comprehensively hot-linked throughout the CD. This provides for adjustments to be made to tasks between cohorts and for these to be automatically marked, with feedback automatically generated by the Virtual Learning Environment software from the server.

A further major advantage of HCI delivery is that it allows students to access tutor support at any stage. E-mail correspondence provides students with a more flexible framework for them to use their allotted tutor time. They can *spend* their tutor time by investing in more email correspondence at the early stages of the course if they are unsure during this phase. Alternatively,

Figure 2. CD main page

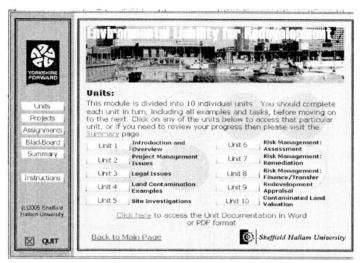

Figure 3. Structure of unit spine and course materials

Unit spine (10 units in all)	Links to:
Unit Objectives and Outcomes	Summary page on CD (includes auto-updated green/red lights to reflect progress on each Unit, and course level aims and outcomes)
Unit Contents	Each content line hotlinks to text page
Examples	Each example hotlinks to audio-visual clip
Stop and Thinks	Questions learning and allows reinforcement and further reading
Summary	Checks against learning objectives and outcomes
Reading and Tasks	Refers to key documents in reader and links to *Blackboard* Web site resources
Assessment	Links to assessment page on CD and *Blackboard* Web site; assignments and related information, reading and links, chat and e-mail facilities, library links, other project document storage and sharing
Completion Box	Checks learning against objectives and outcomes and successful completion of unit task

they can choose to maintain a reserve of e-mail tutor time for later in the project stages if their confidence levels are high earlier in the process. Students combine working individually and in their virtual groups to solve problems throughout the project. There was a clear intent to balance clear structure with flexibility in student learning approaches. Whilst some students may choose to work throughout the spine units sequentially before tackling the project, others might opt to address the problem at the outset, using the units as support. The choice of asynchronous tutor contact was a deliberate decision to allow students to pace their learning according to their personal circumstances and needs.

Figure 4. The Virtual Office project facility

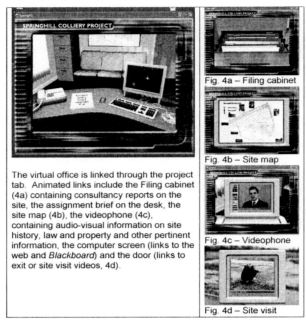

SPRINGHILL COLLIERY PROJECT
The virtual office is linked through the project tab. Animated links include the Filing cabinet (4a) containing consultancy reports on the site, the assignment brief on the desk, the site map (4b), the videophone (4c), containing audio-visual information on site history, law and property and other pertinent information, the computer screen (links to the web and *Blackboard*) and the door (links to exit or site visit videos, 4d).
Fig. 4a – Filing cabinet
Fig. 4b – Site map
Fig. 4c – Videophone
Fig. 4d – Site visit

Figure 5. A model of online learning showing types of interaction

STUDENT
paced, collaborative learning
Independent study
Student-student
Student-content
Communication
Asynchronous or synchronous
Student-content
KNOWLEDGE CONTENT INTERFACE
Content-content
Search & retrieval Tutorials Simulations & games Virtual labs E-books
Peer, family, & professional support
Student-teacher
Teacher-content
Community of inquiry
Structured learning resources
TEACHER
Teacher-teacher
OTHER TEACHERS

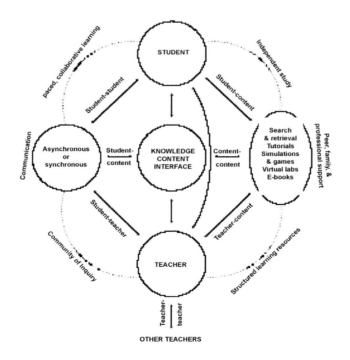

REFLECTION AND FUTURE ISSUES

Full evaluation data is not yet available for the case study. Despite this, and the fact that the main aim of this case study is to document the design process, it is possible to reflect on the value outcomes of the incorporation of HCI. This starts with the fact that HCI facilitates the incorporation of the distance-learning mode, thus providing access to learning to those who otherwise would not be able to travel to points of delivery. However, it also delivers more than what could be gained in the classroom style course, and some of these value additions are unexpected. For example, video clips of outside, sometimes overseas, experts, commenting on liability issues and procedures provide a positive addition to learning materials that were earlier unavailable. Hence, the full time Master's students began using the distance-learning materials during their development and early pilot stages and found them very useful as an additional learning source. Students were able to use the CD to return to issues about which they were uncertain. The formalized collection of material in learning units along with brief learning aids such as the Stop and Think boxes also added value to the existing course delivery. In particular, they began using the online task facility and an early version of the *Virtual Office*, which allowed them to undertake repeat *virtual* site visits to the site. This HCI site is a contrived site based on real data and was not therefore the same site as the project site being used by the classroom-based students. Nevertheless, they found the approach taken in the *Virtual Office* simulation to be a useful example to work with in parallel with their site.

Reflecting on the value of the design process for the HCI innovation, a range of issues was dealt with through the use of the team approach against the sound theoretical and pedagogic background. One key issue was the balance between content and no content. Barrows argues that, "*all the information needed to solve the problem is typically unavailable at the outset. All problem-based learning units should provide this challenge*" (Barrows & Tamblyn, 2000, p. 163). The decision was taken to develop material as a useful resource for potential access by the project team. But it was deliberately placed outside of the virtual office. Teams and individuals could choose whether to access it or not and decide to what extent they wished to use this material. The approach represents an attempt at scaffolding, providing resources, case studies, prompts, and strategic guidance to the learner to enhance performance following the model of Juwah (2004). A further major advantage of electronic delivery is that it allows students to access not only materials, but also tutor support at any stage in the sequence.

The content template was designed to be internationally applicable, both by including examples of international practice in the unit materials and by focusing students' attention on the method and approach rather than on details of rules and regulations. This was a conscious decision to use the problem-based learning approach, with HCI tools, with the stated intent to enhance deep learning. The resultant course is more accessible, flexible, and international than previously, and provides the mechanisms for repeat visits and integrated projects that facilitate such learning. Despite a greater physical distance between the student and the teacher, the course provides an opportunity for a closer and more interactive relationship than is often the case with conventional delivery modes.

Regarding the management of future delivery, one of the course development drivers was university management-led market considerations. The extent to which the potential social and educational benefits can be realized is contingent on the time allocation that tutors devote to course management, especially to e-mail interaction with students. This in turn raises important questions about costing and work planning for teachers who are not physically present in the classroom. The resource intensive nature of the initial development implicitly suggests to some university work planners that course delivery will be less resource intensive than a traditional "chalk and talk" delivery mode. As experience in this area develops, it is expected that appropriate work planning practice will follow. A further question of balance emerges with regard to the distribution of resource input between design and delivery. Educational designers and managers should consider the design approach, along with proper resourcing and standards for HCI course design and development. The assumption that design is simple and it is technology and interface development that is dominant is as misplaced as the idea that the time input is entirely front-loaded with minimal demands at the delivery stage. The growth in experience with HCI and distance courses should ensure that such misconceptions become less commonplace; however, in the meantime, it is a task for HCI developers to continue to ensure due cognizance is given to the resource implications of both the design and delivery.

CONCLUSION

Within the context of the appropriate utilization of problem-based learning and the case considered, it is clear that HCI has provided a major impetus to course design and development, and major enabling factor in the shift to distance mode. Given that the subject area is concerned with professional practice, the final design closely mirrors real world problems, as well as having a sound theoretical and pedagogical basis. Maintaining this sense of reality and managing the complexity of the multidisciplinary course content (with sound reasons for doing so) provided a major challenge, which was only met in the shift to distance mode by the use of HCI. Critical success factors included the design basis and the team approach. Incorporation and integration of appropriate HCI elements were facilitated by the clear method and principles available to the team. As the design process continued, the team

approach was important in ensuring that subject elements were treated appropriately, and that each HCI element was designed to contribute to the integrated learning outcomes being achieved.

The long course history was valuable in informing development of the various HCI course elements. However, the principles and theory of problem-based learning also provided critical underpinning to the design process. This ensured that HCI elements were all linked to learning outcomes and deep learning processes, rather than being peripheral and becoming low cognitive, and therefore of limited value. The design process takes time and resources. Fortunately, the course design project was well resourced, but the challenge to the success of this course lies as much in cost and management decisions regarding its implementation as in its design. There is no single formula for producing problem-based neither learning nor integrating HCI. Drawing on the growing body of literature for guidance is valuable, and concept and practice is continually evolving.

REFERENCES

Anderson, T., & Elloumi, F. (2004). *Theory and practice of online learning*. Athabasca University, Athabasca, Canada.

Barab, S., MaKinster, J., & Scheckler, R. (2004). Designing system dualities: Building online community. In S. A. Barab, R. Kling, & J. Gray (Eds.), *Designing for virtual communities in the service of learning*. Cambridge, MA: Cambridge University Press.

Barrows, H. S., & Tamblyn, R. M. (2000). *Problem based learning applied to medical education*. New York: Springer Publishing Co.

Bentley, R., & Dourish, P. (1995). *Medium versus mechanism: Supporting collaboration through customization*. Paper presented at the Proceedings of ECSCW.

Bridges, D. (2000). Back to the future: The higher education curriculum in the 21st century. *Cambridge Journal of Education, 30*(1), 37-55.

Dennen, V. P. (2000). Task structuring for online problem based learning: A case study. *Educational Technology & Society, 3*(3), 329-336.

Dimitracopoulou, A., & Petrou, A. (2003). *Advanced collaborative distance learning systems for young students: Design issues and current trends on new cognitive and meta-cognitive tools.* Retrieved December 1, 2005, from http://www.modellingspace.net/Documents/Collaborative%20Review%20adimitr%20petrou%20special%20issue%20Theme.pdf

Dochy, F., Segers, M., Van den Bossche, P., & Gijbels, D. (2003). Effects of problem-based learning: A meta-analysis. *Learning and Instruction, 13*(5), 533-568.

Duch, B. (2005). *Problem based learning at University of Delaware.* Retrieved September 21, 2005, from http://www.udel.edu/Problem_Based_Learning

Finucane, P. M., Johnson, S. M., & Prideaux, D. J. (1998). Problem-based learning: Its rationale and efficacy. *Medical Journal of Australia, 168,* 445-448.

Gao, H., Baylor, A. L., & Shen, E. (2005). Designer support for online collaboration and knowledge construction. *Educational Technology & Society, 8*(1), 69-79.

Glasgow, N. A. (1997). *New curriculum for new times: A guide to student-centred problem based learning.* Corwin Press Inc.

Houlden, R. L., Collier, C. P., Frid, P. J., John, S. L., & Pross, H. (2001). Problems identified by tutors in a hybrid problem-based learning curriculum. *Academic Medicine, 76*(1), 81.

Hubscher, R., & Frizell, S. (2002). Aligning theory and Web-based instructional design practice with design patterns. *World Conference on E-Learning in Corporations, Government, Health & Higher Education 2002, (pp.* 298-304). Retrieved January 5, 2006, from http://dl.aace.org/9377

Juwah, C. (2004). *Using communication and information technologies to support problem based learning.* Retrieved June 29, 2005, from http://www.heacademy.ac.uk/resources

Koschmann, T. (1999). Computer support for collaboration and learning. *Journal of the Learning Sciences, 8,* 495-497.

Koschmann, T., Kelson, A. C., Feltovich, P. J., & Barrows, H. S. (1996). *CSCL, Theory and practice of an emerging paradigm.* Mahwah, NJ: Lawrence Erlbaum Associates.

Koschmann, T., Myers, A. C., Feltovich, P. J., & Barrows, H. S. (1994). Using technology to assist in realizing effective learning and instruction: A principled approach to the use of computers in collaborative learning. *The Journal of the Learning Sciences, 3,* 227-264.

Marton, F., & Säljö, S. (1976). On qualitative differences in learning—2: Outcome as a function of the learner's conception of the task. *British Journal of Educational Psychology, 46,* 115-127.

Popper, K. (1999). *All life is problem solving.* London: Routledge.

Preece, J. (2000) *Online communities, designing usability, supporting sociability.* Chichester: Wiley.

Rhem, J. (1998). Problem based learning: An introduction. *National Teaching & Learning Forum, 8*(1), 1-2.

White, H. B. (1996). Dan tries problem based learning: A case study. *To Improve the Academy, 15,* 75-91.

Chapter XIV
An Integrative Approach to Teaching 3D Modelling in Architecture

Carmina Sánchez-del-Valle
Hampton University, USA

ABSTRACT

The argument presented here is that computer courses must reach beyond the comfortable cushion of conventional teaching practices, and provide students with a way to come to grips with complexity. It provides as evidence a digital graphics literacy course for architecture students using transformer robot toys as a metaphor for introducing the concept of adaptive kinetic architecture. The transformer toy provides a manipulative device with which to develop students' 3D modelling and rendering skills. The course approach is described, and observations about the students' work are offered. It concludes further investigation is needed to ascertain the most appropriate delivery for reciprocal and complementary knowledge. Years ago during a summer vacation, I watched my four-year old nephew play with his favorite toy—a transforming robot composed of smaller robots. A transformer robot is a highly articulated figure with specialized joints that allows form to change without disassembly. The joints are simple mechanisms, and transformation depends on a highly orchestrated sequence of moves. My nephew, who was bilingual and illiterate then, focused all of his attention on the five figures in front of him, and one-by-one reshaped them to build the larger robot. His eyebrows were tense; his eyes followed the actions of his hands, and his fingers moved gingerly and precisely over the moving parts. He would not speak until the five would be reconfigured into one large robot. He had simpler transformers that could change from vehicle or animal to robot, and he had mastered them all. Instructions for manipulating the toy are primarily graphical; they use line, color, shades, and arrows to indicate how a part is to be rotated, sledded, pushed, or pulled. I noticed, however, that my nephew never used them to pursue his hands-on studies. I realized then that the transformer robot toy was the vehicle I had searched for that would introduce my students to the modelling of complex geometries and articulations in a way that would cross over to other courses in the curriculum, in particular the design studio.

INTRODUCTION

For years I had observed architectural students struggle to grasp concepts and master various commercial off-the-shelf modelling and graphic software in a range of elective computer courses I had developed. The courses guided students into developing their two-dimensional (2D) and three-dimensional (3D) visualization skills through a series of small playful design problems, drawing and constructing models with computer-based tools. These problems encouraged the exploration of various software package capabilities to address the challenges offered by the designs. The idea was to have each student build his or her own approach to thinking about digital representation, and *computer aided design*, and to develop skills necessary to apply his or her experience in the design studio. I noticed that students would usually utilize what they had learned in the graphic presentation of their design projects, but those same lessons did not carry over to enhance their

Figure 1. Transformer robot toy in the process of change; Hasbro® Energon toy

approach to design. The students were active in resolving the course's projects, but their focus was on developing skills that would make them marketable, not necessarily better thinkers and designers. This was not an exception. Gross (1994) has noted a number of drawbacks associated to *computer aided design* literacy courses in architecture schools, among them a "false sense of achievement" (p. 57), having conquered the difficulties posed by a software package rather than a critical attitude toward design computing.

I decided to investigate with my students a different way to teach about modelling and rendering with the computer. Modelling is used in this context as the building of 3D models, and rendering refers to the painterly manner in which images of the model are further developed to approximate reality. The approach would challenge the students' imaginations and analytical skills. It would require them to question the nature of architecture as they stretched the limits of the software; this would still allow them to meet the fundamental goal of building their computer-based representation skills. It was about initiating change in students' design frameworks so that they could understand the requirements, the nuances, and the possibilities for dealing with the complexity of the world's design challenges. Also, it was important to make a definite connection with the process of design and the applicability of the tools so that the knowledge would be realized as reciprocal and complementary, and would be transferred into studio in a more meaningful way crossing over the existing curricular barriers. A shift from a computer-oriented to content-based model with an architectural design focus—a studio-like environment instead of a lecture and workshop where students complete a series of prescribed visualization exercises—was seen as a way to resolve the gap between support course and studio. The studio-like format also facilitated peer-to-peer learning, a solution to another challenge: a group of students with varying design skill proficiency and levels of experience working with graphic applications. A condition to contend with was a pre-defined software application.

The subject chosen was adaptive kinetic architecture, or folding and transformable architecture. The approach proposed was mixed media, where pencil and paper served to document observations about the form of the transformer toys and the process required to build the parts in the digital environment. The computer-based three-dimensional modelling and rendering provided the means to represent form, material characteristics, and contexts where the design was to operate. The products of the process were a new construction toy set and a very small transformable building. My decision to focus on adaptive kinetic architecture required providing models and precedents as the course's first step. I posited this would accelerate the students understanding of the mechanics embedded and the resulting behavior of the structures. This is also a tradition in architectural education. Initially, precedents considered were construction vehicles and space exploration vehicles, such as a Mars rover. However, these vehicles were made up of complex mechanical and electronic systems, which the students would have to abstract without having the operational knowledge to do so. Then, when I reflected on my nephew's determined struggle and fascination with the intricacies of his transformer robot toys, I realized this was an applicable model that could be used as metaphor for an inhabitable transformable or adaptive kinetic structure. The basic characteristics of robot transformer toys are: specialized discrete parts exhibiting a variety of joint types; capacity to change overall configuration without changing the physical connection between the parts including disassembly; the ability to maintain at least two configuration states, and to reverse its change-states locally or globally. Finally, components can rotate, slide, and act in combination.

The use of metaphors is a well-established teaching practice used to explain concepts. In architectural design, but not exclusively, metaphors are used to stimulate the imagination and spur new directions. There are well known iconic metaphors, such as Le Corbusier's house as *machine for living*, architecture as body, green architecture, as well as newly coined ones such as Santiago Calatrava's *twisting torso*, denoting the cantilevered structure for a skyscraper. The transformer robot toy metaphor did not inherently contain all the answers to the inquiry it facilitated, but experience teaching the course described here has shown it is an acceptable repository for projections, and can serve as a reference.

Schön (1983) identified the reflective practitioner's need for metaphorical transposition decades ago, when he proposed *seeing-as* and *doing-as* are critical ways of knowing in design, because they allow the designer *"to have a feel for problems that do not fit existing rules"* (p. 140). Schön was influenced by Thomas Kuhn's *thinking from exemplars*, and Robert Oppenheimer's discussion of analogies to model new scientific theories on existing ones. For Schön the ultimate metaphor was the generative type *"when the two things seen as similar are initially very different from one another,"* and this difference allows for *"new perceptions, explanations, and inventions"* (pp. 184-185). Yet, a limitation to the use of metaphors is that to recognize its potential to be effective and have an impact, one must have had previous experience working with it. The transformer robot toy is an appropriate metaphor because most students have memories of having manipulated it.

Adaptive kinetic architecture refers to an integrative system that interacts with the environment thus consuming less energy, and requiring less material to build. This type of structure has two distinctive characteristics: it stores and transforms energy, and produces work in the form of controlled motion. Motion is a physical manifestation of its adaptation to changing environmental forces or programmed behavior triggering a major or minor but reversible reconfiguration of components. Motion is produced as a response to excitations,

Figure 2. Diagramming an adaptive kinetic structure

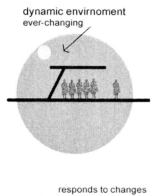

dynamic envirnoment
ever-changing

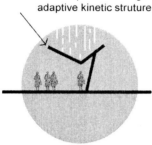

responds to changes
adaptive kinetic struture

such as physical contact, light level, wind speed, sound, temperature, and so forth. In architecture two types of adaptive kinetic structures have been explored: articulated and continuous body. The articulated body structures are like the transformer robot toy, while the continuous ones are like the human body.

The investigation of adaptive kinetic architecture has gained relevance, as the awareness about the role architecture must play in the cycle of material life—production, consumption, decomposition—has grown. An ecological perspective is needed to see architecture as an integrative system in an ever-changing context conforming to environmental mandates. Adaptive kinetic architecture ties well to the concept of sustainability. In addition, the idea of systems thinking, on which sustainability is based, is related to transformable architecture because in this type of architecture "the relationships among the system's parts, [are more important] than the properties of the parts themselves" and because

the relationship "between the parts change to improve performance," (Hjorth & Bagheri, 2006, p. 79) just like a transformable structure can morph adjusting to rainfall, or high winds. Seen in this way, transformation is inherent to the life cycle of a building as it adjusts, or adapts to changes. Sherman and Martini (2002) have called this notion *elastic boundary,* "where the building is viewed as a mediator responding dynamically to natural forces, rather than as a collection of mechanical systems that maintains a static environment." An adaptive kinetic structure is an elastic boundary. In practical terms the challenge is, as explained by Battle and McCarthy (2001), how to create "a single form that can be appropriate to all physical and climatic forces" (p. 17).

The layers of knowledge established in this course respond to a call to overhaul architectural education prompted by the discipline's diminishing ability to make a difference in the world. A 1996 study of architectural education in the U.S. proposed, "Fostering the learning habits needed for discovery, integration, application, and sharing of knowledge over a lifetime" (Boyer & Mitgang as cited in Diaz Moore, 2001, p. 59). Battle and McCarthy (2001) have suggested *"fearless innovation"* is necessary to address the increasingly evident serious large-scale social and environmental challenges (p. 97). Architecture has played a large part in the onset of those problems, and is past due in rousing itself to define a sensible direction. Battle and McCarthy (2001) further propose radically different processes and tools are necessary where the "problem is examined in more than two or three dimensions, but in seven or eight dimensions" (p. 95). This raises a fundamental pedagogical question: How do we guide architecture students into a new framework for design thinking that will responsibly consider the basic terms of complexity?

There are both fundamental and far-reaching goals underlying the series of explorations performed by the students enrolled in the course described here. The first is to introduce architecture

Figure 3. An adaptive kinetic structure is like a rubber band; it stretches and contracts

students to a specific 3D digital or computer-based construction environment, its general interface structure, and its operation rules. Modelling the transformer robot toy's varied geometry presents a challenge to the students' abilities. As models for design, they facilitate a more holistic thinking about architecture. Their investigation provides a space for discovery and invention, thereby creating a referential framework for future inquiries into the imagination.

But beyond that, through the use of the metaphor, students begin to grapple with the idea of complexity, and with methods for discerning its components. The exploration offers an opportunity to consider geometrical, assembly, and mechanical complexity, as well as manifest the concept of work as force multiplied by energy. When the transformer toy is taken as a model for design, students must consider the articulations between materials and between components. They visualize potential states of the structure to predict conflicts. They make joints and parts to effectively interlock. They deliberate on the sources of energy necessary for altering states and where to apply it. They design a structure that locks into alternative positions without falling apart.

This section has presented the rationale for a course that explores a different way to teach about computer-based modelling and rendering:

essentially, it shifts the focus from computer-based to content-based. Also discussed were the need for metaphor in architectural design, and a holistic approach to knowledge integration within the architectural curricula. In the course students were encouraged to think creatively about design representation using a combination of traditional and digital media. This was facilitated by the manipulation of the transformer robot toy metaphor, which served as the bridge to the design of complex architectural systems. The approach was based on the argument architecture must address the increasing view of architecture as a negative component in the larger, complex, and precarious global ecosystem. Tomorrow's architects need to come to grips with the complexity of reality and be able to arrive at effective strategies to respond to it through their designs. This capability will be attained only after requisite skills have been developed in analytical process, systems thinking, and clear presentation of proposals. Dealing with the complexity of design encourages the exploration of the complexity of media, and builds understanding of it.

The background section will expand on the state of the integration of computer systems into the architectural curricula. The variety of approaches introduced will include those from engineering and interdisciplinary product design education. The concept of physical *manipulative* or *transitional object,* of which the transformer robot toy is an example, will be defined and related to a larger class of learning tools—construction toys.

BACKGROUND: TINKERING WITH DESIGN AND COMPUTERS

Architecture is the art and science of designing spaces and the material enclosures for habitation. It mediates our interaction with the physical world. Architects design buildings and landscapes, but typically are not responsible for building them.

Instead, they depend heavily on representations to communicate to others what they will look like and what to build. Consequently, the possibilities of design depend on the quality of its representations, and the depth of thought and breadth of exploration and analysis that went into their conception. The power of ideation, imagination, and highly developed spatial and visual senses are essential. Drawings, paintings, sketches, diagrams, animations, movies, and 3D models generated through physical and digital means are the matter used to design, review, and communicate decisions. A design is built on approximations, and a built project is often its only physical prototype. We evaluate designs through physical testing and simulation and through critical analysis trying to capture all the intangibles that will affect a building through its working life. The process is iterative and reflective.

The application of computers in architectural practice and education is evident in modelling, rendering, and animation. Digital media are used to mimic traditional media, such as in 2D working drawings and digital collages; for design and for presentation; and, for testing conditions and performance of specific environments. They are used to explore new ways of transferring the design information to the built object through *computer aided manufacturing*, to develop new approaches to organizing building information, and facilitate teamwork and collaboration.

Schools of architecture offer courses that build students' representation skills in stand-alone support courses, and embedded into the design studio. The studio is the setting where the knowledge gained in all other courses is synthesized into design. Design investigation can be open-ended or prescriptive, but the conclusion is generally the concretization of a proposal. Some studios are representation-based; a few are design-build, requiring students to construct their designs full-scale individually or in teams. Learning is project-based, hands-on, mixed media, syncretic,

and direct. The space for exploration is usually provided by a design project that is located on a site, real or imaginary.

The integration of digital media, computer graphics, visualization, and representation courses is usually tailored to the resources available and to the specific goals of a program. Some schools have the capability to offer a diverse collection of courses at different levels, while those with limited resources teach the essentials. In the U.S. the architectural education accrediting agency stipulates as one of its student performance criteria the ability to represent designs through traditional and digital media, which implies integration into the design studio. Programs have addressed this requirement in two ways: fusion or focus; the first incorporates computers into the studio, while the latter deals either exclusively with building computer-based tools, or learning how to apply them, as is the case of a software-based visualization course, and a mechanical systems or structures course centered on modelling and simulation. Gross (1994) has classified computer courses into three categories: tool using; tool building; and theory, methods, and computation. Andia (2002) has identified five *discourses of computerization*: design methods, computer aided design visualization, paperless architecture, information architecture, and virtual studios. The content-based course described here does not fall into any of these categories since it is based on a holistic or integrative approach to teaching with computers, rather than fused into, or isolated from other courses.

Aside from the course types just mentioned, there are a variety of teaching modalities. In architecture and engineering the hybrid media or mixed media approach, where digital media are combined with material-based media, is common. Talbott (2003) and others have argued learning digital modelling must occur between the virtual and the physical, where students both work on their designs through software and with tangible materials (p. 154). In engineering, Erdman and

Durfee (1995) have also promoted a hybrid or mixed-world setting to push design abilities where there is a "commitment to hands-on engineering, and developing innovative ways to integrate advanced computer-based design tools with prototype construction and test experiences" (p. 23). Dym, Agogino, Eris, Frey, and Leifer (2005) have used *reverse engineering* or *dissection*—the "taking apart, tinkering, discussing, and reflecting on engineered products" (p. 113), to promote integrative design thinking. In her interdisciplinary design courses Frances Brönet (1999) has tested the concepts *artifact-in-the-making* and *space-in-the-making* to ensure students do not lose sight of the broader societal, environmental consequences of their design decisions. The first calls our attention to the need for constantly reflecting through design about the social implications of our proposals because, she has written, "tools and people...cannot be understood apart from each other." The second reminds us space is fluid and can be manipulated. All of these modalities are geared among other things to develop the students' intuition, *thinking-in-action*, and improvisation as creative forces inventing connections where none seem to be available, to look at everyday objects in a different light.

An attitude of serious play and the elements of gaming are often incorporated into design courses. Nancy Cheng (1999) among others has investigated play as a *"start towards building a comprehensive, balanced digital curriculum, injecting the freedom of childhood play [to] increase student comfort [and] creative achievement"* (pp. 107-108). Burry, Dawson, and Woodbury (1999) and Woodbury, Shannon, and Radford (2001) have used form-making games to teach digital media in architecture because they afford a clear territory for play and exploration. Schön (1983), in the context of design practice, calls this process *exploratory experiment*: "the probing, playful activity by which we get the feel for things" (p. 145).

Engaging in play to learn can involve interacting with physical and virtual objects, or *manipulatives*. These are tangible objects the students can manipulate, typically used in the teaching of math, science, and structures to demonstrate concepts. Construction toys, familiar examples of manipulatives, have long been recognized as important learning tools, especially in the areas of spatial and sensorial-motor skills, intuition, and imagination. In their biographies important architects recall playing with construction toys, most notably Frank Lloyd Wright. My students often cite these along with computer games as their childhood favorites. Origami, solid blocks, connecting blocks, and transformer toys are the four basic types of building toys available today. Solid blocks, such as wood blocks, are not attached and depend on weight and shape. Tinkertoy®, Log blocks, Erector/Meccano®, fishertechnik®, K'Nex®, LEGO®, Öliblocks®, ZOOB®, and Capsela® building sets have specialized parts and articulations that allow motion. Transformer toys, such as Hasbro's Transformers series and Playskool Go-bots™, Mega Blocks Blok-Bots™, and Hoberman's Gro-bots®, also have discrete parts and articulations, but differently from the other toys, transformation occurs without disassembly, and form change can be reversed.

A handful of architectural educators have been introducing their students to cybernetics and computation through toy-like manipulatives. A design seminar at the ETH in Zurich pioneered the use of the LEGO® Mindstorms Robot Invention System to make architectonic objects with a designed behavior. Among them was space with programmed walls that could move on their own will, or triggered by an external event (Engeli, 2001). Gross and Do (1999) have identified construction toys with embedded electronics as a means to introduce architecture students to digital media, and in a "simple and crude way," to introduce the idea of responsive building as a "computational entity." They have also argued "asking students to embed computation into physical environments and models encourages finding elegant ways to integrate digital and physical craft" (p. 7).

The transformer robot toy is a *transitional object*, as defined by Papert (1980) with which the beginning designer can have direct contact and establish a *bridge* to previously gained knowledge, as well as new knowledge. In Papert's case a semi-spherical roving robot programmed in LOGO provided a connection between the *"mathematics and the body"* (p. viii; p. 161). Raffle, García, and Ishii (2003) have developed the latest application of the idea of transitional object with *Topobo*, articulated blocks with embedded electronics to support tangible learning about computing. We have previously noted that in architecture, models are fundamental instruments for representing and testing design ideas.

This section has introduced the precedents that have most influenced the shaping of the course. The next section discusses the objectives of the course, its structure, the response to the challenges presented by the emphasis on designing complex architectural systems, and materials used. It also describes the exercises and the limits placed on the students' play experimentation. It will be followed by a tentative assessment of the results of the course, and reflections on future explorations.

THE HOLISTIC APPROACH: THE TRANSFORMER ROBOT TOY METAPHOR

Believe it or not, drawing robots is easy. It's only a matter of stacking geometric shapes on top of each other and providing details by clipping away at the edges [...] But the transformation process, knowing how it switches into another form and why—that information has always remained elusive. (Jackson, 2004, p. 4)

The main goal of the course was to develop 3D modelling skills using a digital environment. Parameters defining the quality and scope of the course's outcomes: the work had to stimulate the imagination, challenge preconceived notions about form and geometry, encourage collective creation and the exchange of knowledge, provide skill sets and frameworks directly transferable to the design studio, and inspire independent exploration. Finally, the content of the course had to be accessible to the modelling software neophyte, and to a mix of students from all levels in the architecture program. This course used transformable robot toys as vehicles for building and manipulating complex 3D geometries. Students were instructed to approach the transformer robot toys as metaphors for transformable architectural artifacts responsive to their environment, and intended occupant(s). Students were asked to make evident the efficiency and effectiveness of their designs by modelling and rendering them in detail. Meeting these objectives required they develop awareness of structural and spatial dynamics, mechanisms, control systems, and energy flows. The course and the design problem promoted a space for exploration, invention, and innovation.

The course consisted of four basic activities: observation, documentation, design, and evaluation as preparation for the next design iteration. Course grading was based on the precision evidenced in the documentation of parts, and in the subsequent modelling and rendering of their assembly; and, the fulfillment of the requirements of the various intermediate design stages of two design projects. These two design projects were first to design a transformable architectural toy, and second, to design a small transformable building for one occupant referencing the parts of their toy.

The transformer robot toy as a metaphor for adaptive kinetic architecture offered three advantages. First, its immediacy and physicality allowed its easy transposition into a diagrammatic concept to be manipulated, handled, and touched. It offered a process of transposition rather than translation, because the integrity of the toy had to be respected; its joined parts mutating between two stable configurations were to be acknowledged. With hands-on exploration, the toy quickly became a familiar object to students. Direct experience with the toy was expected to develop their intuitive knowledge to approach design with some expertise. In addition, the metaphor itself allowed students to draw upon their imagination while keeping them grounded. By the toy's very existence—it had weight; it had reality—its nature could not be denied. Familiarity was relevant because the intention was to use the metaphor not just to design toys or toy-like buildings, but also to critically consider ways of framing complex design problems. The renowned industrial designer Victor Papanek (1995) speculated that if educational toys were designed like transformers, children could learn about biomorphic design and the connection between nature and the built world. Papanek suggested this type of experience could lead to more versatile product designs (p. 212) and by extension to a new architecture.

Secondly, the geometry of the transformer toy parts required careful study, and its representation demanded multiple geometric construction operations. Most of the pieces were not simple extrusions, but rather complex curved surfaces. The joints were of particular interest, since they required the parts met precisely, and had to move in a predetermined manner. Thus, the emphasis had to shift from appearance to performance. The effectiveness of the configuration was more heavily judged in terms of the object's projected behavior; hence formal criteria such as proportion, rhythm, and balance were secondary. The implication was that students were to establish a literal correspondence between articulated toys and building, where the parts of their buildings had specific functions and behaviors organized in a systematic way as an assemblage.

Finally, students had to make sense of mechanisms through preliminary simple identification and classification of types. A more insightful recognition of the components and alignments of mechanisms would facilitate the demonstration of physical laws of motion, types of motion, and energy required for work or movement.

The problem of highly articulated structures—and thus the robot transformer toy—is that the more parts, the more joints, the more mechanisms, the more chances for failure. Another problem is semantic: is the transformer robot toy like a machine, or like an organism? If it is a machine it is a closed system that operates within known bounds, but if it is an organism it is a flexible, open system. Fritjof Capra (1982) described living systems as *"interlinked by cyclical exchanges,"* (p. 300) and *"there is a continuous exchange of energy and matter"* (p. 270). Organisms have the redundancy and regenerative capacity to respond to failure. Therefore, for kinetic adaptive structures to be considered complex dynamic systems they must approximate organisms. Certainly, neither buildings today, nor the robot transformer toy are such a system. Yet, the application of the metaphor of the transformer toy provides the platform from which to ask questions, identify characteristics, and establish comparisons about this subject.

At the beginning of the course students were introduced to the concept of kinetic adaptive structures, and reviewed its applications in architectural projects built and un-built. They also became acquainted with the history of the digital 3D modelling environment and its theoretical foundation. FormZ was used as the building platform for the design iterations simply because it was the software available. The formZ software has the capacity to generate *developable* surfaces; these are 3D objects that are translated into flat two-dimensional planes using the *unfolding* function. An unfolded 3D object becomes whole again by folding the surface along its edges, as in Origami. Folded edges behave as hinges. A hinged joint could be one of the articulations modeled

Figure 4. Parts sketched by the students

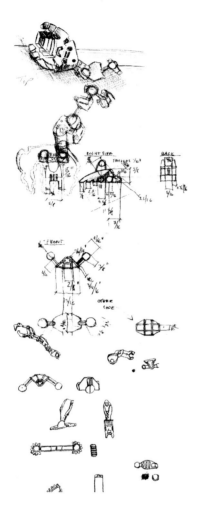

by the students. In addition, formZ supports the modelling and manipulation of solid geometry and surfaces, entities present in a transformer robot toy.

In one class session students had an opportunity to put their hands to work becoming acquainted with the toy and studying its mechanisms by transforming them. In a following session students did not dissect the toy; rather, they were presented with a set of parts collected from a variety of transformer toys such as the Blokbot Megablock™, the LEGO® Bionicle, the Hasbro® Transformer models, and the Hasbro Go-Bots™.

The intention was to avoid the simple translation of the toy's geometric form into a digital 3D model. It also encouraged them to view the parts in a new light. They could consider applications other than the ones given by the original toy part, thereby providing space for innovation and inventiveness. The pieces selected comprised a diverse set based on the type of joint, its geometrical complexity, and its versatility.

Students had to measure and sketch each part precisely. The sketch involved a process of selection. It offered students a chance to observe carefully, to distill the essential attributes of the parts' form, and how parts were shaped to connect to other parts. After documenting the parts, each student modeled in digital space one or two parts. Each part had to be built to its true scale. The students' task was to adjust the environment's grid on the construction plane to work with such small pieces. At this point students confronted the necessity for detail. The modelling of transformable toys presented a considerable challenge given that few of the parts could be modeled with simple extrusion and mirror-copy. Many of the parts were combinations of complex surfaces and solid primitives. This was precisely one of the reasons why the transformer robot toy was chosen in the first place, to face formal complexity and to address it through design.

Students then diagrammed through handdrawn sketches the construction process that led to the finished version of each part. These diagrams allowed them to share experiences and to draw lessons from them. They helped students answer questions about the use of the software, identify best means and methods for abstracting form to build the piece, and ascertain the accuracy of the digital version.

After all the parts were modeled, the best constructions were merged into one file to be distributed among the members of the class. These were the parts' models that offered the closest match to the original set, and had been built as solids rather than as surfaces, which would allow

Figure 5. Diagrams illustrating the process followed to build a 3D part in formZ sketched by students

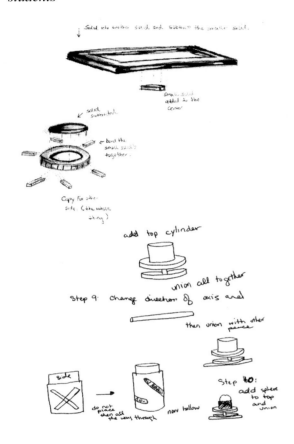

it would have been easy to ignore the toy parts and just build with simple extrusions, or recycle models from other projects, thus eliminating the need to model them again. Therefore, the first rule was the actual size of the new parts had to be comparable to the original ones. Second, the new parts needed to precisely connect to the original parts, or an articulation piece needed to be created. Third, the added pieces had to define space, rather than simply create a dense conglomerate, or solid mass made of parts.

Before building their own architectural transformer toys, students were asked to quickly sketch their initial idea. After they had modeled their designs in digital space, they were asked again to sketch it by hand. The iterative process of moving from hand to computer and back again was a way to verify goals had been achieved. It kept minds active and helped students clarify and maintain their focus. It facilitated the discussion of the differences and similarities between drawings and digital models. It also revealed the students' hand-drawing competence in contrast to their digital modelling skills.

It became quickly evident that the complexity of modelling the new toy resided not so much in the shaping of the parts, but in locating their coupling in space. The students' initial models were of separate, distinct parts; the transformable architectural toy required its constituent parts reconnected. Students had to develop joints for the personal pieces compatible with the original parts kit. In the robot toy few of the articulations had their axes on planes parallel to the default XY, ZX, and ZY construction planes. Most required auxiliary reference planes for each part connected. This made certain the parts were accurately coupled, even if placed in different orientations. *Props* were necessary to mark points in space for proper alignment of joints and positioning of parts. Props were extraneous 2D and 3D objects used to snap a piece to the center of a hole, or to a relevant point in space outside or inside an object. The prop established a singular relationship to

them to be digitally sculpted. This was an important condition because in most digital modelling programs virtual sculpting allows 3D objects to be combined. The task that followed involved designing an architectural transformer toy. All the pieces provided in the set were to be used. In addition, each student was to add two new pieces of their own; this customized each kit of parts. In effect, students had to find among a diversity of familiar forms and components those that would have a scale comparable to the original toy parts. There were three requirements imposed on the students' addition of parts to ensure the first set still related to the second, at least in size. Otherwise,

Figure 6. From toy part, to hand-drawn sketch, to digital model

Figure 7. Toy sketches before building digital models drawn by the students

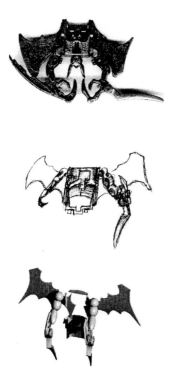

that particular point. This stage was possibly the most difficult. Although modelling software for mechanical engineering applications does have built-in functions that facilitate these procedures, formZ does not. Students needed to be creative and invent their own linking process. Students had to carefully study the fitting of joints, the relationships between the parts shaping the mechanisms they created, and the types of joints that facilitated the intended type of motion.

Students worked through several versions of their toy before the next task. The class determined the fundamental characteristics of a transformable architectural toy. They defined them as jointed, mobile, having interchangeable parts and transformable surfaces, and intriguing to manipulate. Collaboration at this point delivered a clear set of guidelines for design. The preliminary designs were tested by having the students set them in

prescribed conditions: floating in water, placed on sand, placed on the hand, on top of a table lighted by a desk lamp, and on top of a piece of paper containing the preliminary sketches for the design. These explorations introduced students to rendering techniques, and demonstrated how the modelling environment could be used as a tool in design to virtually place the design on a site to qualitatively assess its practicality.

The final task was to design a small building—an adaptive kinetic structure based on the experience gained from the development of the architectural transformer toy. To better transition into this phase, students were asked to sketch by hand the initial concept for the transformable structure. Two rules were imposed on the process: the artifact had to have room for one person, and the enclosed space had to cover not more than 100 square feet. The area limitation was intended to

Figure 8. New toy digital models

Figure 9. Testing the toy designs

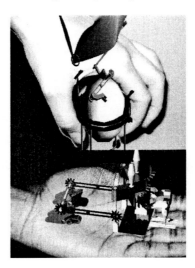

Figure 10. Architectural artifacts set on location

keep all the designs within the same scale; and, the presence of the occupant promoted the design of an inhabitable structure rather than a large-sized sculpture. The architectural program was minimal and incomplete to allow for students' participation in defining its purpose. The model was to be constructed using a natural scale (1:1); it had to be highly detailed; and its parts and articulations were to reference the toy. Modification of both parts and joints to accommodate the larger scale and material reality was permitted. The design had to respond to a specific site and occupant needs, encouraging each student to determine both. The architectural artifact had to be shown photo-realistically in a real setting with corresponding orientation and including the occupant. The last phase reintroduced students to the multivalent world of architectural design—a world where compromises resolve conflicts between the forces vying to shape the resulting form. In this case it involved issues of site, function, habitation, construction, power sources, and transformation.

ANALYSIS

Designing a transformable architectural artifact became the most difficult and misunderstood endeavor proposed to the students. It has been mentioned before that for beginners, the modelling of the toy parts presented a significant challenge. Mixing dissimilar systems and creating new articulations added another level of complexity. However, the transposition of an architectural transformer toy to an architectural structure demands understanding of the physics and the mechanisms that occupy our everyday world. Although not surprising, in most cases the architectural artifacts designed were vehicles with robotic capabilities, because students are sufficiently familiar with their appearance and performance to accept them. It could be argued that this points toward the students' unwillingness to accept buildings as dynamic systems and elastic boundaries, or merely to the foreignness of such an idea.

Students seemed more focused on the final form of their design as a motionless object, than on considering the various form-states and the form of the mechanisms moving the parts. The mechanics of the designs were not verified through virtual simulation, because the software did not have the capability, or through hand-drawn sketches. It is possible students addressed the challenge in purely pragmatic and immediate terms, because they concentrated on fulfilling the requirements as a way to demonstrate 3D modelling mastery. Students dealt superficially with issues of motion control and the physics of motion, while spending most of their energies applying realistic textures to the parts and settings, which they learned to do well.

The students cannot be blamed for overly ambitious course objectives and pedagogical strategy.

Figure 11. From toy to artifact: toy conceptual sketch and 3D digital model of structure

If they lost sight of the more transcendental lesson behind the metaphor—the concept of architecture as a complex dynamic system responsive to its environment—they certainly did catch on to the 3D skill building aspect. They also became critical of the limitations of the virtual space where they were constructing their design. The course demanded a holistic approach, bringing into the students' field of action systems thinking, mechanics, dynamics, and cybernetics, areas that have not been fully integrated into the architecture curriculum. Also, the horizontal connections, the reciprocal and complementary relations, are not yet in place. What has been learned from teaching this course is that if one is to propose thinking outside the confines of the discipline—of becoming aware of complexity and approaches to systems thinking—one cannot teach exclusively from the perspective of architecture, nor explore problems solely targeting the architectural resolutions.

FUTURE WORK

This course provides a first step in getting students to confront complex design challenges through the analysis and exploration of kinetic adaptive structures set in a virtual construction environment. The results are extremely tentative and require documentation of future implementations of the course. The promise of the transformer toy metaphor in the design process—to yield a rich learning environment when the tools are applied with a purpose—was short-changed by an ambitious agenda that did not anticipate and properly resolve gaps in the students' knowledge. The exercises have taught students about complex geometrical modelling and assembly, and have developed awareness of kinetic adaptive structures stimulating their curiosity to learn more. They have also shown major deficiencies regarding the students' knowledge about the workings of the physical world. Future work must be accompanied with more precedents, careful consideration of mechanisms, control systems, smart materials, dynamics, kinematics, motion simulation, and the construction of physical prototypes. Also, the investigation would be more insightful if software capable of simulating behaviors, such as part movement could be used to visualize and analyze mechanism motion and part interference, and software simulating environments, such as wind force could demonstrate the impact of the environment on the structure.

The collection of transformer robot toy parts used in this course can be enlarged to include mechanical and electronic building block sets such as: Capsela®, fishertechnik® ROBO Mobile set, and LEGO® Mindstorms. It can also be extended by considering MIT Media Lab's Topobo, a

programmable set of building blocks with embedded kinetic mechanisms and electronics to teach children about dynamic systems. The *Topobo* blocks record movement that can be physically defined, or can be programmed to move. Finally, Weller, Do, and Gross (2004) have prototyped EspressoCAD and CocoaCAD, building block sets specifically design for architecture, composed by robotic modular blocks that rearrange themselves according to set rules, a design and simulation environment, and a transmission system connecting the design environment to the blocks (Weller, Do, & Gross, 2003, 2004). This last collection has a close link to metamorphic, or self-reconfigurable, shape-changing robots exemplified by ATRON, the Omnitread Serpent, and M-Tran II.

In this section it has been suggested that if the course is to deal with complexity, both its content and structure have to be further revised to broaden its scope to include the demonstration and discussion of concepts that are typically outside the architectural curricula. It has proposed to add the construction of physical models to the range of media available for the course. It also suggests the application of software that can simulate the behavior of the designs so that they can be tested against criteria measuring levels of integration and the enhancement of the transformer toy metaphor to include construction toys that have embedded electronics. Finally, it points to the need to resolve the tension between the acquisition of practice-oriented marketable skills and the less obvious critical thinking skills.

CONCLUSION

The chapter has presented as an exploratory case study a course that utilizes the vehicles of metaphor and transformer robot toys to introduce architecture students to complex systems. It has described the state of computer-based tools' integration into the architectural curricula and placed this case study within the existing context. It has discussed the reasons for the creation of a course that was based on a holistic integrative approach. The idea was to provoke students to deal with complexity and systems thinking to design, and to explore and develop computer-based modelling and rendering skills. The chapter has also posited this course can serve a reciprocal and complementary role within the curriculum to allow the transfer of knowledge to the design studio. It has described the exercises given to the students and the students' proposals, and has assessed the results in terms of their general implications for education and practice. The conclusion suggests the course's experiences can provide insights about future computer-supported design settings. Such settings might allow the combination of different types of media and knowledge in a cooperative and interdisciplinary work environment.

It is necessary to continue building the best ways to develop analytical and synthetic thinking throughout the architectural curriculum. Thinking in 3D is not enough; we need more than space, form, and order. Architecture must serve as an armature for expansive inquiry. New ways of thinking as well as knowledge are accompanied with new conceptual models. In architectural education we have moved from the clay, wood, and plaster models to the digital ones, to virtual modelling and simulation. It has been proposed here that the design environment needs to be populated by a variety of representation tools, which allow considering design problems from multiple perspectives in a fluid relationship with its environment. The assumption has been that assessing a complex problem at multiple levels in an integrative way is a process of learning that must be attained by architectural students, if they are to address the challenges that we are confronting today.

The metaphor of the transformable toy was used to learn about modelling and rendering, and about buildings as assemblages of parts, with fixed or flexible connections. It was used

as an integrative platform on which to consider the idea of dynamic interactive structures as a new type of architecture that is responsive to the environment, and therefore more efficient. The metaphor facilitates understanding the notion of systems, integration, and dynamics. As in systems thinking, components are recognized as parts of many wholes, and as parts defined by the whole; individually, parts lack the characteristics of any of the systems within which they reside. In architectural design this entails dealing with interrelated systems of space, systems of forms, and systems of systems. When students recognize their own designs are dealing with components belonging to multiple systems, barriers begin to collapse. Up to this point, for example, a roof and a wall are merely components of shelter in a fixed relationship. But when they are seen as components of many interrelated systems, roof and wall respond, change, and interact. The knowledge and skills that result from this approach add to those needed to address the accelerated changing needs of our environment, including a judicious use of very limited resources.

One of the obstacles for investigating architecture as a dynamic system is the lack of tools available to evaluate in an integrated manner patterns of behavior and processes existing in a dynamic system. This offers potential for further research in HCI. It is precisely in the shaping of a space for multiple representations, simulation and analysis, where computation can spur architecture out of the defunct Machine Age metaphor of the early 20th century, into the relevant 21st century challenges and opportunities.

REFERENCES

Andia, A. (2002). Reconstructing the effects of computers on practice and education during the past three decades. *Journal of Architectural Education, 56*(2), 7-13.

Battle, G., & McCarthy, C. (2001). *Sustainable ecosystems and the built environment*. West Sussex, Great Britain: John Wiley & Sons, Ltd.

Brönet, F. (1999). *Objects in motion course*. ACSA 1999 Teachers Seminar on Interdisciplinary Design [Presentation transcript, electronic document]. Unpublished manuscript.

Burry, M. T., Dawson, & Woodbury, R. (1999). Learning about architecture with the computers, and learning about the computer in architecture. In *Architectural Computing from Turing to 2000, ECAADe Conference Proceedings* (pp. 374-382). Liverpool, UK. Retrieved May 2005, from http://cumincad.scix.net/

Capra, F. (1982). *The turning point*. New York: Simon & Schuster.

Cheng, N. (1999). Playing with digital media: Enlivening computer graphics teaching. In O. Ataman & J. Bermúdez (Eds.), *Media and design process: ACADIA'99 Conference Proceedings* (pp. 96-109). Salt Lake City, UT.

Diaz Moore, K. (2001). The scientist, the social activist, the practitioner and the cleric: Pedagogical exploration towards a pedagogy of practice. *Journal of Architectural Education, 18*(1), 59-79.

Dym, C. L., Agogino, A., Eris, O., Frey, D. D., & Leifer, L. J. (2005). Engineering design thinking, teaching, and learning. *Journal of Engineering Education*, January, 103-120.

Engeli, M. (Ed.). (2001). *Bits and spaces*. Basel: Birkhauser.

Erdman, A., & Durfee, W. K. (1995). Pac-man, calluses, and the undergraduate engineering design student. *Educators' Tech Exchange*, Spring/Summer, 16-23.

Gross, M. D. (1994). Roles for computing in schools of architecture and planning. *Journal of Architectural Education, 48*(1), 56-64.

Gross, M., & Do, E. Y. L. (1999). Integrating digital media in design studio: Six paradigms. In *ACSA 1999 Conference Proceedings*. Retrieved January 8, 2005, from http://depts.washington.edu/dmachine/PAPER/ACSA99/acsa99.html

Hjorth, P., & Bagheri, A. (2006). Navigating towards sustainable development: A system dynamics approach. *Futures, 38*, 74-92. Retrieved April 8, 2006, from Science Direct database.

Jackson, S. (2004). *How to draw transforming robots*. San Antonio, TX: Antarctic Press.

Papanek, V. (1995). *The green imperative: Natural design for the real world*. New York: Thames and Hudson.

Papert, S. (1980). *Mind-storms: Children, computers, and powerful ideas*. New York: Basic Books, Inc., Publishers.

Raffle, H., García, C., &. Ishii, H. (2003). *Topobo for tangible learning*. Retrieved May 2005, from http://web.media.mit.edu/~hayes/topobo/papers.html

Schön, D. (1983). *The reflective practitioner: How professionals think in action*. New York: Basic Books.

Sherman, W., & Martini, K. (2002). *Teaching a dynamic perspective on building systems*. Retrieved May 2005, from http://cti.itc.virginia.edu/tti/Sherman-Martini.html

Talbott, K. (2003). An inductive approach to digital modelling instruction. In K. R. Klinger (Ed.), *Connecting crossroads of digital discourse: ACADIA'03 Conference Proceedings* (pp. 151-157). Indianapolis: IN.

Weller, M. P., Do, E. Y. L., & Gross, M. D. (2003). Espresso blocks: Self-configuring building blocks. University of Washington Design Machine Group. Retrieved May 2005, from http://cumincad.scix.net

Weller, M. P., Do, E. Y. L., & Gross, M. D. (2004). EspressoCAD: A system to support the design of dynamic structure configurations. Retrieved January 8, 2005, from http://code.arc.cmu.edu/lab/upload/espresso-cad_gcads2004.pdf

Woodbury, R. F., Shannon, S. J., & Radford, A. D. (2001). Games in early design education: Playing with metaphor. In *Proceedings of the Ninth International Conference on Computer Aided Architectural Design Futures* (pp. 201-214). Eindhoven, The Netherlands. Retrieved May 2005, from http://cumincad.scix.net

About the Authors

S. M. Abutarbush is an assistant professor in large animal internal medicine at the Atlantic Veterinary College, University of Prince Edward Island. He graduated from Jordan University of Science and Technology in 1999, obtained a Master of Veterinary Science from the WCVM in 2005, and became a Diplomate of the American Board of Veterinary Practitioners and the American College of Veterinary Internal Medicine in 2005. He has an interest in the different methods of learning and teaching veterinary medicine using multimedia, and improving veterinary education. Dr. Abutarbush was involved in the research and development of the computer-assisted learning modules NGI modules in this book.

M. Axmann has worked for several years at various higher education institutions as an instructional designer developing Web-based course materials. She is currently working as a manager for academic quality assurance at Open Universities Australia in Melbourne, Australia.

C. A. Bagley is a distinguished service professor at the University of St. Thomas and a team leader of The Technology Group, Inc. With more than 30 years in the field of instructional technology, Dr. Bagley has made significant contributions through her work with the Minnesota Educational Computing Consortium (MECC), Control Data Corporation – Plato project, MN Department of Corrections Schools, Future Kids, ISPI, ASCD, U.S. Government Schools, K-12 public schools, virtual schools and universities, corporations, and law firms. Dr. Bagley has provided e-learning leadership, design and strategic planning expertise, workshops, seminars, publications, and keynote presentations within the U.S. and internationally.

M. Berry is a senior lecturer in the School of Creative Media at RMIT University. She supervises postgraduate students at the master's and PhD level in new and interactive media and lectures in content and interaction design at an undergraduate level. She has worked with interdisciplinary production teams to design and develop wizards to assist educational designers to develop online instructional material that is pedagogically sound, usable, and accessible by people with disabilities. Her interests include narrative forms for mobile phones, social practices and new technologies, user experience, and how creative storytellers and designers incorporate emerging technologies into their everyday practices.

C. C. Chou is an assistant professor in the Department of Curriculum and Instruction at the School of Education at the University of St. Thomas. She is in charge of the Learning Technology MA/Certificate Program. As the co-director of the Minnesota Leaders and Educators Technology Initiatives (MELTI), she has worked to bridge the digital divide in the K-12 schools. Her research focuses on the integration of technology into curriculum, computer-mediated communication (CMC) systems, and the design of distance learning environments.

C. Clark is an assistant professor of large animal medicine at the Western College of Veterinary Medicine, University of Saskatchewan. His main interests are cattle diseases, pharmacology, and veterinary education. Dr. Clark is leading the bovine project described in this book.

J. Faulkner is a senior lecturer in literacy in the School of Education at RMIT University. After teaching English extensively in schools, she completed a thesis in popular culture and teenage reading practices, beginning a new career in research and teacher education. As much of what young people find popular is mediated through digital technology, the significance of computers in relation to learning and teaching has become a prominent feature of her research interests. With her colleague, Gloria Latham, she continues to investigate and write about the relationship of information and communications technologies to deep learning.

M. Hamilton is a senior lecturer in the School of Computer Science and IT at RMIT University. She is an active member of the Web research group, and lectures in Web site design, construction, and programming. She has collaborated on several research studies in CS education, including BRACE (Building Research in Australasian Computing Education) and the RMIT mobile computing group. Her interests include investigating how computer scientists adapt new technologies such as mobile computing with the Tablet PC, or wireless keypad voting devices for interactive teaching, and also how lecturers and students manage in large groups, and with plagiarism detection software.

L. Hawkins is a lecturer in social work at RMIT University, Australia: research and practice experience in the flexible delivery of education. She has been a consultant on projects aimed at increasing the use of ICTs to enhance the teaching and learning experience of tertiary students. She was awarded an RMIT Certificate for Scholarship of Teaching for her work in flexible delivery. Much of her research and writing has been on professional expertise and multidisciplinary collaboration, particularly in the field of education. This is within local, national, and global contexts. Research interests include ICTs and flexible delivery of tertiary education, teamwork and multidisciplinary collaboration, standards for practice professional expertise, and field education.

N. Herzog teaches multimedia design in the School of Creative Media. She has extensive industry experience in design and currently supervises the multimedia students in their industry project. She has a specific interest in the relationship between learning and the workplace.

R. Horne is the director of the Centre for Design at RMIT University. Until 2005 he was a senior lecturer at Sheffield Hallam University where he developed a Distance Learning Master's program and collaborated on associated HCI initiatives. Horne has over 10 years experience of designing and delivering postgraduate problem-based learning courses and is particularly interested in interdisciplinary projects. He is currently involved in developing a new master's program at RMIT University.

W. Hürst received his master's degree in computer science from the University of Karlsruhe (TH), Germany in 1997 and a PhD in computer science from the University of Freiburg, Germany in 2005. From January 1996 until March 1997 he was a visiting researcher at the Language Technologies Institute at Carnegie Mellon University in Pittsburgh, PA. From the end of 1997 until March 2005 he was a research assistant the University of Freiburg, where he now works as a teaching and research associate. His main research interests include multimedia technologies, human-computer interaction, information retrieval, and computer supported teaching and learning.

S. Jones is the associate professor of employment relations at RMIT University. She is the recipient of several Teaching and Learning Excellence Awards and has published extensively on how to design and develop student-centered, situated learning environments, particularly for managers and practitioners. Sandra has been invited as an international expert to teach and research in many countries including France, Canada, the United Kingdom, as well as in Hong Kong, Malaysia, and Singapore.

K. Kaur is vice-dean at the Faculty of Education, Arts, and Social Sciences, Open University Malaysia. Her work has focused primarily on teacher education, language, and literacy development, as well as collaborative online learning for distance learners. She is editor of two volumes of research in ESL, *Second Language Writing* (2004) and (with Basil S. Wijasuria) *Transcending Boundaries: Selected Papers on ESL Teaching and Learning* (2004), both published by the Malaysian English Language Teaching Association. She is also co-editor of *E-Learning Readiness in Malaysia* (2005), a study by Open University Malaysia and the Ministry of Energy, Water, and Communications, Malaysia.

J. Kellett is a senior lecturer in urban & regional planning at University of South Australia where he is director of the Undergraduate Planning Program. Until 2004 he was in charge of the master's program in environmental management for business at Sheffield Hallam University, where he project managed the development of a major HCI initiative. His chapter with his former colleague, Ralph Horne, draws extensively on their experience in designing and developing an aspect of this project.

G. Latham is a senior lecturer in literacy in the School of Education at RMIT University. She is a primary school teacher, has been a theatre director, written books, and written for theatre and television prior to moving into teacher education. Over 10 years ago she was given the role of learning technologies mentor for her faculty, and this started intense interest in what ICT can offer learners. For the past eight years she has edited a now completely online guide to the School of Education. A virtual primary school was developed to foster deep learning for teacher educators, and she continues to research, explore, and write about virtual possibilities with her colleague Julie Faulkner.

C-S. Lin earned his PhD in instructional technology and computer science at Indiana University in 1994. He currently is an associate professor at National University of Tainan, Taiwan. With his compelling experience in the field of networked learning, Lin frequently serves as a consultant to numerous governmental digital learning projects of Taiwan and Asian countries. Being an advocate of educational simulation since his graduate study in late 1980, Lin now is focusing his research on blending the strength of microworld, simulation, and role-playing games to create virtual learning environments and content.

K. L. Lohmann received her veterinary degree from the Freie Universität Berlin, Germany in 1995. Following an internship at a private equine clinic in Los Olivos, CA, she completed a residency in large animal internal medicine at Texas A&M University and became board certified in 2000. She then pursued graduate training at the University of Georgia in Athens, GA, and received her PhD in physiology in 2004. Dr. Lohmann is an associate professor in the department of Large Animal Clinical Sciences at the WCVM. Dr. Lohmann's clinical interests include all aspects of large animal, particularly equine, medicine. Her special clinical interests are neonatal medicine and gastrointestinal diseases. Her research interests include inflammation, endotoxemia, and host-pathogen interactions. Dr. Lohmann extended the use of the NGI modules in a new WCVM context and is contributing to the development of computer-assisted learning modules for equine medicine described in this book.

D. Loi is a senior research fellow and lecturer at RMIT University. Since the late 1990s she has been involved in a number of research endeavors: ARC researcher in 1999; member of multidisciplinary THT at the Interactive Information Institute (1999-2001); research fellow in the Australian Federal Government-funded C2C project (2001-2002); and visiting researcher at IADE (2004). Dr. Loi has presented her work in Europe, Australia, the U.S., and Canada, and her practice revolves around arts-based inquiry and qualitative research; participatory design; HCI and tangible media; trans- and post-disciplinarity; collaborative practices; and constructivist learning/teaching. Her work and publications are available at http://www.darialoi.com.

J. Martin is an associate professor in social work at RMIT University, Australia: research and practice experience in conflict prevention, management, and resolution. She has a Bachelor of Social Science, a Bachelor of Social Work, a Master of Social Work, and a Graduate Certificate in developmental child psychiatry. Much of her academic and direct practice work is in multidisciplinary teams. She has developed a model for effective multidisciplinary collaboration. Research interests include conflict prevention, management, and resolution, mental health, and multidisciplinary and cross-cultural communications. She is a practicing mediator and forensic consultant.

K. A. Mohamed obtained his BSc in 2001 at The University of Western Australia, with double majors in applied mathematics and computer science. In 2002, Mohamed went on to receive First Class Honors for his BSc (computer science) at the same university, after solving the problem of constraints satisfaction in industrial manpower allocation by means of conceiving and implementing fast and efficient knowledge- and rule-based techniques. Presently, Mohamed is a PhD candidate at the Institut für Informatik of Albert-Ludwigs-Universität Freiburg, and doing research on gesticulation techniques between styluses and digital boards—particularly in the field of artificial intelligence in multimedia e-learning.

V. K. Murthy is a senior lecturer in information systems at the School of Business Information Technology, RMIT University, Melbourne, Australia. He has carried out research in agent-based systems, knowledge management, e-business, databases, and mobile computing/systems. Murthy has made significant research contributions that are recognized internationally. His international visibility is demonstrated by his extensive publication record, which includes books, book chapters, and journal and conference publications in reputed international journals and high profile international conferences. His publication record includes two books: *Transaction Processing Systems* (Prentice Hall, U.S.) and *Architectural Issues of Web-Enabled E-Business* (Idea Group Publishing, U.S.). He has authored several book chapters and over 75 refereed journal and conference publications in reputed international journals and conferences. He has received the best paper award in the International Conference on Knowledge-Based Intelligent Information and Engineering Systems for his paper on agent-based systems. The extended version of this paper has been published in the *International Journal of Knowledge-Based and Intelligent Engineering Systems*.

J. M. Naylor graduated from the University of Bristol, UK, with a combined degree in veterinary medicine and biochemistry. He obtained his PhD from The University of Pennsylvania and then moved to the WCVM, University of Saskatchewan, where he spent 20 years in the Department of Veterinary Internal Medicine and, later, the Department of Large Animal Clinical Sciences. Currently he is a professor at Ross University School of Veterinary Medicine. His interests are clinical medicine, clinically applied research, and innovation in learning. He designed some of the first interactive large animal computer simulations, wrote the first electronic book on the interpretation of sounds heard by auscultation, and is currently studying methods to improve classroom learning. Dr. Naylor led several initiatives described in this book.

L. Padgham is a professor in artificial intelligence, discipline leader for intelligent systems, and leader of the internationally renowned Intelligent Agents research group, School of Computer Science and Information Technology at RMIT University, Melbourne, Australia. She has a research background in various aspects of commonsense reasoning and for the last six years has been involved in research in intelligent multi-agent systems. Over the last several years Lin has developed (with colleagues) a design methodology for building agent systems, and is one of the leading players internationally in methodologies for building complex agent systems. She has published in 2004, the first detailed book on a methodology for building multi-agent systems, and in 2005, the supporting tool for this methodology, the Prometheus Design Tool, won the award for the best demonstration at AAMAS'05, the major international conference in this area. She also has a background in psychology and has a long-term interest in exploring a variety of pedagogical methods, especially those that engage students actively in their learning.

G. Parchoma is a doctoral candidate in educational administration, an instructional designer, and a lecturer at University of Saskatchewan. Her instructional design work is currently focused on technology-enhanced learning and the creation of virtual laboratories. Her research interests include e-learning policy, learner-centered instructional design, and evidenced-based pedagogical change. She has been involved in several WCVM research and development projects. She researched the background for and coordinated the writing of the chapter.

L. Polley is a professor of parasitology at the WCVM. He received his degree in veterinary medicine and PhD in parasitology from the University of Bristol, has held faculty appointments at Bristol and at Cornell University, and visiting appointments at Texas A&M University, Imperial College – University of London, ENVN-Nantes (France), and Murdoch University (Australia). At the WCVM, Dr. Polley has served as assistant dean (special projects), director of the Veterinary Teaching Hospital, and head of the Department of Veterinary Microbiology. He has taught parasitology to students in veterinary medicine, medicine, and biology. His research interests are focused on parasite ecology, related most recently to Arctic wildlife, climate change, and zoonoses. Dr. Polley has led the research and development teams in the development of parasitology database described in this book.

S. Porterfield spent 12 years teaching in the K-12 system before completing a Master of Education and working as an instructional designer. She has spent five years developing computer-mediated learning resources for the University of Saskatchewan and the Saskatchewan Institute Applied Science and Technology. Sharon contributed to the canine-feline study described in the book.

Carmina Sánchez -del-Valle is an associate professor of the Department of Architecture at Hampton University in Virginia, USA. She received a Bachelor in Environmental Design and a Master of Architecture from the University of Puerto Rico, and a doctoral degree in architecture from the University of Michigan. She has taught at the University of Kansas and the Florida Agricultural & Mechanical University. Her area of expertise is design computing, in particular information management, design process, and representation. Her research has focused on the integration of computer-based tools into architectural education and practice, and developing models for mapping historical districts through relational databases. She is a licensed architect.

K. Schwarz is an instructional designer. She holds an MEd in instructional technology, as well as a BSc and BEd. She is working on a PhD in educational technology. She worked six years as an instructional designer in higher education and in industry, and taught multimedia and instructional design at a community college. Her research interests include quality measures for online courses from a learner's perspective, best practices for facilitating learning, developing virtual learning experiences that require higher order thinking skills, and group dynamics in online environments. Schwarz is the instructional designer for three projects described in the book and in the final preparation of the manuscript.

C. L. Shmon is a professor of and small animal surgeon in the Department of Small Animal Clinical Sciences, WCVM at the University of Saskatchewan. She teaches small animal surgery to veterinary students in the clinic, classroom, and laboratory. Dr. Shmon is involved in the development of the surgical principles computer-assisted learning modules described in the book.

R. Tarsiero, a knowledge management consultant and facilitator for Gionnethics, combines a solid background in medical science with over six years of experience in moderating and facilitating online communities. Her academic publications and conference participations cover a broad spectrum of topics. Of particular interest are her works on online self-help communities, communities of practice, facilitation, ICT, and non-profit and volunteer management.

S. M. Taylor is a professor and small animal medicine clinical specialist in the Department of Small Animal Clinical Sciences, WCVM at the University of Saskatchewan, where she teaches students in the clinic, in the classroom, and in the laboratory. Dr. Taylor was involved in the development and research activities for the canine and feline medical exercises computer-assisted learning modules described in the book.

R. Van Schyndel (BAppSc, MAppSc in computer vision, PhD [Monash] in digital watermarking, MACM, MIEEE) is based at RMIT University. He has been involved in pioneering research on digital watermarking since 1992 and is the co-author of one of the first and most cited papers in the field. Ron has published some 20 papers, and reviewed close to 100 papers and articles in the field over the years. However, unlike many others in the field whose interest is from the security perspective, his interest in this is from the point of view of making media accessible by incorporating meta content in the media itself. Always keen to advance the cause of universal Web access, he has kept close track of the direction of multimedia usage on the wired and now wireless Internet and is concerned about the user behavior in this domain and the interaction of accessibility, multimodality, and personalization and how that will influence interface design toward a common goal of universal access.

C. Waldner holds a Doctor of Veterinary Medicine and a PhD in epidemiology from the University of Saskatchewan. Dr. Waldner is an associate professor in the Department of Large Animal Clinical Sciences, but also participates in the teaching program for Community Health and Epidemiology at the College of Medicine. Dr. Waldner has contributed to the canine-feline study described in the book.

Index